Freedom and the Arts

Freedom and the Arts

Essays on Music and Literature

—

CHARLES ROSEN

HARVARD UNIVERSITY PRESS

Cambridge, Massachusetts, and London, England

2012

Publication of this book has been supported through the generous provisions
of the Maurice and Lula Bradley Smith Memorial Fund.

Library of Congress Cataloging-in-Publication Data

Rosen, Charles, 1927–
Freedom and the arts : essays on music and literature / Charles Rosen.—1st ed.
p. cm.
Includes index.
ISBN 978-0-674-04752-5
1. Music—History and criticism. 2. Literature—History and criticism. I. Title.
ML60.R7849 2012
780.9—dc23
2011044591

For Henri Zerner

Contents

Acknowledgments

ABOVE ALL, I should like to express my gratitude for Robert Silvers's sympathetic and inspiring efforts to make sure that the many reviews of mine he edited were always accessible to readers without a specialized knowledge of the matters at hand. I have written two new and somewhat technical essays for this volume, not so much to supplement as to correct what I have written before, and I must thank Professor Robert Marshall of Brandeis University and Professor Scott Burnham of Princeton University for their really valuable corrections and their encouragement. I owe a great debt to Professor Kristina Muxfeldt of the University of Indiana at Bloomington for helping me put the book together and get the music examples in good order, saving me many hours of labor. I am deeply sensible of the understanding shown by the Harvard University Press, above all the kindness and tact of Lindsay Waters through all the changes of plan, and grateful for the help and patience of Shanshan Wang.

Introduction

WE MIGHT ALL AGREE that a knowledge of the historical and biographical circumstances that saw the production of a work of literature or music or even an analytic study of them may often help us to a greater understanding and to the increase of pleasure that comes with understanding. Nevertheless, one brute fact often overlooked needs to be forced upon our consideration: most works of art are more or less intelligible and give pleasure without any kind of historical, biographical, or structural analysis. There are always some aspects of the work which do not need our critical industry or demand much interpretation. All that is necessary is just some small familiarity, acquired however involuntarily and informally by occasional experience with the stylistic language and tradition of the work.

In the end, we must affirm that no single system of interpretation will ever be able to give us an exhaustive or definitive understanding of why a work of literature or music can hold an enduring interest for us, explain its charm, account for its seduction and our admiration. A recognition of the inadequacy of any system of interpretation is essential to our being able to gain a fresh experience of the work. We need at times to acquire the talent of reading a work of literature or listening to a piece of music with innocent eye and ear, untainted or unblocked by critical studies, a state of objectivity unrealizable in all its purity, but which may be approached. Every fine work has inherent merits easily grasped across the ages and effective in alien cultures, merits that cannot always be convincingly shown to have been imposed by historical, social, or biographical pressures. At the moment of its creation, a work will have different roles to play, different functions to fulfill (some of which we ignore or deliberately set aside), and will develop still new roles and functions as it grows old and passes through history. A piece of Mozart or a poem by Pope for example, both carries with and conveys a sense of the age and the society in which it was created, and yet at the same time it can speak directly to the sensibility of a modern listener who has little knowledge of the original historical context. Merely a nodding acquaintance with the style and language of the time will generally be enough, and this acquaintance may be superficial and still effective. A study of the historical conditions in which the art was created can of course deepen our understanding and make it more complex and even increase our delight, as I have remarked at the opening. But the study is rarely absolutely indispensable, the individual interpretation never exhaustive or permanent. Every critical approach is likely to obscure important aspects of a work that will enter into the experience of a naive reading, Any appreciation of the past must acknowledge that several different critical approaches are valid, and that even in the absence of any formal system of interpretation, the work may still speak to us simply through its intrinsic merit or value.

In these essays and reviews, I have tried not only to benefit from a variety of different critical methods, but above all to keep in mind that listening and reading with intensity for pleasure is the one critical activity that can never be dispensed with or superseded. This will allow us to recognize the muliple possibilities of significance, and to avoid appreciating only those elements of an artistic production that are revolutionary; both Theodor Adorno and Glenn Gould, for example, were incapable of seeing that Mozart was sometimes astonishingly effective and superior to most of his contemporaries even when he was extremely conventional, not only when he was most strikingly original. And to recognize that Mallarmé, who permanently altered the nature of poetry, was nevertheless right when he claimed that he was only doing what all poets had done before him. While a study of the sources of Montaigne's ideas will reveal his debt to the stoic, epicurean, and skeptic philosophers, only a rereading of his essays for the enjoyment of his style and his delight in contradicting himself will tell us that his conclusions are generally provisional and that the interest for the reader lies in the voyage and not in reaching the goal—or, rather, that the voyage (the demonstration of the way the mind works) was the real original goal all the time.

The freedom of interpretation is fundamental to the tradition of music and literature in the West, which continuously demanded innovation, but an innovation that would eventually—often with some difficulty and delay—be assimilated and absorbed by the tradition, which has often, indeed, more influence upon the character of the art works produced than the personal and historical circumstances at the moment of their appearance. Nevertheless, the freedom of interpretation is balanced by a requirement of fidelity—that is, that the identity of the work be preserved and remain coherent.

The essays and reviews chosen here deal largely with the necessity of preserving both a respect for the identity of the literary and musical works and the freedom from coercive interpretation, a freedom which provides the basis and the guarantee of the pleasures of reading, listening, and performing that justify the existence of the arts.

Part One

THE WEIGHT OF SOCIETY

d can be a source of fatigue. With a silly play on words, there is a split second
en a word suspended between two incompatible senses briefly loses all
eaning and becomes pure sound, and for a lovely moment we revert to the
lighted state of the child freed from the tyranny of language. Of all the con-
raints imposed on us that restrict our freedom—constraints of morality and
corum, constraints of class and finance—one of the earliest that is forced
on us is the constraint of a language that we are forced to learn so that others
n talk to us and tell us things we do not wish to know.

We do not learn language by reading a dictionary, and we do not think or
eak in terms of dictionary definitions. Meaning is always more fluid.
evertheless, we are hemmed in, even trapped, by common usage. Senses we
ish to evade entrap us. The greatest escape route is not only humor, but poetry,
art in general. Art does not, of course, liberate us completely from meaning,
ut it gives a certain measure of freedom, provides elbow room. Schiller claimed
the *Letters on Aesthetic Education* that art makes you free; he understood that
e conventions of language and of society are in principle arbitrary—that is,
nposed by will. They prevent the natural development of the individual. The
lash between the imposition of meaning and freedom has given rise to contro-
ersy in ways that Schiller could not have predicted.

The critical problem of the battle between conventional meaning and indi-
idual expression was best laid out many years ago in Mayer Schapiro's appar-
ntly controversial insistence that the forms of Romanesque sculpture could not
e ascribed solely to theological meaning, but were also a style of aesthetic
xpression. What that meant at the time was quite simply and reasonably that
he character of the sculptural forms could not be reduced only to their personi-
ication of theological dogma, but possessed a clear aesthetic energy indepen-
lent of sacred meaning. The fallacy that Schapiro was attacking has reappeared
ecently in musicological circles with the absurd claim that music could not be
njoyed for purely musical or aesthetic reasons until the eighteenth century as
he word "aesthetics" was not used until then. (This naive belief that indepen-
lent aesthetic considerations did not exist before 1750 without social and reli-
rious functions would strangely imply that no one before that date could admire
he beauty of a member of the opposite sex except if it could be related to the
unction of the production of children.) It is true that some thinkers of the
eighteenth century would proclaim the fundamental precedence of the aes-
hetic: Johann Georg Hamman observed with Vico that poetry is older than
prose, and insisted that music is older than language, horticulture than agricul-
ture. We should recall here the extraordinary sixteenth-century controversy
about style between the admirers of Cicero and of Erasmus, the former, led by
Etienne Dolet, believing that style had a beauty independent of the matter of

CHAPTER I

Freedom and Art

THAT GREAT ECCENTRIC of the Enlightenment, Geo
Lichtenberg, who put into his private notebooks just abo
that came into his head, once jotted down: "Whoever decreed
must have a fixed meaning?" He was perhaps the first to recogni:
constraint involved in the perception of meaning and the atte
it firm.

In his discussion of humor, Sigmund Freud deals with this lac
profound reflection. The mechanical structure of psychoanalyti
now rightfully laboring under some discredit, but Freud's literary
him insights that are still valuable. After treating at length the ki
that allows a safe and neutralized outlet for the taboo expressi
desire and of social aggression, he arrives finally at "pure" humor, t
are innocent of repressive fantasies, but just simple word games, sil
are only a form of play. (I can remember a superannuated examp
junior high school days: "Why do radio announcers have such sn
Wee paws [we pause] for station identification.)

To explain our delight in such foolishness, Freud invokes the lalla
small children, who sit and repeat long strings of nonsense syllabl
ma . . . , mow, bow, wow, . . . etc.) at great length for their own a
Learning a language, being forced to attach a meaning to a sound,
to the child, who, in a reaction, strings together senseless rhyming
form of escape. Even for adults understanding speech is not devoi

the literary work, and the latter insisting that the beauty of style was wholly dependent on its consonance with meaning. (Dolet was burnt at the stake, but not for his admiration of Cicero. Montaigne took the Erasmian position against pure stylistic shenanigans, but foreshadowed some twentieth-century criticism by avowing that when the style was as masterly as Cicero's, it could be said to have become its own matter.) The contention that pure aesthetic appreciation was impossible before 1700 would not only make the existence of that controversy as early as the 1500s impossible, but also astonishingly overlooks both the innate aesthetic impulses of any human animal, and the most obvious characteristic of every form of artistic endeavor—that at some point it inevitably draws attention away from its meaning and function to the form of expression, or from the *signifié* to the *signifiant,* to use the well-known structural linguistic terms that were so fashionable only a few decades ago.

This is most obviously the case when the signifier, the artistic form, so to speak, seems to have developed a sense somewhat at odds with the ostensible signified. Perhaps the most spectacular depiction of freedom in music may be brought up as evidence of this, the greeting of Don Giovanni to the masked guests at his party, *"Viva la libertà!"* In the libretto, these words are only an invitation to have a good time, but they have often been understood politically. Oddly, the astute Hermann Abert denied the political implication, basing his stance on the sense of the libretto. However, Mozart sets this as a call to arms, with trumpets and drums unheard in the work since the overture, and with an evident traditional martial rhythm, while the singers forte shout the words *"Viva la libertà"* over and over again. In 1789, after twelve years of political agitation since the American Revolution, it is unlikely that anyone missed the political sense. The message should not be interpreted naively and one-sidedly. *Don Giovanni* is about sexual libertinage; not only was that considered by conservatives to be the inevitable ultimate result of the arrival of political freedom (although in fact many revolutionaries from Robespierre to Stalin and Castro have installed prudish and puritan measures), but the Marquis de Sade in his best known pamphlet, "One Step Further," specifically proclaimed that political freedom had to be accompanied by sexual freedom to be truly meaningful. Mozart's own position on political liberty may be left undetermined by this page, but the evil Queen of the Night in *The Magic Flute* was understood very early as a personification of the Empress Maria Theresa, and the Masonic Order of the time, while certainly not a radical revolutionary group, was at least partly in opposition to the central power, although it contained many of the most influential members of Viennese society of the time. In any case, we can see that the artistic form here in the central or first finale of *Don Giovanni* loosens any fixed meaning dependent on the libretto, and allows for the free play of the imagination. One important note should be added: the amazing exhilaration of this passage is more closely related to the possible political meaning than to the more social welcome implied by the text without the music, as the page is extremely stirring in its traditional martial excitement, unnaturally so in terms of the operatic story.

The partial freedom of, and from, meaning that is the natural result of aesthetic form is made possible by the exploitation of an inherent fluidity, or looseness of significance, naturally present in both language and social organization. This is a freedom often repressed, and attempts at repression and conformity are an inevitable part of experience. That is why aesthetic form—in poetry, music, and the visual arts—has so often been considered subversive and corrupting from Plato to the present day.

Conventions are the bulwark of civilization, a guarantee of social protection. They can also be a prison cell. Of course, any art has its conventions, too, just like every other activity, and an artist is expected to fulfill them. Traditionally, however, for at least three millennia and possibly longer, the artist is also expected paradoxically to violate conventions—to entertain, to surprise, to outrage, to be original. That is the special status of art among all other activities, although it may indeed spill over and make itself felt throughout the rest of life. It is the source of freedom; it prevents the wheels of the social machine from locking into paralysis. From our artists and entertainers, we expect originality and resent it when we get it.

Ideally we expect style and idea, form and matter to be fused, indistinguishable one from the other. Friedrich Schlegel observed that when they are separable, there is something wrong with one or both of them. Nevertheless, the liberty of the artist rests on the ever-present possibility or danger of their independence. The Erasmian principle that style is, or should be, always subservient to idea is essentially naive. It takes little account of experience. Style can define and determine matter. We can see, for example, how the virtuosity of style in La Fontaine profoundly altered the morals of Aesop's fables. The tension between style and idea, their friction is a stimulant.

One aspect of freedom in the language of literature came to greater critical prominence in the twentieth century and was given novel emphasis with the criticism of William Empson, beginning with *Seven Types of Ambiguity,* but systematized perhaps more importantly with *The Structure of Complex Words.* Here, the great English twentieth-century literary critic explored the way relationships between the different meanings of a word could be brought into play, above all in poetry but also in prose. (One example, the Victorian lady's injunction: "No, you may not take Amelia for long walks; she's delicate." This, as Empson observed, asserts an equation between two meanings of "delicate"— refined on the one hand, and fragile or sickly, on the other, and suggests as a subtext that all refined girls are sickly.) These equations depend on whether a principal meaning implied a subsidiary one, or vice versa, and it permits Empson to understand and explain why "God is love" has a meaning so different from "Love is God." It is certain that the most powerful developments of this hidden source of linguistic freedom are found most often in poetry, but Empson is able to explore it not only in *Paradise Lost* and *King Lear,* but in *Alice in Wonderland* as well, on which he remarks that the unpretentious shepherd of the pastoral genre who is able to enunciate profound truths (surprising in one of such a low station in life) is replaced by the young child whose innocent observations rival the sophisticated wisdom of adults. Once again we meet with a freedom of form that amounts to a kind of duplicity.

The ambiguity of spoken or written language is far less than the ambiguity of musical meaning, a disconcerting ambiguity powerfully described by Denis Diderot in his *Lettre sur les sourds et les muets:*

> En musique, le plaisir de la sensation dépend d'une disposition particulière non seulement de l'oreille, mais de tout le système des nerfs. . . . Au reste, la musique a plus besoin de trouver en nous ces favorables dispositions d'organes, que ni la peinture, ni la poésie. Son hieroglyphe est si léger et si fugitif, il est si facile de le perdre ou de le mésinterpréter, que le plus beau morceau de symphonie ne feroit pas un grand effet si le plaisir infaillible et subtil de la sensation pure et simple n'etoit infiniment audessus de celui d'une expression souvent équivoque. . . . Comment se fait-il donc que des trois arts imitateurs de la Nature, celui don't l'expression est la plus arbitraire et la moins précise parle le plus fortement à l'âme.

> In music, the pleasure of sensation depends on a particular disposition not only of the ear but of the entire nervous system. . . . In addition, music has a greater need to find in us these favorable dispositions of the organs than painting or poetry. Its hieroglyph is so light and so fleeting, it is so easy to lose it or to misinterpret it, that the most beautiful movement of a symphony would have little effect if the infallible and subtle pleasure of sensation pure and simple were not infinitely above that of an often ambiguous expression. . . . How does it happen then that of the three arts that imitate Nature, the one whose expression is the most arbitrary and the least precise speaks the most powerfully to the soul?

I have quoted this elsewhere (in *The Classical Style* as an epigraph), but it is important to see how clearly the nature of musical discourse was understood by the second half of the eighteenth century. Mendelssohn found the meaning of music more precise, not less, than language, but that is because music means what it is, not what it says.

The most famous association of music and freedom is illustrated by the première of Aubert's opera *La Muette de Portici,* which is credited with starting the revolution that led to the creation of Belgium, the only opera in history to have had such a powerful political influence. The opera itself has a strong political cast, but if anything in it inspired political action, it must certainly have been the overture, which has a principal theme with a strong jingoistic swing to it like the American "Battle Hymn of the Republic." It certainly sounds exuberantly patriotic, and remained a model for national hymns that superseded the "Marseillaise." Most of the music that celebrates freedom in the nineteenth century has a character that is more nationalistic than humanistic, and the freedom is not expected to apply to humanity in general. The masterpiece of this kind of music is surely Verdi's *Aida.* The late Edward Said wondered what Verdi thought the Egyptians would think of this work, premiered in Cairo to celebrate the opening of the Suez Canal. Of course, for Verdi the opera was not really about Egyptians at all, but about Italy, and the repression of a subject people very like the Austrian subjugation of Italy, although the foreign scene offered a chance for exotic and picturesquely alienating musical effects supposed to be typical of the Near East. It dealt with the very modern case of a cruel society dominated by a wicked clergy; the anticlerical aspect of the opera is emphatic, and certainly resounded strongly in Italy. The portrayal of freedom in the work is best represented by Aida's nostalgia for her native land, reminiscent of Azucena's longing for her native mountains in *Il Trovatore* ("Ai nostri monti"), taken up later by Bizet's *Carmen* ("Là bas, Là bas dans la montagne"). Nostalgia and freedom are often linked concepts. The idea of freedom is usually a vision of a paradise lost. It is probable that Verdi cared not a whit for what the Egyptians thought of his opera, as it was going to be mounted soon afterward at La Scala in Milan, and that was the public he was writing for.

The most famously humane plea for political freedom in music is surely Beethoven's *Fidelio.* His revisions to the first two versions, both called *Lenore,* are almost all improvements of efficiency, tightening up the score by removing repetitious phrases, but the change of the overture from *Lenore* 2 or 3 to a more conventional partially buffa-style introduction reduces the political character of the opera, as the earlier variant overtures clearly foreshadow the prison rescue that will be the climax of the opera. And it has always seemed wonderful that such prominence should be given in the first act to the simple desire of the prisoners for light and air. Some have derided Florestan's cry at the opening of act 2, "Welch dunkel hier!" as unnatural, since he should have noticed it was dark after many years in the cell, but surely any prisoner in solitary must have sudden intense moments of despair at the conditions of his confinement. In the prison quartet, Leanora's passionate intervention, "First kill his wife!" is an unsurpassed thrilling effect in the unexpected change in both harmony and tessitura, and the music is dramatically far more explicit than the text. The effect requires a clearly articulated musical language in which a B-flat in a D major tonality can have a dramatic effect, and the dissonant and startling B-flat is used here to foreshadow the B-flat trumpet fanfare that is the ultimate climax of the quartet and signals the beginning of the resolution of the action.

The "Ode to Joy" finale of Beethoven's Ninth Symphony must be considered here, as there is a well-established theory that the "Freude" of the final ode was intended to be understood as an obvious substitute for the overly inflammatory word "Freiheit." Too enthusiastic or insistent a declamatory use of the word "freedom" would send a message to any government nervous about its power that someone is out to make trouble. Freedom and joy are of course not incompatible and go together remarkably well. Most of the choral finale of Beethoven's last symphony, however, is somewhat more apt for the concept of freedom than joy. The B-flat scherzo variation with the percussive, so-called Turkish, percussion sound effects is in military style, and a combat for freedom is more reasonable than a fight for joy. In the following variation, after the fugue has completed the battle imagery, the great musical representation of the starry heavens implies more easily a spiritual view of freedom, while joy on the contrary lacks the dignity of the spacious sound imagined by Beethoven. It would be a mistake to try and pin down too specific a political meaning for the triumphal air of the last pages, but the sense of victory is everywhere evident.

The spectacular musical representation of freedom in these monumental works is the result of historical conjunction. Political freedom was fashionable just then, although the taste for it had been growing steadily since Machiavelli. After 1776 and 1789, it had become inescapable. Later in the nineteenth century, it would lose some of its golden aura. After 1848, the evident sarcasm in the title of Johann Nestroy's great comedy *Freiheit in Krähwinkel* is telling (*Freedom in New Rochelle* would be a good translation of the title for Americans.) Its central monologue informs us that particular freedoms, like *Gedankenfreiheit* (freedom of thought, valid as long as the thoughts remain unexpressed, for example,) or billiard freedom in cafes—freedoms in the plural, make sense, are comprehensible and available. But what is fashionable now is singular-case Freedom in general—except that this is an unobtainable chimera and nobody knows what it is. The ideological disaster of 1848 throughout Europe as a whole degraded what was left of much of the hope and idealism of 1776 and 1789. (Perhaps particularly in Germany; Lewis Namier called the German revolt of 1848 "a drunken cow.") By the beginning of the twentieth century, when Hugo von Hofmannsthal, in the "Chandos Letter," asserted the inadequacy of language to express anything profoundly individual and subjective, one of the first words to have completely lost its meaning for him was "freedom."

The triumph of Beethoven's musical image of freedom depended on more than just the contemporary popularity and relish for the idea. It needed an adequate musical language for its expression with subtle and complex articulations. These articulations had thickened within a few years after his death, making way for a powerful and rich chromaticism. Art may offer us a chance of liberation, but we are chained by its limitations. When we reach the great works of Verdi, who was so deeply and ideologically involved in the struggle for Italian freedom, the representation of freedom for him, as we have seen, offered a choice between a coarse but thrilling jingoism or a passionate nostalgia for an existence of the past in a country far away. This is a natural process in the history of styles. We are always haunted by the past, even when we try to destroy it. Novalis defined freedom as *Meisterschaft*. When Richard Strauss at the end of *Der Rosenkavalier* needed to represent the innocence of teenage love, all his mastery had at its command was only a flagrant pastiche of Mozart. Our freedom is hemmed in on every side. We must be grateful for what remains.

CHAPTER 2

Culture on the Market

I

Some thirty years ago, the then head of CBS Records, Clive Davis, sent out a directive that no recording was to be undertaken if the recovery of its costs could not be projected within one year's sale in the United States. Accordingly, the plan to record Mozart's Serenade for Thirteen Wind Instruments with George Szell and members of the Cleveland Orchestra was canceled. One of the producers at CBS was properly indignant. "Doesn't he know that we're an international company?" he said to me. "The sale of classical music in Japan is twice that of the United States, the sale in Europe three times as great. We could have recovered the costs of this record in a short time with no difficulty."

Thinking in terms of so long a time as a year was, in fact, unusually broad-minded in the American record business. Normally the goal was nothing more than a fast recovery of costs and a quick profit. A continuously growing profitability was also desirable since selling only the same number of records each year would neither please stockholders nor attract investment. Staying in business merely by sustaining the same level of activity was not commercially appealing. This is part of a general conviction that affects most activities today. Countries must attract more tourists each year, airlines must fly ever more passengers to more destinations, energy companies must supply—or appear to supply—more energy to more customers. This conviction, it seems to me, is less a principle of economics than an article of faith.

If the market does not grow fast enough, the most common commercial policy is not to try to sustain the level reached, but to cut back drastically. Canceling a respectable project if it does not promise a fast return is the easiest road to take. It is often deplored that the market for classical music is not growing or that it is even shrinking, although it is hard to interpret sensibly any of the figures sometimes given. The population in the parts of the world in which classical music is historically most at home—western Europe, for example—is also shrinking. Part of the loss of interest in classical music may, however, be laid at the door of the record industry. At the time that listening to records was beginning to overtake going to concerts as the chief way of staying in contact with the classical tradition, the record companies consistently refused to make records freely or cheaply available to schools. Educating a future public would have meant planning in longer terms than the habits of thought of the modern business world are comfortable with. Nevertheless, this makes a coherent view of our cultural heritage in literature and music an awkward undertaking. Some educators have abandoned the idea as hopeless and (sour grapes!) as unnecessary. Even the idea of a canon of great works of the past can inspire resentment today.

2

At the beginning of the third book of his *Discorsi* (a commentary on the first ten books of Titus Livy), Machiavelli writes, "If one wants a republic or a sect [i.e., a party or religion] to live a long time, it is necessary to bring it back often to its beginnings" *(il suo principio)*. He puts it simply and dogmatically. With the passage of time, a republican system of government and a religious sect will need renovation: "It is as clear as light that without renovation, these bodies cannot last. The mode of renovation is, as I have said, to reduce them toward their origins." These renovations can, he remarks, be brought about by extrinsic causes, as when attacks by the barbarians inspired the Roman state to "wish to be reborn, and in being reborn, to take on new life and new virtue," but it is better when the return to the basic principles comes from "intrinsic prudence," when the origins of the society are systematically rediscovered. "We can see," Machiavelli remarks a few pages later, "how necessary this renovation is by the example of our religion, which, if it had not been returned to its origins by Saint Francis and Saint Dominic, would have been completely exhausted, since with poverty and the example of the life of Christ, they brought it back to the mind of men, where it was already exhausted." The return to beginnings is, for Machiavelli, not only a rebirth but a way of finding new life and new vigor. The sense of a society's origins is embodied in its tradition and guarantees its survival.

I have tried to ennoble these simple home truths by dressing them up with Machiavelli and his awareness of their practical value. It is interesting that he conceives them as having the greatest importance above all for the republican form of government. ("He who wants to create absolute power, commonly called a tyranny, must innovate in everything.") Machiavelli is realist enough to understand that tradition is often an illusion or a fraud: "Whoever wishes to reform the government of a city," he observes, "and wants it to be accepted and to maintain it to everyone's satisfaction, will have to retain at least the shadow of the ancient ways, so that to the people nothing will seem to have changed although in fact the new laws are in all respects completely alien to those of the past." A sensible opportunist will therefore fake a tradition when he has to.

It has often been observed that revolutionary movements generally claim to be restoring the past, to return to an as yet uncorrupted state, an age of innocence. Martin Luther's ideal, like that of Saint Francis, was to restore the earliest decades of the primitive Church; the Jacobins of the French Revolution wanted to return to the naive virtue and courage of the Roman Republic; the early Romantic poets wanted to restore to poetry the simple clarity of everyday speech. The appeal to tradition is useful both to sustain the system in power and to destroy it. This is because a tradition, if it is to function practically, is malleable, not rigid. Returning to one's origins in a moment of crisis will alter the origins, and literally transform the past to fit a new sense of desperation or hope.

A democratic society—at least, a society with democratic elements—functions most cohesively when there is a general knowledge of its laws, its history, and its artistic inheritance. In eighteenth-century England and America, the only part of the literary heritage that one could take for granted as shared by almost everybody was the translation of the Bible, but during the nineteenth century a wider knowledge of fiction, poetry, and drama began to work its way into layers of the population. Since the fifteenth century a knowledge of Roman and Greek literature was the standard way of appearing to return to one's cultural origins. Athens and Rome were the mythical sources of modern society and a superficial acquaintance with their classics provided a certificate that one was a gentleman; even women were reluctantly allowed to acquire this distinction at times. It was, however, female taste in the vernacular literature that was the most powerful force in fixing the criteria that determined the status of writing in English. Eventually an informal canon of serious literature in the vulgar tongue was formed and imposed by education.

The essential paradox of a canon, however—and we need to emphasize this repeatedly—is that a tradition is often most successfully sustained by those who appear to be trying to attack or to destroy it. It was Wagner, Debussy, and Stravinsky who gave new life to the Western musical tradition while seeming to undermine its very foundations. As Proust wrote, "The great innovators are the only true classics and form a continuous series. The imitators of the classics, in their finest moments, only procure for us a pleasure of erudition and taste that has no great value."[1] Any canon of works or laws that forms the basis of a culture or a society is subject to continuous reinterpretation and to change, enlargements, and contractions, but to be effective it is evident that it must retain a sense of identity—it must, in fact, resist change and reinterpretation and yield to them reluctantly and with difficulty. A tradition's sense of identity is dependent on the way it is transmitted, on what kind of access to it is made available to the members of the society concerned, and on whether the transmission makes the canon too rigid or too yielding.

3

To illustrate the strange problems in the definition and the diffusion of tradition in the arts today, I must begin by descending from these grand generalities to personal anecdote. I was in Oxford and thought this would be an opportunity to buy a volume of the early philosophical works of Francis Bacon published by Oxford University Press as part of an ongoing complete critical edition. This was not stocked by most bookstores since the press had decided that it would henceforth publish this kind of book only for libraries and accordingly put an exceedingly high price on it, way beyond the means of most students, teachers, or book lovers in general. (This policy started about twenty years ago and coincided unfortunately with the moment in England and America when most university libraries found themselves strapped for cash, so it became beyond their means as well.)

I went to the store that the press keeps in Oxford and asked for the book. "Not all the volumes of that edition are available," I was told, but the salesman helpfully looked up the edition on his computer. "That's the volume I want," I said, pointing to the item on the computer. "We have zero stock of that volume," I was told; "perhaps you can find it secondhand." This was a strangely defeatist attitude from a publisher—above all since secondhand bookshops, even in Oxford, are closing permanently with the inevitability of leaves falling from the trees in the autumn.

In any case, it has become common enough to find that when the fifth volume of a new, complete, and at least temporarily adequate text of a classical author appears, volumes one to four are already unavailable. It used to be the boast of Oxford University Press that they never let a book go out of print. We

---

1. In his article "Classicism and Romanticism."

can understand that economic pressures in the modern world would not permit such a grandiose policy to continue, but the British university presses have no longer any pride in providing the best possible version of the English classics. These are made available today in the most haphazard fashion, and usually only if each volume is heavily subsidized by institutional funds.

A good deal of writing is intended for a quick sale of six months—or two weeks, a single day, or even a few hours. Modern publishing is geared for the most part to the short term, and in general properly so, although publishers are naturally pleased if a book sells for a longer time than they thought they had any right to expect. (The insane policy of some governments of taxing publishers on their unsold stock makes printing for long-term sale impossible.) However, a short-term policy makes no sense with a volume that presents a classic like Bacon or Dickens in a new text based upon years of research, and doubly foolish when the publication is part of a large project which requires some years to reach completion.

From the middle of the nineteenth century to the middle of the twentieth the greatest part of English literature that had attained some kind of classical authority was available in well-bound, well-edited publications largely available to readers of modest means, and the less expensive paperback versions made some of this even more widely accessible. Various series systematically covered the field: Bohn's library, the Modern Library, Everyman's Library, the World's Classics, the Oxford English Texts, and others. Nevertheless, in the second half of the last century, this representation began to decline, and even to fall apart. Most of these series have disappeared, retrenched, or gone into paperback—in many cases, the latter expedience proclaims the impermanence of the product. No first-rate complete edition with the most modern scholarship at a price affordable for the average reader is available of Wordsworth, Shelley, Dryden, George Eliot, Thomas Browne, or Ben Jonson, to list only a few, and no publisher appears to have any plans to make the English literary tradition more accessible.

There are, of course, libraries from which one can borrow books, and also the new technology of printing on demand, which should replace the need for the publisher to stock books. Until now, the new technology has not developed very far, although it will surely do so in the future. One university press offers to print any book needed within a month, but a bookseller who ordered from them told me that a volume requested a year and a half ago has still not arrived.

Neither the public library nor print-on-demand are satisfying solutions for becoming acquainted with the fundamental works of our culture. Reading the works of Shelley in a copy borrowed for a month or two from a library is not acceptable if you admire his work deeply. A classic may almost be defined as a book to which you wish to return from time to time even if only for a few minutes. When I take a book from a library and find that it is that kind of work, I immediately return it largely unread in order to force myself to find a copy of my own.

The technology of print-on-demand, too, neutralizes an important element of the pleasure of reading: after all, a book is a material object as well as a collection of words, and I do not like to decide to buy one before holding it in my hands for half a minute and glancing at its contents. Typography, page design, the hue and quality of the paper—all this contributes to literary pleasure. Perhaps in the end, however, we shall all have to resign ourselves to reading mainly the texts we can order electronically.

Access to what are considered the great works of painting and sculpture is adequately provided by museums. They stand as a formidable barrier to those who would like to get rid of a canon, or radically alter its character (generally replacing dead white males with candidates selected by ideology, politics, or sexual preference). As I have said, a canon properly resists change, although, in the end, it must change if it is to exert a living influence. However, an abrupt and radical alteration is generally impossible to achieve: the old values spring immediately back into place once the new ideology's back is turned. Introducing new figures into the canon is therefore, with few exceptions, a slow process, the additions generally reaching public acceptance only after decades of professional interest.

The example of two poets, John Donne and Friedrich Hölderlin, often said to have been discovered at the end of the nineteenth century after years of neglect, can show that the pathos of neglect and rediscovery is largely a myth. The present fame of Donne is popularly supposed to be owing to the influence of T. S. Eliot, but he was greatly admired by Coleridge and influenced Browning; and editions of his poetry were available throughout the nineteenth century. Perhaps the most influential academic critic of the time, George Saintsbury, wrote of Donne as "always possessing, in actual presence or near suggestion, a poetical quality that no English poet has ever surpassed." The criticism of Eliot brought Donne to the attention of a larger public, but he had never lacked admirers. Hölderlin is said to have been rescued from complete obscurity at the same time as Donne by the interest of two great poets, Rainer Maria Rilke and Stefan George, but earlier Robert Schumann wrote music inspired by his work, and Brahms set his verses to music. The fame of both Donne and Hölderlin increased greatly at the opening of the twentieth century, but these additions to the canon were made possible by the earlier existence of a continuously sustained admiration.[2]

---

2. The elevation of an absolutely unknown artist to the pantheon is exceedingly rare: among the few examples are the seventeenth-century Thomas Traherne, whose unpublished religious poetry was only discovered in manuscript in the early twentieth century, and the Welsh eighteenth-century painter Thomas Jones, whose works were only released

The efficacy of a tradition, however, can be weakened by swamping it with a host of minor figures, and we have seen this happen in our time. The fashion for Baroque music has awakened the interest of recording companies and concert societies, and the novelty of an unknown figure has a brief commercial interest. A brilliant essay by Theodor Adorno mocked the way the taste for Baroque style reduced Bach to the status of Telemann, obliterated the difference between the extraordinary and the conventional. Concerts of music by Locatelli, Albinoni, or Graun are bearable only for those music lovers for whom period style is more important than quality.

Of greater concern, however, is the way the taste for novelty has made it more difficult to enlarge the canon with more controversial figures today. Some thirty years ago, I was invited by Pierre Boulez to record his piano music for CBS records, which had hired him as both a conductor and a composer with an engagement to make his works available on records. I started by recording Sonata no. 1 and the two movements of Sonata no. 3 then released to the public, "Trope" and "Constellation-Miroir."[3] The composer was present at the recording, which does not, of course, make it official, but I carried out the few suggestions he made, and the record won the Edison Prize in Europe. Then it was deleted from the catalog a few months after being issued. This was not due to any malice on the part of the company, since it kept my album of the last six sonatas of Beethoven in the catalog for more than a decade and reissued it on CD; it was merely the mechanical action of a computer which cut out any disc for which the sale fell below a certain mark. (I could have gone on to record Boulez's Sonata no. 2, which I had performed several times, but Maurizio Pollini came out with a beautiful recording of that work, although with perhaps somewhat less ferocity than I would have preferred. In the end, it seemed to me unprofitable to continue a project that was being treated so cavalierly by the company.)

The policy of either an immediate profit or the withdrawal of any book or record that does not have sufficient commercial interest when issued makes it awkward to establish the achievement of a new figure whose work has a certain complexity. Committing the company to represent Boulez as a composer on records should have required CBS to keep a representative number of them accessible over a period of years, so that a body of work could remain before the public. When Mozart was played in Paris in the early nineteenth century, he

---

to the public by his family in the 1930s. Most resurrections that have a permanent success are of previously successful artists whose fame has been eclipsed for reasons of fashion, like Monteverdi or Vermeer, or has been temporarily obscured.

3. I have seen the manuscript of the three other movements written a half century ago, but Boulez publishes his music with deep reluctance.

was popular neither with the critics nor with the public, but his music kept being frequently performed until both critics and public came around.[4]

The question is not the ultimate worth of Boulez's music, although a great many musicians find him one of the few important composers of the last fifty years, but the possibility for the general music lover to arrive at an informed opinion. His works are rarely played in public in America and not that often in France. When Boulez was director of the New York Philharmonic, he consistently refused to conduct a single one of his orchestral compositions, since the rehearsal conditions would not have permitted an adequate performance.[5]

Record companies have not always been so shortsighted and irresponsible. When Goddard Lieberson ran CBS, all the works of Stravinsky were recorded and remained largely available, and this certainly contributed to the almost complete acceptance of his style in the world of music. The two complete recordings of the works of Anton von Webern that CBS issued have made it much easier to perform this music before the public. There would be much less difficulty with the programming of contemporary work if composers whose musical language has awakened professional respect, interest, and admiration were made substantially available on records which remained in the catalog long enough to give them a chance with the public.

During Lieberson's time, I asked my producer at CBS, Jane Friedmann, how the two largest American companies stood with regard to the classical repertoire. She replied, "RCA has all the big blockbuster recordings, but oddly enough we make more money in the classical field." The secret of the success was that CBS issued many more inexpensive recordings; RCA preferred large

---

4. See below, "The Triumph of Mozart," pp. 73–78.

5. When a piece of Harrison Birtwhistle was performed a few years ago in Paris by Boulez with his Ensemble Intercontemporain, I remarked to Boulez that I had never heard a work by that admirable composer sound so convincing and effective. "We had thirty-five rehearsals," Boulez replied. This may seem excessive and it is beyond the means of most musical organizations today, but when Beethoven's Symphony no. 9 was undertaken during the late 1820s at the Paris Conservatoire, the first rehearsal was so terrible that it was rehearsed every day for a year. Berlioz reported that the result was a triumph, although it was conducted by Habeneck, who was his deadly enemy.

The music world has not changed as much as one might think. Radically unfamiliar works require much more rehearsal than is practical when they first appear, before they can work their way into general musical consciousness: the first performance of Elliott Carter's Double Concerto for Harpsichord, Piano, and Two Small Orchestras needed ten days of rehearsal; several years later, with a different orchestra that had never played the work, it needed only two days—the idiom had gradually permeated the musicians' world. When Hans Rosbaud directed Schoenberg's *Moses und Aron* at the Zürich opera in 1957, he spent almost the entire budget of the year on rehearsals of this one work.

sales figures even when they did not cover the costs of expensive projects. This skewed ideology influences many of the CEOs in the culture business. Even when the company loses money, large sales figures have more prestige and glamour than small but steady sales with a profit.

4

Not only production, but critical interpretation is affected by the market. To attract attention, to sell a critical interpretation, novelty is an aid, but scandal is often thought to be required. Were some of Felix Mendelssohn's works really written by his sister Fanny? Was Huckleberry Finn homosexual? These are the grand questions that provoke discussion. It is true that to create an outrage may often be salutary: for example, William Empson's book *Milton's God* took seriously Milton's intention of justifying the ways of God to man, and claimed that the Christian God was so horribly cruel that no real justification was possible; Empson's study of Milton's arguments and logic made readers attend to the details of *Paradise Lost* with renewed intensity. A traditional interpretation of a traditional work seems to be insufficiently exciting even when it goes more deeply than others have gone before or casts further light on the work. We require the stimulus of shock.

Plays and operas are available in books and scores, so we can imagine what dramatists, librettists, and composers had in mind, but finding this out from almost any staging today has become impossible. It is not, I think, always understood how much imagination can be deployed in an interpretation that remains faithful to the original text: there is always a place for innovation that enhances without deforming the original. However, to be talked about, a production of an opera or play must generally misrepresent the work in a striking way.

For two and a half centuries, serious opera has always been run at a considerable loss, supported by reaching into the pockets of taxpayers. Perhaps a production would not get talked about enough to justify the continuation of this kind of financing unless it subverted the opera and gave the newspapers an outrage to write about. Perhaps, too, any kind of nonsense is judged appropriate for a genre traditionally considered dramatically absurd from its creation in the seventeenth century, if only one can draw in an audience large enough to dazzle the donors with their tax-deductible contributions. A fine production of an opera used to remain for many years in the repertory. Simply sustaining tradition today has become much more difficult.

CHAPTER 3

The Future of Music

I

Since music is a primitive and essential human activity its survival is not in question. By many eighteenth-century thinkers it was held to be the original form of language, the origin of speech. If there is a question of survival, it is of Western art music, or serious music, what is called "classical" music. That its survival is in jeopardy is an opinion expressed largely by journalists and by a few disgruntled critics. This is, however, a view that has been surfacing regularly for the last 230 years. It was even passionately maintained more than four centuries ago. I presume that some conservative Greeks felt that way when the purity of the Doric mode was perverted by the introduction of the lascivious Ionic mode. Perhaps the best plan would be simply to take a summary look at what enabled Western art music to survive in the past, and see to what extent the same factors still apply today.

I should like to start with what may seem like an irrelevant detail from a related art. The troubadour poetry of late twelfth-century Provence was originally written down with the music: the manuscripts contain both the words and the tunes. Toward the middle of the thirteenth century, however, collections of the poems appear without the music. It is also at this time that they begin to be accompanied sometimes by biographies of the poets, called *vidas*, or by critical commentaries, called *razos*. It would seem that when the poetry was isolated from the original musical context that gave it part of its meaning, a new context had to be invented to substitute for the lost significance. (It was sometimes true that the old melodies would have been known without being recopied, but this was not always the case.) Being read without the music, the poems now had a different social function; they were no longer performed to make up a part of a communal experience. The void caused by the disappearance of the poet who sang was made good by his biography. And the critical commentary replaced the experience of hearing together with others.

It was more or less at this time during the thirteenth century that Western music began to draw apart from poetry with the introduction of polyphony, in which two or more strands of music sound simultaneously. The new degree of complexity, which resulted over the centuries in an unprecedented and unequaled richness for music, demanded greater and more intense awareness from both listener and performer, an awareness that was at least partially independent of the words. Words and music developed separate interests, each with an independent aesthetic that was sometimes at odds with the other. The poems now asked to be read on their own, but consequently they now required a new context to make good the disappearance of the musical context. Biography and critical commentary arose to provide a kind of significance that was previously not felt to be necessary. The poetry had to survive without the music, and it stimulated the new setting that allowed it to flourish. Complex vocal music could even, at times, be executed by instruments alone, and the music began to stand by itself.

When we speak of survival here, obviously we do not consider the survival of the art itself, but of the specific works of art. An art can survive simply because its traditions survive, its practices continue. This kind of ritual survival is best accomplished in a society that remains static, and that is culturally homogeneous. The survival of a work in a rapidly changing society, on the other hand, depends not only on whether it is handed down to us unmutilated, but on its ability to adapt to changing conditions of reception, on its capacity, when its original social function has been destroyed or altered beyond recognition, to create or inspire new kinds of significance that allow its vitality full play. Just as troubadour poetry, when its original form of presentation was moving toward obsolescence, found a new social context from biography and critical commentary, so many works of Western music have inspired new forms of presentation from age to age that have brought them back to life again and again.

Essential to Western music is its ability to adapt to different social conditions, or—to put it a different way—to remain independent of the conditions that watched over its creation. By the middle of the fifteenth century, manuscript collections of music mixed together religious and secular music. Vocal works could be performed by instrumentalists; liturgical music—motets and sections of masses—could be arranged for the lute. Church music could be transformed into secular entertainment. As with troubadour poetry, when the art of music began to free itself from any rigid or absolute attachment to its social function in the late fifteenth and early sixteenth centuries, critical writing about composers and their works started to appear as if to justify and give meaning to the existence of an independent art. We learn, for example, that Josquin des Pres habitually withheld his compositions for several years before allowing them to circulate.

The survival of a work of Western music, before the twentieth century, depended essentially on a system of notation. Of course, we must not underestimate the power of memory. Thomas de Quincey, for example, was able to repeat a good deal of Wordsworth's *The Prelude* from memory after having heard it read to him years before (he was certainly not permitted to copy any of it before the publication thirty-five years later). Most of the music in the world is not notated at all: it survives insofar as it does only through repeated performance, through the fidelity of the performers' memory. A great deal of music is not repeated at all, but newly created on each occasion. In any case, some of the finest music does not need notation, or at any rate resists it. Folk music is particularly recalcitrant to being written down, and it is only in recent years that an attempt has been made to notate—with only partial success— some of the best examples of jazz.

In odd corners and pockets of European civilizations, a few fragments of medieval and Renaissance music were perpetuated throughout the eighteenth century, half-alive, like the crumbling Gothic ruins of an earlier culture. A monastery south of Rome continued (and still continues today) to preserve Byzantine chant. The Sistine Chapel choir still had the odd piece of Palestrina in its repertoire. But the history of music came into being inspired by the anti-quarian interests of the end of the 1700s, when, in literature, old ballads were printed along with the legends of Robin Hood, and the Dark Ages became romantically fashionable. The true beginning of musicology was Charles Burney's decoding around 1798 of the puzzling notation of Josquin des Pres's masterly *Déploration sur la mort d'Ockeghem,* a composition in memory of the fifteenth-century Franco-Flemish composer Johannes Ockeghem. For his *General History of Music,* Burney set the parts into score. (In Josquin's time, all music was copied as separate parts for the different performers; whatever full scores may have existed at that time, none have come down to us, and we have no autograph manuscripts from that period.)

The dependence of classical music on the score, or on a system of notation, has given rise to odd and eccentric philosophical speculations. To dispel some of the clouds, we may briefly examine what Burney did. Having copied the parts out into a score, he found that they made no sense. The dissonances were intolerable and absurd. The tenor part, set to the chant of the Requiem for the dead, was marked "Canon." To any eighteenth-century musician, a canon was a piece in which different voices sang the same melody together but starting at different points, out of phase, so that a single melody would make contrapuntal harmony with itself.

This could be presented as a puzzle. Musicians would be given the melody in a single voice, and challenged to find the places where the other voices entered into it to make perfect harmony. That would presume that one had to find how to add a voice singing the chant to Josquin's *Déploration,* but beginning later than the tenor in a way that would make proper sense. However, the dissonance of the piece was already so intolerable that adding notes could only make it worse. Burney's discovery was that "canon" simply meant "puzzle," and this one was resolved by transposing the tenor chant, which was in the mode of church music called Dorian (centered on D), up a step into the mode called Phrygian (centered on E); once this was done, all became clear, and a great work was revealed.

Josquin's canon can stand for us as a symbol of the relation of notation to realization, of score to performance. For practical purposes, not every aspect of music can be written down. Notation is selective: only certain musical elements, or "parameters," are chosen. For this reason, we might consider an art heavily dependent on notation like Western art music as essentially inferior to the musics of other cultures, transmitted orally or by the imitation of practice. That is why we can say of such and such a pianist that he or she may be playing the written notes but has no idea how to interpret the music. It is almost entirely on what is not written down that different schools of pedagogy attempt to base their claims to superiority. However, it is essentially the fundamentally unsatisfactory nature of notation that has allowed the monuments of Western music to survive, to escape the ruinous erosion of time. In fact, it is the basic antagonism of score and performance, of concept and realization, that is the glory of Western music.

One metaphysical aspect of Josquin's canon needs to be set in relief. We hear the tenor part sung in Phrygian, but in reality it is in Dorian. This reality has two facets. First, the original chant is in fact in the Dorian mode; that is the way it came down to Josquin and has come down to us. Second, the chant is written on paper in the Dorian mode: that is the way the singer saw it and still sees it (if one keeps the fifteenth-century notation). The written form acknowledges the "authentic" version of the chant, which is then, as Burney discovered, inflected and even contradicted by what one sings and hears. If the originating form is the written one that is not heard, the emotion conveyed by the music comes from its realization: to our ears, and probably to the ears of a contemporary of Josquin, Phrygian harmony has greater pathos than Dorian, and is most suited to the elegy commemorating the death of Josquin's greatest predecessor.

2

It is sometimes said that the work of music is not what is written down on paper: the score is merely a set of directions that enables one to find or realize the work. This claim, however, leads to an absurd misunderstanding of the way the music works. What we hear, the realization of the score in sound, can never be identified with the work itself because there are many different ways of realizing the score, but they are all realizations of the same work, which in fact remains invariant—remains, we might say, visible but inaudible behind all these realizations.

It is not sensible to claim that for every score there is an ideal realization. The relation between score and realization implies that various possibilities remain open. This is how Artur Schnabel could be justified in maintaining that a Beethoven sonata was greater than any realization could possibly be. The written score sets limits within which many possibilities can find a home. The critical problem remains essentially how to decide which of the many interpretations realize the work and which ones betray it. Some interpretations are, of course, out of bounds, but determining what is legitimate and what is illicit is not as straightforward or as easy as we might like to think. In fact, the most deplorable misrepresentations of a work can often come from those who believe themselves to be the legal guardians of the tradition.

The survival of the Western musical past is due in part to the creation of an efficient system of notation. For the past 250 years, the transmission of the musical tradition has depended on the fact that in Europe, and to some extent in America, the proof that one belongs to a cultural elite has implied that some members of your family have learned to read this system of notation. Even members of the lower classes have been taught to read music, to sing, and to play an instrument—generally a keyboard instrument—as a proof of cultural literacy, as an aid to social mobility, to rising in the world. In particular, most European women in the nineteenth century from a class of even moderate pretensions learned to play the piano just as they learned to read, to sew, and to cook. Playing the piano gave one a certain self-respect, enabled one to judge others, and allowed the amateur to arrogate the right to pass judgment even on the professional.

We think today of music as something public—performed in concerts or sold to the public in the form of recordings. In the nineteenth and early twentieth centuries, the experience of music was altogether different. Most music was heard at home, and was completely private; some of the experience was semiprivate, music played at parties or after dinner by invited professional and amateur musicians. Even symphonies were not solely a part of the public realm; in music-loving families, four-hand piano arrangements of the Mozart and Beethoven symphonies were common enough. Wagner operas and Mahler symphonies were sold in four-hand piano versions for playing with a friend or another member of the family. Just as most of the audience today at a play by Shakespeare have read some of his works in school, so a good part of the audience at a symphony concert seventy-five years ago had received their first knowledge of an important part of the symphonic repertoire at home.

This private and semiprivate experience of music did more than increase one's familiarity with the repertoire. It altered the understanding of music. Playing a symphony at the piano four hands and then hearing it in public with an orchestra made one aware of the existence of the work with a strikingly different realization of the sound. Learning to play a Beethoven sonata as a part of one's education and then hearing a concert pianist perform it in public showed how personal the interpretation of a score could be—and was intended to be, in fact, for a great part of Western musical history. Merely the fact of displacing a work from the private to the public sphere altered its significance. Our assumption today, made unconsciously, that almost all music is basically public, is a radical distortion of Western tradition. We no longer have a public that largely understands how the visual experience of a musical score is transformed into an experience of sound, and to what extent this transformation is not a simple matter, but is capable of individual inflections. If the audience for classical music is not growing fast enough to make the art richly profitable—it never really was so profitable, by the way—the reason is not that there is a diminished response to the art of serious music but that there are fewer children who learn to play the piano. Learning music from records instead of playing it has radically altered our perception of the art.

3

Asking in what ways our musical culture can be transmitted to the future requires us to consider how our heritage has come down to us—which part of the past has been transmitted by being written down and what we have been able to gather only by a continuing tradition. Here it is worth emphasizing that notation only preserves very limited aspects of the music: many parameters are not written down at all.

In the history of European music, pitch is primary. Traditionally what has been notated is largely the pitch of the notes (although the notation of pitch is not as precise as we might think) and, more roughly and grossly, the rhythm. It is not clear how specifically our earliest examples of written music define the pitch: the scores seem to indicate whether the voice went up or down without allowing us to decide exactly what the intervals were. Greater precision was introduced later on and was certainly demanded by polyphonic music.

Nevertheless, what was written down was not always exactly what was sung or played. Singers could alter the written pitches up or down by the introduction of sharps and flats that did not originally appear in the text. These accidentals are called *musica ficta,* fictive music. We have been warned by Professor Margaret Bent of All Souls, Oxford, formerly of Princeton—and we must be grateful for the warning—not to identify the notes in a medieval or Renaissance manuscript with the white notes on the piano. Much of the *ficta* added to the text may have been originally understood as implicit in the notation.

However, the conception of what the pitch ought to be did not remain static over the years, and musicians developed a taste for chromatic harmony which could inflect music written as long as half a century before. To understand the development of European musical history, we should note the curious fact that the notes that were actually sung and heard are called fictive, and this implies that the written notes are somehow more real. What should be emphasized is that the musical text remained invariant while the performances could vary even as regards the absolutely primary element of pitch. Until the eighteenth century—and even later—the ornamentation of the written musical line was left to the performer. Couperin and Bach encroached on the performer's freedom, and wrote out many of the ornaments. It is interesting to note that sometimes in Bach the ornaments infringe the academic rules of counterpoint: ornaments were not subject to the same rules as the underlying text.

Another aspect of Baroque performance left up to the player was the figured bass or continuo—that is, the improvised addition of harmonies to the written-out bass part by the keyboard performer at organ, harpsichord, or early pianoforte in order to fill out the texture. Bach himself wanted the rules of counterpoint to be obeyed within his own part by the improviser of the continuo, who was working only with the bass part in front of him on the music rack; but Bach allowed, and indeed was forced to allow, the rules to be broken by the existence of parallel fifths and octaves between the continuo part and the upper parts (soprano, alto, and tenor) of the ensemble; the keyboard player was not able to see these parts and could not respect the rules.

For Bach, in spite of his desire to control what might normally have been improvised and his understanding of the importance for the music of the ornamentation, there was still a hierarchy of values. Some aspects of the music were primary, and these made up the compositional structure itself; others were secondary, and basically concerned only the realization. It is significant that in his fugues for the keyboard, he largely indicated the ornaments to the main theme only when they were convenient to play. Many editors add these ornaments (sometimes in brackets) each time the theme occurs. We no longer make the distinction so fundamental to Bach between composition and realization, and our error arises to a large extent from his practice of notating some of the elements of the realization with a fullness rare at the time.

In the history of music since Bach, many of the secondary elements have one by one become primary—that is, those aspects of music once left up to the performer have gradually become incorporated into the original compositional process. It would be a mistake to think that this has occurred only because composers wished to exercise greater control over the execution of their works. What has happened is that the secondary elements became primary to the structure. Dynamics, for example, were once a way for the performer to elucidate the structure of pitch and rhythm and make them expressive and even personal.[1] With Haydn and, above all, Beethoven, however, the dynamics are often an integral part of the motif, which has become unthinkable and unintelligible without them.

Gradually through the nineteenth and into the twentieth century, not only dynamics, but tone color are removed from the province of realization and transferred into the basic process of composition. Starting with Debussy and continuing with Boulez, indeed, tone color—balance and equilibrium of sound, pedaling, quality of staccato and legato—sometimes even outweighs the element of pitch in importance. In several pieces of Debussy, it would give the music less of a shock to play a wrong note than to play the wrong dynamics or apply the wrong touch. The composers have little by little invaded the territory of the performers. The freedom of the performer has not been completely annihilated, but it has had to be reformulated.

The distinction between primary and secondary elements has dominated the history of performance in the West, and has influenced even the way music is edited. Pitch, we agree, is determined by the composer. It would be considered immoral for a performer to change Beethoven's pitches. If he wrote a C, most musicians feel that we ought not to play a B-flat just because we might like it better. Rhythm also belongs to the composer, at least to some extent: we are allowed to inflect the rhythm, however, with rubato, with ritardandos, and with various other deformations, in order to make the expression more personal, to impose our own styles. Further, performers and editors traditionally act as if Beethoven's dynamics are merely suggestions: it would seem to be perfectly all right to play a mezzo forte where Beethoven has prescribed a piano mezza voce if we think it more effective.

As for phrasing and pedal indications, editors and performers have ruthlessly disregarded and altered Beethoven's indications—and those of Chopin, Schumann, Liszt, and almost anyone else—at will. It appears to be legitimate to change Beethoven's and Chopin's fingerings even when a different fingering

---

1. In the first part of the eighteenth century, a contrast of piano and forte could occasionally be essential to the structure of the theme, but crescendo and diminuendo were expressive effects largely determined by the singer and performer.

will radically change the sound of the passage. Pitch and part of the rhythm are primary; all the rest is secondary—a conception that, as I have implied, is imposed by the limitations of our system of notation. At times, this has even influenced composition: Schumann's Toccata op. 7 contains almost no indications of dynamics—that is, degrees of volume such as piano and forte—in order not to erode the freedom of the performer. (It should be said, however, that the required dynamics are fairly obvious, and Schumann inserts those few that would not be so evident—the dynamics are, by this time in the history of musical style, incorporated almost directly into the basic musical inspiration.)

The hierarchy of musical parameters has received its blessing from musicology, mostly without musicologists being fully aware of this or of its implication. Most musical analysis deals almost exclusively with pitch. Rhythm gets a smaller amount of examination. Tone color, texture, phrasing, all have to wait patiently in line for a little attention. They are, however, as important a part of our sensuous experience of music as any of the primary aspects, and as we have seen, many of them have become primary in our century. Our way of writing about music, however, is still anchored in the period around 1700. The notation of music makes the pitch and rhythm most precise: anything else is sketchily and subjectively indicated, and, after all, who has the courage to write about something so difficult to pin down? Ethnomusicologists experience this problem at its most poignant.

4

The distinction between idea and realization is built into Western cultural history: in the visual arts it is at the center of the argument that opposed drawing and color. Drawing was the abstract design that held the work together: color was merely the realization in the flesh of the idea. It is the late nineteenth-century painters who showed how flimsy the opposition was. In a dogmatic attempt to assert the old hierarchy, Ingres had claimed that you could not judge an oil painting until you could examine the reproductive engraving made of it; only line was truly important for him, at least in theory. By the time of Cézanne the claim no longer made any sense. In aesthetics, any formal opposition will always be eventually overridden by artists who have learned to blur the contrasts or synthesize the opposing distinctions, as Cézanne learned to compose and draw through color. Composers similarly placed timbre on the same level as pitch, in order to compose with tone color.

Discs and tapes will transmit to future generations what our performances sound like. But what about the sound of music before Edison? What will future generations be able to make of most of our musical heritage? The history of the revival of medieval and Renaissance music, and even of the Baroque, can show upon what a flimsy base our idea of the past can rest.

How did the great masterpieces of the fifteenth-century Flemish school sound when they were performed? I take this body of work as a largely uncontested supreme moment in Western musical history. Performances have ranged in my own experience from executions almost on tiptoe, like musical equivalents of the much-admired contemporary Flemish miniatures, to shouting matches, as if we were witnessing a medieval equivalent of crowd songs at football games or an urform of Carl Orff's *Carmina Burana.* How were the notes sung: with a mellow or an incisive tone, or—inspired by a once-fashionable theory based upon strange pinched facial grimaces of the singing angels in Van Eyck's *Adoration of the Lamb* in Ghent—with a continuous nasal whine? Were the singers doubled by instruments, and if so, which ones? How fast were the tempos? How high or low was the pitch? Some of these questions can be answered only with varying degrees of probability. We do not know exactly what fifteenth-century music sounded like, although we can be relatively sure that performance style and practice varied from country to country and city to city.

Does it matter what the music sounded like? Or sounds like today? This is not a question that I have heard put, perhaps because we assume the answer is an obvious Yes. Indeed, I do think the answer is more or less Yes, but it is not a simple straightforward affirmative.

Sung loud or soft, fast or slow, freely or rigidly—or not sung at all but played by instruments, or indeed, merely imagined from the score—many of the works of Guillaume Dufay, Johannes Ockeghem, Josquin des Pres, and Pierre de la Rue will seem beautiful to most cultivated musicians and amateurs of music. Not because we have been brainwashed or imposed upon by historical reputation, but because of the way the works fit in with our previous musical experience from Bach to Gershwin and Boulez, and make sense to us after a momentary adjustment of our expectations. Not every revival of the past will meet with such assent, but these works are easily embraced by our already habitual musical concerns. That, of course, is because they were an essential part of the historical process by which the musical tradition developed, and these works can still be implicitly discerned within the later developments. To understand how this functions, however, we must turn back to the distinction between score and performance, composition and realization.

In our belief that music is what is made available to the public, we have a prejudice in favor of realization. It is hard to make people understand today that the score may be beautiful irrespective of any realization. The ideal example is, of course, Bach, whose work provided the foundation of music education for two centuries. His compositions from *The Art of the Fugue* and *The Well-Tempered Keyboard,* for example, have been played on the harpsichord, the organ, the clavichord, the piano, and by a string quartet, a full orchestra, the Moog synthesizer, a jazz band, and the Swingle Singers. You may prefer one medium to another (the original intention was two hands at the keyboard, whichever keyboard you had around the house), but all of it sounds pretty good. Which means that in some senses of the word "sound," it does not matter what Bach sounds like. The theoretical structure of pitch and rhythm is successful enough to stand however it is realized. It is not that the realization in sound is irrelevant, but it is not quite so fundamentally relevant as the devotees of authentic sound would like to maintain.

The eminent value of the score—the theoretical structure of pitch and rhythm with some of the other aspects of music indicated generally in a somewhat cursory fashion—is, I think, unique to Western music. It accounts for the reason that we think music is somehow allied to philosophy (although perhaps we have inherited this view of music from the Greeks). There are two consequences: first, the music may be admired even when no one can be quite sure what it sounds like; second, a score can be realized in many different ways, with many different kinds of sonority, as if a purely ideal structure could be made to give life to a multitude of actual forms. (In our time, Boulez has made this almost into a principle of composing, with many different versions of the same structure, but in his case the working-out of a new realization is, in reality, only a later and more advanced stage of composition.) We must conclude that although the musical works of the past have been preserved by a system of notation, what has guaranteed the life of the past through so many centuries, or allowed forgotten music to be revived, is essentially the ambiguity of the notation. The fact that it does not tell us exactly how the music sounded has made it possible for later generations to realize it in their own way, deforming or restoring the past in a variety of forms.

5

The love of music is a natural human instinct, but the love of classical music is something else again: it may even reasonably be considered to be perverse. It certainly demands at least a discernible amount of experience and education to become addicted to it. For serious music to play an important role in a culture requires not only a significant number of professionals who can be hired to perform it, but a dedicated body of amateurs who take an active but occasional part in its production. From the sixteenth to the seventeenth century, art music was upheld by the members of society who learned to sing as well as to listen. Beginning in the eighteenth century, learning to sing was partially replaced by learning to play an instrument, above all a keyboard instrument, and finally, above all, the piano, which ended by ousting all the other keyboard instruments from the province of the enlightened amateur. In the nineteenth and twentieth centuries, the piano at home and in the salon was used not only as a solo instrument, but also to accompany lieder; opera arias were also arranged and played in the home at the piano. The transcriptions of string quartets and symphonies for two or four hands was a common way of getting acquainted with the most important works that one would hear in the concert hall. As a small child I first came into contact, for example, with the symphony of César Franck by reading a transcription for two hands.

In the middle class, knowing how to play the piano was thought to give one a social advantage, as I have remarked, although of course one pretended that it was a purely disinterested love of music that supported the thousands of piano teachers who did their bit for European civilization. The great advantage of this kind of pretense is that in many cases it eventually turns out to be true; social progress is regularly and correctly fueled by forms of hypocrisy. The audience for a concert of serious music always contained an important group of amateurs who had experienced the art at first hand. Most of these had never had any ambition or desire to became a professional, but they combined connoisseurship and enthusiasm.

Learning to sing and learning to play the piano have been supplanted today by collecting records. This is a disquieting development that is already affecting the future. The audience for serious music has become increasingly passive, and there is no longer an important body of educated listeners experienced in the making of music that can act as a bridge between the general public and the professional.

Popular music has today an astonishingly large number of young people who are active in performing it privately, for their own pleasure and for a few friends. This has been true throughout history. But in our time, popular music reverses the classical relation between composition and realization: realization becomes all. Except as a form of nostalgic and commercial kitsch that deforms the original product, popular music is no longer the faithful rendition of a traditional tune. In the great examples of popular music in our century, those that have already attained a classic status like the great jazz improvisations of musicians from Art Tatum to Miles Davis, the original composition becomes identified with the performance. The interest of the tune at the basis of the improvisation—like Cole Porter's "Night and Day," for example—is minimal, except that it is useful and enlightening for connoisseurs to be aware of the tune, just as one recognizes the traditional Lutheran hymn tune in a Bach chorale prelude. Tatum does not realize Porter's composition, he composes an entirely new work into which the tune enters as a structural component. In the early part of the twentieth century, the most advanced forms of popular music were essentially improvised events, each of which was one-off, ephemeral: it was preserved not by a score, but on occasion by a recording, and was basically unrepeatable.

In improvisation, the distinction between composition and realization disappears almost completely. So it does as well in another typical phenomenon of our time, electronic music: the playing of an electronically realized composition on tape is identical with the composer's intention, except where the reproducing equipment or the acoustical setup is defective. The role of improvisation, however, has been reduced in rock music: here, recording has taken over. A public performance of rock music is rarely a newly improvised work or a new realization of a score, but the reproduction of a recording. Most of the audience knows the work from a disc, and has come to experience it communally en masse. (In rock music, too, the creative role of the recording must be taken into account.)

With classical music, the impact of the recording industry has been complex. It has enabled us to grasp how many different ways of realizing a work may exist, how many different and wildly contrasting interpretations of, say, *The Passion According to Saint Matthew* are possible. It has also made the general public acquainted—in a largely haphazard and disorienting fashion—with a bewildering variety of period styles and genres, and helped us to absorb so much of what seems alien at first hearing.

Recordings, nevertheless, stand on its head the traditional aesthetic on which art music has been based. For most of Western history, the composition is fixed, the performance is fragile, existing only for the moment. Recordings, however, privilege the performance over the score. The composition is held at a distance: the performance is up front. This sense of privilege is increased by the possibility of splicing. Performances are no longer flawed except by the idiocy of the interpreters or an injudicious placement of the microphones. Technical mistakes may be easily eradicated.

With recordings, one of the most profound aspects of the experience of art music is almost completely obliterated: the resistance of the work to interpretation. I have spoken of the relation of score to realization as an opposition. The work does not hand itself over easily to interpretation; it does not surrender without a fight; it puts obstacles in the way of the executant. If you have played a Beethoven sonata, then you know what the problems are of looking at a score and how it is to be turned into sound. But with a recording, what you hear is the sound without being aware of the score behind it. Both experiences are fine, but most people today no longer have the experience of knowing what it is to transform a score into sound and the kind of resistance that the work exhibits. With five or ten recordings of the *Matthew Passion,* we can see that they're all different but we're not exactly sure of the process that transforms the score into the sound.

This process is a physical experience absolutely essential to the Western music tradition. Listening to a record, we neither feel the physical difficulty of realizing a musical text, nor can we witness, as in a concert hall, the exciting spectacle of the torments of the performer.

Every musical culture has its own idiosyncratic physical experience. The peculiarity of the Western classical tradition is the difficulty of translating the score of someone else's idea into sound. Recordings have, of course, made possible the expansion of our experience of the musical repertoire, given us an unprecedented contact with past ages. But there is a small qualitative difference between the experience of music on records and the experience of music in concert, and a large qualitative difference between listening to it on records and playing it oneself. Sometimes there are technical obstacles, as in the works of Liszt, which can literally cause physical pain to the pianist. Sometimes the problem is emotional: how to realize the extraordinary passion that lies within a Chopin polonaise without falling into the sentimental clichés of performance style taught at conservatories around the world.

Often enough the obstacle is intellectual: How can one make audible for an audience the intricate interweaving of the voices in a Bach fugue without merely hammering out the theme and without obscuring the affective power of the work? For a great part of the repertoire, including the examples I have given, the difficulties are technical, emotional, and intellectual all at once. Behind all these lies the fundamental one: How is the physical pleasure of performance to be made manifest to the listener—and to oneself—without obscuring the qualities of the original composition that make everything possible?

For centuries, the tradition of art music has rested on this opposition of composition and realization, and on the sense that the composition has a value that transcends all imaginable realizations. Whether this fundamental aesthetic requirement will last into the future, I do not know. It is attacked not only by the replacement of public concerts and private performance by records. It is subtly undermined by directors of opera who think that they can invent stage business, which has no relation or relevance to the music, as if the musical score can be overridden by the stage director's imagination. It is violated by the fans of authentic period style who think that a work of music can be simply identified with the way it might have sounded to the composer. It is misunderstood by the widespread failure to grasp the different ways a work could be realized during the lifetime of the composer and, in addition, the ways in which it is altered by the generations that follow, while retaining an important part of its validity. It is ignored by so many who do not recognize the special character of the Western tradition, and who imagine that it can be treated as another variety of folk music.

The eventual survival of the tradition is ultimately not at stake. There are the documents available—the scores and the recordings and a bewildering pile of published research. If the tradition disappears, it may be revived, as we have revived the singing of Gregorian chant. Nevertheless, there is a difference between the continuous survival of a tradition and one that has to be brought back to life from death or near-death. It is not, however, what might be thought, a difference of authenticity. The continued existence of a tradition brings with it gradual changes and corruptions in the performance and the realization of its works. A Viennese performance of Mozart today is incomparably different from one during the composer's lifetime. Recovering the past with Mozart is as difficult as with Monteverdi, but the problems are not the same. For Mozart, we have to correct and adjust—not only to go back to the earlier techniques and style, but to find ones more adequate to modern concert halls and instruments and modern sensibility than the nineteenth-century stylistic habits with which he has been saddled. For Monteverdi, on the other hand, we have to invent a style of performance, inspired by contemporary documents and accounts, in a process like digging up the ruins of Assyrian civilization. In the twenty-second century, will the monuments of Beethoven and Chopin have to be excavated or merely tactfully restored?

CHAPTER 4

The Canon

I

A museum, it is now generally realized, deforms and disfigures the works of art it contains. It wrenches the pictures and statues out of the churches, palaces, and homes from which they drew their life and much of their significance, and exhibits them in an apparently neutral space, an intellectual void. Some of their functions have been wiped out; a good part of their meaning is lost. The walls have a color and texture different from the ones that originally set off the works of art, so that the harmony of the paint and the marble has been denatured, the space in which the art presents itself to the spectator has been altered. Although we may celebrate the uncanny aptitude of the objects in a museum to adapt to their new home, to present new aspects and even to convey some of the old meanings, historians deplore the inevitable loss that the institution entails. Nevertheless, we cannot do without museums: if they alter the meaning of the past beyond repair, they allow some of it to survive.

Literature, of course, survives physically with greater ease. We do not need to exhibit books: they lie peacefully on the shelves of libraries, and need only a minimum of heat and humidity control so that they do not crumble or rot. There is one function of the museum, however, imperfectly exercised by the library or only haphazardly exercised. The museum conserves the past by

A review of the works of Jean-Jacques Rousseau volume 5, of the Marquis de Sade vol. 2, and of Bettina von Brantano vol. 4.

suppressing part of it: works of art are divided into those worth seeing and junk, the latter consigned to the reserve cellars when it is not shipped out and sold. Our knowledge of the past demands this suppression in order to be manageable. We cannot look at every picture, read every book; critical evaluation is not so much ideological as practical. Some of the past has to be suppressed for the rest to become visible. But it is just this suppression that has understandably and sometimes justifiably given rise to protest in our times.

For literature, the counterpart of the museum is not the library, but the uniform edition of the classics, the publication of the "canon" in a hard-bound, permanent form to be kept on their shelves by the well-to-do and even the less well-off but more ambitious and appreciative readers. These regimented volumes with their similar bindings give their owners a satisfying sense of culture, and define that part of our heritage invested with an aura of prestige. Today, however, large parts of the population in many countries are alienated from a culture they feel has been imposed upon them. There is agreement from all sides that the canon in art, literature, and music needs revision, although less agreement on what kind of revision and even less understanding of how revision might be accomplished. Dragging the neglected artist or writer out of obscurity does not inevitably result in acceptance. The editions of the classics that still manage to survive today reveal the difficulties both of revising the canon and of making long-accepted figures presentable or even legible to the disaffected modern reader.

These uniform editions date back to the late Renaissance, when the Dutch publishing house of Elzevir made the Latin and even some of the Greek classics available in the convenient but elegant pocket format useful for traveling; no gentleman could afford to be without some of these volumes. It is, however, the late eighteenth and nineteenth centuries that were the great ages of printing the classics in the vulgar tongue. Dr. Johnson's *Lives of the Poets* was written as the prefaces to a publishing venture intended to contain all the English poetry worth reading. Almost all female poets were omitted, of course, and so was John Donne, but a place was found for him a few years later when the series was taken up by other publishers. Alexander Chalmers's twenty-two large volumes of 1810 in small print and double columns put a huge body of verse within reach of the general public. Other series in England were published in imitation; publishers in other countries followed suit.

By the twentieth century the Modern Library in America, Everyman's Library and the Oxford English Texts in Britain, Insel in Germany, Gallimard's Pléiade imprint, and Mondadori, Laterza, and Ricciardi in Italy were on the way to making a reasonably complete representation of the national classics of each country. Today, however, most of these ventures have been virtually abandoned. (It is true that the Modern Library and Everyman's have been revived, but with nothing like the old ambition.) The great German publishing house Suhrkamp, famous for its stable of post–World War II avant-garde writers, has initiated a new classical imprint, with complete works of the principal German authors in elegant, large-pocket-size volumes that resemble the Pléiade and old Insel formats, but it is meeting with considerable financial difficulties in carrying out the announced program. There is, in fact, a growing uncertainty about how a project of this kind should be pursued. Only the Library of America, created a decade ago partly in response to the demand of Edmund Wilson that American classics be made accessible to the average reader, and the French Pléiade series continue to publish according to plan in any meaningful fashion, and even they reveal the strains to which such ventures are now subject.

2

Some recent publications expose the contemporary embarrassment. The Pléiade has finally ended its complete edition of the works of Jean-Jacques Rousseau with a fifth volume largely containing the writings on music. The first four volumes were rapidly published between 1959 and 1969. The final volume has taken more than twenty-five years, and it is the only unsatisfactory element of what has been until now the ideal edition of a French classic.

Rousseau is a fascinating and repulsive author. A man of undeniable charm, he longed for the experience of being betrayed by those for whom he had the greatest affection and admiration. There is hardly one of his friends whom he did not accuse of disloyalty: most of them did, indeed, end by slandering him and trying to destroy his career and his influence. This influence was, in fact, enormous. In politics, philosophy, aesthetics, and literature, he was a writer of great eloquence, arguably the most important figure of the eighteenth century in France. His work is embedded in the events of his own present and in the future as well. He is consequently easy to read and difficult to understand, almost impossible to assess. Democrat or protofascist, Romantic or neoclassical, disconcertingly honest or diabolically deceitful, even self-deceiving—all of this applies, but he cannot be circumscribed or defined by any of it.

This makes an intelligent commentary indispensable for an edition of Rousseau. His ideas are bound up with his biography to an extent that those of his contemporaries Voltaire and Kant, for example, are not, and we need to know as well what posterity made of these ideas before we can comprehend how they can speak to us. In this respect, the first four volumes of the new edition are exemplary. The publisher, Gallimard, was forced to adhere to a very high standard of scholarship by the sponsors of the edition, which include Rousseau's native city of Geneva. The commentary was impeccable and lavish, the text reproduced Rousseau's original, including his idiosyncratic spelling and punctuation, and the changes he made in his text were given so that one could follow the development of his thought.

This cannot be said of the new volume. Some of the individual texts are given with the same earlier care: particularly admirable is Jean Starobinski's introduction to, and commentary on, the *Essay on the Origin of Language.* The largest work printed here, however, is Rousseau's *Dictionary of Music,* presented with some explanatory essays and also a splendid introduction by Jean-Jacques Eigeldinger (justly famous as the most distinguished Chopin scholar we have), but with no detailed commentary and without any of the variant readings that all the other works in the edition have received.

The lack of commentary is disastrous. I find it very difficult to read parts of Rousseau's articles on music, since eighteenth-century harmonic terminology is archaic and very specialized, and requires an intimate familiarity with the professional language. Most musicians and amateurs of music will also find some of it almost unintelligible. The absurdity of printing a long text in a way that leaves it inaccessible to most of the readers who will purchase the volume evidently did not strike the publisher.

In addition, many of the articles in the dictionary were originally written for the famous *Encyclopedia* edited by Diderot and D'Alembert. When Rousseau reprinted them in his musical dictionary, he revised them considerably; his feud with the composer Jean-Philippe Rameau had grown in acerbity, and his attacks on Rameau grew more violent. Except for one sample article, the original versions are not given in the new volume. No one will read Rousseau's *Dictionary of Music* to find out about music; it is of interest today only to learn about Rousseau. In this case, his changes of mind are as important as his final statements, particularly since all of them are partially determined by what had happened in his life, which enemies he had most recently made.

He was a musician of very little talent but of extraordinary prestige and influence. A short cantata he had composed was snubbed cruelly by Rameau, who said the melody was incompetent and the accompaniment plagiarized from Italian music: there was something to both these judgments. Nevertheless, his little operetta, *The Village Soothsayer,* had an immense success: its exaggeratedly naive melodies made it a model of popular neoclassical taste. Rousseau's subordination of everything in music—harmony and counterpoint, above all—to the simplest form of melody was an interesting early version of the dogmatic reaction to modernist complexity displayed by recent proponents of minimalism.

The final Pléiade volume was badly planned. It has almost two thousand pages, and the publisher will no doubt allege that it was the lack of space that made the edition of the dictionary almost useless by denying it the necessary commentary. However, the letter to D'Alembert on the theater in Geneva should have been in an earlier volume with *The Village Soothsayer,* and the few scientific writings here could have been placed with the essays on botany. That would have made room for the variants and a decent commentary. It was a pity to spoil the most satisfactory edition of a major French writer.

3

Another recent publication in the same Pléiade series is volume 2 of the works of the Marquis de Sade, containing the novel *Justine* with all three versions complete (each more obscene than the previous version) and an elaborate commentary. It would seem that the Marquis is at last to enter the pantheon of edifying French authors along with Rousseau, Balzac, Racine, Proust, et al. This has understandably been greeted with mixed feelings in some quarters, since the Marquis's pornography is strictly hard-core. However, in reality, the Marquis de Sade has been a part of the canon of great authors for a long time, although there was a certain reluctance to admit this publicly. His reputation stayed underground until well into the twentieth century (French justice ordered the destruction of his books as recently as 1957), but already in the early nineteenth he was read and exploited by Chateaubriand, Hugo, and Lamartine. Flaubert was delighted by him and kept a copy of his works in the guest room, and he became a hero to the surrealists.

It is true that Sade does not write particularly well: at least, his style is not seductive. He has neither the breathtaking verve of Pietro Aretino, the greatest of all pornographers, nor the cynical charm of eighteenth-century smut like *Fanny Hill*. This lack of literary talent is largely irrelevant. I think it would be out of place to demand a stylistically engaging description of the joys of raping a small child or of pulling out all the teeth of a beautiful woman. On the contrary, stylistic pleasures would only confuse the issue. What Sade's work proposes urgently is the delight of naked cruelty independent of any aesthetic cover or charm.

Sade forces his readers to think what most of them would prefer to believe unthinkable. The sober matter-of-factness of Sade's description of horrors was revolutionary; his tortures are neither colorful nor picturesque. They are more or less the average daydreams of every ordinary masochist and sadist, and even of a great many people who would not like to classify themselves as either. Acts of torture have been committed throughout history, and they were basic to the judicial process for both church and state in the past (and are finding a renaissance in our time), as well as to the treatment of civilians by an occupying army; but the inspired originality of Sade was to introduce the excesses of cruelty systematically into the vast corpus of erotic literature which played such an important role in eighteenth-century culture. He was the first to perceive the sexual import of cruelty and torture for the specifically literary imagination.

Perhaps not the first. The fifteenth-century trial of Gilles de Rais is well known, and the surviving documents have been published. This close companion of Joan of Arc raped and murdered dozens of children; his crimes were fully reported, and they read like some of Sade's more extravagant imaginings. (He was accused of hanging the children, cutting them down just in time to console and cuddle them, and then hanging them again.) It has, however, been recently suggested that the details of these crimes were imagined and invented by the inquisitors, and that the witnesses were carefully schooled, the confession of Gilles dictated. If this is so, the inquisitors anticipated the literary efforts of Sade by three centuries.

Sade was able to carry out very few of his reveries and none of the extravagant ones.[1] The actions current in the strange world of S and M make those that he actually committed look, by comparison, like the experiments of a timid beginner; his sadism was almost purely literary. In his writing he revealed the need to defile and disfigure whatever appeared beautiful and pure, and he expressed the desire to be defiled and tortured himself, but there is little realism, little sense of what it would feel like to carry through the ingenious lists of tortures he compiles. In everyday life, even spectacular sadistic acts must be often as disappointing and as unsatisfyingly monotonous as any other form of sex. In fact, the novels of the Marquis tell us little about actual sexual behavior, but they reveal with great power the nature of desire. It is curious that the imagination of the judges of Gilles de Rais was cast in the same mold, if indeed some of his imputed crimes were purely literary inventions from the erotic imagination of the most respectable lawyers.

Whatever literary value one puts on Sade's novels (and they are as repellent as they are fascinating—indeed, fascinating because they are so sordid), in

---

1. Aristocratic debauchery was not then exceptional and was the occasion for numerous popular scandals, rather like the tabloid gossip about movie stars today. The publicity then as now had its political motivation. Sade's youthful behavior does not seem to have overstepped the contemporary aristocratic norms; this, of course, is not reassuring. However, the belief, common to both the eighteenth and twentieth centuries, that sexual excess is confined to the very rich and famous (or, alternatively, to the very poor) does not have much to recommend it. Sade was implicated in two scandals: in the first of these, he was accused of beating a prostitute; the second had more serious consequences, since four prostitutes claimed to have been poisoned by aphrodisiacs, and acts of homosexual and heterosexual sodomy were committed, crimes then punishable by death. Jean Deprun, in his introduction to the first volume of Sade in the Pléiade edition, traces the development in the popular imagination during the last decades of the eighteenth century of Sade as a monster, an ogre, and a blaspheming Satanic figure. His mythical reputation seems to have preceded much of his literary work, or even inspired it, and the publicity given to the scandals was perhaps encouraged by his family, who were tired of his escapades and preferred to see him confined in prison, as he was for a great part of his life.

their sober lack of passion they are instructive. They reveal the paradoxically seductive charm of the most deplorable aspects of the imagination. It is, in fact, his sobriety which is most original. By its icy intensity, his work attains the monumental sublime: in his refusal to dress up his descriptions in the traditional baroque eloquence or the pretty euphemisms of previous erotic writing, Sade is a neoclassical artist of his time, a contemporary of the painter Jacques-Louis David.

Essentially, however, his work is important not as an unveiling of new truths, but as a demonstration of how the old ones secretly operated in Western culture. Already in the sixteenth century, Montaigne, considerably expanding traditional religious doctrine, remarked that public institutions as well as private lives are held together by vices—including cruelty, "that bitter-sweet prick of malignant sensuality at seeing someone suffer—and children feel it. . . . Whoever takes away [these vices] removes the fundamental conditions of human existence."

The world of sadomasochism is surrounded with a sinister and largely unmerited glamour, as if it took place in smoke-filled opium dens. But it is a much more commonplace affair and interacts with our everyday lives. When I was writing a review of Alban Berg's correspondence, I remarked to an elderly and very distinguished psychoanalyst, Sophie Lazarsfeld, pupil of Alfred Adler, that I was surprised by how many of Schoenberg's students seemed to enjoy being so badly treated and humiliated by him. She replied, "I have no time to explain this just now, but I can assure you that there are a great many masochists and not nearly enough sadists to go around." I have since asked around in S and M circles and have found that this was indeed accurate.

In the eighteenth century, the erotic interest of pain became more explicit, but Sade was the first to investigate the erotic implications of all vice, including simple humiliation. With his obsessive clear-sightedness he was a moral and edifying artist. He is very much in tune with our politically correct age, and he would certainly have enthusiastically agreed with Andrea Dworkin that all sexual intercourse is basically an act of violence and rape.

Most cogently, he insisted that the political liberty won by the French Revolution was incomplete and even meaningless without sexual freedom. This is a profound truth that presents insoluble problems, but who would maintain that there are any easy or permanent solutions for a civilized society? Above all, Sade is impressive because he makes hypocrisy almost impossible to sustain in considering the erotic imagination. There are many reasons for thinking that pornography does not actually stimulate or inspire sadistic acts, and if this is the case, Sade's work might reasonably be made required reading for high school students (he is perhaps a bit strong for the elementary level). It is good to see that he has been incorporated into the canon, but it would not have worked if he had not, in fact, been there all the time.

4

In Germany about ten years ago, when the major publishing house of postwar philosophy and criticism, Suhrkamp, decided to publish the German classics and replace the elegant volumes of Insel, a new imprint was launched, Deutscher Klassiker Verlag, with an extraordinarily ambitious program: most of the major German authors, and several of the minor ones, in complete or almost complete editions with an elaborate commentary. The house that had made its name with Walter Benjamin, Bertolt Brecht, Paul Celan, T. W. Adorno, Peter Szondi, and so many others now proposed forty volumes of Goethe, twelve of Schiller, eleven of Herder, and several dozen others with different series representing medieval, Baroque, Renaissance, and eighteenth-century literature, six volumes of art history, twenty-eight of politics and history—more than 250 volumes in all, which were to have been completed in a little over a decade and with further campaigns in view.

The publishers of this series have made few attempts to enlarge the pantheon of acceptable authors. The three volumes of the works of Bettina von Arnim (with a fourth volume of correspondence planned) are perhaps an exception. In any case, her writings have never before received so important and so elaborate a commentary, which deepens our understanding of this remarkable woman.

It is easy to make fun of Bettina: she has been called the ideal "groupie." Her works elevate fan mail to high art. The granddaughter of Sophie von La Roche, who in 1771 wrote the first interesting German novel with a middle-class setting, *The History of Fräulein von Sternheim,* Bettina von Arnim was also the sister of Clemens Brentano, whose poetry is perhaps the most musically impressive of the German canon. She married the Prussian aristocrat, novelist, and poet Achim von Arnim, who with her brother Clemens, compiled the great collection of German folk poetry called *Das Knaben Wunderhorn,* which provided texts for Brahms, Mahler, and so many other composers.

Bettina's specialty was hero worship. She chose her heroes well: Beethoven, Goethe, Hölderlin, the Brothers Grimm—the latter dedicated their collection of fairy tales to her. Her admiration of Hölderlin, which she shared with her brother, was almost unique in her time. With many of her heroes she carried on an extensive correspondence, some of which she published with a considerable amount of free editing and unauthorized revision. *The Correspondence of Goethe with a Young Girl* became a best seller. Her volumes of letters have the passionate intensity of a work of Romantic fiction, particularly those with her brother (entitled *Wreath of Spring*) and with her sister-in-law Günderode. She printed her correspondence with the king of Prussia *(This Book Is for the King),* an ineffectual attempt to persuade him to liberalize his social policies. She also published the exchange of letters with a young man who fell in love with her but developed later, disappointingly, into a conservative mediocrity (Bettina's affairs of the heart were almost embarrassingly platonic).

She was an important figure in Prussian society: her daughters were presented at court, although she herself refused to attend. During the revolution of 1848, her salon was split in two, with Bettina's left-wing protégés on one side of the room and her family and their reactionary friends on the other. Some of her children were ashamed of their mother's politics. With a brother and husband violently and fashionably anti-Semitic, Bettina worked hard for Jewish causes. She even began a remarkable study of poverty in Prussia, a survey of poor families in town after town, with lists of how much money each one disposed of, how they were clothed, in what housing conditions they were lodged. The book was banned by the government even before it was written, but the lists exist and are printed in this new edition, along with the introductory matter that was actually finished. The simple details are very moving. It is an extraordinary piece of early sociological research.

The 125-page introduction to Bettina's political writings brings a new perspective to her work. The Prussian bureaucracy decided to teach her a lesson and attempted to levy the Bürgerrecht ("bourgeois right" or commercial tax) on her as a business rather than as a private person. She refused to pay, but proudly offered the sum as a gift to the Prussian state, a compromise which was declined. In a letter that scandalized the magistrature, she wrote:

> I grant you that I place the bourgeoisie higher than the aristocracy. There we are in agreement.—Similarly I place even higher the class of the proletariat, without whose inborn magnificent force of character, fortitude in misery, in renunciation and restriction of the necessities of life, little profit for the good of the whole would be accomplished.—The wealth of the poor consists in the inborn riches of Nature, the service of the citizenry in the application and cultivation of this natural wealth, which thanks to its active application is bestowed to the advantage of those classes whose arrogance, over-indulgence and spiritual ill-breeding devours everything, just because it has no power to produce.
>
> The basis, therefore, for my placing the proletariat in the highest rank is that it is freed from the baseness of trying to win something from the world by usury, that it gives everything and consumes nothing in return of what it needs, as it develops new force for the profit of others.— Obviously the position of the lowest of the nation is the highest and inspires the greatest veneration because of its helplessness; indeed, working most successfully for poverty in spite of its poverty.

We can see from this that Bettina's politics are essentially conservative, but of a traditional kind of Romantic conservatism that frightens most of the conservatives who have achieved power.

This new edition of Bettina von Arnim, the first with a full commentary, gives greater stature to her work. It also illuminates the difficulties that a woman of great talent experienced in the nineteenth century. Her various collections of correspondence may appear parasitic, dependent on other minds to come into being, but paradoxically her ambition was even higher than that of the great female novelists of the century, whose work rivals and often surpasses the novels written by men. Her intention was to play a role in the politics, philosophy, poetry, and art of her time, and she won her position finally against society, against the government, and against her own family. Like the Marquis de Sade, Bettina von Arnim can join the company of saints because she was, to a certain extent, already there. Rilke and others read her, although with skepticism and a patronizing sympathy. This new edition allows us to see her with all her limitations but without condescension, because it offers a new view of the role she played in her society.

The prestige which these grand, luxurious editions confer on their authors has an advantage which conceals a danger. The uniform bindings confirm us in our belief that we are reading a classic, and they make the authors appear in some timeless space in which they all coexist together: Ben Franklin cozily conversing with Henry James, Sade arguing with Montaigne, Bettina von Arnim and Grimmelshausen meeting as coeval equals. The illusion that these bindings are designed to foster, and it is not an ignoble one, is that these authors all speak to us directly as our contemporaries. This facility of discourse, however, only becomes fully effective as we understand how alien these writers are to us, and we become able to translate them for ourselves. For this reason, an adequate historical commentary is a necessity, since it repositions the text in real time, and marks out the difference from our world. Even the variant readings of a critical edition are a help: they make us realize that the work itself has a history, and did not spring into the world a full-grown classic.

Like a museum, a publication of the classics in a series not only preserves, but partially invents a past, a national identity. Those who are dissatisfied with the culture in which they live and would like to alter it will naturally try to construct a new canon. The past, however, is not infinitely malleable; it frustrates many of our efforts to change it. Tradition is resistant. On the other hand, it is not monolithic; it is, in fact, continuously being reshaped. Nevertheless, tradition has to appear to cooperate with the reshaping. Ignorance and a contempt for the past are often a prerequisite—and even a wonderful inspiration—for the creation of new styles and new forms of art, but the restructuring of the canon that many of us hope for can only be accomplished with a sympathy even for those aspects of the past most antipathetic to modern ideals.

Part Two

MOSTLY MOZART

CHAPTER 5

Dramatic and Tonal Logic
in Mozart's Operas

I

Writing in 1966, Meyer Schapiro explained more persuasively than anyone else why writing about the unity of a work of art has given rise to so much dubious critical speculation and, at the same time, why the subject is not one that can be evaded or dismissed:

> I have argued that we do not see all of a work when we see it as a whole. We strive to see it as completely as possible and in a unifying way, though seeing is selective and limited. Critical seeing, aware of the incompleteness of perception, is explorative and dwells on details as well as on the large aspects that we call the whole. It takes into account others' seeing; it is a collective and cooperative seeing and welcomes comparisons of different perceptions and judgments. It also knows moments of sudden revelation and intense experience of unity and completeness which are shared in others' scrutiny.[1]

Any treatment is bound to be provisional, subject to reinterpretation, but it is also an essential aspect of critical experience.

Two excellent papers of the 1990s treat of the question of the tonal organization of Mozart's operas: James Webster's "Mozart's Operas and the Myth of

1. Meyer Schapiro, *Theory and Philosophy of Art: Style, Artist, and Society* (New York: Braziller, 1994), p. 49.

Musical Unity," and John Platoff's "Myths and Realities about Tonal Planning in Mozart's Operas";[2] they both clear away much nonsense and show that the wrong questions are often asked on this subject—generally "What relation do Mozart's operas have to sonata form?" or "Is there a single systematic approach that can account for all of Mozart's procedures?"—and these naturally produce unsatisfactory answers. Nevertheless, there has always been a persistent feeling that each of Mozart's mature operas hangs together efficiently with an individual character of its own.

Without attempting to construct a speciously uniform global theory, we may set down simply what is definitely known and obvious about Mozart's operatic practice and ask a somewhat different set of questions.

The following characteristics are certain:

1. Every opera that Mozart wrote after the age of nineteen ends in the key with which it began. This is not true of all the operas before that, so it is certainly an aesthetic decision on the composer's part.

2. Every number ends in the key of its opening.[3] Ending in a new key is possible only after an interruption either of spoken dialogue or of secco recitative, making what follows an independent number. (An accompanied recitative may begin outside the main key and lead to it.)

3. A finale is a set of pieces uninterrupted by recitative or spoken dialogue, and the first and last pieces of the finale must therefore be in the same key.

4. There are generally two important finales, a concluding one (in the key of the overture) and a central one. The central one begins and ends in a tonality that is always harmonically distant from the key of the overture. The relation between the keys of the two finales in the different operas is:

> *Die Entführung aus dem Serail:*
> Overture and conclusion (act 3), C major
> Large final ensemble of act 2, D major
> *Le Nozze di Figaro:*
> Overture and concluding finale, D major
> Central finale, E-flat major
> *Don Giovanni:*
> Overture and concluding finale, D minor- D major;
> Central finale, C major

2. Respectively: *Cambridge Opera Journal,* vol. 2, no. 2 (July 1990); *Cambridge Opera Journal,* vol. 8 no. 1 (March 1996).

3. A rare exception is found in *The Abduction from the Seraglio,* Osmin's lied "Were ein Liebchen hat gefunden," which surprisingly turns into a duet with Belmonte in D minor-major.

Così fan tutte:
  Overture and concluding finale, C major
  Central finale, D major
Die Zauberflöte:
  Overture and concluding finale, E-flat major
  Central finale, C major

All these are dissonant and distant relations, although the C major of *Die Zauberflöte*'s act 1 finale is somewhat closer than the others to the opening and closing key of E-flat major through the relation of the relative minor of E-flat, C minor.

5. Mozart was deeply aware of the expressive character of the distance of one tonality from another. In a famous letter concerning an aria of the bass, Osmin, in *The Abduction from the Seraglio,* he explains to his father that Osmin loses his temper, and there is a change of key, and the change must be to a distant key to reveal the dramatic character of rage, but not so distant as to be unmusical. *Even in this aria, the break between F major and A minor is justified by a few words of spoken dialogue.* Although it is a single aria, the principle of ending in the opening key is therefore preserved, as the spoken dialogue implies a new beginning. The very few spoken words do not weaken the tonal contrasts, but it is interesting to note that even here Mozart preserves the principle of the tonal unity.

As we can see, Mozart was particularly sensitive to the juxtaposition of tonalities, but we cannot make any general rule applicable at every point for how he exploited this, as there are different reasons for using a tonality. One reason that must certainly have played a role is the expressive character of the relation to the previous number, but another reason is the fact that in the eighteenth century some instruments sounded remarkably better and more at ease in some keys. E-flat major, for example, was particularly welcome to wind instruments, horns above all. D major was much appreciated by violinists.

One important aspect must be considered briefly later: closely related keys create what might be called a key area, above all a tonic with its dominant and subdominant. That is why Mozart feels that A minor is dramatically distant from F major, but musically not too far away, as the two keys each contain only one note not in common with the other, B-flat or B-natural. As Mozart grew older (the *Seraglio* is relatively early), I think he became willing to countenance more distant relations, as the extravagant development section of the Piano Concerto in B-flat Major, K. 595, demonstrates, as it goes with only the most laconic and summary transition directly from F major to B minor, and that is about as far as eighteenth-century harmony can take you. It is true that in one of the melodramas of *Zaide,* Mozart follows a dominant seventh of E minor with a chord of C minor, but then he puts a fermata over a rest between the two, indicating a theoretical break.

The hierarchy of key relations is simple and not entirely related to the circle of fifths. The closest keys are dominant and subdominant:

C major, G major, F major

The next least dissonant, juxtaposed with increasing frequency in instrumental pieces after the 1780s, are the mediant and flat mediant tonalities, the flat mediants having, of course, more tranquil character than the sharp directed mediants:

E major, A major, E-flat, A-flat

The next most dissonant are the keys of the supertonic and the flatted leading tone as they attack the tonic note (C) of the original tonic key:

D major, B-flat major

Still more dissonant are the flat supertonic and the leading tone, and most dissonant of all is the key of the augmented fourth:

C-sharp major, B major, F-sharp major

2

From the preceding list of simple facts, let us ask how the tonality of the central finale and the tonality of the overture (or conclusion) are employed by Mozart. We may start with *Le Nozze di Figaro,* as that is traditionally the one to try on the dog, but we must not expect to get exactly the same answers with the other operas, although we may hope that the differences are related to the different character and structure of each opera. Webster reasonably maintained that we cannot exactly hear D major as a tonic for the whole of *Figaro* (he says that since the overture is followed by a G major duet, that we might think of it as a dominant). However, when we have heard the opera, and realize that it ends in D major, and when we learn that Mozart always ended his operas in the key of the overture, we may consider D major as a temporary tonic. We might even consider it at the very least as a theoretical tonic, a frame for the beginning and the end, much as J. S. Bach framed the chorale preludes of the third volume of the *Klavierübung* with the Saint Anne prelude and then the fugue. It is a presentation that has nothing to do with a performance of the prelude and fugue, but the relation of D major to the opera as a whole is surely much more intimate than that. The eighteenth-century listeners certainly perceived this consciously or unconsciously, and we can today as well, when we become very familiar with eighteenth-century practice.

More cogent is the question: How is E-flat major, the key of the central finale, employed throughout the opera?

1. It first appears in act 1, for Cherubino's expression of adolescent sexuality ("Non sò più").
2. It next turns up at the beginning of act 2 in the Countess's first aria, "Porgi amor," lamenting that she has been neglected by her husband.
3. The long finale to act 2 is one of the most spectacular constructions of Mozart's career in its harmonic drive and excitement. Beginning with the Count's jealousy, and gradually increasing the cast of characters from duet to septet, the finale ends in E-flat major, of course, with the arrival of Marcellina and her suit against Figaro for breach of promise.
4. Figaro's satirical and misogynist aria in act 4, "Aprite un po' quegl'occhi," naturally has to be in E-flat major, since horns are the symbol of cuckoldry.
5. At its last appearance, and most significantly, E-flat major turns up dramatically within the concluding finale in D major, at the exact moment that Figaro believes Susanna is betraying him with the count. Psychologically, this may reasonably be considered the most extraordinary effect in all of Mozart's dramatic work. This moment of extreme tension is rendered with tranquil lyricism. The tempo slows immediately from the direction *Con un poco più di moto* to larghetto; the shift from G major to E-flat major takes less than a second, and horns and clarinets softly sustain an expressive motif. Mozart is inspired as much by Da Ponte's genius here as by his own instinct. "Everything is tranquil and placid [Tutto è tranquillo e placido]," Figaro sings, comparing himself to Vulcan as his wife, Venus, couples with Mars, and the atmosphere is classical pastoral. E-flat major continues into an allegro molto in a duet for Figaro and Susanna, whom he mistakenly takes for the Countess. The resolution back to D major goes first through B-flat major, and then a lengthy subdominant G major as the Count begs for forgiveness, as D major arrives with the full orchestra.

It would be a mistake to conclude that E-flat is being used as a symbol for troubled sexuality, because that is not how musical symbolism works. But it does act as an agent of dramatic tension throughout the opera, a fundamental opposition or dissonance that throws things off balance. That is why the lyricism that characterizes some of the appearances is so remarkable.

No other opera except *Die Zauberflöte* makes quite so powerful a use of the key of the central finale, but it is not isolated and there are parallels. Does the D major of *Cosi fan tutte*'s central finale appear in the C major of the closing finale? It does, at the precise moment of dramatic crisis, when the men pretend to return from the war and precipitate the final panic of the intrigue: the D major military music of the first act is repeated literally. Does the C major of the central finale of *Die Zauberflöte* appear in the long E-flat major concluding finale? Yes, at the critical moment of the trial by fire and water with Tamino's flute solo, and the effect of a return is very striking as the central finale in C major begins with Tamino's aria with a flute solo.

3

Mozart's operatic finales are very complex constructions, sometimes lasting more than thirty or forty minutes. No other composer, not Gluck, Haydn, or Beethoven, equaled Mozart in the elaboration of a finale. He had to find a compositional trajectory that encompassed more than half a dozen numbers, all performed generally with no pause at all, and a tonal plan that expressively mirrors the stage action, and ends convincingly and logically with a return to the opening key. When the action and the intrigue proceed smoothly, the change of tonality will be to the most closely related keys—that is, dominant or subdominant. A surprising action will be set in relief by a change to a more distant key—often the mediant or flatted mediant, or by a significant alteration of instrumentation or dynamics.

The central finale to *Figaro* is often considered Mozart's most exemplary, and shows the tonal structure in its most convincing form. It begins with two closely related keys, E-flat major and its dominant, B-flat. This corresponds to the intimate relation of the opening scenes, beginning with the Count's decision to smash down the door behind which he thinks Cherubino is hiding, and this will enable him to prove his wife's infidelity; the second number is a direct continuation of the first, as it is Susanna who comes out, to the surprise and consternation of both Count and Countess. The following, more radical change from B-flat major to G major signals a brusque new situation as Figaro enters. From there the finale moves systematically to a return of E-flat major. Each number is the dominant of the next one—G, C, F, B-flat to E-flat, a construction often used in the eighteenth century for its simplicity. This results in the smoothest and most impeccable logical drive, with an increase of complexity in the texture as the intrigue moves from duet to quartet to septet. Much of the credit for this structure must be given to the librettist, da Ponte, and he was justly proud of his contribution.

In *Don Giovanni*, the concluding finale is relatively short and the central finale very long and complex. Some of the differences between the two works arise from this. The key of the overture appears as a separate section in the central finale of *Don Giovanni* for the only time in a Mozart opera.[4] D minor accompanies the Commandant and Donna Anna at each appearance, including Donna Anna's entrance into the great E-flat major sextet in act 2. Her first scena is in D minor, her first aria in D major (with a long accompanied recitative that concentrates on D minor); and her F major aria in the second act, "Non mi dir," has an impressive introduction ending on a half cadence in D minor.

The act 1 finale of *Don Giovanni* (C major by contrast with the D minor-major overture) is also the only finale in which the contrasting initial tonality of the central finale reappears not only at the end, but is repeated in the middle. It is sometimes claimed that the central finale of Don Giovanni is composed according to very different principles from the central finale of Figaro. This, however, is not strictly true. The first four tonalities of the central finale of *Don Giovanni* are the same as the last four of the central finale of *Figaro,* with the efficient scheme in which each one is the dominant of the next: C, F, B-flat, and E-flat. The forward drive embodied by this progression launches this finale, but it ends in the confusion provoked by Don Giovanni's attempted rape of Zerlina.

The F major section, however, frames at its center a trio in its relative minor, D minor, with the entrance of Donna Anna and Don Ottavio, and Elvira:

C, (F – D minor – F), B-flat, E-flat

The first, more distant mediant modulation is then found only at the end of this sequence, with a move from E-flat major back to C major, the opening key of the finale, and this harmonic change is electrifying.

The return to C major is necessary, given the construction. Starting modestly in C Major, the finale continues with the stage orchestras behind the scene beginning the dance music for the ball in the subdominant F major. However, if the minuet is to be played with the other orchestras tuning up, then it has to be transposed to G, so that the violins and cellos can tune to the open strings C, G, and A. The move to G is preceded by first going from F major to B-flat major for an expressive trio scored only for wind instruments and voices. The change of scene for the ball is marked by a swift move to E-flat major with brilliant orchestration. The brilliance is increased with the arrival of the vengeful masked guests, with full orchestra including trumpets and percussion heard for the first time since the overture, with a military return to C major, *Maestoso,* and the full cast shouting "Hurray for freedom" ("Viva la liberta"). Mozart must have felt it important to reaffirm the opening key in what is clearly heard as a political provocation. That political freedom implied

---

4. In *Cosi fan tutte,* the C major of the overture briefly appears in passing in the central finale when Despoina pretends to bring the mock suicides back to life.

sexual freedom was a popular idea during the 1780s. The C major will lead naturally to its dominant G major.

We must distinguish close modulations from more radical ones for the dramatic effect. At first, all changes of key in the finale have been to closely related keys, either a subdominant or a relative minor (C, F, D minor, F, B-flat major, E-flat major): this first mediant modulation in the finale, from E-flat to C-major, creates a shock, above all because it is accompanied by a change from piano to forte, a martial rhythm, and the addition of trumpets and drums. We cannot abstract tonal structure from dynamic and orchestral effects, or from the action on the stage.

C major introduces its dominant G for all the dance music. The next modulation is appropriately not to a closely related key, but to the mediant E-flat that arrives with the attempted rape of Zerlina. Starting in E-flat major, the resultant confusion is pictured musically by several rapid and unstable changes of key, ending triumphantly with Don Giovanni's escape in a cadential sequence of F major and C major.

4

To what extent are tonal relationships in Mozart based on theory planned or partly instinctive? We have seen that conscious planning certainly had to play a role along with a desire for closure and a sense of harmonic distance. To what extent did he expect that connoisseurs would be able to hear these relationships? Or, indeed, more important, to what extent do they affect our experience of the operas even without our being aware of them? It would be absurd to believe that one cannot appreciate the operas without analyzing or identifying the compositional process, or, on the other hand, to claim that harmonic structure has no effect on the unlearned listener.

It should be noted that harmony in the late eighteenth century was considerably simpler in some respects than it became afterward. Many members of the audience may unconsciously or consciously have recognized each reappearance of D minor in *Don Giovanni* as a return.[5] E-flat major and D major-minor, for example, sounded very different on the instruments of the eighteenth century, but it became harder for us to distinguish today, particularly after all those years of Chopin, Wagner, Debussy, and Schoenberg.

5. A failure to analyze correctly does not imply a lack of understanding, just as we can understand language without being able to tell a subject from a predicate or an adverb from an adjective.

Mozart sometimes goes out of his way to set in relief some of these relation-ships. *The Abduction from the Seraglio* has no very weighty finale, but the first act concentrates heavily on C major, and Mozart forced his unwilling librettist to give him at least an elaborate ensemble to finish the second of the three acts, which he set in D major. One parallelism easy to remark concerns the aria of Osmin discussed above, which begins in F major, and then is followed by a raging A minor. The opera ends with a vaudeville (that is, a number in which every member of the cast lines up and one after the other sings a stanza, while the others join in a refrain); this begins in F major, but when it comes to Osmin, he once again loses his temper and goes from F major again to A minor and repeats the end of his aria. Even if one does not exclaim "Ah, F major to A minor again!" some feeling of symmetry must present itself. This time Osmin rushes off the stage, and every one else placidly finishes the vaudeville in F major, which leads to a short chorus of the Janissaries rounding off the opera in the C major of the overture.

It is not always important for a composer to feel that his listeners are con-sciously aware of the compositional procedures. Schoenberg was surprised when his performers could figure out the twelve-tone row. However, it is clear that Mozart sometimes goes out of his way to reinforce and clarify the listeners' sense of the harmonic movement. Two points should be made here. From what was said above it should be obvious that Mozart considered dry or secco recita-tive to be in some sense equivalent to spoken dialogue. It does not enter pre-dominantly with any great force into any larger sense of tonal planning. I should imagine that the secco recitative was probably composed after the rest of the opera was finished, except for the overture, always written last. Mozart could do small things exquisitely with secco recitative, but it almost never establishes a key with any final definition (there is mostly just a perfunctory cadence that allows the following accompanied music to create the effect of standing on solid ground), and when he felt that a transitional modulation to an aria or ensemble was important, he required a recitative accompanied by the orchestra. In my own experience, during a succeeding dry recitative, the tonality of the last number performed is still present in my ear.

Furthermore, we might think sometimes of closely related tonal areas as well as specific keys. What happens at the beginning of *Figaro* is a good example. The overture in D major is followed by a closely related G major duet in which Figaro and Susanna prepare the furnishing of their room. A new duet follows in the more distant mediant key of B-flat major: this effectively renders a change of atmosphere; the view of connubial happiness of the first duet is succeeded by Susanna's warning that the Count has designs on her, and the new key area signals the danger. The menace of the Count and the new key area continue with F major, in Figaro's cavatina threatening the Count, dominant of B-flat but mediant to D major. The two duets are lightly scored, but with Bartolo's aria, "La vendetta," the full orchestra with trumpets and tympani returns, along with a return to the D major of the overture. The reaffirmation of D major is partially confirmed by a duet for Susanna and Marcellina in the closely related dominant key of A major; the relation is justified as Marcellina and Bartolo are a close-knit pair. This makes a tripartite arrangement of two D major areas flanking a flat mediant and submediant section dealing with the Count's designs on Susanna.

The only other appearance of D major in *Figaro* until the last act finale is the brilliant aria of the Count in the third act. It follows a passionate and erotic duet for Susanna and the Count beginning in A minor, but with a long final section in the dominant A major. The Count's aria has trumpets and drums as well, and is preceded by a long and impressive accompanied introduction. This does not mean that we should call D major a tonic throughout—that is a foolish way to regard the score of an opera—but it certainly sets D major in relief with the most brilliant orchestral instrumentation of the work, along with the C major of "Non più andrai" and some of the wedding music. If we know that Mozart will make a weighty return to D major at the end, a sense that D major is playing a central role can be maintained without exaggeration.

Much more important considerations for Mozart's constructive sense oblige us to return briefly to the opening scene of the work. The succession of D major, G major, B-flat major, F major, D major, A major is followed by Cherubino's aria in E-flat major. This is the first appearance of E-flat in the opera, and coming after A major makes a modulation of a tritone. That is the most dissonant relation possible at the time and sets the change of key in high relief and gives the initial appearance of E-flat major unusual prominence. The succession of two pieces related by a tritone is rare in Mozart, possible only in an opera.

The most astonishing example is the great quartet in *Idomeneo,* Mozart's favorite number (he could never listen to it without tears). The E-flat major quartet is set in relief by being framed by two numbers in A major, the latter introduced by a long accompanied recitative. The preceding duet is also followed by a recitative, but after only a few seconds the orchestra crashes into the recitative with a brusque cadence in E flat marked *forte,* making the contrast of key ostentatious. It is certainly a striking way to underline a new key. Mozart generally reserves the effect for a moment crucial to the drama.[6]

---

6. Another example is Fiordiligi's aria in *Cosi fan tutte,* "Per pietà, ben mio," the most elaborate and pretentious aria of the opera. It is in E major and follows an aria by Ferrando in B-flat major; but here the startling juxtaposition is bridged by a very elaborate accompanied recitative, which does not, however, approach closely to E major until the very end. Cherubino's aria succeeds a long secco recitative that also only at the end approaches the dominant of E-flat. In any case, it sounds like an entirely new tonal region.

5

Not only in *Don Giovanni* and *Le Nozze di Figaro* does Mozart return during the first half dozen numbers to the key of the overture, but in *Die Zauberflöte* as well. A brief consideration of the opening scenes of *Cosi fan tutte* can show us how Mozart's sense of the key of the overture was somehow basic to the work, and, in particular, how radical changes of tonality mirror the atmosphere and the action. After the C major overture, Mozart continues with a trio in the closely related dominant, G major, in which young men sing the praises of their beloved ladies to the cynical Don Alfonso. There is a marked change of key for a second trio in E major as the cynical proposals of Don Alfonso present a radical change of atmosphere. A third trio where the lovers accept the challenge of Don Alfonso returns triumphantly to C major to round off the first scene. (This follows the pattern of *Figaro*, a first number in a key closely related to the key of the overture, a mediant modulation when a new topic or situation is broached, and an emphatic return to the key of the overture.)

The second scene begins with a duet for the two women in the submediant A major. The next change of key is appropriately dissonant and even brutal, as Don Alfonso enters with the news that the men have been called away for military service. This brief aria is in the very surprisingly distant key of F minor. A quintet deploring the news follows in E-flat major, not too far harmonically from F minor. Then in a duet for the two men in B-flat major, the dominant of

E-flat is succeeded by a mediant change which adds a certain brilliance to a military chorus in D major.

This chorus frames another modulation to a mediant, a quintet in F major that should be considered Mozart's greatest masterpiece of ironic humor, setting the words "Da scrivermi ogni giorno—Due volte" ("Write to me every day—twice a day") to music of an exquisite pathos never surpassed. After a repetition of the D major chorus, an E major trio accompanies the departure: "Soave sia il vento" ("Let the winds be gentle"), a triumph of tone-painting.

The close of this long second scene is a recitative for Don Alfonso, starting secco, and finishing with thirteen bars accompanied by the orchestra of an astonishing character—astonishing, that is, in that they seem to have a purely formal function.

These leisurely bars of Allegro moderato are quite simply only two simple and commonplace cadences in C major: ii, V, I, and IV, V, I. This does nothing but close the second scene of the opera in C major like the first scene, and this is the sole function of this page, as if, after a long voyage through varied changes of key, Mozart needed to reaffirm the basic tonality briefly once more before continuing with the rest of the opera.

In *Don Giovanni,* a clear attempt to unify the opera is made, in addition to the various significant appearances of D minor, by reminding us of the beginning of the overture in the middle of the concluding finale. In *Cosi fan tutte,* the end of the overture is quoted literally before the beginning of the concluding finale, making the identification of the return of C major inevitable, and we learn only here that the last chords of the overture were saying Co-, si-, fan-, tut-, te.

Mozart's treatment of the key of the overture and final number and its contrast with the central section developed gradually during his mature life, and gained in subtlety. The earliest of his great operas, *Idomeneo,* simply ends every one of the three acts in the D major of the overture. Perhaps the simple closure of each act in the same key seemed pedantic or confining afterward to Mozart, and he changed his strategy. The next opera, *The Abduction from the Seraglio,* makes an initial massive use of C major. The overture is in C major, with a central section in C minor; the first number adapts the minor section of the overture into a C major aria. The key returns several times in the act, which closes with a C major chorus. In the second act, two numbers bring back C major, including the longest and perhaps the most spectacular aria Mozart was ever to write, "Martern aller Arten." This act, however, ends far from C major: first, there is an aria in B flat major, and then, with no intervening dialogue, the extensive ensemble, amounting to a small finale, that Mozart insisted on having to round off the act. Starting in D major, this quartet returns to the preceding B-flat major key, finally returning to a brilliant finish in D major. Both the D major and the B-flat major are then recalled in succession with exceptional symmetry at the end of the next act immediately before the resolving F major vaudeville (with its little excursion in A minor) and the final chorus in C major.

Mozart here sets up a tonality distant from the initial key to create a powerful harmonic tension that can be recalled and resolved at the end. He made the process still more effective afterward. In *Le Nozze di Figaro,* and later in *Don Giovanni* and *Die Zauberflöte,* as we have seen, he succeeded in strengthening the tonal opposition and integrating it within a structure of two complex finales. Even if Mozart did not choose to make it more explicit, a distinct sense of polar opposition between the center and the opening and closing sections governed the way he made each opera sound so characteristically different, so individual.

CHAPTER 6

Mozart's Entry into
the Twentieth Century

I

Another book in English on Mozart might not seem to be a pressing need just now after the extravagant outpouring of the 250th anniversary of his birth, but we have waited a long time for this one. When, eighty-eight years ago, Hermann Abert's *W. A. Mozart* appeared, it was recognized as the most authoritative survey of the composer's life and works. (It claimed to be a revision of Otto Jahn's pathbreaking life of Mozart of 1882, but in fact almost nothing was left of Jahn; when one of Jahn's observations does appear in Abert, it is quoted as if from an external source, so it is just as well that Jahn's name is no longer displayed on the title page.) Abert managed to set down everything of interest about Mozart's life that was known in 1919, and he added a complete overview of Mozart's works, very many of them discussed in great detail and related to a masterly account of the music world in Mozart's time and the different musical traditions of the age. Over the years the project of translating Abert often came up, but until now, no one had the courage, the good sense, or the resources to carry it out. The fifteen-hundred-page monument has finally been issued in an excellent translation by Stewart Spencer (even Mozart's letters in rhyme when quoted by Abert appear like reasonable verse), and it has turned out to be not

A review (1996) of *Wolfgang Amadeus Mozart,* by Hermann Abert, edited by Cliff Eisen and translated from the German by Stewart Spencer.

only the most satisfactory, but also the most readable and entertaining work on Mozart available in English.

Nevertheless, so much research has been expended on Mozart since 1919, so much more is known, and so many dates and facts have been corrected and revised, that the book could not simply be translated. It had to be brought up to date. This has been done with full respect for the original by one of the most brilliant Mozart scholars of our time, Cliff Eisen. He has himself written profoundly on Mozart, above all on the viola quintets, and his knowledge of the composer and the musical life of his time has no superior and few equals. Without altering the original, he has added thousands of footnotes that correct or expand the text, indicating the most useful of recent publications on almost every aspect of Mozart taken up in the book. An immense bibliography has made this publication not only a pleasure to read, but extremely useful for music-lovers, students, and scholars alike. We may well ask, however, after so much recent scholarship and revision, how a work of almost a century ago can retain its importance not just as a document of the past but as an adequate presentation of Mozart for the modern listener.

In his introductory editorial note, Eisen may give us a clue to an answer when he sets forth his main disagreement with Abert. He presents his case eloquently:

> The heart of Abert's book is chapter 31, "Mozart's Personality." For all his discussion of biography, of social circumstance, of commerce and industry, patrons and the public, it is Abert's firm belief that, above all, Mozart's music expresses Mozart himself, his keen observation of, and boundless empathy for, his fellow man: ". . . it is impossible to separate his life from his music: in both, the same force is at work." And it is here that I profoundly disagree with Abert: as I see it, Mozart was a keen observer of mankind, and boundlessly empathetic, but what he expressed in his music was us, not himself. Put another way, Mozart was the consummate artist, able to manipulate and cajole his listeners, to draw them in and draw them out, to create art, to construct art not for the sake of self-expression but to allow us to express ourselves.

Yet this fundamental difference with Abert is exactly why I like the book so much: if I could, I would say exactly the same things about the music, I would describe it in exactly the same words and with the same images, for Abert's words and images correspond more or less exactly with how I hear the music. At the most basic level, then, Abert and I agree, not only that Mozart's music is profoundly expressive but also as to what it expresses. So it is really of little consequence, in the end, whether Mozart is expressing himself or expressing his listener. Either way, Mozart's is a compelling story: to whom, or to what, we attribute meaning in his music only determines the thrust and trajectory of the narrative, not its substance and not, ultimately, its effect. It is a story that can be read and told in a multiplicity of ways and Abert's, because his understanding of the music resonates so strongly within us, no matter what our view of Mozart's creative personality, remains perhaps the most compelling of all. (p. xi)

Eisen's point is subtle, and provokes elucidation, but this is not simple. He is ill-at-ease, and to some extent rightly, with the old-fashioned and only too well established idea that the composer is simply expressing himself; this turns the composition of music, a social activity, into a purely personal performance, and it is true that some critics of the past and even of our time have absurdly treated works of art as private creations, published so as to allow readers, listeners, and spectators to eavesdrop on the artist's intimacy. When Eisen, however, says that what Mozart "expressed in his music was *us,* not himself," it is not easy to identify the "us." Who are we? Mozart's contemporaries, or his patrons, or the connoisseurs of his work, or the listeners of his posterity? To choose any one of these makes expression too narrow, too limited. To choose all of them makes it too vague to be given a precise meaning. When Eisen, after declaring a profound disagreement with Abert about expression, then writes: "At the most basic level, then Abert and I agree, not only that Mozart's music is profoundly expressive but also as to what it expresses," he seems to b trying to take back, at least, in part his initial objection. Yet his disquiet is well founded.

To justify Eisen's dissatisfaction, we should turn not to the chapter on Mozart's personality, but to a passage in Abert's own preface that reveals his great strength, but also betrays a methodology that is at the root of some less than satisfactory emphases in his book. Here, he pays generous tribute to his predecessors, in particular the work of the French team of Wyzewa and Saint-Foix, but he makes one sharp criticism of their work:

> For them, Mozart's art is like a mosaic, made up of a series of influences to which he succumbed in the course of his life as a result of chance. This rationalistic desire to bring clarity and order to a varied picture is typically French, but quite apart from the fact that it is a fatal error to see genius as the sum total of the influences that affect it, this approach provides us with no answer as to two main questions: how did Mozart choose which of his many models to adopt? And which elements did he appropriate from them and make his own? Why did Johann Christian Bach and Schobert, for example, affect him more deeply than the incomparably greater Gluck?[1]

---

1. We must not mind the touch of Gallophobia in the reproach of French rationalism, natural enough in a German in 1919, and Abert's initial praise of the French team is

This is a profound indictment not merely of Abert's predecessors, but of an enormous amount of research on Mozart between Abert's death in 1927 and our own time, so often devoted to a demonstration of how frequently Mozart borrowed from his contemporaries. Much of this is already in Abert (a great deal of subsequent research reads, in fact, like footnotes to his work): he constantly reveals what Mozart took from J. C. Bach, Schobert, Paisiello, and others. He observes, for example, that the opening theme of the famous Symphony in G Minor is an eighteenth-century commonplace (and that it is found yet again in Tamino's first aria in *The Magic Flute*), but he also points out the two details that Mozart added to the motif that transformed the banal into something new.

Immediately following the above quotation from the preface are a few sentences about the difference between a genius and the common man that will provoke a shiver of distaste from the majority of modern scholars:

> Not even ordinary mortals imitate things if they do not already contain within them the nucleus of what they are imitating. In the case of the genius, this selective process already bears within it the stamp of creativity: it is his first attempt to assert himself in the face of tradition, to cast aside what inhibits him and is alien to his nature and not just to imitate all that he feels drawn towards but, at the same time, to recast it and make it his own.

Today, no one (or few, at any rate) denies that there is a difference between a genius and an ordinary craftsman or hack, but it is felt to be not very nice or democratic to mention it. Of course, we know that an uncritical ascription to Mozart of Romantic nineteenth-century ideals of revolutionary originality gives a false picture of the career and thought of a late eighteenth-century composer. The problem is, nevertheless, to claim that the ideals of originality and revolutionary inspiration do not apply in any way to Mozart (a claim sometimes made today in the newly fashionable view of Mozart as a simple professional craftsman only out to please the patrons who commissioned his work) gives a picture equally false, and one that impedes any workable view of the music.

Abert's view of genius, however, leads him into a typology of Mozart's works that, while it does not actually do much harm to his book, is nevertheless dubious. He depreciates the importance of the traditional division of musical works into sacred, dramatic, instrumental, and vocal, because that would mean

---

evidently wholehearted. At the opening of the book, Abert makes it clear that he thinks Mozart was not really Austrian but Swabian, as his father was born in Augsburg. It might be objected that Augsburg is not actually in Swabia but in Bavaria, but it is on the border of Swabia, and Abert himself came from Stuttgart, which is the main city of Swabia.

examining trivial works of Mozart alongside more important ones, but does not reject it. He sets up new divisions, however, partially based on the way Mozart's works were responses to commissions and to external circumstances. He writes:

> A living tradition still existed at this time, a summation of formal and stylistic rules acknowledged and felt by all, whether they were the patrons responsible for issuing the commissions . . . or the artists responsible for carrying them out. No artist could afford to ignore them. (p. xxv)

There are three groups of works for Abert: first, those written to fulfill a commission,

> in which his genius conformed to tradition without further ado, in some cases even subordinating itself to that tradition . . . works written for various celebrations, the pieces intended for pupils and individual singers, with their specific demands, and so on. The second group consists of those works that are still part of the tradition described above, but where the tradition is permeated and hence transformed and enriched by the elemental force of the artist's own experience, its range of forms increased in consequence. Typical of this group are the great keyboard concertos of the 1780s, which still clearly embody the old ideal of music written to divert society. . . . In the works of the third group, finally, the artist's archetypal experience, his basic emotion comes to predominate, with the result that the tradition is completely overshadowed by it. Here the focus of the artist's interest passes from the receptive element—his audience in society—to the artist himself. In these works, tradition is annealed by the fire of Mozart's genius to the point that it falls away like ash, allowing entirely new shapes to emerge. (p. xxv)

To this final group for Abert belong "the great symphonies and string quintets" as well as the great operas.

This system of classification is neither entirely misleading nor indefensible, but it is tendentious. It preempts judgment. Abert himself admits that the distinctions are not hard and fast, and even observes that it is a pleasure to try and decide in which category a work belongs. Excluding the wonderful concertos of the 1780s from the category of the sublime because they are sociable, is certainly a dubious point. This distinction of categories inclines us to underestimate the role of tradition in the most radical works of the third group (a tendency that Abert, however, largely resists successfully in spite of his programmatic statement above). It also assumes unwarrantably that the composer always expressed his art more personally when transforming tradition than by conforming to it, that Mozart, in short, was most Mozartean only when most radical. That is particularly dangerous with this composer because it may prevent us from recognizing that Mozart could be as inspired when he conformed to tradition as when he was revolutionary. The refusal to acknowledge that Mozart often showed his genius when he was most conventional has inspired such foolishness as Adorno's rueful assertion that Mozart, unlike Beethoven, could not always write the way he wanted, or Glenn Gould's attempt, by performance as well as writing, to demonstrate that Mozart in his last years had become an inferior composer.

Abert's preference for the most radical and revolutionary works is certainly due in large part to the contemporary situation in the arts in 1919: this was the moment of German expressionism in painting and literature, with Kirchener, Kandinsky, Beckmann among the artists, Hauptmann, Wedekind, and Thomas Mann among the writers; the era of the French Fauves and cubism, of Joyce and Proust; the period dominated in new music by Richard Strauss, Arnold Schoenberg, and Igor Stravinsky. A new view of Mozart was required.

Abert's preference for the Mozart that could seem, at least, most personal and radical did not, in fact, infirm his judgment except in minor ways. The only important exception to this is his treatment of the piano concertos. This is not to say that he was insensible or unappreciative of their extraordinary qualities; it would not be easy to find a treatment that was fairer. But he treats them oddly as a group, and does not give them individually the space extended to the viola quintets and the symphonies, not to speak of the operas (the field of Abert's greatest expertise). He does not trace the extraordinary change in the style of the concertos from the A Major, K. 414, to the C minor, K. 491, and while he is aware that Mozart transformed the tradition of the concerto as greatly as he did the opera and the symphony, he does not choose to set this in relief. He does not even treat the early masterpiece of the twenty-year-old Mozart, the Concerto in E-flat Major, K. 271, separately from the two concertos that preceded it: this is the opus that Alfred Einstein called Mozart's "Eroica" Symphony, the stylistic breakthrough that confirmed his mature style, and about which H. T. Robbins-Landon remarked that with it, Mozart "quietly bursts the form which was bequeathed to him by his predecessors: for K. 271 is indeed far removed from the form and content of the pre-classical concerto."[2]

---

2. *The Mozart Companion*, ed. H. T. Robbins-Landon and Donald Mitchell (New York and London), 1956, p. 249. Earlier in his article, Robbins-Landon had insisted that Mozart's concertos are incomprehensible without knowledge of the preclassical form, and he seems to contradict that here. He is, I suppose, right on both counts; it depends on how you think music is—or ought to be—understood. It should be added that, if Abert's treatment of the individual concertos is disappointing by comparison with the passionate discussion of the other works, the chapter ends with a very long section with two dozen examples on the virtuoso figuration and texture of the piano style in the concertos that is more interesting and informative than anything else I have seen on the subject.

It is clear that Abert's aesthetic risks a distortion of history, and we can see why Eisen should be made uncomfortable by it. Yet it has had two admirable effects, and these are strangely contradictory, or at least paradoxical. The first effect is that it has increased our appreciation of Mozart by setting in relief, for the most part, those works which appeal to musical taste today. Our interest in the art of the past is necessarily discriminating, and we must not expect to admire with an equal passion everything that our ancestors valued before us. Abert and his generation put new life into Mozart by making him into a composer that appealed to the twentieth century. They brought out what they felt to be the demonic aspect of Mozart; the dramatic force, and even the violence, and created a figure that was very different from the more graceful and charming, but blander Mozart; generally conceived by the nineteenth century (with, of course, a few notable exceptions from E. T. A. Hoffmann and Kierkegaard to George Bernard Shaw, who were aware of Mozart's power).

The expressionistic aesthetic, historically flawed as it is, had, as its second effect, a historical restoration of the way that Mozart was viewed by the late eighteenth century. For his contemporaries, Mozart was a difficult composer, not only hard to play, but hard to listen to. Most of the greatest works, they felt, could only be performed by the finest professionals, or else they made a poor impression. Not only were there too many notes (in most operas by other composers, the second violins played the same notes as the first violins most of the time, but in Mozart they are more often given an independent line, and the violas, as well, are allotted interesting phrases), there were above all too many new ideas and new themes, all coming one after the other in a profusion that was painful to follow. And the harmony was often outrageous and impossible to understand (to this complaint E. T. A. Hoffmann replied that connoisseurs understood Mozart's most radical harmony without difficulty, the uneducated public was emotionally stirred by it, and only the half-educated music amateur was bewildered). Abert and his generation restored Mozart's difficulty and made him definitively the dramatic equal of any composer in history.

2

Nowhere does Abert shock modern scholarship more than in his low estimate of Mozart's last opera, *La Clemenza di Tito*.[3] This work has been revived with some success in the last two decades, and is sometimes advertised as a seventh great opera along with *Idomeneo, The Abduction, Figaro, Don Giovanni, Cosi*

---

3. The overture to *The Magic Flute* was written after Tito, but the rest had been composed before.

fan tutte, and *The Magic Flute.* This was a work that Mozart wrote hurriedly in ill health, and had to get someone else to write the recitatives. With all his other operas he almost certainly had something to do with the choice and even the construction of the librettos,—he forced rewriting of *Idomeneo,* messed up the libretto of the *Abduction* to get a more effective finale for the second act, chose the Beaumarchais *Figaro* himself, and must have influenced *Figaro* and *Die Zauberflöte* with their profusion of ensembles and a Protestant chorale for *Die Zauberflöte*—but not *Tito.* With this work, he was not, as Abert remarks, able to create something original, but only to set quickly an old libretto of Metastasio, fixed up and abridged in advance.

Abert gives a sympathetic account of the work, admiring above all the first act finale, "one might even say that it is the spirit of classical tragedy that finds expression here" (p. 1237), but his final judgment is severe:

> Any comparison between *Idomeneo* and *La Clemenza di Tito* is bound to be to the latter's disadvantage, as the later work lacks the sense of profound personal experience that we find in the earlier piece. In *Idomeneo,* Mozart still believed in his artistic mission even in the field of *opera seria.* By the time he wrote *La Clemenza di Tito,* this world lay far behind him, and his only concern was to carry out his professional duty and complete a task that only sporadically engaged his interest.

His severity is, I think, justified. There are a number of fine things in the opera, but for most of it Mozart's ability to give new life to the commonplace, to transfigure the banal has deserted him. One has only to compare the fine rondo of Sesto in the second act with the similar but much more affecting rondo of Fiordiligi in the second act of *Cosi* to see the lower level of inspiration.

In one sense, the way Abert privileges the most radical works gives a truer representation of Mozart in history than an effort to reconstruct an eighteenth-century mind set; it sets in relief those works that changed the course of music. It is these radical works that have had the greatest effect on composers after Mozart. The progeny of *Don Giovanni* is innumerable. The *Abduction from the Seraglio* changed the way the *Singspiel* was composed afterward. *Cosi fan tutte* was imitated by Beethoven and Stravinsky. Schoenberg said that he learned the secret of eccentric phrasing by studying Mozart's works. In short, the demonic composer that Abert partly discovered and partly created restored Mozart to history.

On two largely neglected works of Mozart, Abert gives a lengthy and brilliant account that makes their importance convincing. One is the unfinished German opera on a serious Turkish theme, *Zaide,* written just before the comic Turkish opera the *Abduction.* Abert is understandably repelled by the disgusting style of the libretto (all the spoken dialogue has disappeared except for two experimental sections called melodrama—that is, spoken dialogue with orchestral accompaniment) but gives full justice to the music, which presents some of Mozart's finest arias and ensembles. Except for the overture (always the last piece to be written, because it needed no stage rehearsal) and the final scene, the work is complete.

The other work to which, as far as I know, only Abert has done full justice, is *The Musical Joke*. This is a sextet for string quartet and two horns that Mozart wrote in 1787. Abert relates it to "a venerable tradition of caricaturing worthless and incompetent colleagues" (p. 1001), and observes that "the real parody is directed at the work's imaginary composer." This is Mozart's Art of Music that takes the form of an example of how not to do it, and it makes a wonderful introduction to his conception of composition. What is magnificent is that Mozart's imaginary idiot blunders into every possible clumsy mistake, and yet Mozart succeeds in making the piece sound delightful. Abert goes into great detail explaining each error and so giving a beautiful résumé of Mozart's aesthetic, and remarks "Rarely has so much wit been expended on creating an impression of such witlessness."

I have only one serious disagreement to offer with Abert; he does not believe that Mozart's setting of "Viva la libertà" ("Hooray for liberty") in *Don Giovanni* has a secret political meaning. It is true that the overt significance at Don Giovanni's party is an invitation to his guests to enjoy themselves, but Mozart's setting is clearly martial and stirring with trumpets and drums reintroduced for the first time since the overture of the opera, and resonates like a call to arms. In any case, the belief that the setting was subversive was later accepted, as the words were fearfully and prudently changed to *Viva la società*.

One important aspect of Abert's view of Mozart was omitted by him, and appears only in the short introduction to his edition of *The Marriage of Figaro;* that is the harmonic construction and logic of the opera as a whole. On this subject Abert's considerations have become unfashionable, and some critics have tried to deny that a Mozart opera has the unity that so many have felt about each of the mature works. Of course, the unity of an opera is not the relatively closed structure of a sonata or symphony, which is not, in turn, the even denser structure of a single movement, or the absolutely closed form of a rounded melody. Nevertheless, the way Mozart worked out the harmonic relationships in his later operas has logic and a symmetry that has convinced many listeners, and they were best indicated and described so far by Abert in his Eulenburg edition of the orchestral score. Recent writing on this subject does not seem to have understood or paid much attention to his arguments, and it would be a good idea to add these few pages as an appendix when this book is reprinted, as I expect it will be.

CHAPTER 7

The Triumph of Mozart

J AMES H. JOHNSON's *Listening in Paris* is an original book filled with
good things. It takes up the way people listened to music in Paris, starting
with the operas of Rameau in the mid-eighteenth century, and ending with the
chapters "Beethoven Triumphant" and "The Musical Experience of Romanticism." Johnson traces the development of attentiveness, the change from an
audience that chattered sociably during fashionable operas to a public that
listened in religious silence. His book is an essay in the history of aesthetic
"reception," that is, it deals with the public response to the revolutionary transformations in the nature of Western art music that took place during the life of
Beethoven.

Johnson makes an observation about the concert programs in Paris in the
early nineteenth century which reveals the strengths and the limitations of the
history of reception:

> There was also the dogged presence of Mozart, whose symphonies and
> operas were roundly denounced in the first decade of the century yet
> remained just as surely on programs. Already in the 1810s some of the
> initial bemusement was giving way to interest, and by the 1820s Stendhal

Originally written in 1995 as a review of *Listening in Paris: A Cultural History,* by James H.
Johnson.

could claim that the true dilettante was as enamored with Mozart as with Rossini. (p. 218)

If Mozart was disliked by the public and roundly denounced by critics, how can we explain his "dogged presence" on musical programs? The answer is that the music which is performed is not so much the works that the public wants to hear, as those that musicians insist on playing. Public demand counts for something, of course, but a musician's life is often enough hard, disagreeable, and monotonous, and it would be intolerable unless he could play the music he loved.

This is not a question of elite preference, but of professional ideals, a subject that the history of reception deals with very badly. That is because practitioners of this important discipline generally refuse to admit anything like an intrinsic interest to music. Johnson writes:

> Musical meaning does not exist objectively in the work—or even in its composer's intentions. It resides in the particular moment of reception, one shaped by dominant aesthetic and social expectations that are themselves historically structured. (p. 2)

This may be true on a high epistemological level, but it is a vacuous and uninteresting truth when it comes to explaining something like the eventual triumph of Mozart. No doubt, the admiration of professional musicians for the works of Mozart was shaped by "dominant aesthetic and social expectations," but the musicians were also reacting to specific qualities and characteristics in Mozart's music that they found nowhere else. Some works have demonstrably a capacity for generating and sustaining interest, and that is why we can often learn more about the history of reception by looking at the music itself than by studying the specific interpretations it has inspired. Interpretations change, of course, but not nearly as radically as some historians think, if one considers specifically the reactions of professionals, and if one also considers not only the reactions to a first performance, but to the second and third ones as well. As long as the history of reception concentrates solely on the attitudes of the general public and on journalistic criticism, it chooses to ignore the central forces for change in the history of music.

Some composers are able to inspire an almost fanatical devotion; it does not necessarily lead to popularity—but it does lead to survival. Schoenberg is not, I think, a composer who will ever be genuinely popular, but there has always been an important body of musicians who insist on playing him, and they eventually find enough of a public to justify it, even economically. Put on a concert of Schoenberg string quartets and you will not make a fortune, but you might break even and have some loose change left over. This is why a study of public reception is so often an illusory and imperfect way of determining the prestige and even the economics of music.

Johnson's choice of Paris for his study is both a limitation and a strength. In the late eighteenth century, the city that produced the music that would have the greatest influence on the future of music was Vienna. The public concert life of both London and Paris in the early 1700s, however, was much more developed than Vienna's, and we have a rich documentation for these cities available (Viennese scholars have tended to sit on what evidence there is for the concerts in Vienna, releasing it with the kind of prudence reserved for the Dead Sea scrolls). By the mid-eighteenth century, the center of European musical activity was Paris. That was where Italian composers hoped to be invited in order to achieve international prestige. Johnson was inspired when he chose Paris for a study of audience behavior: it was the true commercial center of European art.

By contrast, Vienna did not develop any extensive public concerts until the 1770s—that is, concerts at which all the tickets were sold and the musicians paid from the proceeds. The musical life of Vienna was dominated by the court; in fact, New York had extensive public concerts before Vienna. (It is true that tickets left over from the court concerts after the invitations were exhausted were sold to the public.) What Vienna had was a more intense semiprivate musical life, performances that were for a small audience and not strictly commercial. During Beethoven's lifetime only two of his thirty-two piano sonatas were performed at a public concert in Vienna; on the other hand, all of his string quartets were played by virtuosos in public as well as at private gatherings. The idea that string quartets were a private form of chamber music for the delectation of the players while piano sonatas were for public consumption is a myth. It ought not to be a paradox that the instrumental style best suited for public exploitation was evolved in Vienna. In fact, the richness of the semiprivate tradition nourished the new music that would finally triumph in Paris, London, and elsewhere. As we learn from Johnson's book, Haydn was an immediate success in Paris already in the 1780s. It took a longer time for musicians to impose the works of Mozart and then of Beethoven; and *Listening in Paris* gives a fine account of how Beethoven achieved enormous popularity.

Unfortunately, Johnson writes as if listening in public were the only kind of listening that mattered. In the eighteenth century, even in Paris, the public concert was a relatively recent creation, still something of an anomaly. To talk about listeners' reactions only to public concerts is to cut oneself off from the main activity of listening, although the documentation of public performances is more abundant than it is for private ones. For this reason, Johnson is obliged to limit himself for the first part of his book largely to opera. This does less harm, perhaps, when dealing with French musical life compared with the tradition in Germany and Austria, but it is still one-sided.

As the book goes on, we seem to witness the victory of German seriousness over French frivolity; essentially this amounted to a victory of instrumental music over vocal. Not that opera did not remain popular, and we might even cite the extraordinary popularity accorded to Schubert's lieder in Paris during the 1830s, something that Johnson does not mention. Nevertheless, it is the German instrumental style that gained philosophical prestige as the model of the art of music.

The great success of Johnson's book lies in its anecdotes. (Never underestimate the power of anecdotes: they can be more profound, more creative, than generalizations.) He gives, for example, a fascinating account of an elephant ballet staged during the Revolution and of the experiments made at the time on the effect of music as an erotic stimulant for the mating of elephants. He is not only entertaining, but instructive about the connections that were developing at the time between art, sensuality, and science (he even reproduces an engraving of elephants beginning their foreplay in response to the music).

However, Johnson is less sure-footed about aesthetic theory, although he provides a lot of fascinating quotations from contemporary writers on the expressive or nonexpressive nature of music. It is particularly unfortunate that he fails to consider German and English speculation on music and aesthetics, since France was much less isolated from foreign influence than has sometimes been thought. He fails, for example, to convey the complexity of Diderot's thought and its English influences. And the treatment of Michel de Chabanon is also curious, since this interesting writer does not appear in the index, although his provocative essays on expression in music are listed in the bibliography. He is even mentioned on pages 37 and 75, but not his ideas, which attempt to deal directly with the perverse nature of aesthetic theory. (He remarked, for example, that when sailors are happy they sing sad songs.)

On the music itself, Johnson does not distinguish well between those characteristics that were developed in response to changing public taste and those that were already frequently employed before. For example, he quotes a sextet in Méhul's opera *Euphrosine* of 1790 to show the new concern with illustrating distinct sentiments, but in fact the music does not differentiate very much between the six characters, except for the bass singing "My blood freezes in my heart" with his musical line frozen on one note. Not only would the second act's famous "jealousy" duet, which made Méhul's reputation, be a more apt example, but the great quartet from Handel's *Jephtha* almost forty years before, in 1751, did a considerably better and more effective job of radically expressing four different kinds of emotion.

In trying to relate changes in musical style to social developments, we stumble against the problem of musical meaning, and the difficulties of pinning down meaning with any confidence were only recognized with real clarity first in the late eighteenth century. Johnson appreciates the fluid nature of musical meaning, its ability to support multiple interpretations, but his view of how this is done is too lax, no doubt because he wishes to displace the meaning from the music itself into the mind of the spectator, while, as he himself remarks, to do so only opens the music to radical and uncontrollable forms of misreading. Nevertheless, he underestimates certain conventions, and writes, astonishingly:

> It is difficult to imagine how a melody might paint such words as *triompher, gloire,* or *victoire,* and in fact there is no characteristic movement these *melismas* [successions of different notes sung on one syllable] take to suggest that composers had any more precise motive in mind than simply to draw attention to the words with a punctuated phrase or flourish. (p. 43)

I do not understand this point, and would think that an example of the chorus from Handel's *Saul* would explain how music could, in fact, reflect triumph and victory, and do so in a way that continues from Handel until the second act of Verdi's *Aida* and beyond. Not even early eighteenth-century theorists were naive enough to think that it is entirely by melodic types that music imitates, leaving out rhythm and orchestration.

At the end of the book, Johnson confronts what he feels is the "irreducibility of musical meaning," and writes:

> The only solution is to resort to the language of metaphor, with its inevitable approximations, to discuss musical meaning. Without metaphor we are reduced either to silence or to highly technical structural analyses like those of Heinrich Schenker—analyses that tell us about as much about musical meaning as a purely grammatical analysis might reveal about the meaning of Saint John's Gospel. (p. 282)

There is a double misunderstanding here: Johnson thinks that metaphor is necessarily imprecise, and he does not realize that technical analysis, certainly Schenker's, is fundamentally metaphorical.

Some metaphors are fuzzy, of course, but others are as precise as a proper name. There is nothing approximate about

> Her Voice was like a hidden Bird that sang:
> The thought of her was like a flash of light
> Or an unseen companionship, a breath
> Or fragrance independent of the wind.
> (Wordsworth, *Home at Grasmere*)

And simply to say, for example, that a harmony is dissonant is to use a metaphor. A dissonance is literally a disagreeable sound, but there is nothing disagreeable or unpleasant about a "dissonance" in tonal music; many dissonances are much nicer to listen to than consonances. A dissonance in triadic tonality, the musical language from 1550 to 1900, is a chord that is "unstable," "needs" to be resolved, "calls for" resolution, "demands" to be followed by a consonance—use whatever metaphor you find suitable. Metaphors work by analogy, by resemblance. Music acts on us by metaphor, by its analogy with our sensations and our emotions, our impulses. In short, like almost all elements of music, a dissonance itself is a metaphor and is described by technical terms which are themselves metaphors.

The basis of Schenker's theory, furthermore, is that a work of tonal music is a large metaphor for a single tonal phrase. The whole piece works by analogy with the simple phrase, it acts by "suspending" and "prolonging"—metaphorically, of course—various parts of the basic "line" until the final chord. Even this final tonic chord has a metaphorical power conferred by the piece as a whole, as the tonic is conceived as a satisfying resolution of all the preceding tensions.

It is only when the historian's account (largely metaphorical, I might add) of the social and historical setting of music is tied to the metaphorical power of the technical details (or can clearly be related to this aspect) that we have any chance of saying something that is not either a form of free association or idle guesswork. And, of course, all analyses, technical as well as ideological, are controlled by our knowledge and experience of the traditional metaphors in the history of music, the conventions of meaning that have been given to the grammar and syntax of music, as well as to the elements of harmony and melody.

In turn, if a technical analysis of a work of music is not a dramatic scenario, an account of the power that enabled the music to act directly on the composer's contemporaries and on successive generations of listeners, then it is an empty academic activity. It is true that most writing about music is either insubstantial speculation or a mechanical exercise, but then so is much writing about anything else. I take it that Johnson is bored by most technical analyses, and so am I, but if he is incapable of appreciating the dramatic power implicit in the best of them like some of Schenker's, he ought not to boast about it.

CHAPTER 8

Drama and Figured Bass in Mozart's Concertos

I

In his excellent book on Beethoven's concertos, Professor Leon Plantinga has written that I claim that Leopold Mozart (and, by implication, Wolfgang as well of course) "made use of continuo playing for concertos only at home, and only in the absence of winds."[1] In fact, I never denied that Mozart played continuo in public performances of his concertos. I did, however, claim that it was largely inaudible except to members of the orchestra, and I also asserted that although continuo playing still had a practical function in the late eighteenth century, it was "musically, if not practically, dead."

I see that the evidence for this needs to be spelled out more clearly, as it concerns both the character of concerto form and the varied social conditions of its performance. In particular, the extent to which the practice was still carried on with the Beethoven concertos needs to be considered, because ignoring it has led to mistakes in most of the editions of Beethoven's piano concertos—including one important mistake that has still not been corrected in the most authoritative recent edition, and is unremarked by Plantinga.

The Baroque Age in music (roughly 1600–1750) is sometimes called the "Age of Figured Bass" or the Age of the Continuo, because music was now conceived

1. *Beethoven's Concertos: History, Style, Performance* (New York: W. W. Norton, 1999), p. 367.

not only by the horizontal lines of separate vocal or instrumental parts, but vertically by the series of harmonies defined by the bass line with numerical figures underneath, which indicated the intervals that made up the chords. For the performance of most of the music of this period, these chords were realized on a keyboard. This realization could take different forms, since, for example, a C in the bass line with the numbers 3 and 5 could be realized by placing the 3d degree (E) below the 5th (G) or above it, and the bass note could be doubled above as well. It was therefore possible to write down a composition with only one vocal or instrumental part over the bass, leaving all the inner parts to be worked out by the keyboard player from the figures given. Even when the inner parts had been written out separately for other instruments, the keyboard player still realized the series of harmonies from the figures, adding sonority and rhythmic guidance to the performance. By 1775, this method of composing was obsolete.

There is, however, no question that, in the eighteenth century and the earliest years of the nineteenth, a continuo was played in parts of the tutti sections of Mozart and Beethoven concertos, and in the symphonies as well. There are, indeed, a very few places in the concertos that suffer today when the keyboard omits the bass notes and the harmonies. Nevertheless, the right questions, it seems to me, are not being asked about the practice, which cannot be understood as an absolute without considering its multiple functions and its decay.

The purposes of the continuo were manifold:

1. To fill out the harmony
2. To strengthen the bass
3. To add sonority when necessary
4. To help keep the ensemble together, particularly when the music was directed from the keyboard
5. To be used as a score if the work was to be conducted from a keyboard. A full score was never provided. Direction was often done from a copy of the first violin part. When the soloist conducted the orchestra, the bass part with figures for the harmony provided the necessary information (this was equally true for the performance of symphonies, when they were directed from a keyboard)
6. To serve as a guide so that the keyboard player could keep his or her place. Unlike tympanists, keyboard players were not expected to be able to count empty measures

Function 6 is clearly operative as late as Beethoven's *Missa solemnis,* where the bass is written into the organ part even when it is marked *senza organo* or *organo tacet,* and therefore the organist plays nothing at all at these points, but can follow the bass part. Function 1—to fill out the harmony—had, nevertheless, completely disappeared by the late eighteenth century. There is no contemporary evidence whatever that the continuo was necessary to fill out or complete the harmony in symphonies or concertos. A belief that in works of the time some bare passages in two-part counterpoint were juiced up by the keyboard player is simple fantasy, unsupported by any witness or document from the late eighteenth century.[2]

Function 2—to strengthen the bass—may possibly have continued in the last decades of the eighteenth century. The survival of this function would depend on the power of the bass instruments and on how many there were. The frequent indication *Tasto solo* ("just touch") is generally taken to mean "do not play," but it may have meant literally "just touch or play the bass line but add no harmonies." The weak pianofortes of Mozart's time, however, could not compete with any number of bass instruments, although they, too, were weaker than they are now, so this would not have had much effect for what the public heard, although the light percussive sonority of the keyboard may have aided the ensemble. Perhaps when economic conditions today make it too expensive to hire enough bass and cello players, the pianist should occasionally help with a tactful *tasto solo,* but this is not an interesting problem.

Function 4 of the continuo—to give precision to the ensemble—should not be dismissed. After a performance of *Die Zauberflöte,* I told the director, Sir Charles Mackerras, who knew more about late eighteenth-century performance than anybody else, that I was surprised to hear the sound of a harpsichord in two or three numbers; he replied, even more astonished, that he had used a harpsichord in every number throughout. Placed in the center of the orchestra, he said, it helps the precision of the ensemble and gives a bite to the sound. When a pianist directs a performance of a concerto or a symphony from the keyboard (as Haydn conducted the symphonies in London), the percussive sonority of piano or harpsichord increases the accuracy of the ensemble. Played on an eighteenth-century instrument, it is heard well by the members of the orchestra, but is largely inaudible to the public unless the continuo is played during the softer passages of the tutti (but that is largely where, with very few exceptions, all the evidence we have shows that it was generally avoided). That Haydn directed the Salamon Orchestra in London entirely by thumping the

2. Keyboard players were, of course, still taught to realize figured bass at the time, but so was I when I was eleven years old. No one was ever told that it was structurally necessary for the harmony of the music written after the third quarter of the eighteenth century.

keyboard is untenable, as a London critic remarked on the beauty of Mr. Haydn's gestures, so he must have been waving his arms at times like Mackerras, Toscanini, or Karajan, but if he was seated at a keyboard he surely played at least some chords. Today's technique of conducting an orchestra was only tentatively and sketchily introduced and developed, and methods of directing an ensemble had not yet been uniformly codified.

Directing an orchestra from a keyboard lasted in the early nineteenth century. A criticism of an instrumental performance of Rossini in New York in the 1820s by an orchestra of twenty-four musicians describes how the keyboard was used:

> Sometimes the direction was divided between the concertmaster, who had only the violin part, and the pianist, who had the bass part. The violins might be a little too loud; but one soul seemed to inspire and a single hand to guide, the whole band being throughout the mazes of Rossini's most intricate flights under the direction of M. De Luce (the first violin and concertmaster); while M. Etienne presided in an effective manner at a piano, of which every now and then he might be heard to touch the keynote by those whose attention was turned that way, and just loud enough to be heard throughout the orchestra, for whose guidance it was intended.[3]

There is evidence that a conspicuous presence of the continuo was avoided in the late eighteenth century. In his son's Concerto in E-flat Major, K. 271, Leopold Mozart wrote out the figures for a continuo part, and he added figures in only six bars when the orchestra is not marked *forte;* all the other soft passages are left bare or specifically directed *tasto solo.* Given the weak sonority of a late eighteenth-century piano, the continuo presence must have been very unobtrusive unless the orchestra was reduced to little more than a string quartet with solo winds, and even then it would not be particularly prominent. At places in this work, Mozart himself specifically wrote rests into the solo part to render its succeeding entrance more effective, or removed all harmonization by ending the orchestral section with unison octaves in all the instruments, and these should certainly not be harmonized by the keyboard. This practice can already be found in other composers like Johann Christian Bach, who marked the keyboard part at these places *unisono.*

Even Leopold Mozart may not have fully understood how far in the revolutionary work K. 271 his son was playing with the relation of solo piano and

---

3. M. Sterling Mackinlay, *Garcia the Centenarian and His Times* (New York, 1906), p. 76. Mr. Will Crutchfield provided me with this source.

tutti. The last bars of the first ritornello of the Andante slow movement and the last bars of the whole movement are similar, but Mozart in the final bars added arpeggiated chords in the solo piano to the unison octaves in the orchestra. In my opinion, the penultimate dominant chord added by Leopold to the end of the opening ritornello is a mistake, and would spoil the more elaborate and dramatic effect Mozart reserved for the very end, although Mozart himself added a little harmony to the final chord in the horns:

This is confirmed by the ending of the first solo, which exactly repeats the unison cadence at the relative major without the addition of harmony, and Leopold does not suggest harmonizing the bare final notes:

This extraordinary concerto (Alfred Einstein called it Mozart's "Eroica Symphony") is famous for the continuous interference of the solo piano during the orchestral sections, each interference a dramatic surprise, and Mozart predicted that the Viennese public would be astonished by the novelty of his new concertos. For its effect, the work depends on a perception of the clear demarcation between tutti and solo sections. This is generally recognized about the first movement, where the piano constantly interrupts the orchestra with a solo passage. Equally astonishing, however, is the return of the main theme in the slow movement. The theme is first presented by the strings in imitative counterpoint, clearly marked *tasto solo* by Leopold:

The first solo section then places an expressive obbligato over a literal replaying of the ritornello:

At the recapitulation, however, there is an unprecedented effect as the piano appropriates the orchestral role for two bars:

A further solo intervention in a tutti occurs six bars before the end of the movement, at a climax where the violins remove the mutes, used throughout until then. That, however, does not give enough sonority for Mozart, and he has the pianist play the bass seven times in octaves, but marked *tasto solo:*

Here, the soloist, having briefly taken over the orchestral role, now enters into the orchestra, and acts as tympanist with seven percussive beats (there are no tympani in this concerto).

This is a good example, although astonishing in character, of function 3—to add sonority. The only realized continuo in Mozart's handwriting, that for the Concerto in C Major, K. 246, constitutes the principal evidence for how this was done. When the orchestra is not marked *forte* in K. 246, Mozart invariably directs *tasto solo,* except in a single half measure, the repetition of which has a crescendo. Not even all the forte passages are supplied with keyboard harmony in the realization. See the following passage:

The most significant detail is a place in the slow movement where the oboe melody is now written into the solo piano part! As I have pointed out,[4] this realization was therefore written for a performance without winds, possibly a private one with a string quartet, as this is the only place in the concerto where the winds play a melody not doubled by the strings. The missing wind parts have, therefore, to be supplied by the solo keyboard:

Supplying the melody—not just filling out the harmony—was therefore necessary when some of the instruments were absent.

4. *The Classical Style: Haydn, Mozart, Beethoven* (New York: W. W. Norton, 1997), pp. 191–193. In a Princeton Ph.D. dissertation of 1983, "Col Basso and General Bass in Mozart's Keyboard Concertos," Linda Fay Ferguson oddly suggests that the solo keyboard cooperated with a second keyboard to represent the orchestra. This implies that someone (Mozart himself?) transcribed the orchestra for a second piano but omitted the oboe melody not doubled by the strings. Why would anybody make a transcription that foolish? Why would the only realization of a general bass part that has come down to us from Mozart himself be written down to be intended to accompany a piano transcription? We have here an example of what I have called the fetishism of performance practice studies. Treating the continuo in the late eighteenth century, Ferguson

A further demonstration of this point is the fact that the significance of a similar place in the later "Coronation" Concerto in D Major, K. 537, seems to have gone generally unnoticed, where an oboe part is not doubled by the violins. This work, written late in Mozart's life, is scored for an unusually large orchestra; besides the strings, there are one flute, two oboes, two bassoons, two horns, two trumpets, and tympani, but Mozart's own catalogue tells us that all this large force, except for the strings, is optional. Every important note necessary to the melody or harmony is doubled by the strings, but this is not true of bars 137–138 and 141–142 of the finale:

feels that you cannot have too much of it, and chooses to ignore the implications of the modest realization for K. 246. I still believe that if Mozart exceptionally wrote out a continuo part in which the pianist only reinforces the loud and never the soft orchestral sections, and adds the only melodic line in the winds not doubled by the strings, it would be obvious that he took the trouble for a performance with no winds and a reduced string section.

Here, the oboes and bassoons are not doubled, but only the oboes are essential, as the bassoons who reinforce the rhythm also give the harmony, but that is sufficiently provided by the violas and cellos. However, exactly as in the similar place of K. 246, Mozart has left the right hand of the pianist free and only the left hand is occupied. For a performance with reduced orchestra without oboes, the pianist must be expected to play the oboes' melody. As in K. 246, a written-out continuo would have to signal this to the performer, so the practice must have continued until the end of Mozart's lifetime.

Ellwood Derr was right to insist that pianists should finish the phrases at the end of the Concerto in D Minor, K. 466, and elsewhere by playing along with the orchestra.[5] Of course, they have mostly done so, and played with the final

5. in *Mozart's Piano Concertos: Text, Context, Interpretation*, edited by Neal Zaslaw (Ann Arbor: University of Michigan Press, 1996).

chords of the orchestra at the end of Beethoven's C Minor Concerto as well, as it looks silly not to join in the last two bars, but Derr's suggestion for filling out the bars that precede the *Eingang* or entrance of the soloist in Concerto in B-flat Major, K. 450 (bar 59), is absolutely unacceptable, because it is awkward and makes the entrance much less effective.

This is exactly the kind of place where Mozart himself, or his father, often indicates *tasto solo,* or else explicitly writes rests. Gradually, during the first half of the nineteenth century, the contrast of solo and tutti was made more effective by leaving out the continuo and finding more efficient ways of conducting the orchestra during a concerto; it is ironic that scholars today should seek to spoil the performance by adding a continuo where even Mozart would invariably have omitted it.

Even more regrettable was Paul Badura-Skoda's proposal to add harmonies to an exquisite piece of two-part counterpoint in the ritornello of the same concerto, K. 450:

This passage is immediately repeated with a lush third voice added. Furthermore, when this passage reappears in the recapitulation, the pianist accompanies the simple two-voice with a spare trill on the dominant, and then adds a third voice followed by an elaborate arabesque based on the earlier luxuriant counterpoint, and all this enriching transformation from two- to three-voice polyphony would be marred by imposing banal, clunky harmonies to the initial two-voice presentation of the theme.

In this case, filling out the two-part counterpoint in the orchestra is a project equivalent to Robert Schumann's misguided proposal to provide a piano accompaniment to Bach's unaccompanied violin sonatas.

2

By the middle of the nineteenth century, the continuo had been dropped and all the indications in the concertos of Mozart and Beethoven were removed. This, however, led to the falsification of certain passages in the concertos of Beethoven, notably no. 4 in G Major. Important bass notes were removed, which were not continuo notes at all but solo notes, written not as single notes but as octaves, and which were supposed to be not only played but held for a long stretch with the pedal. Franz Kullak pointed out the mistakes in his edition at the end of the nineteenth century, but it took a long time for other editors to make the correction. The most important of these is at bar 402 of the finale:

The following is the correct version:

Without the initial pedaled bass octave and right-hand chord held for four-teen bars throughout this page, the harmony is exceedingly ugly, merely emphasizing a tritone in the bass: with it, a powerful and traditional climax on a dominant seventh chord is achieved. We must return briefly to this example, but another place is the opening of the recapitulation in the first movement:

The bass note here was written as an octave in the manuscript (which means that it was not an indication of continuo but part of the solo text), and Czerny—who had heard Beethoven play this piece—indicated that it also needs to be held with the pedal, although that was not specifically indicated by Beethoven. With the octave bass and pedal support, the passage becomes very grand, and sounds better than the oddly anemic version traditionally printed.

Still more must be added to the solo part of the Fourth Concerto, however, as an examination of the final page of the first movement of the Third Piano Concerto in C Minor will suggest. In this work, Beethoven evidently set out to imitate Mozart's concerto in the same key, K. 491. Mozart interrupts the final ritornello with arpeggios in the piano.

Beethoven's imitation is flagrant, even to the point of doubling the last arpeggios in the left hand, but he took care to add original touches and make it even more spectacularly effective. He starts by ending his cadenza not on a tonic chord but on V7 of IV and adding a new motif as the coda proceeds:

He adds new motifs, and the final arpeggios are no longer soft as in Mozart, but fortissimo:

There is, however, something illogical and certainly wrong with these last arpeggios. The right hand starts on the first beat, but the left hand waits until the second. Why? There is no musical reason to emphasize this second beat and leave the first beat void in the left hand. Evidently the left hand was otherwise occupied on the first beat. What has happened is that function 3 of the continuo—to add sonority to the preceding two fortissimo bars of the tutti—is still operating, and the pianist should play the logical and sensible realization implied by the structure of the preceding bars:

Here, the soloist enters into the orchestral climax. Beethoven's pianos were already somewhat larger than Mozart's, and cooperating in the orchestral climax may have made more of a difference.

This suggests that in the two examples given in the G Major Concerto, the pianist was supposed to play and reinforce the preceding bars in the orchestra as follows:

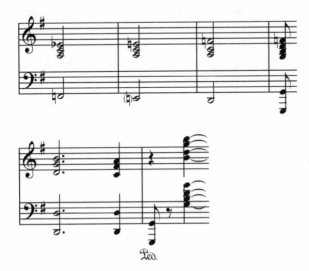

The realization of the continuo in these places is a dramatic improvement of the text. It is significant that the only three places in all of the Beethoven concertos where the removal of the indications for the continuo resulted in a misreading of the solo text should all be a solo entrance immediately following an orchestral fortissimo. That the soloist collaborated with the orchestra when the tutti was that loud is also the evidence of Mozart's realization of the continuo and Leopold's as well, as we have seen. (All of the other early published directions for the continuo—the figures given in the first editions of Mozart—may be dismissed out of hand, as they were the work of a publisher's hack; the numbers of the figured bass sometimes indicate the wrong harmonies and cannot have stemmed from the composer.)[6]

Plantinga has an interesting discussion of the changes that Beethoven sketched into the solo part of the Fourth Concerto some time after its publication to make use of the increased range of upper notes added to the new instruments at that time; none of these changes were ever published by him or, in fact, as we shall see, even seriously worked out. Some conventional arpeggios placed over an expressive orchestral theme at bar 286 of the opening movement, and doubled in the left hand two octaves below, Plantinga thinks may represent the way that Beethoven played during the orchestral passages and relates this to his discussion of continuo, but it is unlikely that adding virtuoso figuration—particularly arpeggios, which were a staple of concerto style—has anything to do with the realization of figured bass. In any case, the variant seems to me a terrible idea, and we must be thankful it was never carried out. Two other suggested variants in the first movement raise much greater problems. Plantinga believes that they represent the "mischievous" *(muthwillig)* way, according to Czerny's description, that Beethoven played this concerto in public. One is a rewriting of the opening of the second solo (or development section), the other some difficult virtuoso leaps added to the double trills at bars 166–169 (the double trill was a great specialty of Beethoven as a performer). Unfortunately, neither variant can bear witness to the way Beethoven actually performed the concerto,—at least one must hope so, as both of them have one bar too many;—if he did play it that way, he would have ended one bar behind the orchestra with cacophonic results (both variants would have required a revision of all the orchestral parts).

Plantinga also suggested that since Beethoven added figures in the manuscript to the bass part of the *Emperor* Concerto, he expected the pianist to play continuo throughout. Since the continuo was still used as a guide for cues and as an aid in making an arrangement of the concerto to be played with a reduced force, I assume that Beethoven preferred the indications to be correct, rather than leave them to the publisher, which at that time courted disaster. Plantinga

6. See Rosen, *Classical Style*, p. 191, for mistaken figures in the general bass indications.

does not suggest a single phrase which would be improved by the continuo, and I can think of many where it would be ruinous (including the one Plantinga gives as an example from the manuscript.) However, the pianist should certainly join in the last two or even four bars of the finale to avoid giving the impression of being ready to leave before everybody else.

The fashionable musicological favor enjoyed by the continuo in recent years has given rise to strange speculation. Scholarly research has an energetic momentum, a vitality independent of history and sometimes of logic. Having established correctly that the continuo was used well into the nineteenth century, students of performance practice would like to make this knowledge interesting, widely available, and manifest. They wish to resurrect, to breathe new life into, a convention that was, in fact, in the process of slowly dying out throughout Europe. Like justice, scholarship must not only be done, it must be seen, or rather heard, to be done. Even Neal Zaslaw, normally the most judicious of all experts, writes that in a private performance of a concerto with strings alone, "the soloist (at least, if he or she was a professional musician) presumably provided some of what was lost by the absence of the winds by improvising imaginative continuo realizations in the tuttis."[7] There is no reason to think that the realization of any continuo after 1770 was ever imaginative, or that an imaginative one would be desirable or even acceptable. Everything that we know about the use of the continuo at this time indicates that it was completely conventional and never ostentatious. Of course, in an earlier time, an imaginative or an elaborate realization of the continuo (for the trio sonata in *The Musical Offering,* for example) was a good idea, and we know that Bach expected a realization of the figured bass in four full voices correctly following the rules of counterpoint, although parallel octaves with the other instruments were permitted, but in Mozart's works it is hard to see which of the various functions of the continuo would have been enhanced by the slightest originality or imagination. Any attempt to make the continuo interesting would, in fact, interfere with the music. Imaginative embellishments are needed in several places in Mozart's concertos, imaginative rubato and phrasing as well, but any realization of the continuo that calls attention to itself is, as far as I know, inauthentic.

The following questions need to be posed. If the clarinet player plays along with the first violins throughout the tutti of the Clarinet Concerto (it was written into his part, and the solo violinist of a concerto as well could look at the complete first violin part of the tutti), how does that improve anyone's appreciation or understanding of the work? This indication has been cited as support for reviving the general bass, but surely it only gives us cause for doubting the rationale of the revival. Is there any reason to think that if, in the

7. in Zaslaw, *Mozart's Piano Concertos,* p. 10.

eighteenth century, the clarinetist did actually double the first violin in every bar of every tutti, it was done in such a way that it could be clearly heard? Knowing Mozart's exquisite sense of wind doubling in all other works, we would find it hard to accept the policy of relentless doubling in the concerto. It would certainly exhaust the player and spoil the performance of the solo passages. What reason is there for thinking that playing the continuo throughout the tutti of a Mozart concerto is musically more significant or more desirable than playing it in a late Haydn or early Beethoven symphony? Was the disappearance of the continuo a perverse aberration on the part of musicians who misunderstood the Mozart concertos, or was it not, on the contrary, a response to the new dramatic deployment and opposition of soloist and orchestra achieved by Mozart and others, and also to the recently developing conditions of directing an orchestral performance? Is not the disappearance, in fact, foreshadowed by Mozart's writing pauses into the solo part just before important entrances of the piano?[8]

The emancipation of the solo keyboard from its role as an accompanying member of the orchestra is strikingly accomplished by Mozart's K. 271. The solo entrances in most of his concertos afterward are very striking and not improved visually by making it look as if the keyboard had a double function. Mozart's inspiration in K. 271 to confound the audience's general expectation that a concerto would begin with an orchestral ritornello was magnified by Beethoven in the last two concertos, and was continued with new dramatic emphasis by Schumann, Mendelssohn, and Liszt.

3

The modern revival of the continuo in Mozart concertos has had unfortunate consequences in historical interpretation. It is the lynchpin of Professor James Webster's contention that the Mozart concertos are not dramatic, and his refusal to acknowledge the almost complete emancipation of the form of the Mozart concerto from the earlier eighteenth-century concerto grosso, as well as the influence of the Italian opera aria, an influence that reaches an absolute identity of form with many of the movements of the concertos.[9] It is true that the Mozart concertos are perhaps not as dramatic or as loud as those of Liszt

8. See Christoph Wolff's remarks in the critical notes to his edition of K. 271 in the *Neue Mozart Ausgabe,* Bärenreiter; the critical notes were completed only after the original manuscript was rediscovered with the hitherto unnoticed rests in the solo part, and the concerto had been printed.

9. "Are Mozart's Concertos 'Dramatic'?" Concerto Ritornellos versus Aria Introductions in the 1780s, in Zaslaw, *Mozart's Piano Concertos.*

and Tchaikovsky, but they are considerably more dramatic than any earlier concertos of the eighteenth century in the way they exploit the individuality of the solo instrument. Traces of the old concerto grosso form do indeed continue, notably in the use of a reduced string section or *concertino* during the solo sections. However, for the most part this *concertino* plays a purely accompanying subsidiary role, and it is by no means certain that the reduction of the strings to a string quartet was carried out in all performances, although it was certainly done so at least in the case of the Concerto in G Major, K. 453, and in the Concerto in B-flat Major, K. 595. There are also very rare moments in the Mozart concertos (the canon toward the end of the slow movement of K. 271 and the last appearance of the main theme in the slow movement of K. 595) where the first violinist indeed plays as a solo with the pianist (the use of the full violin section doubling the melodic line of one flute and a pianoforte of the 1780s is absurd, although unfortunately that is the way it is almost always performed).

In the latter example, the pianist should probably add an ornamentation that blends tactfully with the flute and violin lines.

The combination of solo wind with piano in several Mozart concertos is no more typical of the earlier concerto grosso style than it is of Brahms's concertos and other Romantic works, and the wind solos often resemble those in late eighteenth-century opera arias—except, of course, that a singer cannot accompany horn or oboe with something like an Alberti bass as the pianist may. Even the cadenza-like introductory passages *(Eingänge),* adduced as an example of the difference of aria and concerto, that Mozart writes for the pianist to interrupt the orchestra have their precedents in the operatic aria, although the instrumental character of the pianoforte can make them more elaborate than the vocal examples. These sudden appearances of the solo in the orchestral texture at the end of the first ritornello (as in the concertos K. 271, K. 450, K. 467, and K. 503) add, in fact, to the dramatic character, and affirm an opposition to, and tension with, the orchestra rather than an integration.

However, Webster insists rightly that the forms of the Mozart concertos do not resemble the arias in his operas of the 1780s. Nevertheless, he does not point out that the arias in Mozart's earlier operas of the decade before (in *Ascanio in Alba* and *La Finta Giardiniera,* for example) often display the direct model for many of his concerto movements after 1775. Several arias in the first act of *La Finta Giardiniera* exhibit an opening ritornello with two independent motifs in the tonic and a final tonic cadence, and this is followed by a solo with the first motif still in the tonic, a modulating passage, and the second motif at the dominant with a cadence on the dominant. This became a fairly standard form for a large number of concerto movements.

In the 1780s, however, the opening ritornello of the aria often disappeared, while that of the concerto became more complex and massive. This however, only emphasized the dramatic contrast of the first solo section of the concerto (see, for example the great slow movement of the G Major Concerto, K. 453).

Webster's perception, however, is fully justified when we reflect how concerto and opera moved in new and different directions as Mozart matured. Concerto and opera forms did not remain the same for very long, and the evolution of both was radically opposed, although the links between them were never completely severed. The influence of the prestige of operatic forms had already shaped Mozart's concerto movements into a dramatic confrontation between an individual instrument and the larger band. The influence was not altogether in one direction. The first aria of the Podestà in *La Finta Giardiniera* is almost a Sinfonia Concertante, a sort of young people's guide to the orchestra, containing a splendid moment with *divisi* violas, announced with the words, "What is that black harmony I hear, it is the violas" (perhaps the first testimony to Mozart's passionate attachment to the viola). Of course, even more of a symphonic concerto is the great aria "Martern aller Arten" in *Die Entführung aus dem Serail.*

In fact, the reason that the indications for continuo were removed from the later publication of Mozart's and Beethoven's concertos was that the evolution of concerto form and the growth of public concerts made the soloist even more like a character in the theater, and emphasized the derivation of concerto from aria form, and this had gradually demanded new and more effective ways of directing and executing the works. It is true that, as I have tried to show, a few places in the concertos have suffered from the confused and uncritical erasure of all the notation of figured bass.

Above all, the history of performance practice has to be conceived dynamically, not as a series of independent fixed states. Old techniques of performance continue to be practiced for some time after they are no longer suitable. We will not understand the continuo from 1770 to 1830 until we study the process of its disappearance, instead of speculating solely on the way it might be reinstated. Our present understanding of it is too shaky to support a novel rethinking of

Mozart's concertos. We cannot reasonably maintain that the innovations in late eighteenth-century concerto style were irrelevant to the gradual decay of the continuo function. The abandonment of the continuo was a welcome reform—and, in my experience, most reforms are finally completed only when they are long overdue. Most important of all, musical style in the late eighteenth and early nineteenth centuries depended on well-articulated and even violent contrasts of musical texture very rare in the early eighteenth century (for striking and famous examples, see the beginnings of Mozart's Jupiter Symphony or Beethoven's "Eroica," or the opening of Mozart's Concerto in C Major, K. 503), which are not improved by a continuous vertical realization of the harmonies of the figured bass on a keyboard. The keyboard general bass imposes a uniformity of rhythmic texture that was no longer attractive or suitable for the more recent works. That is why it was ultimately abolished.

I do not want to leave the impression that the late twentieth-century fashion for the continuo in Mozart makes enough difference to spoil performances of the concertos. It is largely inaudible, except when miked up in a recording. I have witnessed, in a performance directed by Christopher Hogwood, a forte-pianist enthusiastically and vigorously attacking the continuo, most of which I could not hear, although I was sitting only five rows from the stage. Of course, playing the continuo weakens the visible dramatic impression of the solo entrances, and the impression of public performance depends on sight as well as sound. It is astonishing how little effect changes of critical fashion can have; most of the time, in fact, they do very little harm. In any case, even if we disregard the only model given by Mozart (for K. 246) and absurdly play the continuo ostentatiously and with irrelevant fantasy, its weakened survival during the late eighteenth century does not justify the view of the solo piano in the concerto as merely primus inter pares, as simply the chief member of the orchestra, a view democratically but perversely maintained by several musicologists today. Any attempt to set the continuo into relief, or to give it any importance beyond that of keeping the orchestra together when conducting from the keyboard or adding sonority to a performance with a reduced ensemble, only compromises the originality of those passages in the solo sections of the concertos where Mozart reverses the roles of soloist and orchestra and has the piano accompany the orchestra (good examples of this can be found not only in K. 271, but in the opening movement of 459 and the finale of K. 503). These passages were intended as a novelty, not as an affirmation of the tradition in which the keyboard discreetly filled in the harmony. The pianos available to Beethoven were more powerful than those used by Mozart, and perhaps joining in the fortissimo moments of the orchestral section may have had greater importance for Beethoven's compositions.

Plantinga cogently remarks that concerto performance in public until

Beethoven's death was considerably less formal than it became later. We may reflect that, although it is, as I have observed, absolutely absurd to think that the solo clarinet in Mozart's concerto for that instrument played every note of the first violin part during the long opening ritornello, the clarinetist may have thought it a good idea to warm up for the solo passages by joining in the louder sections of the tutti. The violin soloists could have played throughout the tutti probably without getting too tired, but there is no reason to think this was done relentlessly throughout a concerto. Just as the bass indications were finally removed from the solo piano parts, similarly the solo violinist was eventually expected to make a dramatic entrance with the first solo section. Whether or not joining in was practically useful, it was at no place musically necessary. Perhaps socially it is a way today for the soloist to exhibit a democratic solidarity with the more lowly colleagues of the orchestra, in the hope that this will create a warm glow of sympathy from the audience or camaraderie from the orchestra. Musically, however, it makes little or no difference.

As public concerts became commercially more successful and widespread, the enhancement of the dramatic character of the solo instrumentalists—transforming them into stage personalities, in short—became the preferred way of performing concertos, of exploiting the relation of the form to the opera aria present from the 1770s or earlier, and always influential, a relation that later composers, including Liszt and Chopin, continued to develop in their concertos. Isolating the soloist in this way was as much an improvement in the method of execution as, in the performance of opera, the substitution of the silent gestures of the conductor for banging on the floor with a heavy stick. We must avoid the ingrained pessimism that drives so much study of performance practice, the belief that every innovation is a change for the worse.

CHAPTER 9

Mozart and Posterity

I

In 1783, when Mozart was only twenty-seven years old, the teacher of the thirteen-year-old Beethoven in Bonn said that "he would certainly become another Wolfgang Amadeus Mozart if he continues as he has begun." Evidently Mozart had recovered from the often damning reputation of a child prodigy and was already accepted as one of the leading European masters, although outside the German-speaking countries (and even within them) his music was often contested for its difficulty, complexity, and unintelligibility until well into the nineteenth century. We may conveniently assess the character of Mozart's fame by the poets and artists to whom he was compared. In a conversation with the emperor of Austria, Joseph II, in the 1780s, the composer Carl Ditters von Dittersdorf compared him to Klopstock, a poet renowned for his difficulty and his pretensions to the grand style, who transferred the meters of classical Greek poetry to German verse.

Less than two decades later, Mozart's glory had reached the summit from which it could no longer be dislodged, although it could be shaken, and different views of his music would develop over time. In a novel of 1803 by the Romantic master Jean Paul, who would be the favorite writer of Robert Schumann, there is a discussion about music in which Haydn, Gluck, and Mozart are compared grandly to Aeschylus, Sophocles, and Euripides. One of the company objects that "it was all right about Gluck and Haydn, but Mozart was more like Shakespeare."

Only four years after this, a disciple of Jean Paul wrote a review of Beethoven's *Eroica* Symphony, in which he compared Beethoven to Jean Paul, for his fantastic imagination and humor, and Mozart to Schiller for his passion— "unfortunately we have no composer like Goethe," he added. This is the figure of Mozart exploited a few decades later in 1843 by Søren Kierkegaard in *Either/Or:* he had become the model Romantic composer, with *Don Giovanni* as the ideal, or, indeed, for Kierkegaard, the only possible, opera, embodying the essentially erotic nature of music.

In the nineteenth century, however, the standard coupling of Mozart with another artist was to be Raphael, a comparison possibly initiated by the painter Ingres, who idolized both, and Mozart was transformed into an icon of classicism, an emblem of grace and purity. As the century proceeded, both Mozart and Raphael suffered, not from a loss of prestige—that was only too firmly in place—but from a growing disdain among the avant-garde of practicing artists and composers for the established classicism in favor with the academies of art and music. Bernard Shaw protested acutely that people did not realize how powerful Mozart was because his music was so beautiful. Brahms's appreciation of Mozart was equally passionate and nostalgic: how wonderful it must have been to be a composer at the time of Mozart, he thought, "when it was easy to write music," as if Mozart was the great representative of a prelapsarian age, before the exile from paradise.

The view of Mozart as a master of a conventional, respectable style obviously called for revision, and it was sensibly provided by an age of expressionism in the early twentieth century. With the generation of Arnold Schoenberg, the qualities of morbid passion, tragedy, complexity, and radical experiment were restored to Mozart: he became a modern composer. The most systematic expression of the new view was found in the work of the biographer of Mozart, Hermann Abert. He also wrote the article on Mozart for the 1929 *Cobbett's Cyclopedic Survey of Chamber Music,* a once indispensable reference book. The editor, shocked at its dark revisionist view of Mozart, printed it out of respect (Abert had just died) but protested that Mozart had always been compared to Raphael, while this made him seem much more like Michelangelo.

It is significant that this new view restored the sense of difficulty that Mozart's contemporaries had found in his work, but making it a virtue rather than a failing. As late as 1812, the novelist Ludwig Tieck, protesting the latest works of Beethoven, had written: "If we may call Mozart mad, Beethoven often cannot be distinguished from a raving lunatic." The difficulties of Beethoven's art were correctly attributed to his adherence to the tradition of Mozart.

2

Today, the most recent generation of music historians has attempted to dismantle the view of Mozart as a radical visionary and reduce him to an ordinary artisan, better at his job than anyone else, of course, but just trying to make a living. Nicholas Kenyon, after an excellent summary of the changes of Mozart's reputation in his *Faber Pocket Guide,* gives a sympathetic account of the new perspective:

> We cannot be sure if "composing freely" is a concept that Mozart would have understood or desired: all the evidence is that he yearned to be needed and appreciated—to be asked to write music because people wanted it, to show off the skills of his singers and players as well as possible, to make the most of whatever practical performing circumstances he was faced with. Yes, he wanted his audiences to enjoy his music, and to show by their attention that they were enjoying it. Yes, he wanted his music to be better, cleverer, more passionate, and more memorable than everyone else's, and probably believed it to be so, but there is not a shred of support for the idea that he ever consciously wrote for some far-distant future. (p. 27)

We have, however, more than a shred of evidence that Mozart thought beyond the immediate practical circumstances suggested by Kenyon. In a letter on February 12, 1778, Leopold Mozart went somewhat beyond his usual exhortations to his twenty-two-year-old son to make enough money to support his parents:

> Now it depends solely on your good sense and your way of life whether you die as an ordinary musician, utterly forgotten by the world, or as a famous Kapellmeister, of whom posterity will read.

There is, after all, something missing from Kenyon's picture of Mozart's ambitions. He wants to be a success, he wants to be loved by his performers and his public, he wants his music to be acknowledged as better than everyone else's— but he seems not to care what kind of music it is, he has no artistic principles, he never tries to win over listeners or musicians to music they might not have expected. That is not the Mozart of history. Already at the age of twenty-two, when the leading singer at the Munich opera complained that in the quartet of *Idomeneo* ("the highest musical achievement of the opera," according to Julian Rushton) he could not *spianare la voce,* that is let the voice float lyrically and evenly above the orchestra, Mozart retorted that the singer didn't seem to know that in an ensemble you were not supposed to sing *spianato* but *parlando,* with a speaking effect. In fact, if Mozart had not so often been intransigent about imposing his own standards, his own vision of music, he might have been given the permanent post in a large city that was always refused him and that went to more accommodating composers like Salieri, about whom posterity reads only because they had some contact with Mozart.

Each of these successive views of Mozart has its merit. He was, as so many of his contemporaries thought, a difficult composer whose music was challenging to follow. More than twenty years after Mozart's death, E. T. A. Hoffmann was still defending him against claims by other musicians that his harmony was incomprehensible. The comparison to Shakespeare and Schiller made sense, as the dramatic power of his work is still astonishing today. Kierkegaard's insistence on the erotic element in his work was certainly accurate. Mozart could write a love duet as erotic as any other composer in history (in *Così fan tutte,* the music of the duet for Guiglielmo and Dorabella graphically illustrates the caresses of his hands as he feels her heart beat).

Mozart as the correct composer, the Raphael of music, is equally persuasive: he was a master of all the conventional tonal procedures of his time, and the correctness of his counterpoint impressed Chopin as much as the work of Bach (when he tried to explain counterpoint to a layman like Delacroix, he was just as likely to refer to Mozart as Bach). The early twentieth century's image of a turbulent Mozart drew attention to his expressive power, and it is still to some extent the approach of those who are most passionate about his achievement. It has, however, the disadvantage of diminishing an appreciation of his technical skill. In spite of his radical experiments, Mozart could be one of the most conventional composers of his time—except that no one ever handled the basic conventions with such skill and such ease, and he must have gloried not only in his ability to shock, but also in his facility at producing the conventional with such purity and grace.

Long phrases of absolutely conventional figuration and banal motifs articulate his works at the end of short sections, and give the structure its clarity. (Beethoven imitated Mozart closely in this respect, but he had the knack— already to be found in Mozart, but with less panache—of making one think that he had invented the most conventional motif expressly for each piece.) Writing about Mozart, we are always tempted to dwell on the extraordinary purple passages without noticing that in every case they are followed or preceded by the most conventional devices. They complement and support each other.

After a century of modernism, it is hard for us to delight in the simple craftsmanship of Mozart. The advantage of the most recent approach, above all in the brilliant researches of Neal Zaslaw and Cliff Eisen, is that it restores this craftsmanship, makes us understand Mozart as artisan, not working in a void but with the everyday problems of singers, instrumental performers, impresarios, and patrons, and it has enlarged our understanding of how his art came into being, and how it worked in his world. The preoccupation of both writers with the everyday aspect of music production, however, tends to impose an image of Mozart as an accommodating fellow, always giving his patrons, singers, and public what they wanted. But there are too many cases of Mozart willfully going his own way to make this tenable. After receiving the first of three commissioned piano quartets, for example, the publisher canceled the contract: the music was too difficult.

A comic example of Mozart's suiting himself rather than his clients is the Sonata in D Major for Piano, K. 576. In *The Cambridge Mozart Encyclopedia*, there is some difference of opinion about this work. According to Cliff Eisen (on p. 184), this is one of the easy keyboard sonatas that Mozart said he was writing for Princess Frederika of Prussia, but John Irving writes that "the whole of the sonata K576 is technically beyond all but the most experienced performer" (p. 470). Eisen is right, as a glance at the slow movement will show (there is a beautiful section of exceptional simplicity where the young pianist need play with only one hand at a time), but I have heard great pianists like Walter Gieseking and Solomon mess up the first movement.

What happened is that Mozart was unable to resist showing off his polyphonic ingenuity; the main theme lends itself easily to stretto. In K. 576, the second voice enters and combines with the first after one beat, then after three beats, then again after six beats, and some of this is difficult to play, particularly when the two voices are only one beat apart, because the strong accent of the theme no longer coincides in the two hands. The only phrases of the first movement that are difficult to execute are in simple two-part counterpoint (that is, when each hand has to play only one note at a time), and Mozart mistakenly seems to have thought that this was easy—much like J. S. Bach, whose Two-Part Inventions were also intended for beginners and are actually very hard to perform. It is clear, however, that Mozart miscalculated out of vanity or exuberance, displaying his contrapuntal skill just as he did in the finale to the *Jupiter* Symphony, the Wind Octet, the second-act finale of *Così fan tutte,* and so many other works. In any case, the rest of the sonata is easy, unless one tries to make the last movement, which should be played at a sedate tempo, into a stormy virtuoso piece.

3

No one really writes for posterity. Occasionally a stubborn, hardheaded artist produces work that is not immediately popular, but hopes that the public will eventually come around. Nevertheless, the concept of posterity had a clear and novel importance for musicians in Mozart's day: he arrived on the scene together with the invention of the history of music. The first significant attempt to write such a history came from Giuseppe Martini, called the Padre Martini, a Bolognese composer and scholar, with whom Mozart studied briefly when he was fourteen—he always mentioned him with reverence afterward—and from whom he derived much of his contrapuntal learning. It was at this time that the Padre was working on his history: the publication did not get very far, only through classical Greek music theory, but some of the medieval material was in manuscript. He certainly intended to include the contemporary scene, since he collected portraits of all the important musicians of his day, including one of the young Mozart.

The first publication of a history of music that dealt with both the medieval and the contemporary age arrived from Charles Burney when Mozart was twenty years old in 1776. Burney did not really know Mozart (although Mozart, at the age of four, had sat on his lap), and he later recorded another musician's opinion that the prodigy had not lived up to his early promise. His interest in the history of music, however, marked a radical change in the conception of the art. For the first time, musicians could be placed on a level with painters, writers, and architects: they could be compared to Sophocles, Shakespeare, and Michelangelo.

This was a moment of crisis for composers. Patronage and support for music from church and court was diminishing and even being withdrawn. Haydn, professionally imprisoned in a small court at Esterhazy, found his independence and international prestige by exporting his symphonies to Paris, by publishing his quartets, and, released from his duties at Esterhazy, by traveling to London and directing his works in concert—that made him a fortune. Furthermore, like Figaro in Mozart's opera, composers were beginning to resent their status as servants to the aristocracy. An enhancement of their prestige had become imperative.

Mozart was perhaps the most ambitious composer in the history of music. He produced at least one, and generally several imposing masterpieces in almost every genre of music—concerto, song, opera (serious and comic, German and Italian), string trio, string quartet, string quintet, quintet for piano and winds, trio and quartet for piano and strings, quintet for wind instrument and strings, divertimento for wind octet, double concerto for violin and viola, symphony, piano sonata, violin sonata. Although he left no completed major work of religious music, his two fragments—the C Minor Mass and the Requiem—are monumental even in their unfinished state. In comparison, Haydn's major successes were largely restricted to the two genres of symphony and string quartet; only when he was much older than Mozart ever became did he create his most impressive piano sonatas, piano trios, and the important vocal works with the late masses and the two oratorios. And only after Mozart's *Prague* Symphony had surpassed in size and weight any of Haydn's orchestral works, setting an example, did he expand his symphonic style.

Mozart enlarged the forms of his time by combining genres. The finale of his Piano Sonata in B-flat, K. 333, is a large concerto movement, with imitations of the contrast of orchestra and soloist, and a huge cadenza like an improvisation. He introduced operatic effects in his chamber music, and symphonic and concerto passages into his opera arias. His concertos have moments of intimate and complex chamber music. The finale of the *Jupiter* Symphony has an unprecedented display of learned counterpoint, simultaneously combining six themes. He magnified almost every genre in which he worked.

Mozart's string quintets and string trio have a spacious gravity never before achieved in chamber music. The power and drama of his Fantasy and Sonata in C Minor were not to be found again in piano music until Beethoven appeared on the scene. *The Marriage of Figaro* was much longer and more serious than any comic opera before; Da Ponte apologized for the length by claiming that he and Mozart had created "something absolutely new."

Mozart was to trump that achievement two years later with *Don Giovanni,* in which a mythical, iconic figure of two centuries of European renown was given a tragicomic artistic form that crushed most of the previous incarnations, as well as those still to come. In a spectacular effort in the first-act finale, Mozart placed three dance orchestras for the ball on the stage, each one tuning while another plays, and each playing entirely different and even contradictory rhythms, but in perfect harmony, the greatest pyrotechnical display of contrapuntal art ever put on the stage. With *The Magic Flute,* he went still further, combining popular Austrian style with music of religious gravity, a double fugue for an overture, a chorale prelude on a Lutheran hymn (in Catholic Vienna!) in the style of J. S. Bach, a virtuoso display of coloratura passagework that is still dazzling, and music of the most exquisite and moving simplicity to celebrate the ideal of fidelity in marriage.

No wonder he was never, until the last years of his brief life, offered an important official position at court, too late for him to derive much profit from the post.[1] Although famous and even celebrated, he had to live by occasional, well-paid commissions and by teaching piano.

---

1. In 1787, a modest function with a modest salary was created for Mozart in Vienna to supply dance music for the court balls.

CHAPTER 10

Structural Dissonance and
the Classical Sonata

RULES OF MUSICAL FORM are of two kinds. Some are simply conventions of the age in which the art work is produced: eighteenth-century sonata rondos, for example, often have a central section in the subdominant. Eighteenth-century minuets generally have a three-phrase form, the first phrase repeated, and the second and third phrases repeated together. The development section (sometimes called the second solo) of a piano concerto almost always has lots of arpeggios. These are rules, subject to exceptions, of course, like the rule that sonnets have fourteen lines, since we find extravagant sonnets with long codas and eccentric minuets with two or five phrases.

Other formal aspects, however, are embedded in the language itself, and are conditions of intelligible expression. The rule that an eighteenth-century work of music should end with the tonic harmony with which it began belongs in this category, and so does the rule that any material in a sonata exposition that has a memorable profile presented outside the tonic in the dominant (or sharp modulatory direction) must be returned in the recapitulation in the tonic area. These are rules like the one that every sentence should have a verb. This kind of rule may indeed be overridden as well, but the justification for doing so must be apparent and convincing for emotional or dramatic reasons ("My kingdom for a horse!" for example); if not, we are likely to conclude that some printer's error or other incompetence is responsible. (Similarly, there is the requirement in sixteenth-century art that a painting or drawing should exhibit a correct perspective: distortions of perspective in Renaissance art needed to be expressively justified.)

In eighteenth-century music, this closing transposition into the tonic of a theme that was originally in the dominant or sharp area (or in the relative major for works in the minor mode) implies that it was in need of resolution; it would, in fact, be more literal than metaphorical to say that the theme was dissonant until so resolved. (A dissonance in tonal music is not a disagreeable noise but simply a harmony that must be resolved into a consonance, and a consonance is a harmony that can be used to end a cadence, the ultimate consonance being the tonic triad.) Writing many years ago, I called this "structural dissonance," that is, dissonance on a large scale, encompassing a whole theme or section, not just a single interval or harmony. I was, of course, aware that the requirement was sometimes overridden, and I even examined several works of Haydn and Mozart where this was the case, to point out that there was a good reason each time for the lack of resolution in the recapitulation—for example, that the theme in the dominant had already appeared briefly in the tonic in the development section or in the subdominant (transposition in the flat direction of a theme being an acceptable traditional method of resolution in the eighteenth century, and, in fact, theorists insisted at the time that an allusion to the subdominant at the opening of the recapitulation was an important way of reinforcing the resolution of the tension caused by the movement to the dominant).

In an essay of 2002, "Beyond the Sonata Principle," Professor James Hepokowski of Yale University expressed his distaste for the concept of structural dissonance, claimed that there were many examples of dominant material left unresolved with no justification, was not happy with my explanations for the lack of resolution in the few examples that I had given, and felt that there were different reasons for the nonappearance of the theme in the recapitulation. Of course, there is always more than one reason for anything to happen in a work of music—characteristic of any work of art is the fact that most details are overdetermined (to use the once popular term of psychoanalysis).

Although I did not find Hepokoski's counter examples persuasive, I saw no reason to answer his essay,[1] but I do so now, largely because I wish to correct a crucial mistake of my own in a discussion of an example from Mozart demonstrating the action of structural dissonance, and I can add some new points to show briefly how it works. The example was a motif in E-flat major from the great Sonata in C Minor, K. 451, that I claimed never reappears in the tonic in the recapitulation, but only in the subdominant minor in the development. This claim, however, is not quite right. The theme is a two-bar motif, immediately repeated with an extra expressive feature. Here is the motif, bars 22 to 25,

---

1. In a review of *Elements of Sonata Theory* by Hepokoski and his collaborator Warren Darcy, *Musical Times* (Winter 2007), p. 96, Wlliam Drabkin indicated his dissatisfaction with Hepokoski's dismissal of structural dissonance.

with the context of a few bars before and after (bars 19–35), and its reappearance at the subdominant F minor in the development:

Hepokoski correctly reproached me with treating the original playing of the motif as if it were a part of the "second group" of the exposition (i.e., appearing after the new tonality of E-flat major has been established), although it is really still part of the first group. However, he did not appreciate the importance of his observation. As we can see from the bars that follow this repeated motif (bars 26–35), Mozart does not consider the relative major to be properly established as yet even by the two dramatic forte bars of the dominant seventh of E-flat that precede the motif, and he writes a full eight-bar conventional cadence properly to confirm E-flat major.

This explains why the motif cannot be literally transported to the tonic in the recapitulation; it has a transitional function to establish a new key, and it would make no sense to repeat it in C minor, since at this point C minor has already been fully reestablished sixteen bars before. Nevertheless, to say, as I did, that it does not reappear is not strictly true, since Mozart replaces it with a very similar and analogous two-bar motif, also immediately repeated with extra expressive features. Both motifs go from the leading tone to the fifth scale degree above, and repeat the pattern while adding notes above for more intense expression. The parallel is evident:

This is done, not with a simple C minor harmonization, but nevertheless *within* the harmonic territory governed by C minor, its Neapolitan D-flat major, with its traditional implication of pathos carried by the Neapoliutan harmony. The original motif established the move from C minor to E-flat major, and reemploying it to go from C minor to C minor would have been absurd. The change of harmony with a parallel Neapolitan motif now justifies the explicit and fully literal return of the following elaborate and conventional cadence that we found earlier in the exposition to establish E-flat major, here used to reconfirm C minor, while avoiding an initial C minor harmony that would make the process redundant. In this way, the structural dissonance or sonata principle functions without producing nonsense: the E-flat motif was too important, too expressive, and too easily remembered to leave unresolved in the recapitulation, but could not be simply played in the C minor tonic. It is therefor rewritten as a strictly symmetrical analogue with the same structure and much the same character, a two-bar motif repeated at once with extra expressive detail, and the parallelism of exposition and recapitulation is preserved, the necessary resolution accomplished, with a moment of pathos that enriches the recapitulation.

This technique is by no means isolated in Mozart's work, and a more spectacular example may be found in the A major slow movement of a string quartet, the Quartet in D Major, K.575. In the exposition, the second group is closed by a lovely E major phrase, relatively high first in the violin, and repeated immediately in the violoncello.

Hepokoski claims that this expressive motif never returns at the tonic A major in the recapitulation. Like my claim about the E-flat motif in the C minor sonata, this is only half true. At the place where it is expected in the recapitulation, Mozart composes a new but closely similar four-bar melody in the same register but now in the tonic, first for the violin and, as before, immediately repeated by the cello.

The parallelism is evident, and so striking that we must hear this as a return. I suspect that Mozart realized that when the E major melody was transposed to the tonic A major, the range of the original motif for the two instruments was less effective, either too high or too low, and supplied an analogue with an equivalent lyrical and cadential character to take its place, but in the same more comfortable part of the instruments' register we found in the exposition, instead of the fifth lower or fourth higher entailed by the transposition of the original motif to the tonic. In addition, he produced a theme with an almost identical character but with a slightly more conclusive air, which is apt, as the end of the movement is only four bars away. Not comprehending the function of this passage (and the intimate parallel relationship with the four-bar motif in violin and cello of the exposition), Hepokowski calls this form "eccentric and deformative." It certainly does not sound like that, and I believe that Mozart would have considered it to be more eccentric to transpose a theme of the exposition into a return a fourth higher or a fifth lower that was less effective and less agreeable for the instruments to play, and he created instead this exquisite effect of a theme reshaped and reconceived.

Similar examples of such rewriting in a recapitulation to reproduce the register of the exposition may be found throughout Mozart's operas. On a grand scale, however, is a page of the great E-flat major quartet in *Idomeneo* (a number that Mozart said he could never listen to without tears): an exquisite phrase in the exposition at the dominant, B-flat, goes into the minor mode and continues in D-flat major, the relative major of the dominant minor, before returning to B-flat major to close the exposition. This should, of course, return at the tonic, and then go to G-flat major, but this key would be very ungrateful for the voices in the quartet, either too high or too low. The melody accordingly reappears in toto in C-flat major, closer to the range of the original D flat. The harmony is more chromatic, exotic, and penetrating and in the right range, and even admirably serves the purpose of resolution, as C-flat major is the relative major of subdominant A-flat minor. The effect is far more expressive than a return in the more traditional transposition to E-flat minor and its relative major, G-flat, would have been.

When a literal resolution at the tonic is inconvenient, the illusion of return must be constructed to satisfy the sensibility of the time. These examples serve to demonstrate that the return and resolution of dissonant material are subject to conditions of range, harmonic expression, and the relation of the original function of the material placed in the new situation, confirming the tonic and resolving tension in a recapitulation instead of increasing it in the exposition. Still other pressures may come into play.

In his discussion of structural dissonance, Hepokoski offers a grab bag of examples of second-group themes that do not return in the tonic at the recapitulation. Even if they were all convincing, the number of his examples barely makes a dent in the statistics that in over 99 percent of the sonatas of 1780–1830, the second group returns later at the tonic, very often in an almost completely literal and mechanical fashion. When it does not happen, the overwhelming weight of the tradition of the tonic return should surely inspire us always to ask why, and in each case we will get a variety of answers even from the rare examples that we find, and we need to inquire what compensates for the omission.

The overture to *Idomeneo*, cited reasonably by Hepokoski, is a case in point; much of the second group does indeed not return at the tonic. Mozart here forgoes traditional sonata structure for dramatic effect: he ends the D major overture in the minor mode, and so sweeps his public directly into the opening number of the stage action. Mozart abandons the symmetry of resolution here for a special dramatic effect. The purpose of resolving a motif of the second group by bringing it back in the tonic is to conclude in the proper way, by resolving a dissonance. The overture to *Idomeneo,* however, does not properly conclude, but evades the traditional ending in order to merge with the initial action of the opera.

The overture to the next opera of Mozart, *Die Entführung aud dem Serail,* also ends a form in the major mode, once again in a minor mode, in order to merge with the following action, but in an even more intimate fashion. Opening with a sonata exposition in C major, the overture then goes to a central trio section in C minor and in a slower tempo. What seems to be at first a sonata recapitulation of the opening section (and part of the second group does reappear convincingly in the subdominant) soon produces an inconclusive ending in C minor that goes directly into the opening aria, which takes up and repeats the C minor middle section of the overture, but in C major. If the resolution of the overture is incomplete, the rewriting of the C minor section in major makes the first aria appear to be a resolution and completion of the overture. Once again, the omission of any material presented only outside the tonic is given a grand and even ostentatious justification. The overture must end in C minor in order to make the repeat of its central section by the aria in the major dramatically comprehensible and effective. To eighteenth-century sensibility, the resolution of dissonance was absolutely essential. When dramatic exigency made it difficult to achieve completely, the suggestioin or appearance of resolution had to be imposed.

In most of his other examples of material outside the tonic, too many to deal with here, Hepokowski adduces passages that function in an exposition as a transition from the tonic to the dominant, or else simply develop motifs of the first group already heard in the tonic. What needs to reappear in the tonic in the recapitulation is only the individual profile of any new theme in the dominant. Development of the material to confirm the move to the dominant would have no logical place in a section that stays in the already reconfirmed tonic. For example, all the bars of Haydn's Quartet, op. 33, no. 1 *(The Bird),* that Hepokowski claims as exceptions to the sonata principle (bars 27–42) are nothing but reworkings of first group material used to establish the dominant, and each such motif has already been heard at the tonic and does not need a resolving tonic restatement. These passages would be illogical in a recapitulation: motifs used in a transition from C major to G major would have no reasonable function if the music remained in C major. Haydn's omission of them at the return is therefore only good sense, not "eccentric and deformative" (as Hepokowski would have it).[2]

One anomaly needs to be mentioned that does not concern the exposition, but a new theme in the development. On rare occasions Mozart begins a development section with a new theme at the dominant. In two cases it is not a

2. The passages from the overture to *Cosi fan tutte* that Hepahowski finds omitted from the recapitulation are all made up of motifs from the first group, or closely resemble passages from the first group.

theme with any contrast to the main theme, but one of similar character. In the Sonata in G Major, K. 283, it is clearly a variant of the opening theme:

In the Sonata in F Major, K. 331, the new theme is very close in character and harmony to the opening theme:

This procedure, I believe, is a borrowing from a variant of the opera aria. It reflects the occasional appearance in an aria of different text in the center of an otherwise binary form, or the outer sections of a da capo aria. This generally has only an exposition and a recapitulation, the latter opening with the main theme in the dominant, and quickly turning back to the tonic.[3]

In one sonata, where the theme is clearly contrasting, the Sonata in C Major, K. 330, Mozart feels the need for resolution, and even brings back the motif in the tonic at the end in a coda. Mozart's chamber music forms are, more often than Haydn's, heavily indebted to opera as well as to concerto.

Hepokowski sees tonic resolution not as an essential of eighteenth-century musical sensibility, but as a default position in a computer program. He is influenced by recently fashionable psychological theories that equate the brain with a computer, a once useful and challenging metaphor that has revealed its limitations. This aspect of his thought is emphasized by his fascination with acronyms, which lards his texts with dozens of capital letters, giving his analytic prose the semblance and concision of a computer manual.

We come up in his article constantly against these acronyms: EEC; TR; TMB; FS; GP; and MC. For those of us for whom a GP is a doctor in general practice and an MC a master of ceremonies, this is hard going. For Hepokowski, the grandeur of the capital letters gives the illusion that these acronyms have a real, fixed, and individual identity. MC, for example, is a medial caesura, but much of the time Hepokowski uses it essentially to mean almost any articulation of the necessary late eighteenth-century point of distinction between tonic and dominant areas in an exposition. This articulation was essential to the clarity and the dramatic impact of late eighteenth-century style. It can be achieved in many ways; an effective pause, restating a theme at the dominant, introducing a new theme, playing a half cadence on the dominant of the dominant, a full cadence on the dominant, a half cadence on the dominant, the introduction of a new rhythm, or simply a change in dynamics. Hepokowski's use lacks clarity and often confounds and merges several of these methods. Very often with his "medial caesura," there is no actual pause or caesura proper at all. This is a pity, as Hepokowski has a great deal of interest to tell us about sonata technique.

---

3. For example, in the second act of *Idomeneo,* Arbace's aria in C major, "Se il tuo duol," has a central section with new words and new material in G major that behaves harmonically like a typical development section of the time by modulating to a cadence in the relative minor before the recapitulation begins. This is a traditional procedure in an aria of this form.

CHAPTER II

Tradition without Convention

I

Some years ago, when I was practicing a difficult passage in the Concerto in B-Flat Major, K. 450, by Mozart, I found that I had absentmindedly strayed into a similar virtuoso phrase from another B-flat Concerto, the last one, K. 595:

Both these phrases represent typical Mozartean virtuosity in B-flat major. We can find other examples in the Finale of the Sonata in B-flat Major, K. 333 (this movement, indeed, is written like a concerto rondo arranged for solo piano and mimics the relation of orchestra to soloist throughout)—

—and in the Sonata for Piano and Violin, K. 454, also in B-flat Major:

These passages are formed out of the basic elements of tonality: placing them well requires a certain mastery, but the invention of material here may be said to be almost at the zero degree. It is easy to see how any one of these passages may conveniently be replaced by a similar one from another work. The kind of mistake I made, however, is unlikely to happen with a later composer. During the nineteenth century an important change took place in the history of musical style in the West—a progressive change, and we are still living with it. Late eighteenth-century music depended on a number of conventional formulaic phrases that might be transferred at will from one work to another. Of course, almost all musical styles depend on some sort of conventional repertoire of motifs: in most periods the main body of this repertoire generally consists of cadence formulas, ways of ending or rounding off individual phrases or complete works. These cadence formulas, in fact, may often be said to define the style. What is striking, however, about the second half of the eighteenth century is the grand dimension of these formulas, their imposing length—how long they last and what a large role they play temporally in the structure. They are not simply, as in other periods, motifs or short sequential sets of harmonies, but elaborate phrases lasting several bars, sometimes, indeed, a succession of several phrases. They act within large forms as a kind of stuffing. They fill out the work. They also articulate the form, occurring most often at cadences. In concertos (and sometimes in sonatas), these formulas are virtuoso arabesques woven out of scales and arpeggios: for the most part they are derived from the coloratura passagework developed at that time for the operatic stage, and the technique is transferred to the keyboard concerto and sonata or, less often, to the violin concerto. It is essential to the tradition that these conventional passages of virtuosity be executed with grace and ease. In symphonies and quartets, on the other hand, the conventional phrases tend to be elaborate and lengthy flourishes or fanfares. They mark the spaces between the end of one melody and the beginning of another, or between two playings of the same theme. We may take an example from one of the more symphonic of Mozart's piano sonatas, the A Minor, K. 310. The rounding-off of the main theme is marked by a lengthy but conventional half cadence:

Later, the end of the exposition is articulated by an equally conventional phrase. Here there is standard virtuoso figuration in the left hand and a military fanfare in the right.

These banal phrases are a stumbling block today to critics of Mozart, who prefer to gloss over, or even forget, the conventional aspects of his work and concentrate on the more original inspirations, which are often very radical indeed. This modern prejudice, however, does a disservice to Mozart's accomplishment, as his handling of the most conventional material reveals an easy mastery denied to almost all his other contemporaries, and we therefore fail to see how the more eccentric aspects of his style depend on a purely conventional context to make their effect. I have written elsewhere that when there is a convention of form, it is always found completely and elaborately fulfilled and even nakedly revealed in Mozart, while Haydn deals with the conventions as quickly as possible, even sometimes attempting to disguise or skate over them. This explains why the amount of "stuffing" is so much greater in Mozart's work than in Haydn's, where, nevertheless, it still plays an important role.

One might speculate that the expansive treatment of the traditional filling material has made Mozart an easier composer for today's audiences to listen to than Haydn with his more summary way of dealing with it, now that we have absorbed, and are no longer disconcerted by, the radical innovations in Mozart that made him such a difficult composer for his contemporaries. The conventional passages functioned as an aid to intelligibility, and still work as such today. It is worth considering briefly one of the most radical passages in Mozart to see how it depends on the most conventional setting. The most routine procedure for rounding out a development section in the last quarter of the eighteenth century is a cadence on the relative minor—or a half cadence on its dominant (V of vi)—followed by a return to the tonic. The second solo, or development, of Mozart's Concerto in B-flat Major, K. 595, begins with his most astonishing modulation—from F major to B minor, the interval of an augmented fourth ("the devil's interval"), the most destructive of a stable tonal sense—and continues with a series of surprises:

The progression, perhaps the most extreme in all of Mozart, goes from B minor to C major, C minor, E-flat minor, V of B major, V of A-flat major, V of F minor, and finally V of G minor, the relative minor, the most conventional way to round off the development section of a sonata form. The last three moves are accomplished with banal passagework, and, indeed, at the arrival at G minor, we reach another convention of the second solo of concerto form during Mozart's lifetime, the use of arpeggios. These arpeggios begin the retransition, and the harmonic progression is a strikingly conventional ascent to the subdominant: G minor, C minor, F minor, B-flat major, E-flat major.

Then Mozart reaffirms the conventional relative minor by its dominant (D major), and then, with a set of arpeggios, accomplishes the return to the opening theme and the tonic. The conventional detail is as exquisitely handled as the unprecedented and eccentric harmonic progressions. In this extraordinary work, the conventional elements of structure, the banal figuration, and the arpeggios help Mozart to solve the problem of an expansive form. They allow the composer to slow down the momentum as the development section reaches its end after the disconcertingly swift changes of the opening, and they endow the return to the opening theme with the necessary breadth. They announce the resolution while suspending the movement toward it. The passages of conventional filler—arpeggios, virtuoso figuration, or fanfares—are essential to the late eighteenth century's project of enlarging the shorter binary forms of the first half of the century into the more imposing sonata forms.

The growth of public concerts at that time made the larger forms desirable, and what was wanted were forms more tightly organized than the relatively loose sectional forms of the da capo aria or the concerto grosso, in which the dramatic climax cannot be focused as successfully and as lucidly as in the later symphonic structures, where the moments of extreme dramatic tension are far more clearly articulated than they could have been with early eighteenth-century style.

On lowest level, the long passages of stuffing in the late eighteenth century simply helped to pass the time, to extend the dimensions of the form, to make it more imposing. However, the emphasis they added at cadences had powerful consequences for the large-scale harmonic structure as well: they enabled the composer to transform with ease the standard half cadence on the dominant at the end of the first part of an early eighteenth-century binary form into a full cadence that affirmed the dominant in what would later be called a modulation, raising the long-range power of the harmony to a higher level. The conventionality was, in fact, an asset; it made the form more easily intelligible in public performance. The audience did not have to strain to understand something original or eccentric. In concerto and aria, the conventional virtuoso figuration may be said paradoxically to have combined physical excitement with intellectual relaxation. They made it possible for the audience to admire the performers without having to strain to admire the composition. The moments of purely conventional material that essentially resolved any previous harmonic and even melodic tension were basic to the style we call classical, which required, at a point about three-quarters of the way through the movement, an emphatic and lengthy resolution of any form of structural dissonance, a resolution that could not, as later in Chopin and Liszt, be postponed to the last page. The conventionality is also derived from improvisation, which is almost never original and, in general, is dependent on a repertory of standard figures. For example, in the keyboard concertos of the third quarter of the eighteenth century by Wagenseil and others, the second solo (or what, in a sonata form, we would later call the development section) was sometimes notated only as a series of harmonies that were to be arpeggiated at will in any way the soloist pleased. Later in the century these arpeggios were written out and specified by the composer. The standard formulas did not disappear. A page of sketches by Beethoven once puzzled experts, as it consisted entirely of a series of these standard figures, all relatively banal. It was realized that this was a repertory of figures that Beethoven could use in improvisation—he was, in fact, famous for his extempore powers, and he had his collection of formulas just as the poets who improvised oral epic poetry had their repertory of standard phrases, images, metaphors, and epithets. Beethoven was, however, to effect a profound change in the use of conventional material.

2

The aesthetics of the late eighteenth century developed a fixed prejudice against the conventional as part of the widespread and even fashionable contemporary speculation on the nature of language, a prejudice extending into our own time. There is a double significance to the word "conventional," and the two meanings cannot be completely separated in eighteenth-century aesthetics. The conventional is both commonplace (that is, familiar and banal) and arbitrary (that is, imposed by an act of will). A convention is accepted by everyone precisely because it is arbitrary, because it is imposed. There can be no disagreement because there is no argument. For the eighteenth-century critic, the signs of painting are "natural": that is, the painted image of a tree signifies a tree because it looks like a tree. The arbitrary nature of language, however, has been acknowledged at least since Aquinas: a word signifies its meaning by convention, not because it sounds like, or imitates, its meaning—even when it does, as with onomatopoeia (words like "buzz" and "gargle"), the meaning is still fixed and imposed by arbitrary convention. The word "tree" signifies a tree just because it does: it neither sounds nor looks like a tree. That is why language is essentially social, not personal, and makes available only the meanings that society has agreed upon, not the inimitably individual significance that each of us might like in order to express something absolutely unique. The most famous eighteenth-century discussion of the arbitrary character of linguistic signs is G. E. Lessing's *Laokoon*, written in 1766, in which it is maintained that the arbitrary signs of language can only describe in temporal succession those qualities in Nature that coexist simultaneously:

Es ist wahr; da die Zeichen der Rede willkührlich sind, so ist es gar wohl möglich, daß man durch sie die Teile eines Körpers eben so wohl auf einander folgen lassen kann, als sie in der Natur neben einander befindlich sind. Allein dieses ist eine Eigneschaft der Rede und ihrer Zeichen überhaupt, nicht aber in so ferne sie der Absicht der Poesie am bequemsten sind. Der Poet will nicht bloß verständlich werden, seine Vorstellungen sollen nicht bloß klar und deutlich sein; hiermit begnügt sich der Prosaist. Sondern er will die Ideen, die er in uns erwecket, so lebhaft machen, daß wir in der Geschwindigkeit die wahre sinnlichen Eindrücke ihrer Gegenstände zu empfinden glauben, und in diesem Augenblicke der Täuschung, uns der Mittel, die er dazu anwendet, seiner Worte bewußt zu sein aufhören. (sec. 27)

It is true, the signs of speech are arbitrary, so it is indeed possible that through them one can let the parts of a body follow each other when they are to be found contiguous in Nature. But this is, above all, a characteristic of speech and its signs, not, however, insofar as they are most convenient for poetry. The poet does not want simply to be understood, his representations should not be simply clear and intelligible: that would content the writer of prose. But the poet wants the ideas that he awakens in us to be made so lively that we immediately believe that we feel the real sensuous impressions of his objects, and, in this moment of illusion, gives us the means to cease to be conscious of his words.

In short, poetry must claim to transcend the arbitrary nature of language. Ideally, the words in the poem do not merely signify the meanings established by convention; they make the reader seem to experience the meaning sensuously and directly. The words are transformed from arbitrary signs into natural ones: the words of a poem, if the poet is successful, appear to convey their meaning by their sound and rhythm and by the way they are ordered. The significance arises not only by the conventions of meaning recorded in a dictionary, but out of the poem itself, which gives the illusion of newly inventing or recreating the meanings of the words. In his essay, Lessing was influenced by Denis Diderot's *Lettre sur les sourds et muets* of 1751, which asserted that in poetry, sound, rhythm, and word order are all so many "hieroglyphics" (or symbols) that combine to remove the arbitrary character of meaning. For Diderot, language in poetic discourse takes on a kind of organic life:

Il passe alors dans le discours du poëte un esprit qui en meut & vivifie toutes les syllabes. Q'est-ce que cet esprit? j'en ai quelquefois senti la présence; mais tout ce que j'en sais, c'est que c'est lui qui fait que les choses sont dites & représentées tout à la fois; que dans le même temps que l'entendement les saisit, l'ame en est émue, l'imagination les voit, &

l'oreille les entend; & que le discours n'est plus seulement un enchaîne-
ment de termes energiques qui expose la pensée avec force & noblesse,
mais que c'est encore un tissu d'hiéroglyphes entassées les uns sur les
autres qui la peignent. Je pourrais dire en ce sens que toute poésie est
emblématique.

There takes place in the poet's discourse a spirit that activates and enlivens
all the syllables. What is this spirit? Sometimes I have felt its presence, but
all I know is that it causes things to be both said and represented at once,
that at the same time that the understanding grasps them, the soul is
moved, the imagination sees them, and the ear hears them, and that
the discourse is no longer only a series of energetic terms that display
the thought with force and nobility, but also paint it by a web of hieroglyphics piled on top of each other. I might say that in this sense all
poetry is emblematic.

This astonishingly early proclamation of symbolist theory implies that
poetry appears to transform the signs of language, the words, from arbitrary
into natural symbols. The poetic technique breathes life into the words: they
no longer signify by simple convention, but by stimulating and awakening the
listener to their meaning. For Diderot, this poetic sophistication is a sign of an
advanced state of civilization, and he also proposes to carry his analysis of the
effects of poetry and its hieroglyphic character into the arts of painting and
music. But not everyone, he claims, is capable of appreciating the subtleties of
poetry: those who are sensitive to them form an elite (although not, it must be
said hastily, an elite defined by class). As Diderot remarks, the symbolic nature
of poetic discourse makes even the easiest poet hard to read if we wish to
understand him fully, and impossible to translate.

3

The identification of the commonplace with the arbitrary is profound, but it
obscures the dynamic process of stylistic development: a convention only
becomes commonplace when it loses its logical reason for existing—when, in
short, it becomes arbitrary, when its justification becomes dubious. A convention remains alive when it seems inevitable; but when we become aware that we
can do without it, it begins to be tiresome, and even to seem vulgar. It is not
frequency that makes repetition appear commonplace, but the lack of evident
necessity. A slice of bread at every meal will not seem tiresome to those who
find it unthinkable to go without it. When the classical conventions were still
vigorous, they were felt to be as indispensable as bread or potatoes. When, for

example, the convention of the final cadence in tonal music or the modulation to the dominant in an exposition went unchallenged, it did not then feel banal or commonplace.

In the final quarter of the eighteenth century, however, the demand for originality, perhaps imperceptibly at first, stimulated musicians to question certain aspects of the tonal language. It has sometimes been claimed that composers like Haydn and Mozart thought of themselves as craftsmen writing only for their contemporaries rather than as original and even radically innovative artists with at least one eye on posterity. This will not hold water, however. Connoisseurs insisted on originality—and of course, as they do today, resisted it when it came along. One sign of this was the despairing sense that the conventions of tonality had now been exhausted. Charles Burney's conversation in 1770 with the Roman opera composer Rinaldo di Capua is instructive in this respect.[1] Music was finished, the Italian composer asserted—all possible beautiful melodies had already been invented, all the beautiful modulations discovered. The best one could do was to create an ugly modulation to set the beautiful one in relief. The modern dogma that the shock of the ugly is the inevitable and only road to original creation has begun to rear its head.

Novalis was to be even more incisive when he wrote: "Alles Ausgezeichnete verdient den Ostrazism. Es ist gut, wenn es ihn sich selbst gibt." (All excellence merits ostracism. It is well when it ostracizes itself.) This is one of the fundamental tenets of modernism. By 1828, the Italian poet Giacomo Leopardi was to claim that any truly original melody was bound inevitably to displease a public that was content only with the familiar.

4

In the process of the destruction of conventional material, Beethoven is a pivotal but ambiguous figure. The conventional material does not disappear from his music—on the contrary, there is perhaps even more of it in his work than in Mozart's. But it loses some, or even most, of its conventional aspect. The traditional, conventional use of arpeggios in the second solo of the concerto will give us a good example: they are present in every one of Beethoven's concertos. Ostentatiously present, in fact, and that makes all the difference. The clearest example is the *Emperor* Concerto, bars 273–301:

1. See my *The Frontiers of Meaning* (New York: Hill and Wang, 1994), lecture 2.

Following Haydn rather than Mozart, Beethoven arrives at the relative minor early in the development instead of waiting for the more traditional end of the section, and the soloist accompanies the melody in the orchestra for sixteen bars with varied arpeggios. With bar 289, the arpeggios are no longer an accompaniment but have taken over the texture aggressively. Fragments of the main theme in the orchestra now become the accompaniment to the relentless and energetic arpeggios of the soloist. The arpeggios have ceased to appear conventional: they have become thematic, the principal motif, the bearer of meaning on which we concentrate all our attention. In short, the "arbitrary" has been "naturalized"—that is, given an immediately perceptible meaning unforeseen by the tradition and independent of it. It now sounds as if Beethoven had created the idea of arpeggios specifically for his concerto: with that, the existence of a tradition has been made irrelevant. Beethoven does not simply employ the traditional stuffing with the mastery of Mozart: he reinvents it. In the development of a Mozart concerto, the standard arpeggios may be played with an improvisatory quality—for example, the opening of the development in the first movement of the Concerto in G Major, K. 453. Mozart recalls the origin of this convention. In this section of the *Emperor* Concerto, however, all sense of improvisation must be left behind. These arpeggios are no longer improvised; they are composed. They must be played strictly as part of a symphonic texture. It has often been remarked, furthermore, how much of Beethoven's thematic material is not merely derived from the conventional filling of the classical technique but reproduces it nakedly, generally in his most important works. The opening themes of the Ninth Symphony, the *Eroica,* and the *Appassionata* all start as simple unadorned arpeggios, as if the basic building blocks of tonality were enough of a stimulus to create a form.

It is easy to find examples of Beethoven's rethinking the major conventions in order to give the impression that they have been invented for the particular work; and, as I have implied, this is a sign that the conventions were beginning to lose their authority for the musical imagination. I mention only one example here—briefly, as I have written about it elsewhere,[2] but its importance is fundamental in its large-scale exploitation of the most banal possible conventions. Perhaps the dreariest of academic procedures is the use in fugue of the devices of inversion, augmentation, and diminution. In the finale of Opus 110, Beethoven employs these devices as if each had been invented specifically for this one work. After the exhausted character of the second *Adagio arioso* marked *ermattet* (exhausted), the rising theme of the fugue is inverted, now descending

2. See *The Classical Style: Haydn, Mozart, Beethoven,* rev. and enl. ed. (New York: Norton, 1998), penultimate chapter.

and so losing its force. The return to life *(poi a poi di nuovo vivente)* is represented by the augmentation of the theme in a tempo twice as slow that gradually accelerates back into the original tempo, and by the diminution of the theme, now three times as fast, signifying the sense of new vigor. These old-fashioned and banal devices are here given a meaning within a dramatic scenario for, as far as I know, the first time in the history of music. The conventions of the fugue are naturalized, and this would have been unnecessary if they had not been felt to be in need of justification, to have outlived their usefulness. Beethoven gave them a reason to exist in the modern world.

5

The generation that followed Beethoven—Chopin, Schumann, Liszt, Mendelssohn, Berlioz, Wagner—was torn between the need to master the classical conventions and the desire to ignore them. Liszt's one attempt at the classical sonata is clearly a reformulation and deformation of the conventions for the purpose of constructing a new type of dramatic form. It is not program music like some of the sonatas by Clementi or Dussek or like Beethoven's *Pastoral* Symphony, all of which work by mimesis: the now conventional structure of sonata-form is reworked by Liszt from within, to create a progressive scenario of despair, consolation, Satanism, triumph, and death (for the layout of the work, he followed in the steps of Beethoven and Schubert, using the finale of the Choral Symphony and the *Wanderer* Fantasy as models). It was not with full respect for, or obedience to, the classical sonata conventions that Schumann created his most successful works, and he almost always displays a certain awkwardness with them, with rare exceptions, as in the slow movement of the C Major Symphony. He achieved his most distinguished and popular achievements in large forms when these appear to be invented with relative freedom, as in their recasting of the concerto or the program overture. Chopin's two mature sonatas have always been brilliantly effective in public, but the principal movements are idiosyncratic and even eccentric. The large works of Chopin and Schumann that have had the greatest prestige evade classical sonata modules: the ballades, scherzos, and polonaises, the F Minor Fantasy and the Barcarolle, the *Davidsbündlertänze,* the *Carnaval,* the C Major Fantasy, *Dichterliebe, Frauenliebe und Leben,* and so on. More significant, however, is the disappearance from the music of both Chopin and Schumann of the conventional passagework still found in Beethoven and Hummel, an almost total disappearance in Schumann after Opus 1, and a drastic reduction in Chopin after the Andante Spianato and Grande Polonaise. Any simple scales or virtuoso "filling" that remain in mature Chopin are no longer purely cadential in nature, (with rare exceptions, like the end of the E Major Scherzo, or the return of the main theme in the Nocturne in B Major, op. 62, no. 1) but are idiosyncratic thematic figuration reworked with astonishing originality, above all in the final sections of the Ballades.

The late 1840s, however, betray a new musical conservatism, a desire to return to the past evident in the work of Liszt and Schumann. Even Wagner and the so-called Music of the Future did not remain untouched by this change in musical ideology: we can see this not only in *Die Meistersinger* and *Parsifal,* but also in parts of *Der Ring des Nibelungen.* The leading figure in the reaction is, of course, Brahms: the reminiscence of Beethoven's Opus 106 in Brahms's Opus 1 and the allusion to Beethoven's Choral Symphony in Brahms's Symphony No. 1 were manifestos, and were understood as such at the time. Chrysander even shrewdly interpreted the reference to the Choral Symphony as a signal that Brahms intended to lead music back to a pure instrumental style. We are beginning today, however, to understand how radically Brahms reinterpreted classical forms and technique, how he attempted to revive and preserve the style while getting rid of many of its most conventional aspects. The basis of classical triadic tonality is the relation between tonic and dominant. This was considerably weakened by the composers of the 1830s, who were more interested in mediants than in a classical tonic/dominant polarity. The diatonic purity of triadic tonality was attacked from the beginning by the minor mode, which always introduces chromatic elements. In the eighteenth century the minor mode is essentially an exception, an agent of trouble. It is therefore significant that all the sonatas for piano, or for violin and piano, or for cello and piano by Chopin, Liszt, and Schumann are in the minor mode, which traditionally uses the mediant as an immediate secondary key instead of the dominant (although the dominant minor can turn up later in the exposition in a succeeding tonicization). What is essential to classical triadic tonality, however, is the major dominant.[3]

In a number of works, Brahms goes farther than anyone to weaken the tonic/dominant polarity by substituting the dominant *minor* for the major.[4] The dominant minor lacks precisely the sharpened leading tone necessary to the strong tonal cadence. The exposition of the first movement of the Third

---

3. Beethoven's occasional substitution of a mediant for the dominant is always preceded by an elaborate preparation on the dominant of the mediant chosen. This is largely evaded by Chopin, who prefers a rapid change using a pivot note (e.g., shifting from A-flat major to E major by holding the tonic note of A-flat and simply putting an E-natural under it). For an elaborate form like the first movement of the B Minor Sonata, he moves in the exposition from B minor to the relative major D major by first shifting astonishingly to D minor and then changing the mode.

4. See my *Sonata Forms* (New York: Norton, 1980), final chapter.

String Quartet in B-flat Major mixes the major and minor modes of F major very ambiguously, and this removes some of the power of the dominant. (The theme of the variations in the last movement uses D minor instead of the dominant F: the exotic harmonic structure is B-flat major/D minor :‖: D major/B-flat major.) The solo exposition of the D major violin concerto goes to A minor, and the solo exposition of the B-flat major piano concerto goes to F minor (this makes a problem for the opening ritornello, since returning directly to B-flat major from F minor is not possible, but it is cleverly solved by Brahms's placing of the secondary material at first in D minor). Brahms also uses the mediant minor instead of the major in the Cello Sonata in F Major, where the exposition of the opening movement goes to A minor. In a study of the proportions of Brahms's sonata forms, James Webster found the coda to be anomalous for its length: there was, however, no way to avoid a long coda, as logic forced Brahms to end his recapitulation correctly in D minor, and it was necessary to find the way back to F major. In short, these are all, superficially, classical eighteenth-century forms, but the harmonic structures are profoundly subversive of the traditional stylistic language: the procedures weaken the foundations of the old style by adding an anomalous chromatic emphasis at odds with the very tradition that Brahms was claiming to revive. Carl Dalhaus has cogently remarked that in Wagner's *Die Meistersinger* the frequent diatonic pages presuppose a basic chromatic background.[5] In spite of the opposition of Brahms and Wagner, we may say the same of Brahms. And we should go further: with both composers, the purely diatonic in their music has come to sound exotic, the chromaticism normal. In one respect Brahms goes more radically in the direction of twentieth-century modernism than Wagner does: the dissonant contours of his melodic shapes are insistent and spiky, and the dissonances carry more weight than their release and resolution into consonance, which are always correct but for the most part deliberately underplayed. The interior cadences are generally weak (this is a characterization, not in the least a value judgment), rarely decisive: moreover, the cadences in the melodies are often out of phase with the cadences in the bass, which serves to increase their weakness. By softening the force of the cadence, Brahms attacked the principal conventional element of the classical system while, at the same time, he reproduced with extraordinary cunning the proportions, the procedures, and many of the lineaments of the style. He studied the composers of the past and recreated their techniques with material or procedures that would have been previously rejected or would have been unthinkable. The transition to the opening of the recapitulation of the first movement of the B-flat Concerto is an example of his sophistication:

5. See his article "Wagner," in *Grove 2* (1981).

A V–I cadence that prepares the return of the tonic and the main theme depends traditionally for its effect on the sense of a strong downbeat on the tonic chord. Brahms reproduces here the standard dominant preparation, even at great length, but the arrival of the tonic is placed as if it was still part of the dominant harmony, and the articulation is blurred. The blurring continues with the replaying of the two phrases of the opening theme, originally heard in the horn with echoes from the soloist: here, theme and echoes are merged, the antiphonal clarity of the opening of the movement becomes complex, the contours fluid. (In what follows, Brahms seems to have taken to heart Donald Francis Tovey's much later observation that in the concertos of Mozart, the recapitulation is a synthesis of the first ritornello and the first solo.) The reentry of the main theme at the beginning of a recapitulation is the most important tonic cadence in the classical scheme next to the final cadence itself, and Brahms's treatment affects the structure of the movement as a whole.

His attempt to evade the most conventional effect here can be compared to Wagner's treatment of the tonic cadences in the most diatonic of his works, *Die Meistersinger:* a very large number of these all-too-numerous cadences avoid the final tonic chord for a surprise resolution into V_7 of V—or what would be a surprise if it did not occur so often in this work that it almost hardens into a new convention. What is most remarkable about the return in this concerto of Brahms is the lack of forward drive and the sense of suspended rhythm. The end of the development appears to dissolve into the recapitulation. The tension of the lengthy dominant preparation of a return in the classical manner is not so much grounded as dispersed. Perhaps Brahms was influenced here by Mendelssohn's lyrical technique of ending a development with an air of exhaustion, but he has transferred that effect here to the return itself. The classical resolution on the tonic midway in the second part of the sonata is achieved on paper, but the dramatic scenario is completely subverted. Brahms seems to me far more radical in this instance than Beethoven in the *Appassionata*, where the tension of the development is prolonged into the recapitulation by a dominant pedal. The recapitulation of Brahms's Second Piano Concerto is very much like the recapitulation of his Symphony no. 4, where the opening theme returns in a stillness marked *dolce,* with the rhythm arrested and even suspended by the augmentation. This extraordinary passage is often performed with an unnecessary *ritenuto,* spoiling the subtle effect of the pianissimo arpeggios in the strings, which create two written-out four-bar fermatas.[6] Brahms may seem to be preserving the classical conventions, but in fact he reformulates their function in ways that attack the foundations of the style. Perhaps Haydn was equally revolutionary for his period, but Beethoven never altered the premises of the musical language to the extent that Brahms does in many of the large works.

6. The aesthetic implied by these striking moments lies behind the even more unclassical return of the opening movement of Symphony no. 3: not only is there no dominant preparation of the return of the tonic F major (except at the last possible and very brief moment), but any sense of a dominant is contradicted by a repeated emphasis on an E-flat over an E-flat pedal and then a brief tonic pedal. Perhaps this derived from a study of Beethoven's Symphony no. 4, where the return of the tonic had been prepared paradoxically by a long tonic pedal, but Brahms has subverted the essentially classical aspects of Beethoven's device. In any case, introducing the tonic through an emphasis on the flatted seventh must have been unprecedented when Brahms did it here.

But then Brahms had the radical experience of the generation of Schumann as part of his equipment, to say nothing of the contemporary challenge of Wagner, for whom Brahms had a grand but suitably nuanced admiration.

The Second Piano Concerto makes more use of conventional virtuoso figuration than, for example, Schumann did in the first movement of his piano concerto, from which it was virtually eliminated. (This opening movement was originally the entire concerto, already containing, fused together, an allegro, slow movement, scherzo, recapitulation, cadenza, and coda—the lyrical intermezzo and the more conventional virtuosity of the finale were only added later.) Nevertheless, Brahms's use is idiosyncratic and, we might say, fundamentally unconventional. He does, naturally, follow Beethoven in naturalizing the conventional by making it thematic. The arpeggios that begin the cadenza right after the opening of the concerto provide an example:

This makes the opening page of the *Emperor,* on which it is clearly modeled, seem by contrast extremely conventional, and the free tempo of Beethoven's cadenza, traditional for the classical cadenza, has yielded to a much stricter tempo. Not all of the conventional elements, however, are given a similar thematic character. In this concerto, which is famous for its exacerbation of the virtuoso element, the conventional arpeggios, scales, and figuration of the concertos of Mozart are not absent. Nevertheless, one essential character of the conventional filling in a classical concerto is canceled by Brahms: the grace and ease with which it should be performed. Almost without exception, the conventional material is slightly altered by Brahms so that it sounds awkward as well as difficult; the pianist not only has trouble playing it, but—against the grain of the convention, contradicting its purpose—clearly appears to everyone to be having difficulty. The tradition demanded that the difficulties of display be solved with an apparent ease of execution: the virtuosity was an impersonal or neutral element of the composition; the ease of the performer allowed the admiration of the spectators to be concentrated entirely on the execution of the purely mechanical. Our consciousness of the deliberate awkwardness of the passages of display in Brahms, by contrast, adds an impure element that partially blocks the audience's surrender to the interests of the performer; the awkward alterations divert attention to the composer, even in passages of almost completely mechanical content:

The extra note A-natural in this arpeggio of the dominant seventh of F minor makes this bar horrendously difficult to perform, and almost impossible to execute with any sense of ease. The most difficult passages in a concerto by Rachmaninov or Tchaikovsky allow the soloist an appearance of facility and grace refused by Brahms. This imposed awkwardness oddly transforms the mechanical into the expressive—or, in other words, the arbitrary sign into a natural signifier. Similarly with the famous parallel thirds in the final movement:

This reproduces part of the scheme of the opening strain of the finale of Beethoven's Concerto no. 3 in C Minor that Brahms followed almost slavishly as a model for the finale of both his piano concertos, and is a substitute for the brief cadenza that Beethoven inserts after the second phrase of his main theme to introduce the return of the opening motif, except that Beethoven's trill precedes the scale, and his scale is only a single line, not in parallel thirds. Brahms later reinforces the new complexity by demanding that the parallel thirds be played by one hand alone. Even if the soloist plays all the notes *leggiero* as marked, this never sounds like the more freewheeling cadenza style of the Beethoven concerto. It is only when we compare this with the model, in fact, that we realize that these bars actually function as a cadenza written out in strict time and that Brahms, as he did with the first concerto, has adhered faithfully to the Beethoven scheme, with a motif repeated several times followed by a cadenza leading directly back to the opening phrase of the main theme:

In short, Brahms has rewritten the classical cadenza so as to remove the basic convention and function of a cadenza, its sense of free improvisation. One idiosyncratic employment of convention should be mentioned: the use of a convention so old-fashioned, so archaic, that it had ceased to be conventional, but had become an original and almost exotic effect. In Brahms's Violin Sonata no. 2 in A Major, the development section begins by playing the main theme at the dominant and then replaying it at the tonic.

Beginning a development with the main theme at the dominant was a convention that was still alive; beginning with the main theme at the tonic was an experiment of Beethoven in Opus 31, nos. 1 and 3. But playing the main theme at the dominant and immediately after at the tonic is a form so archaic that, as far as I know, it had not been practiced by anyone since the 1760s, when it was commonplace and almost standard. Derived from the midcentury opera aria, it can be found frequently in works of Haydn from that early period (Oliver Strunk called it a "premature recapitulation" and thought it a banal device, which it was), but Haydn later abandoned the scheme, perhaps not only because it was banal, but also because it inconveniently reduced the tension of the development. Brahms revives it, but with great originality. He exploits the inconvenience, as the relaxation of harmonic tension increases the lyricism. It is also the fruit of a musicological study—a convention so buried in the past that it has been forgotten and is no longer conventional. Brahms is not only continuing a classical tradition, but amusing himself here, I think, by resuscitating the dead.

6

The project of purging art music of its conventions continues after Brahms into the twentieth century, and is still active today. Debussy almost always used only compound arpeggios, complicating the triadic nature of the device, and consented to write simple scales only ironically, as in the Etude for Five Fingers "in the style of Mr. Czerny." (As far as I can remember, Ravel wrote scales only *glissando* on either the white or black keys, which changes them from a witness to the harmonic language of tonality into examples of pure sonority.) The disappearance of scales and arpeggios is a great hardship for performers today, causing much misery above all perhaps for pianists, as the arrangement of the black and white keys of the keyboard was specifically designed to facilitate their execution and to make anything else more onerous. With instruments constructed for tonality, the loss of conventional material has made music harder to play, and, as we all know, harder to listen to. In the general development in the nineteenth century of all the arts—music, literature, and painting—the attempt to rid the arts of the standard conventions is the villain in the wicked creation of a difficult style and the consequent alienation of that large part of the public that resents any heavy demands made upon its attention.

The difference between art music and popular music is, in fact, largely a question of how much close attention is required or demanded for appreciation. Of course, when so-called classical music is familiar enough so that it no longer makes us uncomfortable, we can listen to it happily without paying much attention to it and think about more pressing and more practical considerations. The once controversial work of Wagner or Stravinsky can now be transformed into Muzak and performed in elevators without inspiring a public outcry.

Sustaining the classical tradition while weakening, or even dispensing with, so many of its conventions was a paradoxical activity. The classical language of music was largely dependent on these conventions: getting rid of them attacked the musical tradition and injured it almost beyond repair—at least, the music language was radically and systematically altered in the process in ways that were probably not completely understood, the consequences certainly not clearly foreseen. That the greatest and most durable masterpieces from 1750 to the present were composed through this project is not enough to make the fundamental loss of eighteenth-century tonality less poignant. Musicians were vaguely and intermittently aware of the danger of this loss of the tradition long before the present day: how wonderful it would be, Brahms once observed, to be a composer at the time of Mozart when it was easy to write music. The demand for innovation, the prejudice against convention, has made music not only harder to play and harder to listen to, but also harder to compose.

In the twentieth century, a reaction against the sensuous delights of unlimited chromaticism and atonality brought an attempt to return to diatonic tonality in the work of composers as disparate as Virgil Thomson, Samuel Barber, and Philip Glass, to name only a few. But the tonal system they employ is by no means that of the eighteenth century or even the nineeenth: the symmetry of dominant and subdominant directions of the 1700s has disappeared, and there is no longer any of the rigor with which chromatic tonal relations were regulated in Haydn and his contemporaries. The radical chromatic harmony of the nineteenth century is no longer fashionable. It is not that the eighteenth- or nineteenth-century conventions are infringed or violated: on the contrary, they are ignorantly or innocently disregarded. In general, tonal relations are loosely conceived by neoconservatives and neo-Romantics today, and their laxity has not permitted a renaissance or revival of the structural richness of the earlier tradition.

Exceptionally, the most surprising and effective use of a diatonic language in the last century has been that of Stravinsky after *Les Noces,* who exploited the conventions and formulas of tonality ironically and perversely. The main theme of his piano sonata shows his method:

The harmonies are all tonic and dominant, but their function has been subverted: every melody note of the tonic triad after the first is harmonized by a dominant, every melody note from the dominant is harmonized by a tonic chord. Here there is a direct and consistent violation of the tonal significance, a systematic destruction of the conventions of tonality that undercuts any nostalgia or sentimentality that might arise from the composition of a sonata in C major. In *The Poetics of Music,* Stravinsky observed that in the 1920s he used the formulas of classical tonality the way he had previously employed the motifs of folk music. The technique in both cases was fundamentally one of alienation. The trill at the opening of the melody of the sonata reveals this as clearly as the harmony: a classical trill of a minor second on the leading-tone prepares the resolution of the cadence as the leading-tone goes into the tonic; but transforming the trill into a *tremolo* on the interval of a ninth blocks resolution, as the dissonance of the ninth hangs over unresolved (above all because the composer has incorporated the dissonance into a semblance of resolution), and even this semblance is undercut by a dissonant harmony. The technique of alienation is basic to Romanticism (defined succinctly by Novalis as "making the strange familiar and the familiar strange"), and the neoconservative Stravinsky, like the neoconservative Brahms, continued the revolutionary development initiated by the late eighteenth century. Both subverted the conventions as they transformed them.

How is a convention established? Clearly by repetition. Of course, the conventions that have been most firmly set in place are those that are consonant with the basic nature of the musical language and style—but that, too, is established by familiarity achieved through repetition. Perhaps the most profound aspect of serious music today is its disdain for repetition. This is not a new phenomenon, but the end of a long and gradual development: the essential difference between an early eighteenth-century da capo and a late eighteenth-century sonata form is that the da capo is structurally a literal repeat sometimes with added ornamentation improvised on the spot or planned by the soloist, while the return of the opening section in the sonata has to be completely rewritten with an altered harmonic structure. Simple repetition (even with improvised decoration) no longer satisfied the new sensibility. The prejudice against unvaried repetition became firmly ingrained during the nineteenth century. By the early twentieth, Strauss, Debussy, and others have renounced the repetition of even short sections, unless they were completely rethought and reformulated. With the second half of the twentieth century, the avant-garde foreswore even the repetition of a theme. In the music of Luciano Berio, Karl-Heinz Stockhausen, Pierre Boulez, Elliott Carter, and others, we come upon the return of textures and even the return of certain kinds of harmonic configurations, but there is never a return of a theme and even no simple recurrence of a motif. It would seem that the most interesting composers of our day have determined to block what might result in the creation of new conventions for future generations. We can be sure, however, that convention will find itself a way back by stealth, and it is probably already doing so.

Part Three

CENTENARIES

CHAPTER 12

Felix Mendelssohn at 200:
Prodigy without Peer

I N HIS NEW BIOGRAPHY of Mendelssohn, R. Larry Todd recounts the story of Berlioz and Mendelssohn and their heated argument in 1831 about religion, while walking in the Baths of Caracalla in Rome. Mendelssohn defended his Lutheran faith while Berlioz expressed his more outrageously modern views. Mendelssohn then slipped and fell on some ruins. "Look at that for an example of divine justice," Berlioz exclaimed. "I blaspheme, you fall." The two composers were then very young—Mendelssohn was twenty-three and Berlioz only a few years older, but Mendelssohn was already internationally famous, while Berlioz remained a controversial figure for all his life and for many decades thereafter. Throughout the nineteenth century, Mendelssohn was accepted, particularly in England, as one of the greatest composers of all time, a position from which he was dislodged only in the twentieth century as Berlioz ascended into the pantheon. The precipitous decline in Mendelssohn's reputation is clearly an injustice, but putting it right is not a simple matter.

Professor Todd is our most distinguished authority on Mendelssohn; he largely owns the subject and rightly so, given the years of research he has spent, the judicious viewpoint free of polemic that he manifests, and also the clear appreciation and respect that he has for the man and his work. His new volume gives not only a remarkably full and detailed picture of Mendelssohn's career, but also a rich and satisfying account of the European culture in which he lived out his short life.

Review (2004) of *Mendelssohn: A Life in Music,* by R. Larry Todd.

This has an importance for Mendelssohn perhaps greater than for any other composer: no other musician had such intimate contact with the whole range of European culture. His grandfather was the philosopher and religious thinker Moses Mendelssohn, the most distinguished Jewish figure of the eighteenth century. His daughter Brendel, later Dorothy, Felix's aunt, eventually married Friedrich Schlegel, who gave us our first definition of Romanticism. Her children by a first marriage, Philip and Jonas Veit, were two of the painters of the Nazarene Brotherhood, the movement to transform contemporary art by reviving the primitive religious style of Germany and Italy. Felix studied music with Carl Friedrich Zelter, one of Goethe's closest friends, and came to know Goethe himself by the age of fourteen. The poet Heinrich Heine, too, was a friend of the family, although Felix's father, Abraham, did not view him with favor. One of Felix's most intimate friends was the historian Johann Gustav Droysen, who wrote *Historik,* the fundamental treatise of the nineteenth century on historiography. When he was at the university in Berlin, Felix went to Hegel's lectures on aesthetics, and was in close contact with Friedrich Schleiermacher, the leading Protestant theologian. Another friend was Adolf Bernhard Marx, perhaps the most important music theorist of the period. Marx even influenced Mendelssohn's work, but they had an eventual falling-out when it became clear that Mendelssohn thought very little of Marx's attempt to write an opera. In the musical world, Felix was very close, in spite of some disagreements on style, to Chopin, Meyerbeer, Schumann, Liszt, and Berlioz; he performed with Clara Schumann and wrote some pieces especially for her. Intellectually, he was the most cultivated musician of his time, with a command of Greek and Latin literature. He was also a superb draftsman, and several of his landscapes are reproduced in the book.

There has never been in the history of music a child prodigy to equal Mendelssohn. As a teenager, he was a much better composer than either Beethoven or Mozart at the same age. Two of his masterpieces—the Octet and the overture to *A Midsummer Night's Dream*—were written when he was sixteen and seventeen years old. The early string quartets of a year or so later are unparalleled in the music of the time; they are the only works influenced by the last quartets of Beethoven which were able to deal successfully with the radical, still controversial, and largely misunderstood style of the old composer. In these first two published quartets, Mendelssohn's imitation of Beethoven is flagrant, particularly of the Quartet op. 132, but the young composer creates forms that amazingly stand up on their own.

(To understand the achievement, one might compare the efforts of nineteenth-century playwrights to imitate Shakespeare. They invariably made fools of themselves, and arrived at either melodrama or pompous academic fare, with the exception of Heinrich von Kleist, who learned both from

Shakespeare's prosody and his sense of dramatic movement, and produced the masterly *Prince of Homburg.*) Not until a century after Mendelssohn's youthful essays would the late style of Beethoven be absorbed again into the mainstream of music by the quartets of Bartok and Schoenberg.

With the imitation of Beethoven's late piano style, Mendelssohn was less successful, although the Sonata in E Major, written when he was seventeen and openly modeled on Beethoven's Sonata in A Major, op. 101, contains some beautiful things and is remarkable for the fact that the more closely it sticks to Beethoven, the more it sounds like genuine and even typical Mendelssohn. It was as if the young composer had discovered himself in one aspect of late Beethoven, and this is, of course, the proper course of action for a young genius. On the other hand, his attempt to profit from the example of Beethoven's Hammerklavier Sonata op. 106 does not work at all, and ends in fact as a silly and superficial piece—but then, Mendelssohn never published it (after his death, his heirs had it printed as op. 106; it would have been better to leave it in obscurity).

Todd deals fairly with the musical talents and achievements of Felix's sister Fanny, a controversial subject today, and perceptively and sanely with the question of Mendelssohn's Jewish heritage, often the occasion for biographical mythmaking. The family had tried to distance itself from the Jewish culture by adopting the name of Bartholdy, and to achieve integration into German society by a conversion to Protestantism. Felix's Lutheran faith was clearly both deep and sincere, and he was not, in fact, circumcised. Nevertheless, he was profoundly conscious of his Jewish background, and the frequent anti-Semitic attacks on him would not have allowed him to forget it. He sponsored a complete edition of his grandfather's works, and his two oratorios allowed an open reference to the heritage. The first, *Paul,* may be thought purely Christian, but the conversion of St. Paul, a Jew, is the great event of the work and carries a personal burden and message. *Elijah* is more ostensibly Hebrew, but it is also a work that points to the coming of Christ. In both works, the more modern oratorio style of Haydn and Beethoven is abandoned in favor of a dogmatic, conservative, and ostentatious revival of the Lutheran world of Johann Sebastian Bach. Mendelssohn was, it is well known, the leader in the revival of Bach's *Passion According to St. Matthew,* performed by him (when he was twenty-one) after it had lain untouched for three-quarters of a century, and he began the transformation of the accepted view of Bach as a great composer of educational keyboard music into the more modern one as a master of religious music. Throughout his biography, Todd treats the question of Mendelssohn's religion and his Jewish background with great sympathy, acknowledges its importance, but points out that there is no evidence that Mendelssohn ever entered a synagogue.

Todd provides fascinating details of Mendelssohn's activity as a performing musician. As a conductor, he was often attacked for his fast tempi in the symphonies of Beethoven, but today this looks like a preservation of the original tradition against the increasing taste for slower tempi that began to appear soon after Beethoven's death and continued to grow throughout the nineteenth and twentieth centuries. Mendelssohn performed Handel's oratorios with the more modern instrumentation that the later eighteenth century had already imposed (extra wind parts) but interestingly planned a revival of the old performance practice. Most remarkable was his interest in Renaissance music, and his performances of sixteenth-century works by Orlandus Lassus and Palestrina.

With his deep knowledge and understanding of Mendelssohn's procedures, it is a pity that Todd avoids an explanation of his catastrophic loss of reputation. Paradoxically, this would call for an account of the reasons for Mendelssohn's immense and easily won prestige. His weaknesses were a corollary of his extraordinary gifts, and these gifts demand a more specific and detailed appreciation than Todd is willing to grant in this biography, although he has written elsewhere more cogently on the music. (There is an excellent account of some of these matters in *The Early Works of Felix Mendelssohn,* by Greg Vitercik, 1992, missing from Todd's bibliography.)

What was amazing from a very early point of Mendelssohn's career was his extraordinary facility in construction. It is true that he possessed to a satisfactory degree most of the talents necessary to a composer. He could write beautiful melodies, but they are rarely as striking as Chopin's or Bellini's, or as hauntingly eccentric as Schumann's. His handling of harmony was impeccable, but he never ventured anything like the radical experiments of Chopin or Liszt: even his profound study of Bach did not induce him to imitate that master's complex forays into chromaticism which so inspired Mozart and Chopin. He was an exceedingly fine master of counterpoint, but he never developed the extraordinary versatility and richness of voice-leading of Mozart or Chopin, or aspired to the daring of Beethoven in these matters.

What Mendelssohn had, already at the age of fifteen, was an unerring sense of how to make a work move; how to put it together. There are no awkward transitions in his music. Everything he wrote has grace and fluidity of construction. At first sight, this may seem less exciting than a strikingly beautiful melody or a revolutionary deployment of harmony, but at its best, the grace of his constructions is so breathtaking as to inspire the same kind of emotional response, of ecstasy, indeed, that we get from the greatest music. He was perhaps the supreme master in introducing—above all, in reintroducing—a theme. Todd observes that the device of bringing back the scherzo in the finale of the Octet is derived from Beethoven's Symphony no. 5, and that is, indeed, the source. But Beethoven brings back the scherzo in that work as a quotation, an intrusion in the finale. In Mendelssohn's Octet, it arises naturally—"organically" used to be the accepted expression—from the finale itself. The way he does it is quite simple. One of the themes of the finale is like a skeleton of the principal theme of the scherzo, which springs out of it with such ease that we are back in the scherzo almost without being aware of it.

Before Mendelssohn, there are two approaches to cyclical form, to the concept of an earlier part of the work returning in a later movement. Both approaches were practiced by Beethoven. The first is the quotation of an earlier movement in the finale. The second, a procedure already recognized in Beethoven's work in 1811 by E. T. A. Hoffmann, was to build the successive movements on the same musical material (as both the first movement and the finale of the *Appassionata* are based on the alternation of tonic minor and Neapolitan harmonies).

Mendelssohn united the two techniques in his early works, combining the ostentatious intelligibility of the quotation with the more subtle motivic working-out, and created cyclical forms in quartets, sonatas, and symphonies that mix clarity and fluidity, so that the reappearance of the earlier music never seems willful. This grace of construction was dazzling from the outset of Mendelssohn's development. It renewed the classical forms while removing the harshness of articulation, softened the contour of forms, made the affective character of the whole work and the relation of one part to another more easily graspable.

In the scherzo of the Octet, the repeat of the exposition with the reappearance of the first theme and the tonic G minor harmony is the most exquisite return. What the sixteen-year-old composer did was to introduce a brief moment of the D major dominant of G minor into the second theme in B-flat major, and pause briefly on it for three bars before returning to B-flat major and a repeat of his second theme. When he arrives once again at the D major dominant, he now sustains the harmony for the astonishing length of twenty-two bars, with the scherzo movement continuing, but all harmonic movement withheld. This creates a sustained tension resolved with ease by returning to the opening bars. What is impressive is the economy of means and the sophisticated simplicity. It required a profound instinct for proportion, rhythm, and large-scale harmonic significance.

All of Mendelssohn's most striking innovations arrive with the same ease and conviction. Todd rightly singles out the placement of the cadenza of the Violin Concerto in the middle of the first movement, not at the end (contradicting the very idea of the cadenza as a cadence). The justification for this, however, is significant. Mendelssohn often altered the traditional conception of sonata form by making the end of the development a lowering of energy instead of the point of extreme tension, so that the return of the opening theme steals in subtly rather than emphatically.

(He took this from Beethoven's Pastoral Sonata op. 28, but added greater continuity and lyricism.) In the Violin Concerto, the end of the development reaches a point of exhaustion, and the solo violinist begins to improvise quietly with increasing virtuosity. The greatest innovation is left for the end of the cadenza: when the orchestra enters with the return of the first theme, the soloist continues virtuoso figuration and, for the first time in history, a solo violin accompanies the full orchestra. (Mozart had the pianist accompany the orchestral soloists, and Beethoven had gone further, making the piano accompany the strings, but that does not detract from the originality of Mendelssohn's conception, above all its unprecedented sonority.)

The decline of Mendelssohn's prestige lay in his refusal to venture beyond the realm in which such ease and grace were possible. Above all, the oratorios were tainted with respectability. (The heavy hand of decorous piety lies upon almost all nineteenth-century oratorios, including those by ostensibly radical composers, such as Berlioz's *Enfance du Christ* and Liszt's *St. Elisabeth*.) Mendelssohn never experimented with the daring chromatic harmony that caused Chopin's later works to be labeled morbid and sick, but which had such a powerful influence on Wagner. He was incapable of the ironic, anticlassical and disconcerting structures of Schumann, which could be integrated into a new classicism by Brahms. Except in the extraordinary central section of *Fingal's Cave,* he could not match the radically new sonorities of Liszt, despised by so many of Mendelssohn's contemporaries, but which became so important for future composers, such as Ravel. In spite of the admiration of Schumann and Brahms (and even Wagner, who stole from him), Mendelssohn seemed the ideal Victorian composer, with his greatest reputation in England and his greatest influence on figures like Sir Arthur Sullivan.

He was perhaps the prisoner of his genius. Life was easy for him. A banker's son, he never had to make his own way. He had the best education money could buy. Above all, he never had to conquer his own failings to arrive at greater heights. He had no failings. Raised on the music of Bach, Mozart, and Beethoven, who gave him a ready-made tradition as a backup, he was a master of melody, harmony, and counterpoint by the age of fifteen. In the following year, he achieved a grasp of large-scale rhythmic form, musical construction, and syntax that other composers needed many years of experience to achieve. He revised with great care and polished diligently, but music came easily to him.

Haydn had to struggle for decades to create a new style. Beethoven could write great melodies but it was hard work for him. Chopin and Schumann lacked Mendelssohn's innate instinct for large structures, and that lack drove them to the creation of new, idiosyncratic forms. Even Mozart had to work for years to master the stylistic innovations of Haydn; the discovery of the music of J. S. Bach represented an extraordinary challenge to him, and his over-weening ambition led him to expand every genre he touched.

Wagner was almost forty before he found his own voice. Most of the artists who survive the selection of history had a deficiency to overcome that inspired them to alter and expand the language of their art. Mendelssohn's precocity was a curse as well as a gift. Because of it, he never matched the extravagance of his greater contemporaries. It has often been observed that his melodies, with a few remarkable exceptions, do not sustain the lyricism of their openings to the end. The increase of intensity that characterizes the typical melodic conceptions of the Romantic School, of Chopin, Schumann, and Berlioz, is generally absent from Mendelssohn's. His unparalleled facility with traditional forms led him to round off his melodic ideas sedately, even when his style implied the more fluid, unresolved energy that had become the new ideal of advanced musicians. The great work that came later—the Italian Symphony, the *Fingal's Cave* overture, and the Violin Concerto—never go beyond the achievement of the sixteen-year-old. With all his learning and mastery, he remained essentially a child prodigy to the end.

There is the occasional awkward heaviness in Larry Todd's biography. He uses the word "eschews," and speaks of Scarlatti's "zesty sonatas." Discussing Mendelssohn's criticism of French musical life, Todd writes that "Fanny chastised him for ignoring nonmusical experiences"; I have no idea what he means (sex, politics, cuisine, literature?). He tells us twice that the scherzo of the Octet reminded contemporaries of mosquitoes, and I am sorry to know that, as it does not help my appreciation. But these are minor matters. *Mendelssohn* is a splendid and deeply satisfactory achievement.

CHAPTER 13

Happy Birthday, Elliott Carter!

TURNING ONE HUNDRED years old on December 11, 2008, Elliott Carter must have found the experience exhilarating and rejuvenating. When I went to see him on the afternoon of his birthday, he was hard at work on a song cycle for soprano and clarinet on poems by Louis Zukofsky. He looked younger than six months before—in fact, younger than six years before. That night, the Boston Symphony, directed by James Levine, played a new work of his, *Interventions for Piano and Orchestra,* with Daniel Barenboim as soloist. A few days later, a party of a dozen of his friends heard four of the new songs splendidly performed by Lucy Shelton and Charles Neidich; they are among his most lyrical and wittiest inspirations.

The Paul Sacher Foundation in Basel, Switzerland, has produced a large, handsome book, titled *Elliott Carter: A Centennial Portrait in Letters and Documents,* with many photographs of Carter, his friends and family, and with many photographs of manuscript pages as well. This is natural as the Sacher Foundation is the world's greatest repository of twentieth-century music manuscripts, possessing most of Igor Stravinsky, Béla Bartók, Anton Webern, Pierre Boulez, Elliott Carter, and many others. The foundation aids scholars and students throughout the world in their studies of the music of the twentieth century, and the collection is housed in a temperature- and humidity-controlled

Originally written in 2009 as a review of *Elliott Carter: A Centennial Portrait in Letters and Documents,* by Felix Meyer and Anne C. Shreffler.

environment in an old house on the cliffs overlooking the Rhine. The book, written and edited by the director of the foundation, Felix Meyer, and by Professor Anne C. Shreffler of Harvard University, gives a detailed visual image of Carter's career, interspersed with discussions of many of the works. The photographs and the letters make up a wonderfully personal account of a lifetime.

One might say that Carter's musical life began in 1924 when, fifteen years old, he heard the American premiere of Stravinsky's *The Rite of Spring* by the Boston Symphony and decided that he wanted to be a composer. In 1925, his father, a lace merchant (who knew twenty languages or dialects, and could speak the tongue of wherever lace was produced), took him on a trip to Vienna. The boy bought a copy of Arnold Schoenberg's Suite for Piano, op. 25. This was the first publication of a twelve-tone piece, and Carter was introduced to the controversial dodecaphonic style that was to dominate so much of European, and then American music for the rest of the century.

Carter's purchase was almost fortuitous, and paradoxical as well, since most Viennese music lovers of that time, and for several decades to come, remained curiously unaware of Schoenberg's recent music. Nevertheless, it is interesting that Carter, fascinated by the new work, was one of the few major avant-garde composers of the century never even to try his hand once at writing a twelve-tone piece, as he found the technique too constraining.

He decided to go to Harvard largely so that he could hear the Boston Symphony, more adventurous in contemporary work than other American orchestras, and went every week to its concerts. He naturally found the Harvard music department stodgy. The conservative British composer Gustav Holst, who taught there, remarked, on hearing Carter play the piano, that if he didn't play so many wrong notes, perhaps he wouldn't write so many in his compositions.

One of his high school teachers in New York had introduced him to Charles Ives, who became his mentor and played part of his Concord Sonata for him, so that he was already in touch with the most radical elements of American serious music. He later, somewhat to the shock of Ives's greatest admirers, expressed his disappointment at Ives's refusal to commit himself fully to a pro-fessional activity in music, abandoning composition for so long, and leaving so much unfinished or only half finished.

Carter's commitment to the profession was total, disappointing his father, who expected him to join the lace business. Like so many American com-posers, he went to Paris to study with Nadia Boulanger, who was the interna-tional pedagogical representative of Stravinsky's style. ("Why should I teach, when there is Nadia?" Stravinsky is supposed to have said.) Carter helped in organizing concerts of new music, and worked with the Balanchine troupe that was to become the New York City Ballet.

For a time, to make a living, Carter took a job at St. John's College, teaching Greek and mathematics among other subjects, but he never ceased composing or trying to find ways for American music to get a hearing. His early style was not only influenced by Stravinsky and Aaron Copland and even Paul Hindemith (in the 1930s this was hard to avoid), but his compositions already had an idiosyncratic rhythmic energy, with surprising assymetrical twists and a wonderful verve, perhaps partially derived from the great jazz performers of the 1930s. His works before 1945 are accomplished and easily enjoyable, and the Holiday Overture became particularly well known.

A Centennial Portrait has some fine pictures of Carter's wife, Helen Frost-Jones, an extraordinary woman who retained her beauty until the latest old age (she died in 2003) and who was loved, admired, and feared by all of Carter's friends and acquaintances. She was a sculptress, very much part of the advanced New York art scene (she used to play chess with Marcel Duchamp), cultivated, and witty. Nevertheless, she abandoned her sculpture when she married Carter in 1939, and authoritatively and sternly made sure he had the leisure and the peace to compose, as in the 1940s and 1950s he worked very slowly on large projects.

On one occasion, I was present when there was a telephone call from the Ford Foundation, inquiring about a commission which Carter was already almost a year late in delivering. I heard Helen say, "Yes, Mr. D'Arms, Mr. Carter is thinking about your commission. A great deal too much in my opinion. Goodbye," and she hung up quickly. "That should hold them for another year," she said to me. Both Helen and Elliott were generous to musicians when they could be, and many performers and composers were helped by them over the years. I remember that Elliott once had to rent a dress suit to attend a dinner at the White House, because he had given his tails to a member of the Parrenin Quartet.

It was in 1945, when Carter was thirty-six years old, that he moved in a new direction, stimulated by the idea of exploiting the characteristic sound of an instrument, the concert piano. He derived the basic motivic material of his Sonata for Piano from the idiosyncratic sonority of the instrument and its harmonic overtones, the way the strings vibrate sympathetically with each other. The *Centennial Portrait*'s observation that this work includes a "large-scale Beethovenian fugue . . . like Samuel Barber's Piano Sonata," written around the same time, is misleading. Neither fugue is Beethovenian, Barber's being an imitation of the fugue in Brahms's Handel variations, and Carter's is also a Romantic concert fugue like others from Liszt to Hindemith, but without a stylistic dependence on a single model. The sonata is inventive throughout in developing the strange sonorities that only a piano can produce, for example changing the pedal rapidly after hitting one note hard, so that most of the sonority is damped and then suddenly recaptured with the sound of an echo.

Three years later, Carter produced an even more important work, the Sonata for Violoncello and Piano, in which new conceptions of music were developed that later became the foundation of his international reputation. The significance of this work seems to escape the *Centennial Portrait*, as the article on it discusses only a minor passage of changing rhythms in the fourth and last movement, and completely neglects the first movement, which was written last, and which is the most radical of all (Carter himself has said that he is sometimes disturbed by how much more progressive the first movement is than the rest of the work). The whole sonata is remarkably effective in concert, but only a consideration of the opening will explain why many musicians find it the finest work for cello written since Debussy's sonata for that instrument.

A letter of Carter's written many years later, in 1959, will give us the key to the originality of this work. The letter is to Peter Yates, the founder of a concert series in Los Angeles, and is mostly about Carter's String Quartet no. 1, but clearly alludes to the cello sonata:

> Certainly my music has sought mainly two things—to deal with vertical and horizontal dimensions in a more varied way than is usually done—I try to find continuities that gain meaning, change, and operate in time on a level of interest that is parallel to our present experience of living. Thus there are textures and shifts of character that feature very contrasting musical behaviors, simultaneously or one after the other, but linked together by phrasing. The other aspect is an attempt to use the performing situation, the instrument, its player, and the combination of instruments as a means of individualization. To find the special music, so to speak, that needs the 'cello and the piano—which don't go together very well. To bring out their differences and make a virtue of that, even a means of expression.

The cello sonata opens with the piano in strict time, ticking away in moderate tempo with a quiet percussive staccato. The cello, however, exists in a different space-time, with a long, lyrical, and eloquent line, irregular and seemingly improvised, very few of its notes coinciding with the beats of the piano. The opening may be the first example of Carter's use of the long, expressive, singing arabesque line that was virtually absent in modernist style (Carter's direction of espressivo for this kind of writing has shocked some of his modernist admirers, who find it absurdly old-fashioned). In the cello sonata and later works, this singing line will often employ and unite the entire compass of the instrument from the lowest to the highest registers.

No previous work for cello and piano had ever differentiated the two instruments so distinctly, and exploited the individual sonority of each. Even in the finest works of the small repertory for cello and piano before this—those of Beethoven (who wrote the first great cello and piano sonatas), Brahms, Debussy, and Rachmaninov—it will sometimes sound as if the piano is given a musical effect that should really belong to the cello and vice versa, making a sense of necessary compromise.

At the end of Carter's sonata there is, in fact, an interchange of material, but without compromise. On the last page of the finale something like the first movement returns, but now it is the cello that is quietly ticking away metronomically with the only percussive sound a cello can make, a pizzicato, and the piano tries modestly to imitate the cello's initial lyricism with very long, quiet notes in the deepest bass register in an irregular rhythm that seems to pay no attention to the cello's strict tempo. This beautiful passage that returns to the earlier movement is prepared by one in which the slower tempo of the first movement in the piano is superimposed over the uninterrupted faster movement of the finale in the cello, mixing the two tempos. A continuous movement of fast notes is played by the cello accenting every fourth note, while the piano plays on every fifth note of the cello part, making not only a counter-rhythm but a counter-tempo, 20 percent slower, with the effect of a jazzy syncopation.

This is the device called "metrical modulation" so often associated with Carter's music. The *Centennial Portrait* describes an example, earlier in the finale, of this method of superimposing one pulse over another, but the most important justification for its use in this movement is the reappearance of the opening tempo. Unless we account for the dramatic and affective reason for its existence, metric modulation can seem like a gimmick.

Both of the editor-authors of the book are fine and perceptive musicologists, but they do not always recognize, or at least treat, the psychological importance for the listener of the musical techniques of which they give an accurate account. For example, in the article on the piano work *Night Fantasies,* they describe at length a complex, slow polyrhythm between the pianist's left and right hands. They seem to think the rhythm very difficult (it isn't), and they miss the only real, although slight, technical difficulty in this passage because they neglect the most important auditory aspect—that one hand is playing right on top of the other. For the listener's ear, in consequence, since both of the lines are in the same register with the same instrumental sound, one line gets tangled up with the other, just as the fingers of one hand get in the way of the other hand, and every pianist has to decide individually how far to clarify the two lines by touch, and how much and where to allow the momentary confusion of one line with the other that is part of the effect.

In Carter's writing for piano (in the Cello Sonata, the Piano Concerto, *90+*, and Dialogues for Piano and Orchestra), there are several examples of this play of confusion in one register. In painting, an oscillation between definition and sfumato is a source of visual delight, and music can provide a similar pleasure, so it is essential to Carter's work to permit a unifying blur to enter at moments into all his examples of highly contrasted opposition of musical character.

Three years later, the String Quartet no. 1 of 1951 was Carter's most ambitious work to date. This was, he has admitted, his first work written to please only himself, with little thought of anyone else's approval. It made his international reputation, winning prizes, and was soon in the repertory of several ensembles, becoming for a while, in spite of its formidable difficulty, his most popular and most often performed piece. After pointing out the influence of recent American composers like Ives, Conlon Nancarrow, and Ruth Crawford Seeger, the *Centennial Portrait* gives a succinct account of this composition, including a brief quotation from Carter:

> The quartet sent a clear signal that Carter's shift away from neo-classicism, which had begun some time before, was finally complete. In this work, he successfully merged the European traditions that had shaped his music until then with the "dissonant, 'advanced' music [of the American ultramoderns], the kind that I'd first liked and that had first attracted me to music."

Of course, what had originally attracted Carter to music was Stravinsky's *Rite of Spring,* but it is a treat to see the familiar Romantic paradox in action, to find that when Carter wrote to please himself alone, he finally achieved his first durable popularity.

The Second String Quartet exploited even more sensationally than the Cello Sonata the individuality of the different instruments. Carter wanted the four players to sit farther apart than is usual with chamber players. "They generally manage to move an inch or two away," he has said sadly, and reported that the composer Walter Piston remarked that if he had composed the piece, he would have put each player in a different room and shut the doors.

From then on, a series of works exploited the idea that simultaneously conflicting perceptions of the passage of time were essential to the modern urban experience, the most famous of which are the Double Concerto for Harpsichord and Piano and Two Small Orchestras and the Symphony of Three Orchestras. The Double Concerto has two orchestras of six players each and four percussion players positioned separately at the back of the stage from far left to right, and playing forty-four percussion instruments. The work uses space as well as time in a novel way; in the slow central movement, the wind instruments play a quiet chorale in strict time while the pizzicato strings, piano, harpsichord, and percussionists, all playing staccato and very softly, perform a gradually accelerating pattern, each musician playing a single note before the next player comes in. This accelerating pattern of single notes describes patterns in space moving from left to right and front to back in a series of circles.

Everyone who loves Carter's music has a favorite moment. Mine is perhaps the trumpet solo toward the opening of the Symphony of Three Orchestras, a virtuoso lyrical page inspired by Hart Crane's image of the seagull descending on the Brooklyn Bridge. The most recent works have become leaner and sparer, without losing their radical expression, although they require as much concentration to appreciate as the earlier pieces. It must be admitted that the great works of the middle period can often appear to be overloaded with detail difficult for listeners to perceive unless the performance is able to clarify the texture. Even in the new works, loud forceful chords in orchestra or piano should not be punched out with all the notes exactly alike, but with varied dynamics, either to bring out an interesting line or to make the sonority of each chord effective. Richard Strauss once complained to Arturo Toscanini, "My music has bad notes and good notes, and when I conduct it one hears only the good notes, but when you conduct it, I hear all the notes."

As horridly difficult as Strauss's music once seemed ("vulgar and unintelligible" was the most famous London critic's reaction to the premiere of *Elektra*), much of the new repertory today in an unfamiliar style is even more so. This, however, requires more rehearsal time than orchestras can provide economically, and more intelligence or goodwill than pianists and other soloists are always able to call up, but without these requirements, the music cannot fully make sense and will remain opaque.

This is not a new problem, but a perennial one. In the years right after Beethoven's death, the orchestra of the Paris Conservatoire tried to play his Ninth Symphony; the first reading was so awful that they rehearsed it for a full year, and Berlioz reported that the effect was superb even with an unsympathetic conductor. So many musicians passionately insisted on performing Beethoven that after some decades, his work had entered into the general musical consciousness and become easier to perform. Schoenberg once said, "My music is not modern; it's just badly played." I heard Pierre Boulez direct his small chamber ensemble in a work of Harrison Birtwhistle, and when I said I had never heard a work of his sound so wonderfully effective, Boulez explained: "We had thirty-five rehearsals." At the Paris Opera, when Boulez conducted the first production of Alban Berg's *Lulu* with the third act that had been withheld for so long, I went to both the second and the last of thirteen performances. At the last performance, the orchestra seemed to be playing almost by heart, and when I remarked to Boulez that I had never heard an unfamiliar modern opera executed with such confidence, he said, "We had forty-five recording sessions."

It is no wonder that the public finds difficult contemporary music so irritating. However, since Beethoven, it is the difficult music that has eventually survived most easily; the originally unintelligible Wagner, Strauss, Debussy, Stravinsky, and all the others that were so shocking are now an essential part of the concert scene. Some of this music is accepted because of its prestige; an average audience would find Beethoven's Grosse Fugue for string quartet as annoying as Schoenberg or Stockhausen if they were not told the name of the composer. In fact, as recently as the 1950s, when the Budapest Quartet programmed a late Beethoven quartet, there were towns in the United States that would threaten to cancel their concerts.

Carter is as intransigent as Wagner or Beethoven. Not only has he refused ever to write a piece of twelve-tone music, but he has never succumbed to the neotonal fashion, a style that annoys today's audience somewhat less than the modernist style because it has familiar-sounding triads—they still rightly prefer Mozart and Brahms. But it should be clear that today's neotonal music is not tonal like Mozart's, which was much more highly structured and ordered. All the modern tonal music I have heard is loosely and simply organized, incapable of the subtle articulations and complex significance we find in Haydn or Beethoven.

Every note in a work by Mozart is related to the basic key of the entire piece and acts in accordance with that relation. This well-defined coordination was slightly loosened in the nineteenth century, blurred by the increasingly rich chromatic palette. Composers from Schumann to Wagner and Debussy had to unify their pieces by an obsessive use of short motifs that would dominate the texture; different motifs for each piece would give individuality. However, the renunciation of motivic repetition by modernists from Boulez and Stockhausen to Carter, Milton Babbitt, Brian Ferneyhough, and many others has made new work initially even more difficult to comprehend. The Carter centennial celebrations have been a joy to those who knew and loved the music, but there have been a few scattered critical protests from journalists who find the music antipathetic or simply puzzling, protests that are the sign of a genuine and healthy interest in the contemporary scene.

It is sometimes thought that if one can first recognize the emotion or the sentiment represented by the music, then one can end up understanding the music. This is a serious misapprehension. When I played Carter's *Night Fantasies* some years ago in Toronto, a local journalist complained that there was no emotion in the music except what the pianist put into it. I thought then, and still think now, that I was bringing the emotion out, not putting it in. Only when one understands how the music works (that is, consciously or unconsciously, feels at ease with the music) can one perceive the emotion.

At the end of the eighteenth century, the editor of the most distinguished music journal complained that Johann Sebastian Bach, suddenly more in view in the 1780s, was a great contrapuntal technician but had no knowledge of the human heart. Decades later, the emotional power of Bach became obvious, but it took a lot of careful listening.

How does one understand a new style? Not by studying music theory, but the way children learn language, by listening to their parents and siblings. Unlike language, music cannot convey information (like "Meet me tomorrow for lunch"), so we have only to learn how the sounds are ordered, and not an elaborate vocabulary. We listen until the ordering becomes familiar, and we absorb the style and learn what to expect.

But why would anyone ever listen again to something that is irritatingly unintelligible? In a museum, when I dislike or don't understand a picture, I pass on to the next wall or the next room. But in a concert hall, I am obliged to sit there listening to something of which I can make neither head nor tail, feeling like an ignoramus—which, indeed, I am for that moment. (My first experience of a Bartók quartet, when I was sixteen, produced a sensation of nausea.) Why would I continue listening and try again? Because a friend or a professional has told me that the music is great, or because I know that it is fashionable and I wish to be in the swim. There is always a certain amount of snobbery about culture, and sometimes it is pernicious (and we pretend to like what we secretly detest), but sometimes it is useful and we get hooked on a new style that will give us pleasure for years to come.

The last hundred pages of the *Centennial Portrait* are a witness to the passion that Carter's music has stimulated in so many performers. To understand the power of the work of the recent decades, one might try the inspired recorded performance of the Cello Concerto by Fred Sherry, conducted by Oliver Knusson, a lyrical and even tragic work, written when Carter was only ninety-two, which escapes all the generalizations often made of intransigent modernism. It is from performances like this that one realizes that the music of Elliott Carter offers pleasures and delights that no other composer can offer.

The *Centennial Portrait* excels in its account of Carter's steady development and his integration into the musical life of the last half of the twentieth century. Not often discussed in the literature devoted to him, however, is the richness of his contacts with the long history of the Western tradition. Some years ago, I spoke to him of my admiration for the originality of a few measures of virtuoso figuration in his Piano Concerto. He smiled and said, "Oh, that just comes from the Chopin Études." And so it does. However, it does not sound like Chopin, but only remarkably like Carter.

CHAPTER 14

Frédéric Chopin,
Reactionary and Revolutionary

W HEN CHOPIN, born two hundred years ago in 1810, died in 1849 at
the age of thirty-nine, his work was firmly established as a permanent
part of the central musical tradition, his influence felt throughout the musical
world of the West. Critical opinion, however, even among his greatest admirers
was by no means wholeheartedly favorable. Having devoted himself almost
entirely to the piano (along with three works for the cello), and with no symphony, no opera, no liturgical work, he could not be granted the status of a
truly major figure. Because of his fragile health and the extraordinary grace
and delicacy of some of his compositions, he was labeled effeminate. Indeed,
most of the students who took lessons with him were women—but the same
was true of Liszt, who did, however, teach some famous masculine lions, like
Karl Tausig, Emil von Sauer, and Moriz Rosenthal, who roared interpretively
at the piano.

Chopin's concentration on the genres of salon music considered trivial—
nocturnes, mazurkas, waltzes—placed him among the miniaturists. Critics
could not grant unqualified approval to his often unconventional forms, and to
the disconcertingly modern chromatic harmony of his last pieces. These compositions, they felt, were the morbid work of a sick, dying man—this was even
the verdict of Liszt, who wrote a little book on Chopin soon after his death
(most of it actually put together by his mistress, the Princess Sayne-Wittgenstein).
Liszt regretted this judgment soon after, but even in the book he had observed
that the sick and morbid works had the most interesting and fascinating

harmonies. As an emigrant Pole living in Paris, Chopin appeared to stand outside the main lines of nineteenth-century tradition—German instrumental music and Italian opera. Nevertheless, although he never published a fugue or composed an opera, his work reveals a deep understanding of both traditions.

This reputation of a limited miniaturist remained critical orthodoxy until well into the second half of the twentieth century. Pianists, on the other hand, have never paid any attention to the critical consensus. The most influential writer on Chopin in English before the 1990s, Gerald Abraham, remarked that although Ballade no. 1 in G Minor is impressive, no one could consider it formally a masterpiece. Few pianists have had any difficulty appreciating the mastery of its eccentric form, breaking most of the classical rules with panache, unifying all its different textures into a narrative whole.

The orthodox view of Chopin as a miniaturist is now pretty much obsolete, exploded, discredited. Many of the large works—ballades, scherzi, sonatas, great polonaises, fantasies, barcarolle—are longer than an average movement of Beethoven. Chopin was, in fact, the only composer of his generation who never, after the age of twenty-one, wrote a long piece that was ineffective. Many of Schumann's larger works (although not, of course, the finest) have uninspired moments that raise problems for their interpreter of sustaining the interest. There are deserts with few oases in a number of works of Berlioz; and there are not many works of Liszt that are completely exempt from some facile and even trashy pages. But the elegance, distinction, and efficacy of Chopin's large forms are almost unique for the time in their success.

For interpreters, the difficulty of playing Chopin is most often found in realizing his most original ideas, not in covering up or glossing over an occasional miscalculation or lack of inspiration as we have to do with Schumann, Mendelssohn, and Wagner. Even Chopin's two piano concertos have always worked successfully in public, although they are perhaps his weakest large-scale works; they were written between the ages of seventeen and twenty-one, after which he significantly abandoned the form for the rest of his life, but they are beginning to find new critical favor today (in spite of the orchestration, about which we are not certain how much of it is authentic or the result of later interventions.)[1]

To accompany another pianist with a reduction for a second piano of the orchestral score of one of these concertos is an interesting experience. When I did this once, I felt as if I were playing the accompanying continuo or figured-bass part for organ or harpsichord of a Bach cantata. Chopin made a lifelong

1. The only one of his large-scale pieces that is somewhat unsatisfactory, the Allegro de Concert, is clearly the draft for a third piano concerto that he never finished, but published years later as a solo piece.

study of Bach, and the results are perceptible in all his work: he knew mainly *The Well-Tempered Klavier, The Art of Fugue,* and a few keyboard concertos, since Bach, whose educational works were already familiar for many decades to professional musicians, was only beginning to be brought to the attention of a larger public.

Chopin, like Beethoven, Schumann, and Liszt, was raised on *The Well-Tempered Klavier.* He never performed any of the fugues in public, but when he warmed up for a recital, he always did so by playing a Bach fugue. And he declared that the music education of his time was fundamentally wrong, because it now started with harmony, reserving the study of counterpoint for a following year, instead of beginning with it, as had been the case throughout the eighteenth century.

In this respect, Chopin, although among the most radical musicians of his time, was deeply conservative and even reactionary. For him, counterpoint was the basis of all composition, and in conversation with friends like the painter Eugène Delacroix, he illustrated this point by citing Mozart rather than Bach. It was not just the learned and ostentatious display of fugues and canons that he thought important, but the hidden contrapuntal mastery—the voice-leading, as it is called—of the different inner and outer lines in all music.

Except for a few very early virtuoso pieces, he rarely used Polish melodies in his work, even in the mazurkas and polonaises. Indeed, in the mazurkas, he draws on, and very often mixes, the radically different mazurka rhythms in a highly original fashion with little regard for the authentic reproduction of the folk elements. He even wrote a mazurka in Scotch style with bagpipe effects, and another mazurka quotes an aria from Rossini. In fact, his treatment of Polish folk style anticipated the freedom of Debussy's Spanish music—Debussy never went to Spain, but used flamenco motifs and rhythms heard in Paris—a freedom that inspired the admiration of Manuel de Falla, who declared that Debussy taught Spanish composers how to write Spanish music. In the same way, Chopin used fragments of melodies, short rustic motifs, harmonic turns of phrase, and guitar sonorities, and produced new forms of music that were sui generis, without precedent in either folk or art music. According to recent research, however, he seems to have been influenced harmonically by chromatic Jewish folk music heard in Poland, which did not prevent him from being offhandedly as conventionally anti-Semitic as many other Poles.

His command of the style of Italian operatic melody was astounding. Most composers were indebted in some way to this most popular of all musical styles of the early nineteenth century, including Beethoven, Schubert, and Liszt; but in some of Chopin's nocturnes—the B Minor Sonata, and the Barcarolle (modeled on the barcarolle duets for two sopranos that Rossini produced for Parisian salons)—he showed a mastery that brought him very close to Vincenzo Bellini, one of the few contemporaries whose music he genuinely admired. He had already developed his skill in Italian style with the Andante Spianato, probably before becoming well acquainted with Bellini's works. He did adapt the opening of a cello melody from *Norma* in an étude, but he transformed it into an imitation of an operatic duet for tenor and soprano.

The spianato style (letting the voice float smoothly and in long, unbroken lines over the accompaniment) was typical of Bellini, and it is the foundation of some of Chopin's most powerfully expressive and idiosyncratic achievements. The style of Italian opera even appears frequently in the most ethnic and folk-like of Chopin's Polish works, the mazurkas, generally in a central lyrical interlude that provides a contrast to the emphatically rustic outer sections.

Not only do his mazurkas incorporate operatic style, but it is also in the late mazurkas that Chopin most openly dared to show off his study of Bach. There are mazurkas that tactfully demonstrate the formal procedures and textures of the fugue, and his last published mazurka even plays the main theme as a two-voice canon at the end. Most editors give an easy fingering for this canon that divides some of the notes between the two hands, but Chopin clearly indicated that he wanted the two voices of the canon played by the right hand alone, making it excessively awkward; it would seem as if counterpoint for Chopin was something to be felt physically, through the nerves and muscles as well as the ear. Gluck was known as the German who wrote Italian music in France: we might call Chopin the Pole who wrote Italian and German music in Paris.

Polonaises had been written by many composers before, including Bach, Mozart, and Beethoven; Schubert, in fact, wrote lots of them. But nothing like the violence of Chopin's military polonaises, for example the polonaises in A Major and A-flat Major, had been heard previously. Even more original were the tragic polonaises, which reveal a passion and despair unknown in salon music and generally reserved for the operatic stage or the most dramatic sonatas and symphonies. The military polonaises were certainly understood as political statements of patriotism for his country, which was struggling to obtain its freedom. While these military polonaises have a decidedly popular character, the tragic polonaises are too radically personal to be understood simply as public statements.

The études of Chopin are a triumph of the ambition of Romantic ideology: to raise an insignificant and despised form of art to the sublime, as William Blake had transformed doggerel moral poems for children into the *Songs of Innocence*. They had a profound influence on later generations, each étude using only one specific technical difficulty, resulting in a limited, unified, idio-syncratic, and striking sonority in every case. The étude in thirds uses only thirds in the right hand, and this opened up the possibility for later composers to create works in which one sonority obsessively dominated the whole, a possibility exploited later by Debussy, Ravel, Scriabin, Prokofiev, and Berg.

In the Preludes, Debussy wrote a piece with nothing but thirds ("Les tierces alternées"). Debussy originally intended to dedicate the twelve études, his last great piano work, to Chopin, but substituted Couperin because World War I made him patriotically feel that a French composer should be honored; yet the inspiration of Chopin is evident throughout, even when it is manifested chiefly by the desire to do something different. Chopin's thirds are all in the high register, for example, while Debussy's étude in thirds puts the thirds mainly in the bass. Debussy's étude for eight fingers (using the thumbs would only get in the way of the continually crossed hands in this piece) is indebted profoundly to Chopin, since it is a monophonic piece in rapid perpetual motion like the finale of Chopin's Sonata in B-flat Minor, an extreme work that shocked even Chopin's admirers. Schumann wrote that one could be impressed but could not praise it, for it was not music. Chopin retaliated by telling a French publisher not to bother to publish Schumann's *Carnaval,* for it was not music; he probably did not appreciate the parody of himself in the *Carnaval,* which is indeed not like his style except for a passionate, arabesque-like ornament with some Chopinesque fingering.

Chopin's influence on piano technique was individual. As a pianist, he was an autodidact and did not believe in the current orthodoxy that one should practice to make all the fingers equally powerful. On the contrary, he felt that delicate passages could best be executed only with the fourth and fifth fingers, and that emphatic and eloquent phrases could be realized with the thumb or third finger alone.

His influence is hard to calculate because it appears where one would never suspect it. Wagner, for whom Liszt often played a good deal of Chopin, was heavily indebted to his work (the development section of Chopin's B-flat Minor Sonata already shows a typically dense Wagnerian texture combining continually repeated leitmotifs, a sequential chromatic phrasing that became typical of Wagner, and powerful rhetorical phrases that remind us of Amfortas in *Parsifal*). Brahms studied him carefully (but when somebody remarked on his borrowing early on, he testily claimed that he had never heard nor seen a work of Chopin in his life). Later Brahms edited one of the finest and most faithful publications of some of Chopin's works, including the ballades, sonatas, and mazurkas, almost the only one of its time to reproduce correctly Chopin's own phrasing and indications for the pedal. He learned from Chopin how to use a strict eight-bar phrase rhythm without monotony, by beginning the melody sometimes on the second or eighth bar instead of relentlessly on bar 1; in other words, he imposed a supple melodic rhythm over a strict rhythmic background.

Liszt and Rachmaninov borrowed openly and extensively from Chopin. So pervasive was his influence that it reached technically into all forms of piano writing and harmonically into the whole of Western style, including the avant-garde modernism of Elliott Carter.

Chopin's music has no humor, except for a certain elegant wit present in some of the preludes and mazurkas. However, the intensity of most of his works, large-scale and miniature, generally surpasses that of all his contemporaries. It is perhaps not hard to pinpoint the source of this extraordinary intensity. It arises from the strange combination, on the one hand, of the techniques he mastered, the long-breathed sustaining of Italian melody, supported as no Italian opera composer knew how to accomplish, by the contrapuntal texture, and on the other, with the richness and continuous expressive interest of the inner voices that he learned from his study of Bach and Mozart. To this he added his adventurous and radical experiments in chromatic harmony that appalled his contemporaries but were exploited by later generations. Rarely disturbed by the ostentatious virtuoso effects of Liszt, never diluted by sallies of eccentric humor as in Schumann and Berlioz, and never hemmed in by the prudent classicism of Mendelssohn's art, much of his music has an intense, focused passion hardly ever equaled in the years between Beethoven and Wagner.

CHAPTER 15

Robert Schumann,
a Vision of the Future

O F ALL THE COMPOSERS who have made a permanent contribution to the standard concert repertoire and who have radically altered the subsequent history of classical music, Robert Schumann, whose bicentenary we celebrate this year, has inspired the greatest misunderstanding. The misunderstanding began with his own conception of his genius and his place in history.

As a young man in Leipzig, by the age of twenty-nine he created a revolutionary new form of piano music, a collection of character pieces—portraits of friends, popular dances, landscape or mood pictures—that were not just heard as individual numbers but that formed a whole. Each set could be experienced as a single work and astonishingly, each even had something like a narrative structure, starting with stability, increasing in dramatic tension, and ending with a resolution, sometimes triumphant and brilliant, sometimes movingly poetic. Among these works are *Papillons*, *Carnaval*, the *Davidsbündlertänze*, the *Kinderszenen*, and *Kreisleriana*. Schumann himself remained ill at ease with his achievement, claiming that we had enough composers who could write short character pieces and what we needed was truly serious work—sonatas, symphonies, and quartets. In other words, what the age called for was a successor to Beethoven.

When his great series of piano works came mostly to an end by 1840, Schumann began to write songs. This was a musical form he had previously considered unworthy of the consideration of a truly ambitious composer. Now he set poems by Heine, Eichendorff, Chamisso, and others, and in a year and a half he had produced 125 songs. Building on the work of Franz Schubert, he revolutionized the German lied with a new understanding of the relation of the sung melody to the accompaniment. He created song cycles like his great piano sets in which all the songs were understood as part of a single unified work, but in which the piano accompaniment played a role equal in importance to the vocal line.

Schubert had often set the scene of his songs with an opening phrase in the piano, but Schumann's most striking innovation was the occasional long postlude in the piano, sometimes incorporating entirely new material, making an elaborate, pure instrumental commentary on the matter of the song. He also expanded the range of musical representation far beyond any of his predecessors, with effects of irony and sarcasm, ecstasy and desperation.

After that, he devoted himself largely to composing ambitious musical forms that were supposed to be important—symphonies, oratorios, quartets, and so on. He occasionally wrote some songs later, but they are rarely as effective as those from the monumental production of his twenty-ninth and thirtieth years. Among the works in large classical forms such as his symphonies, there are many fine things to be found, but they do not often compare in power, energy, and originality with the great piano sets and song cycles of the previous decade.

One pattern emerges in Schumann's life: with each new form or medium, he tended to write himself out as if possessed. The wonderful piano concerto that came shortly after the song cycles was originally a single-movement work (like Schubert's *Wanderer* Fantasy) that really encompassed four movements—an allegro, a slow movement, a scherzo, and a return with final coda. His wife, Clara Wieck, a famous pianist, demanded two more movements, and he supplied them—and they are excellent, but much lighter and less passionate, with more of the brilliance and character of salon music. Two other works for piano and orchestra came later and have never won favor, and are far less interesting in almost every way.

The only one of his large works of chamber music to achieve real popularity is the first, the Quintet for Piano and Strings. During the 1840s, he became briefly interested in a piano with a pedal keyboard like an organ and composed six exquisitely beautiful canons for it (Debussy arranged them for two pianos to make performance more convenient). Four later pieces for this instrument are sadly of little interest. The creative drive of the decade from the age of twenty-one to thirty-one largely dissipated, in spite of a few extraordinarily fine pieces like the slow movement of the C Major Symphony and the first of the *Songs of Spring* for piano, based on poems by Hölderlin.

A composer's greatest achievements are often inspired as much by his deficiencies as by his natural talents. Beautiful melodies did not come as easily to Beethoven as to Mozart, nor did he have that easy facility for counterpoint that

Mozart possessed, but he managed to come out with some of the most original melodic ideas when he needed them, and by sheer force of will he elaborated a new kind of counterpoint that rivaled J. S. Bach and Mozart—in fact, it seems to me that his difficulty in working it out is perceptible to listeners, and this gives his counterpoint a force that we find nowhere else, as if we experience the willpower necessary for its conception.

In the same way, it was Schumann's weaknesses that inspired the most original conceptions that had the greatest influence on later composers. In his famous essay on Berlioz's Fantastic Symphony (Schumann was a great musical journalist), he characterizes the contemporary metric system of music as a prison. He was inspired in this by a passage from a novelist, Johann Ernst Wagner, a disciple of Jean Paul (Schumann's favorite contemporary writer), who remarked that the nightingale pours out her song in free rhythm, unconstrained by the strictly and uniformly measured bars that afflict composers. Basically, almost all music of the time was measured out by two to four beats to a bar, with a clear strong downbeat at the beginning of each bar that defines the rhythmic shape. In addition, from about 1730, a slower beat was almost always superimposed, grouping all the bars by four or eight, the first of which had a heavier accent.

This convention has lasted until our time; it articulates the harmony clearly, and was certainly influenced by the conventions of dance steps. The four- or eight-bar grouping, largely regulating the harmony as well as the rhythm, made possible the great jazz improvisations of the twentieth century from Art Tatum and Teddy Wilson to Miles Davis (if one could take for granted the background harmonic structure, one could imaginatively overlay the improvisation without fear). The regularity of the four-bar phrase is also useful as it has an almost physical effect, nearly hypnotic in carrying the listener along with the music, a characteristic absolutely crucial from boogie-woogie to rock music.

Nevertheless, the rigid and banal grouping by four bars was very often felt as a burden that limited creation. Schumann suggested that perhaps Berlioz might become the composer to recapture the liberty of the nightingale with a more spontaneous rhythm. Quoting Johann Ernst Wagner, he writes that "he who is destined to conceal and render imperceptible the tyranny of the bar in music will, at least apparently, set this art free." Schumann, indeed, affirms this aspiration as an ideal of his age, a return to the freedom of the state of Nature:

> It seems that in the present instance, music is trying to return to its origins . . . and to achieve on its own a prose style or a higher poetic articulation [as in Greek choruses, or the language of the Bible, or Jean Paul's prose].

It is true that composers after 1830 were attempting to find a more continuous and unified flow, free of the sharply defined separate phrases with short contrasting motifs found in eighteenth-century music. Unfortunately, however, no important composer was more constrained by the law of the downbeat and the four-bar phrase grouping than Schumann. Mozart, when he wanted, could compose five-bar and seven-bar phrases that sounded very natural. When Schumann on a rare occasion writes seven-bar phrases (as in the eighth piece of the *Davidsbündlertänze*), it is clear at once that a bar is missing, and the listener is jolted eccentrically.

Chopin, in the ballades, could create irregular phrase lengths that were always convincing; when he kept to rigid eight-bar phrase sets for harmonic organization, he generally achieved effects of great variety and suppleness by beginning the melodic phrase sometimes on the second or the eighth bar. Schumann, on the other hand, frequently betrays a difficulty in varying his rhythm without giving an impression of willful awkwardness (sometimes exploiting the awkwardness for dramatic effect in his finest works).

Critics have long complained of his relentless and unvaried use for successive pages or even for whole movements of one rhythmic figure, particularly dotted rhythms. At times, the performer is saddled with the difficulty of trying to avoid monotony by changing tone color and dynamics. It is true that Schumann's lack of ease in varying the basic rhythm often produces a powerful, impelling drive to the music, and it also accounts for the unparalleled frequency in his music of indications of very brief tempo changes. Schumann's manifold indications of *ritardando* generally last only for a second or fraction thereof.

Nevertheless, it is from this weakness that in many experimental pages, Schumann evolved a novel technique of attacking the downbeat and blurring the meter. No other composer so frequently made it impossible for a listener to perceive where the downbeat is for long sections without looking at the printed score. The standard technique is a simple one: if there are four notes to a beat, the accent will be ONE-two-three-four; but Schumann will suddenly shift to one-two-three-FOUR repeated many times. If this new emphasis is sustained long enough (as in the Toccata for Piano and parts of the great Fantasy in C Major), the listener will think that the downbeat, indicated by the bar line, has shifted. In the Toccata, at the final climax, the shift is sustained for a very long section, and then with greater violence the left and right hands, playing fortissimo, suddenly closely alternate both downbeats on the fourth and first notes, as if two metric worlds astonishingly and confusingly coexisted.

At the opening of the important set *Kreisleriana,* for seven bars all the left-hand accents are on beats 2 and 4, and then in bar 8 there is a surprising fortissimo crash on 3, muddling the listener's rhythmic expectations, and when the theme returns at the end, all the accents are now on beats 1 and 3. In the second scherzo to the Sonata in F Minor, the downbeat is not made clear for several pages.

These experiments anticipate many of the developments of the twentieth century from Stravinsky and Schoenberg to Pierre Boulez and Elliott Carter, and were supplemented by those pages of Schumann, like the last piece of *Kreisleriana,* where the left hand consistently comes in most often harmonically as well as rhythmically on the wrong beats, creating what may be called a rhythmic as well as a harmonic dissonance.

In these experimental pages, Schumann found small-scale, eccentric ways of undermining the conventional rhythmic system of his time. He was the most literary of all composers, modeling some of his pure instrumental works like *Papillons* and *Kreisleriana* on novels by Jean Paul and E. T. A. Hoffmann and on poems by Heine and Hölderlin. The puzzling and disturbing effects are musical parallels to the deliberate cultivation of irrational traits in Romantic poets from Blake and Coleridge to Hölderlin, Heine, Lenau, and many others.

In Schumann, the effect of destabilizing the expectations of his listeners is idiosyncratic and very personal. How deliberately personal his aesthetic outlook was may be seen in his double self-portrait in *Carnaval,* "Eusebius" and "Florestan," respectively the names of the introvert and extrovert sides of his personality. Neither piece ends conventionally with the tonic key note in the bass. Indeed, "Florestan" does not properly end at all, but explodes in exasperation with a repeated and violently hammered dissonance, left hanging in the air, and after a pause we just go on to the next piece.

A controversy twenty years after Schumann's death casts an extraordinary light on another of his innovations, one even more fundamental and influential that radically changed the history of music. In 1879, in a journal controlled by Richard Wagner in Bayreuth, a vicious attack on Schumann appeared, written by Joseph Rubinstein, a young Jewish idolater of Wagner, who had persuaded Wagner to engage him as an assistant and served faithfully until Wagner's death (shortly after which he committed suicide). The article attacked Schumann's great songs, characterizing them as cheap salon music.

The great Norwegian composer Edvard Grieg, grateful to Schumann for the inspiration of so much of his music (the piano concerto, in particular), wrote an indignant answer to the article. He was shocked above all that the attack should come from the circle of Richard Wagner because, as he correctly pointed out:

> In his treatment of the piano, Schumann was . . . the first who, in a modern spirit, utilized the relation between song and accompaniment, which Wagner has later developed to a degree that fully proves what importance he attached to it. I refer to the carrying of the melody by the piano, or the orchestra, while the voice is engaged in the recitative.

What Grieg means here by the contrast of melody and recitative is the appearance of the melody in both voice and piano or orchestra, with a regular rhythm in the instruments but a more idiosyncratic rhythm for the voice that reflects the rhythm of the words as they might be spoken. Playing the same melody simultaneously in differing rhythms is called heterophony. It is presumed to have existed in classical Greece, when voice and instrument would execute the same phrase with different rhythmic inflections. Grieg tactfully does not ascribe conscious plagiarism to Wagner, adding, "for all that, it is a fact that contemporaries influence each other whether they want to or not."

One must go further, however. Related to this heterophonic aspect is the practice of Wagner, already found in the songs of Schumann, of leaving the vocal line fragmentary and unresolved, to be completed by the instruments. Or vice versa—to have an incomplete instrumental line finished by the voice, an essential Wagnerian technique already demonstrated to a sophisticated degree by Schumann. Essentially, they both often conceive a melody differently realized by both voice and accompaniment, sometimes one superimposed over the other, or incompletely by one to be finished by the other.[1] In both, the melody is independent of its specific realization by voice or instrument, and comes into being only as a collaboration. In the second song of the *Dichterliebe,* for example, the singer never gets to finish the melody, ending three times with the penultimate note on a dissonant harmony, leaving the piano to resolve the phrase with an offhand and simple pianissimo.

It is wrong to see this as the result of Schumann's songwriting alone. The technique was elaborated by his great piano works in the decade preceding the songs. Here, the melody is often independent of whether the range is treble or bass, existing simultaneously in the right and left hands, with a regular rhythm in one hand and an expressive, almost speaking rhythm in the other. Above all, in hundreds of places, neither right nor left hand has the complete melody, but requires a continuation in another part of the piano to be resolved. A dissonance unresolved in the register where it is found never gives the feeling of complete resolution when the resolution is in another instrument or in another part of musical space. No composer before Schumann ever made such expressive use of unresolved cadences, forecasting a fundamental change in the view of the musical language of tonality.

The contrast with Schumann's immediate contemporaries—above all, Chopin—is very great. Almost every bar of Chopin can be analyzed as the realization of four-voice harmony that was academically correct. That came from his lifelong study of J. S. Bach, and one is always aware of the independence of the inner voices in his music. Not so the piano music of Schumann,

---

1. In Isolde's *Liebestod,* for example, the first phrase of the soprano is doubled by the clarinet and violin in even notes while the soprano sings a rhythm closer to the spoken word, and the most expressive motif is first played by the clarinet and then finished by the soprano.

who is in this respect the first truly modern composer for today's piano with the sustaining pedal. For him the piano was not the medium for four separate contrapuntal lines but a vibrating instrument for the realization of a single line and its dependent harmonies.

At the opening of the Fantasy in C Major, the right-hand melody is fortissimo and the rapid accompanying notes in the left hand are very soft with the sustaining pedal held throughout, as if they were all echoes of the melody notes in a lower register like the accompanying chords from a string section tremolo. In a performance, if you can clearly hear all the left-hand notes separately, then you know that the pianist has understood nothing about Schumann's conception. He wanted a powerful melodic line and an accompanying blur. Schumann's use of the pedal was often a new aural experience, while Chopin's use always clarified the individual inner voices and the relation to the bass line. It is from Schumann that not only Wagner and Brahms were to develop, but also Debussy and Ravel (the latter with the important influence of Liszt).

This development is also a result of a weakness of Schumann. He did not have the natural gift for counterpoint and voice-leading that we find in Mozart and Chopin. Like Chopin, he studied Bach, but less intensely, and his fundamental lack of appreciation is revealed by his having composed unnecessary accompaniments for the solo violin sonatas of Bach. His condemnation of the great monophonic finale of Chopin's B-flat Minor Sonata is also indicative: "We cannot admire it, for it is not music," he wrote. He could not admire Chopin's ability to create four-voice harmony like Bach from a single line. In his own work, however, reconceiving the different voices of a piece as a single line over different registers required an extraordinary effort of originality. His heterophony was a magnificent substitute for academic counterpoint.

One important, also far-reaching innovation remains to be briefly mentioned: the employment of popular music—not folk music or picturesque ethnic style as his predecessors had used, but cheap urban music, like band music in the public garden and vulgar student songs. The great soprano Elisabeth Schumann always disliked singing the eleventh number of the *Dichterliebe,* a song cycle from Heinrich Heine's collection of lyric poems, *Lyrisches Intermezzo.* It is a brutal poem, and an even nastier song:

> A young man loved a maiden,
> she loved another,
> who preferred still another,
> and she married the first man to come along.
> It's an old story,
> and to whomever it happens,
> it breaks his heart in twain.

Schumann's setting is a shock, jolly, and vulgar. The melody is exceptionally ugly and makes the sarcasm of the music more powerful than the words. Along with the band music in *Papillons* and the Promenade in *Carnaval,* this is a forecast of the dramatic use of cheap urban music in Mahler, Berg, Ives, and Weill. Its insertion into a serious masterpiece is groundbreaking and may be said to anticipate the brief modernist use of the style of cheap fiction in a serious literary work like Joyce's *Ulysses.*

In the *Dichterliebe,* the contrast of this coarse song with the most delicate and intensely poetic sentiment is breathtaking. Of all the Romantic composers, Schumann was the most eccentric and the most private. No one else could achieve both the comic grotesque and the expression of the most intimate pathos. He signed some of his most important early works pseudonymously with the names Florestan and Eusebius. His piano work of the greatest intensity is perhaps the *Davidsbündlertänze* (*Carnaval* was "masks," he said, but this piece was "faces"). He was momentarily indignant when he learned that Liszt and Clara had played it in public.

All his life he feared insanity, and pruned his earliest works on reediting them of any evidence of irrational eccentricity, thereby removing some of the most original and impressive details. After an attempted suicide, he voluntarily consigned himself to an insane asylum, where he died two and a half years later in 1856.

Part Four

LONG PERSPECTIVES

CHAPTER 16

The New Grove's Dictionary Returns

THE BIBLIOPHILE and founding father of French Romanticism, Charles Nodier—or, rather, his invented alter ego, the bibliomaniac Théodore—walking in Paris along the quais of the Seine lined for several miles with secondhand booksellers, was appalled at the vast quantity of recent books remaindered and exposed to the rain and the urban dust, "the inept scraps of modern literature never to be ancient literature. . . . The quais henceforth are only the morgue of contemporary celebrities!"[1] The miles of dead literature arranged in rows were, and still are, terrifying to behold.

Contemplating the development of *Grove's Dictionary of Music and Musicians* from Sir George Grove's personal and almost intimate four volumes of the nineteenth century into the double columns of the twenty tomes of *The New Grove* of 1980 and the twenty-nine of the present revision published in the year 2001, invokes a comparable despair and terror as well as considerable admiration. There are many splendid new articles that delight as well as instruct, but the spectacle of so many thousands of musicians and musicologists of the present and the past whose modicum of interest has either long since evaporated or will

Originally written in 2001 as a review of *The New Grove Dictionary of Music and Musicians*, 2nd ed., edited by Stanley Sadie.

1. Charles Nodier, "Le Bibliomane," in *L'Amateur de livres,* edited by Jean-Luc Steinmetz (Paris: Le Castor Astral, 1993), p. 33.

soon disappear in a few years or even months is awe-inspiring in its breadth. This is heightened by the ambition of the new edition to be up to date, to include recent trends, so many of them clearly unpromising—but who knows, after all, what posterity may find stimulating? Alongside the ephemeral present, *The New Grove* rightly preserves the memory of the once fashionable but now insignificant darlings of the past.

Everything in the universe is, I presume, potentially interesting when seized from the right angle, but all too often an encyclopedic dictionary must simply record the data without indicating where any interest might possibly lie. It is unfair, of course, to judge a specialized encyclopedia by riffling through the pages, particularly one that reads in part like a union directory to the present state of the profession of music history. One will properly consult *The New Grove* from time to time only for a single article, to look up a date, to check a reference. Going through it to see how it has been revised and improved is less like entering into a historical museum of music than into a musicological flea market in which a few treasures are hidden away under immense piles of bric-a-brac. So many articles represent the jetsam washed up by the millennial ocean of music history; and the detritus has only been increased by the new lists and bibliographies, more copious and more useful than before.

Some of the new articles are triumphs. Elaine Sisman's "Variations" will be the definitive treatment of a major musical form for many years to come; its forty-two large double-column pages amount to a small book (although I think that the Brahms-Handel variations are more indebted to Beethoven's *Eroica* variations than to his Diabelli set, as she has it). Andrew Bowie's contribution on Romantic aesthetics to "Philosophy of Music" is equally satisfying (perhaps Johann Wilhelm Ritter's *Fragments of a Young Physicist* should have been mentioned, since his assertion that not only is music the original form of speech, but that everything spoken is accompanied by an inner song, was repeated by E. T. A. Hoffmann in his *Kreisleriana,* and was therefore known to, and influenced, Schumann). David Fanning's welcome new version of "Expressionism" is more cogent than the previous one of Arnold Whittal.

James Webster's "Haydn" is so good that one does not regret the disappearance of the article from the previous edition by the great Jens Peter Larsen. Nicholas Temperley's "Chopin" of 1980 was already an improvement over the account in earlier editions of Grove's, but Kornel Michaelowski and Jim Samson's is still better. John Daverio's "Schumann" is considerably more satisfying than the earlier accounts, and Anthony Hicks's replacement of Winton Deane's elegant "Handel" is fine throughout, well balanced and critically distinguished, as is Roger Parker's new "Verdi." Robert Winter's "Schubert" is as brilliant as one would expect, although more space should, I think, have been devoted to the song cycles. The new "Brahms," by George Bozarth and Walter

Frisch, is an immense improvement on the old article—but why, in the extensive work list and bibliography, is there still no list of the works of other composers that Brahms edited?

The text tells us, for instance, that he edited Chopin, but not that he was responsible for his ballades, sonatas, and mazurkas. Since he was an excellent editor (the mazurkas were the best edition before the new Polish critical edition which just came out last year, since Brahms respected the source he had available), readers should be informed, particularly when one considers the extensive bibliography accorded to so many scholars of lesser competence than Brahms included in *The New Grove*.

Political correctness has had a beneficial influence in the fuller representation accorded to non-Western musics, one of the most important improvements of the new edition, but it has had an influence as well on the article "Exoticism," which concentrates almost as much on fashionable theory as, in a way, on the history of the importation of music from exotic climes into European style. I learned from it that Benjamin Britten used gamelan style to "signal homosexual desire." Did he do so successfully, I wonder—that is, do members of the audience feel or recognize stirrings of homosexual desire when they hear the gamelan style in Britten? "Sex, Sexuality" by Jeffrey Kallberg, and his "Gender" as well, are succinct and persuasive, free from special pleading, and make a case for the importance of these subjects in modern study, and Kallberg is not as defensive as Ruth Solie is in her otherwise excellent "Feminism." The latter subject is allotted double treatment, as it has made its separate way into the article called "Musicology."

In an article in the *New York Times* of January 21, 2001, James R. Oestrich awoke the indignation of Stanley Sadie, editor of *The New Grove*, by claiming that my review of the 1980 edition in these pages was responsible for many of the revisions.[2] In a letter to the *Times*, Sadie insisted that what he called my "animadversions" had nothing to do with any of the changes.

It is only fair to set the record straight: Sadie is perfectly right. As far as I can see, my review can have had no effect on the editorial policy of *The New Grove*. For example, I pointed out twenty years ago that the article "Characteristic [character-]piece" misleads the reader into "the polar opposite of the original meaning." The term "characteristic" here does not mean typical, as *The New Grove* thought, but signifies a work of individual and unorthodox character. It is not clear to me whether Sadie was claiming that he paid no attention to criticism in general or just to my criticism, but in any case his proclamation of editorial independence was fully justified. Here in the newly revised *New Grove* is the article "Characteristic [character-]piece" reprinted in all its glorious idiocy.

2. *New York Review*, May 28, 1981.

In my previous review I quoted two examples of the various foolish statements in *The New Grove*'s article. Let me quote another one for its documentary value:

> Schumann gave the subtitle *18 Characterstücke* to his *Davidsbündlertänze* op. 6. His use of the term there perhaps refers to the characters of Florestan and Eusebius [the two pseudonyms that Schumann used on the title page in place of his own name]: the pieces bear the initials of one or the other (sometimes both) and are accordingly either passionate or meditative.

The eighteen pieces are called *Characterstücke* because they each have an individual character, not because they illustrate two sides of Schumann's personality: they are what the late eighteenth and early nineteenth centuries traditionally called characteristic music. Schumann's Sonata in F-sharp Minor is also signed on the title page by Florestan and Eusebius; it is not, however, a characteristic piece, but an orthodox—or semi-orthodox—sonata without a program. (Symphonies and sonatas with a program, like Beethoven's *Pastoral* Symphony or *Les Adieux* Sonata, were called characteristic symphonies or sonatas.) The attempt to create a basically unique character and form for each piece was one of the central ideals of the period.[3] (Many other small articles, equally mistaken, have been left uncorrected in the new edition.)

Important contributions have not always been newly commissioned, but sometimes only revised—or, on occasion, merely tinkered with—either by the original author or by a second party called in to help. In one case, recourse to a new scholar has resulted in a resounding success. The article on Beethoven by Alan Tyson and Joseph Kerman, one of the most admirable in the 1980 edition, has been brought up to date by the Princeton scholar Scott Burnham (with, I understand, the help of Kerman). More important, Burnham has added a long and brilliant section of nine columns, "Posthumous Influence and Reception," outlining the creation of the mythical figure of Beethoven, his influence on music and musical thought, and his political reception. This superbly extends the original article.

It also reveals the unfortunate lack of editorial policy. There seems to have been no guiding control about what should go into a biographical article. Some have many musical examples; others have none (the excellent notice of Domenico Scarlatti of 1980 with many musical examples has been replaced by an excellent one with none at all). Some end with an account of the reception of the composer's work and his influence after his death: others omit any mention of the subject. This is particularly unfortunate in the case of Johann Sebastian Bach, who, perhaps even more than Beethoven, is the most influen-

---

3. The *New Harvard Dictionary of Music*, in one volume, gives a longer article on characteristic music than the twenty-nine-volume *New Grove*, and it is an excellent account that fully recognizes the importance of the subject.

tial composer in the history of Western music. The editors may think they have covered the posthumous reception of Bach with the article "Bach Revival," but this is parochially confined to England, Germany, and Austria, and is concerned only with the history of performance and stops at 1870. The development of the performance of Bach in the twentieth century, crucial to an understanding of serious music in our time, goes absolutely unmentioned.

Even more serious is that the influence of Bach on composers from Mozart to Saint-Saëns to Schoenberg and Stravinsky, basic to the history of music, is only a vacuum in *The New Grove*.[4] The fundamental role of Bach in music education from Beethoven to Boulez does not exist for its editorial board. The interference of the editors with the contributors' work may have been often exasperating (stories about this are legion), but it seems also to have been capricious, unmotivated by any coherent policy. That is why there is no authoritative voice in *The New Grove:* what distinction the dictionary has, and it is sometimes considerable, comes almost entirely from the independent individual authors.

There is an excellent new article on Richard Wagner by Barry Millington, replacing a hybrid of 1980 in which the life was written by Curt von Westernhagen, and the aesthetics and music were left to the distinguished Carl Dahlhaus, now unfortunately deceased. The new version of the life is very welcome, and Millington's account of the music is interesting and persuasive. However, the twenty pages of Dahlhaus's essay on the music were among the half dozen most distinguished entries in the previous *New Grove,* and some of the finest writing on music of the past half century. To give an idea of what is now missing, I quote two extraordinary paragraphs on *Die Meistersinger:*

> An active element in the plot of *Meistersinger* is the conflict between musical conservatism and innovation, represented respectively by Beckmesser who, as a caricature of a critic (more precisely, of Hanslick), is endowed with the attributes of envy, sterility and the inability to understand anything new, and by Walther von Stolzing, the "natural genius." This contrast becomes confused in the musical realization. It is true that Beckmesser's creative efforts—the serenade and the mangled Prize Song—are given some of the obvious characteristics of outmoded musical practices: mechanical coloratura, modal melodies and perfunctory accompaniments.
>
> On the other hand, Stolzing's songs are anything but "new" music. They are lyrical, in the form of "infinite melody," but in the second half of the nineteenth century "new" music was not lyrical but "characteristic," and the supreme example of stylistically advanced, characteristic music in

4. The article on Bach's son, Carl Philipp Emmanuel, ends with two brief paragraphs on his influence, but stops at 1800. The importance of C. P. E. Bach for Heinrich Schenker, one of the most important twentieth-century theorists, goes unremarked, and a revival of interest in his work today is also overlooked.

Meistersinger is the pantomime for Beckmesser, the traditionalist, in the third act. Wagner as a dramatist may have had the idea of furnishing Stolzing, as the representative of musical progress, with the kind of music that was recognized as progressive in the mid-1860s, but as an experienced man of the theatre he knew better: his triumphant heroic tenor needed music that would have an immediate appeal for the audience, who would identify with the crowd on stage.

With the disappearance of these observations went the last trace of evidence that anyone connected with *The New Grove* had any idea what characteristic music was.

Millington does not remark on the contradiction between Walther von Stolzing as a representative of the avant-garde and the conservative style of the music given to him. He does take up, like Dahlhaus, the music of Beckmesser and the third-act pantomime, and writes:

> The irregular phrase lengths, false accentuations and disorderly progress of the Serenade depict Beckmesser's agitation and supposed artistic sterility, and should not be regarded as symptomatic of an "advanced" musical style (unlike the Act 3 "pantomime" in Hans Sachs's study, which does look to the future in its graphic musical pictorialism).

This is certainly judicious, although Wagner and his more sympathetic contemporaries must have enjoyed the disorderly rhythms of Beckmesser's serenade just as Mozart must have enjoyed all the dissonances and mistakes of composition in his *Musical Joke*. Stylistic progress is often first accomplished by introducing the radical innovations as if they were not really serious; the Romantic play of subjectivity first appears in the comic tricks of *Tristram Shandy*. But what does Millington mean by Beckmesser's "supposed artistic sterility"? There can be nothing supposed about it: Beckmesser is not a real person slandered by Wagner even if he was at first conceived as a caricature of the critic Hanslick (who was not exactly artistically creative), but ultimately a creation of Wagner. If Wagner portrays him as artistically sterile, then that is what he is. Yet if not as profound as Dahlhaus, Millington is always interesting. There is, however, less about the music in the new article than in the old, and far too little about the *Ring* cycle.

The New Grove is not very good on pianists. It tells us that Moriz Rosenthal's "acquaintance and friendship with Brahms began when the composer heard Rosenthal perform his Paganini variations," but it began, in fact, when he listened to Rosenthal play Liszt's fantasy on Mozart's *Don Giovanni*, and invited him to perform the Paganini set. *The New Grove* says nothing about Carl Tausig's important relation to Brahms. About Josef Hofmann, still considered by many as the greatest pianist of the twentieth century, we read "the popularity of his narrow repertory and free, Romantic style of performance waned considerably." Born in 1870, Hofmann's repertoire was immense (he once played twenty recitals in one season without repeating a piece), but he was slightly dyslexic: his repertory was learned by the time he was twenty, and he never played Rachmaninoff's Third Piano Concerto, which was dedicated to him. ("Too many notes," he said.)

Hofmann was certainly Romantic, but his rhythm was far from free: compared to pianists like Busoni, it was often almost metronomic. The problem with *The New Grove* is its policy of refusing to give a discography or to discuss recordings critically when they are occasionally mentioned in the text.[5] In Hofmann's records of 1923 (two Scarlatti sonatas in the Tausig arrangements, the gavotte from Gluck's *Alceste* transcribed by Brahms, the Chopin Waltz in C-sharp Minor, the transcription of the "Magic Fire Music" from *Die Walküre*, and other works), the occasional sensitive rubato is enormously effective by being imposed on an almost absolute regularity. His recording of Liszt's Second Hungarian Rhapsody is, in fact, so rhythmically exact in the opening pages as to be out of style, although still musically extraordinary (Liszt directs *a capriccio*, which implies a free rhythm that was evidently not to Hofmann's taste).

The refusal to include a discography reaches the heights of absurdity with the treatment of jazz. Since most jazz is improvised, unnotated performance, if you do not talk about recordings you are not talking about anything at all that can be documented. The omission of a critical discography for the most important jazz musicians is crippling. Even here, the policy of *The New Grove* is comically inconsistent. To take two jazz pianists, a tiny discography is offered for Bill Evans, but none at all for the great Art Tatum. And there is none whatever—believe it or not—for Miles Davis (although a few lines notated of one of his improvisations are offered, without the harmonization which would make it completely intelligible). A discussion of some of the records in the text is no substitute for a proper list: the same respect should have been paid to the great jazz musicians that was given to the composers of classical music.

This will very probably be the last *Grove's Dictionary* published between hard covers. It is difficult to believe that historians as distinguished as Taruskin, Kerman, and Lockwood will consent to do any important work for future revision that will appear only on the Internet. We must resign ourselves to what we have, and be thankful that some of it is of such high quality.

5. There are, after all, bibliographies and work lists for François-Benoît Hoffman, Richard Hoffman, Jaromír Hoffman, Eucharius Hoffmann, Melchior Hoffmann, Richard Hoffmann (not to be confused with Richard Hoffman), and Lothar Hoffmann-Erbrecht (who is granted not only a bibliography but, unlike Brahms, a list of composers and works he edited).

CHAPTER 17

Western Music:
The View from California

I

A history of Western music is, more or less, a history of all the music that has a history—that is, a large body of musical works that stretch from a distant past to the present through a series of stylistic revolutions. Other civilizations, India in particular, have magnificent musical traditions, but few authentic, documented musical works survive from their past. Only in the West was there an elaborate system of notation that delivered the musical artifacts of more than a millennium to the future, and, as a consequence, only in the West has there been an extravagant historical development from the Gregorian chant of the tenth century to the symphonic complexities of Wagner and Stravinsky, and the triumphs of modernism. Western music, in short, has a history that can be placed in richness and complexity by the side of a history of literature and a history of the visual arts.

The distinguished musicologist at the University of California at Berkeley, Richard Taruskin, has wisely made the invention of a system of notation the basis of his long history (wisely, that is, until the twentieth century, when the decision hits some snags, as we shall find). This is, like almost all others, a history of "literate" music in the West—that is, a history with verifiable historical

Originally written in 2006 as a review of *The Oxford History of Western Music,* by Richard Taruskin.

evidence, the notated scores from the eleventh century to our time. This "literate" body of music existed alongside an important unwritten tradition of folk music and popular music, handed down orally and by demonstration. Of course, "literate" music, too, has never been taught or communicated by notation alone: how to read and interpret the texts has been transmitted by example from one generation to the next. No notation (except that for electronic music) can indicate every detail of performance, much of which has been left to the individual performer, but within a tradition learned by experience and imitation.

This makes for a difficulty that has irritated philosophers of aesthetics and their readers for a long time: Is the work of music to be identified as the written text or its performance? Is a symphony of Beethoven the printed score or the sound in the concert hall when it is played? The printed text is invariable while two performances are never exactly alike. Most histories of music, therefore, have settled for being histories of texts, but this has become more and more unsatisfactory as our knowledge of the performance practice of the past has been widened by research into old accounts, and as we have realized how much we have to know about the habits of performance transmitted "orally" simply in order to be able to read our texts properly. An admirable aspect of Professor Taruskin's project is his intermittent attempt to discuss the parallel "oral" tradition that accompanied our immense heritage of musical scores, including the improvised ornaments often added in the written scores, to take into account the way these scores were actually performed during the composers' lifetimes (although he unwisely assumes that the documents recording these improvisations are a faithful reflection of the practice).

The best part—indeed the glory—of his overstuffed six volumes is the analyses of a huge number of printed examples (the public he has in mind is, of course, the undergraduates who take a general introductory course in the history of music, and his aim is to replace the textbooks that now dominate this lucrative field). His analyses are generally both cogent and entertaining, written in a rambunctious style that conveys technical information with great lucidity.

His intentions, however, are far more ambitious than simply enabling his readers to listen with understanding. He maintains that this is the first history of music which not only relates what was done, but how and why. He aims, he writes, to present a social history of music; that is, he attempts to place the development of music in the general culture of the place and time it was created, to describe it in its social setting, to explain its genesis and its significance for the composers' contemporaries, and at times, for their posterity. He gives a bird's-eye view of the history of Western culture filled out by piquant details (he is particularly assiduous at searching out examples of anti-Semitism). He claims, in short, that he has written the first sociological history of music comparable to Francis Bacon's attempt to embrace the entire history of culture in

The Advancement of Learning, and he observes with a certain satisfaction that Bacon "never lived to complete [his task]: I have—but only by dint of a drastic narrowing of scope."

His inspiration, avowed in his acknowledgments, is the old textbook by his teacher Paul Henry Lang, *Music in Western Civilization,* but unlike Lang, much of whose book was written by his graduate assistants, Taruskin completed his formidable 3,825 pages on his own; never, he declares, has he had a research assistant. He has written a very personal history, often entertaining, self-indulgent, long-winded, occasionally brilliant, and even sensible. He is very levelheaded, for example, on the scarcity of women composers, affirming that it is society, and not any lack of innate talent, that is the reason, but that it is unconvincing to claim that great women composers have been overlooked. (It is a curious misjudgment on his part, however, to give more space to Lili Boulanger than to Ruth Crawford Seeger: of the latter, one of the most interesting composers of the twentieth century, he treats only very minor pieces, neglecting the important string quartet and violin sonata for which she is most admired.)

He claims not to have followed his own taste on what to include: "I hope readers will agree that I have sought neither to advocate nor to denigrate what I did include." His hope has been thwarted. In writing about art, a pretense of objectivity never succeeds: clearly, Taruskin writes much better about music he likes than about music to which he is indifferent. Unacknowledged prejudices loom large throughout the volumes.

2

The opening chapters of Volume 1 on the invention of notation and on the origins of the first written evidence of music, Gregorian chant, are lively and lucid. With the troubadour poets of twelfth-century southern France, the earliest secular musical repertory that is documented, however, we arrive at our first chance of interpreting a musical art with respect to its social setting. Most social interpretation of art views a body of work as the production of a class, generally a dominant or governing class, imposing its ideals. Taruskin affirms it in its simplest form. One of the enduring characteristics of "high art," and a perennial source of contention, is the fact that it is produced by and for political and social elites. Troubadour songs offer a set of works for interpretation that seem to inspire no problem for social interpretation: they are "knightly songs in a European vernacular," as Taruskin puts it:

William, (Guillaume), seventh count of Poitiers and ninth duke of Aquitaine (1071–ca. 1127), was the first European vernacular poet whose work has come down to us. The tradition, socially speaking, thus began right at the top, with all that that implies as to "highness" of style, tone, and diction. . . . A troubador's subject matter was the life he led, viewed in terms of his social relations, which were ceremonial, idealized, and ritualized to the point of virtual sacralization. In keeping with the rarefied subject matter, the genres and styles of troubadour verse were also highly formalized and ceremonious, to the point of virtuosic complexity of design and occasional, sometimes deliberate, obscurity of meaning.

In short, troubadour songs were a courtly art, reflecting the ideals of the feudal aristocracy.

The true heart of troubadour poetry, as Taruskin says, was the love poem, the *canso*. In this form, the loved one is always a young, married woman never to be possessed by the singer, whose love is always hopeless. This is indeed a refined and artificial kind of art, and cannot have corresponded very closely either with the reality or even the ideals of life in twelfth-century Provençal courts (there was a less-refined but also less-admired form in which the two lovers wake up in bed in the morning). There were two kinds of troubadour verse, clear and hermetic (or "closed"), and there were heated defenses of each style, some troubadours practicing both. It has been remarked that it is not always easy to tell the clear from the closed, and that some of the clear is sufficiently complex to have caused difficulty in understanding even to twelfth-century contemporaries.

Troubadour songs were obviously a rarefied, aristocratic form, but what does this mean? Were they written by aristocrats? Sometimes, but many of the troubadours were not at all upper class. Taruskin tells us that Bernart de Ventadorn, one of the most famous and popular, was the son of a furnace-stoker, although he oddly does not tell us that the furnace-stoker was his mother. He claims that Bernart was a commoner "like many of the later troubadours," but some of the best early troubadours were commoners as well—Cercamon and Marcabru, for example. Taruskin also relates that Bernart "rose to prominence, and received noble patronage, strictly on his merits as a poet," but the little we are told by Bernart's biography informs us that his first patron found out that his wife was in love with Bernart, had her locked up, and threw Bernart out. His next patron was the duchess Eleanor of Aquitaine, and, again according to his biography, he fell in love with her and she with him *(s'enamoret de la duchessa, et ella de lui)*. The biography, written a century after Bernart was working, may be fiction, but at least it has more chance of being authentic than Taruskin's speculations. Anyway, the idea that Bernart de Ventadorn made a successful career solely on his poetic merit and not on his personal attraction has no basis except for the evident technical virtuosity of his poetry.

Taruskin knows that the troubadour songs were generally not performed by the nobles but by minstrels, called jongleurs, and affirms that most of the non-aristocratic troubadours started out as minstrels. However, he strangely imagines: "A noble poet would compose a song and teach it to a minstrel, thus sending it out into the oral tradition from which it might be transcribed, with luck, a hundred years later." But, as we have seen, the poet was not necessarily noble, many of them being children of furriers, or notaries, or clerks; the jongleur could have been taught by a poet from the middle class. We do not know how far the art of the troubadours penetrated into the lower classes, but it is unlikely that the popular minstrels confined their performances to the courts. It is also exceedingly snobbish as well as improbable to assume that the complex and often obscure art of the troubadours was appreciated only by the upper class. Does Taruskin think that songs about a pure love for a titled lady would not have appealed to twelfth- and thirteenth-century peasants and urban clerks? It might have been just what they wanted.

The manuscripts containing the troubadour songs were compiled a century after the troubadours had disappeared—or, rather, after their art had migrated to northern France after being wiped out in the south by the Albigensian Crusade. For a hundred years, the songs ceased to be sponsored by the courts. How did they survive if not in other venues, although little is known about them? The evidence for troubadour art is skewed in any case. As Taruskin relates, the manuscripts compiled after a hundred years were all illustrated luxury items, a medieval equivalent of coffee-table books, paid for by later aristocratic courts. How much of the poetry and music was preserved either by the minstrels' memory or by some notation before the surviving written evidence was transcribed we do not know, nor can we tell to what extent the selection made for the manuscripts was representative or biased.

In short, the art of the troubadours was indeed elitist. How could songs in a complex style, some of them difficult to understand even after several hearings, not be so? Perhaps no art has ever been more elitist. Nevertheless, Taruskin's terse formula—"'high art' . . . produced by and for political and social elites"—while obviously true, is uninstructive and unedifying. It is only a fashionable critical slogan. What made up this elite? How did it affect the art? The social situation was more than slightly ambiguous, and the slogan only hides to what extent the poetic and musical art corresponded to the interests of a small class (perhaps, in fact, a small part of a small class) or reflected the ideology of feudal society in general—or, indeed, represented the interests of a professional caste which cut across social distinctions of class.

3

Taruskin returns over and over again to the question of elitism. "Elite" used to have an agreeable connotation, like "liberal," but is now used as a term of reproof.[1] Taruskin approaches the subject with an air of apology or guilt, as if he felt uneasy about enjoying and teaching an art that is accessible only to a minority with the money to pay for it and the leisure to appreciate it. He does not make a sufficiently clear distinction between two different ways that art can be "produced by and for political and social elites." The first way is for a member of the elite to engage a well-known artist to produce something for display. If you commission a famous architect to design your house, that may reflect great credit on your taste, even if you find the house impossible to live in. The second way is to create, or have created for you, a work that will express and mirror your ideals and your way of life, like Raphael's frescoes in the Vatican apartments commissioned by the pope. The second way is preferred by sociological critics because it enables them to construct a subtle analysis of the way the art embodies the ideology of the elite, whatever the identity of the artist. For this to work, however, the elite—political or social—must not only have a recognizable identity, but display some kind of consensus about the world and the way life is to be lived, and we must be able to eliminate the possibility that the artist engaged is not subverting the ideals of the patron for reasons of his own.

The two social classes that generally have the power to commission art are the bureaucratic governing class, either aristocratic or plutocratic, and the well-to-do middle class, or what used to be called the bourgeoisie. The taste of the aristocracy and the upper middle class is not always apt to produce an art that endures, and the more talented artists must sometimes find a place in the margins of the establishment—a rich patron with eccentric tastes, for example. In his characterization of nineteenth-century English culture, Matthew Arnold identified the aristocracy as Barbarians, interested largely in fox-hunting and gaming, and the middle class as Philistines, obsessed with respectability. A great deal of art that goes against the grain is paid for by the establishment unwillingly, and with misgivings. When some of it endures, the sociologist must engage in an agreeable analogue of Freudian analysis, and claim that in hidden ways the work embodies the ideals of the class in power, unaware of

1. "Liberal," which used to be a term of approval, is oddly pejorative in politics today for different sides of the political spectrum on the two sides of the Atlantic—for the right wing in the United States but for the left in Europe, while "elite" is a term of opprobrium on both sides of the Atlantic for both left and right for entirely different reasons—for the right, an "elitist" is an unpatriotic, degenerate left-wing fan of the avant-garde; for the left, he is an undemocratic enemy of the people.

what is revealed by an art of which it overtly disapproves. This is the stimulus for a good deal of criticism today.

Meyer Schapiro, one of the most distinguished art historians of the last century, was reproached by one of his students for having lavished praise on Arnold Hauser's *The Social History of Art*. Schapiro replied that he knew it was bad, "but it's the only one on an important subject, which should be encouraged." A sociological history of art is, as we would all agree, very desirable, but there are difficulties that stand in the way.

To understand the problems of a social history of music, however, let us step back, or rather aside, for a moment, and consider a fascinating essay on the water mill by the great French historian Marc Bloch.[2] In this story of the invention and exploitation of the water mill to make flour, two anomalies stand out. The first odd fact is that the water mill was invented as early as the first century BC, but it took an astonishingly long time—at least five centuries, in fact—for this extraordinarily practical machine that made life so much easier to be widely used. That is because during the Roman period, slave labor was plentifully available. As slavery declined, the expense of building water mills paid for itself, above all when the lord who owned the water rights could make his tenants pay for grinding their grain. The second anomaly is that in the nineteenth century, when steam power provided an even more practical way of making flour, the water mills continued to be used because the local lord could force his tenants to continue bringing the grain to his mill. The processes of invention and exploitation are out of phase. Inventions arrive before they are needed and continue to be employed when they are no longer useful. The history of society and the history of scientific invention do not fit neatly together.

Nor does the history of music fit neatly with social history. Of all the arts, music has the greatest kinship with science, even abstract science: Greek and Roman philosophers speculated about the relation of music to mathematics, and in the latter part of the eighteenth century the philosopher and economist Adam Smith remarked that listening to a fine symphony was like contemplating a great scientific system (it took the long development from the monodic Gregorian chant and the gradual emancipation of music from words for this observation to become possible). A musical system has important attributes of a language, like grammar and syntax, although some of the aspects of communication are very rudimentary—that is, you can convey emotion with music, and imitate cuckoos and babbling brooks, but you cannot make a dinner appointment without words. Nevertheless, as the musical system

---

2. "Avènement et Conquête du Moulin à Eau," first published in *Annales*, vol. 7, no. 36 (November 1935), pp. 538–563, reprinted in Marc Bloch, *Mélanges Historiques* (Paris: SEVPEN, 1963).

changes over the centuries, possibilities of exploiting the musical language suggest themselves that are too fascinating to ignore, but the works inspired by this stimulus may possibly have to wait a long time for their exploitation. A musical system appears to have a logic of its own that can be inflected but not completely controlled by social pressures; it can act as an inspiration to composers, who often feel as if they were discovering rather than inventing. That is what the greatest of music critics, E. T. A. Hoffmann, conveyed when he wrote that Beethoven was not the wild, untamed genius as so many of his contemporaries believed, but the soberest of all composers, because everything he wrote came from the nature of music itself.

Bach's great Mass in B Minor was never performed during his lifetime: as a Catholic Mass, it could not be played in a Protestant church, and the use of an orchestra was forbidden in Catholic churches during Bach's lifetime, although he hoped it might eventually be possible. His *Goldberg Variations* is the most successful of all his works in concert performance today, yet the kind of concert in which it can be performed did not exist for another century, and it had to wait for recognition and acclaim for still another hundred years. Both these works fascinated many musicians during the long period before they could find a niche in the social world of performance. The first great set of works to become the staple of serious public piano performances was the thirty-two Beethoven piano sonatas: only two of these were played in a concert hall in Vienna during Beethoven's lifetime. To judge a work, as Taruskin often does, by how it sounded in the conditions that existed when it was written is useful and even necessary, but it can lead at times to profound misunderstanding. This is where the irritating contradiction between the work as written and the work as heard begins to rear its ugly head.

In any case, many works of music like Beethoven's Great Fugue for String Quartet appear principally as a response to possibilities of the musical system of the time, possibilities that are irrelevant to any kind of contemporary social conditions, and the system itself develops both as a response to social pressures and in ways that are completely independent. No social history of music can succeed that does not acknowledge the partial independence of the musical language, the way it can offer abstract possibilities to the imagination irrelevant to the social and economic world of the musician, but often too tempting to turn down.

4

For the beginning of the period from 1300 to 1600, Taruskin offers a splendid account of Guillaume de Machaut—the first composer to make a four-voice polyphonic setting of the entire ordinary of the Mass. The ordinary of the Mass is the text that is repeated at every service: the Kyrie, Gloria, Credo, Sanctus, and Agnus Dei; in between these sections, the text changes from day to day. Machaut's setting of the ordinary around 1360 is the first large-scale musical work in several movements in history, and it elevated music to the level of greater ambition. Taruskin's writing has the great virtue of making the reader want to hear the music. Equally illuminating is Taruskin's chapter on the next important stage in this development, the use in 1430 of a single liturgical chant to unify the setting of all the sections of the ordinary of the Mass, each section now clearly based on the same easily recognizable melody. This endowed the composition—which came to be called the cyclic mass—with an easily perceptible unity.

A Mass written by a single composer is not only held together by his style, as with Machaut, but is now given a specific identity by the liturgical chant, which appears prominently in every movement. (The practice seems to have started in England, which played a leading role in the musical development of the early fifteenth century, but it quickly spread to the Flemish and French musicians, who were to dominate all European music until the middle of the sixteenth century, even at the Italian and German courts.) These chants were at first taken from the liturgical repertory, but very soon secular songs were used as the basic unifying melodies, a practice that would eventually provoke consternation in ecclesiastical circles, particularly when some of the choir sang the words of the secular tune instead of the liturgical text it was now supposed to serve.

The cyclic mass had enormous prestige from 1450 to 1550, and has been compared to the symphony of the late eighteenth and nineteenth centuries; Taruskin has some persuasive remarks about the comparison:

> It is easy to forget (or ignore, or minimize) the fact that the "movements" of a cyclic Mass Ordinary, the first pair excepted [the Kyrie and the Gloria], were spread out in performance over the whole length of the service, spaced as much as fifteen or twenty minutes apart, with a great deal of liturgical activity, including other music, intervening.

It is indeed difficult to appreciate the musical qualities of the cyclic mass in modern public performance conditions. We should add that some of the cyclic masses contain learned musical procedures which can only be understood by, and give pleasure to, the singers—procedures of a complexity that has never been exceeded, and rarely equaled in the history of music. Taruskin prints one example from a mass by Johannes Ockeghem, in which two choristers (almost certainly solo voices) are given the same musical line to sing at the same time, but one of them sings it eight times as fast as the other and a fifth higher, all this making perfect harmony.

Taruskin's view is strongly argued, and largely convincing, but there are two troublesome points. It is odd to insist so exclusively on the "liturgical and spiritual purpose of the music" when secular tunes were absorbed to become the main melodic interest of the work. Above all, there are the overemphatic scare quotes—too many of them, in fact, placed twice around "esthetically" and twice around "as music." The idea that it was impossible before the late eighteenth century to experience music "as music" is an obsession with Taruskin that reappears many times in the opening tomes. The exaggerated overemphasis here is a sign of anxiety, well founded in my opinion, that the idea is not getting across.

Interestingly, the very aspect of the cyclic mass that makes modern concert rendition ineffective is, in fact, a sign that the composers were eager for their music to be heard "as music" as well as to serve a ritual purpose. Starting each section not only with the same chant, but often presented in exactly the same way, made it possible for the auditors to comprehend the relation of the different sections, even if they were separated by fifteen or twenty minutes of liturgical activity. In any case, it is easy to experience the music as music even while acknowledging the importance of the spiritual or social function. Only too easy, in fact, when dealing with a musical art as extravagant as the Flemish style of the late fifteenth century. We must remember, too, that the religious music of Josquin and his contemporaries was often arranged for instruments like the lute and played privately with no ceremonial function intended: for this to happen, the music must have been appreciated "as music" before the arrangement was made.

Taruskin's eccentric fallacy is his belief that because the word "aesthetic" was not coined before the middle of the eighteenth century, nobody was capable of appreciating an art for its own sake. It is not anachronistic, as Taruskin insists, to think that the public before the late eighteenth century enjoyed music as music, literature as literature, art as art. I am astonished that the old theory current in the 1930s that art and life in medieval society were organically integrated in contrast to modern art is making the rounds again. I thought that we had gotten rid of that foolishness a long time ago. It was not suddenly in 1770 that we acquired the ability to enjoy a work of art either divorced from its ritual or ceremonial use, or sometimes with these ritual meanings absorbed as an integral part of the artistic experience. It is true that the word "aesthetic" does not exist before the eighteenth century, so no one before that time could speak of "aesthetic experience": the terms traditionally employed were "pleasure" and "delight."

5

An extraordinary figure, the Flemish composer Johannes Ockeghem (circa 1410–1497), is not given his due in these volumes, since Taruskin, like so many previous historians, concentrates only on the works with complex musical puzzles, and they are unrepresentative in spite of their fame. He himself remarks on the unfair picture this gives, but does nothing to rectify it. Ockeghem was perhaps the first composer to compose polyphonic music for four voices not by adding one voice after another, but by thinking initially of the complete four-voice texture. The sustained flow of intertwining voices in his music is as fascinating as it is unpredictable. To appreciate Ockeghem's work, one must turn back to Manfred F. Bukofzer's brilliant *Studies in Medieval and Renaissance Music* of 1950.

Immediately following Ockeghem, whom he claimed as his teacher, is Josquin des Pres, the first composer to benefit from the recent invention of printing, and the first composer easy to appreciate by listeners today with very little effort of adjustment to an old style. He is also the first composer to win the kind of fame accorded to literary figures like Dante and Petrarch, or a contemporary painter like Leonardo da Vinci. At the end of the eighteenth century, when scholars attempted to write the history of music of centuries past, he was the first composer to be rediscovered. (Only Palestrina, who came a few decades later, retained his renown until the present, as his works continued to be performed at the Vatican.) Indeed, Josquin was so idolized in the years after his death in 1521 that almost any anonymous piece of music that found favor was attributed to him. In recent years scholars have been pruning the list of his works, and scotching some of the anecdotes of his genius that made the rounds of writers on music in the middle of the sixteenth century.

All this scholarly activity is salutary, but it has given rise to the most unsavory aspect of modern sociological criticism, the attempt not merely to separate legend from reality in the fame of the most important artists of the past, but to dynamite these legendary reputations, to claim that the prestige of whoever seems fair game—Josquin, Beethoven, Shakespeare—is entirely due not to any innate genius, but to a process of brainwashing by the cultural elite in power. This facile and practical substitute for criticism is sometimes mistakenly called deconstruction: one needs no interest in art, music, or literature to pursue it. All references to commonly shared and recognized values can be dismissed since these values are simply a successful imposition by an elite upon the society as a whole. Taruskin is far too intelligent to be taken in by this position in all its crudity, influential as it may be, but traces rub off on him as he tries to remain abreast of the latest developments in his field.

He tells us about the famous letters received by the Duke of Ferrara from two of his agents who were scouting for the best composer to hire for his court. One scout in 1502 wrote that Josquin composes better than Heinrich Isaac, but advised the duke to hire Isaac since Josquin composes "only when he pleases not when he is requested to," and he also demands more money than Isaac. This is the document that allowed historians to refer to Josquin as the first temperamental and difficult genius in music. The other letter, a month earlier, recommended Josquin warmly—"there is neither lord nor king who will have a better chapel than yours if Your Lordship sends for Josquin"—and added "by having Josquin in our chapel I want to place a crown upon this chapel of ours." Taruskin observes: "The Josquin legend had been born, and was already doing its historical work."

However, as we can see, the reputation of Josquin was not a legend but a historical fact. He was considered the finest composer during his lifetime. That his reputation became inflated later with stories, probable and improbable (much like the story of George Washington and the cherry tree), justifies correction, but that still leaves us with the fact of Josquin's immense prestige. It is true that his preeminence has caused scholars to neglect some of his contemporaries who deserve attention, like Pierre de La Rue, a wonderfully original figure whose name is only mentioned in passing by Taruskin. He does not go all the way with the present fashion for cutting Josquin down to size, and actually believes in his superiority. About the motet Ave Maria . . . Virgo serena, which was misdated too late and accepted as a prototype of sixteenth-century style when it really belongs to the period in the 1480s when Josquin worked at the court of Milan, Taruskin remarks, "Far from the revolutionary work that [Edward] Lowinsky sought and found in it, it now appears to be fully representative of its fifteenth-century parent repertory, even if, *as we are all likely to agree, its artistic quality far outstrips that of its companions.*" Nevertheless, he treats the question of Josquin's reputation so exhaustively that, in spite of a few excellent observations on short passages from a motet and a mass, he has no space left to explain why Josquin was accorded such extraordinary reverence.

One reason may be mentioned briefly here: no composer before him (or after him, for that matter) could make such effective use even on a first hearing of the complex imitative devices of Flemish style—the passing from one voice to another and the repetition of short memorable motifs which command the texture of the polyphonic work. This was a technique that was to govern almost all Western music for centuries, and was the glory of Johann Sebastian Bach's style, and the basis for musical style from Haydn, Mozart, Beethoven, Chopin, and Brahms to Schoenberg—all the most famous classics, in fact. Only in the twentieth century was there finally an attempt to escape from what began to be felt as the tyranny of this procedure, a reaction initiated cautiously by Debussy and carried out fully by composers like Varèse, Boulez, and Stockhausen.

Disappointing on Ockeghem and Josquin, Taruskin makes up for it by forty brilliant and satisfying pages on Palestrina, which elucidate his creation of a style so clear and suave that it was to remain a model for many decades, and even a basis for teaching counterpoint for centuries to come. The pages on William Byrd and the way his music reveals the tragic situation of a repressed and defiant Catholic in a Protestant culture are almost as good, although heavily indebted to the researches of Joseph Kerman.

However, when we reach the Italian madrigal, one of the most impressive creations of Western music, we can see why Taruskin's 3,825 pages of text (plus ten pages of introduction, and a whole volume of indices, credits, and chronology) turn out to be paradoxically skimpy. He spends so much time on his theories of the why and how of the music and on his lively and entertaining potted history of culture that there is little space left to do justice to major elements of music history. For many scholars and music-lovers, the greatest composer of madrigals is Luca Marenzio, whose production was immense, and difficult to characterize because, as Alfred Einstein observed, every poem for him needed a different approach and a different solution. Taruskin comments only on the opening of one madrigal. His choice, an extraordinary piece with an immensely long chromatic line, illustrates both the melancholy and the halting steps of the lover in a poem of Petrarch, "Solo e pensoso" ("Alone and pensive"). Taruskin's presentation of this is sensitive. But then he appends the astonishing comment: "The opening couplet of Marenzio's setting of Solo e pensoso is miraculously precise in depicting the poet's pensive distraction, but can an ensemble of five voices represent his solitude?" This is like complaining about a lack of realism in Shakespeare because the actors are all speaking in iambic pentameter. Ninety percent of madrigals must be settings of love poems, and this would imply to Taruskin that four to five lovers are all wooing the same harassed lady. He tries to justify this outlandish position by claiming that Marenzio was aiming at "a literary, not a musical exactness," and in this, he is deeply mistaken, as a single listening will confirm. The modulation of Marenzio's opening, rising over an octave, is grave, wonderfully smooth, and deeply moving even when one takes no account of the words.

Equally unjustifiable is Taruskin's hasty dismissal as "negligible" the chromatic experimentation on instruments contemporary with the similar experiments in the madrigals of Marenzio and Carlo Gesualdo. He even claims that Nicola Vicentino's famous monster keyboard with fifty-three pitches within the octave, which foreshadows twentieth-century experiments with quarter-tones, came to nothing. However, a well-known madrigalist, Luzzaschi, was reputed to have played very successfully on this keyboard. On the outrageous harmonic effects of Gesualdo, Taruskin astutely remarks (it is one of his most brilliant points) that they are not the effects of a composer ahead of his time, as Stravinsky and others have maintained, but are perfectly familiar ingredients of sixteenth-century style. But then so are the weird keyboard experiments, and they are part of the same world as the madrigals.

This is not an anachronistic view: the madrigals of Monteverdi, a composer a generation younger than Marenzio, were attacked by his contemporaries as the accidental discoveries of a man who had just been strumming randomly at a keyboard. (Marenzio's audacities were, in fact, as great as Gesualdo's or Monteverdi's.) The dismissal of the instrumental experiments is a grave methodological error: the history of art can only be understood if the most extreme and eccentric phenomena can be integrated into our view of the whole picture. The extreme cases illuminate the conventional phenomena, the statistically normal. They mark the limits of a style and a period.

In Taruskin's Volume 2, on the seventeenth and eighteenth centuries, a brilliant chapter on Monteverdi's operas brings us to the threshold of music in the modern world, to a repertory that can be performed successfully for audiences today, and it is vivid and satisfying. The social aspect of the music is lucidly dealt with: the first opera, *Orfeo,* was for an invited audience at the court of Mantua in 1607; the last, *L'Incoronazione di Poppea,* thirty-six years later, was for a commercial theater in Venice (the scores of all of the other operas of Monteverdi in between the two were destroyed in a fire during his lifetime). Here, instead of trying to explain the music factitiously by nebulous social ideals, Taruskin shows specifically how the two operas worked within their societies, the solemn ceremony of *Orfeo* contrasted with the sensational and even pornographic aspect of *Poppea.* The musical analysis in this case is as solid as we have come to expect from Taruskin, and facile social generalizations are happily kept at bay. But the modern repertory in the volumes to come will make greater demands on the historian

6

By the middle of Volume 2 of his entertaining, provocative, and massive *Oxford History of Western Music,* Professor Richard Taruskin reaches the repertory familiar to all music-lovers—Bach, Handel, Haydn, Mozart, and Beethoven, with the Romantics from Chopin to Tchaikovsky and Wagner following in the next volume. The landscape changes; writing about the familiar presents new problems. Perhaps the chief one is finding something novel and interesting to say about the most famous figures of the past, revered, written about, and over-analyzed for more than two centuries.

Taruskin's solution has had a certain currency since Lytton Strachey turned his satirical attention to Victorian figures like Florence Nightingale and Cardinal

Manning, casting a cold eye upon the respectable glories of the past, taking them down a peg or two. Taruskin's reassessment is thesis-driven: for him, classical music and all high art in general is produced by and for a social and political elite (although it is not always clear just who belongs to the elite and whether the art created for it was always to its taste), and he feels this to be ignobly undemocratic. Beethoven is his first principal target; his reputation as a heroic figure struggling against critical misunderstanding must have appeared an easy mark.

Taruskin characterizes Beethoven's political opinions as ambiguous at best. While they may have been somewhat inconsistent, his fierce resentment of aristocratic privilege was reported by no less a figure than Goethe. It is true that Beethoven was generously supported by some members of the aristocracy, above all by the most aristocratic of all next to the emperor, the Archduke Rudolph, brother of the emperor and Beethoven's pupil (Beethoven certainly considered Rudolph an exception to his class, observing that he treated people with civility even if they were not well-born).

Taruskin fails to mention Beethoven's democratic leanings, fashionable enough in the decades after the American and French revolutions, but he refers only to his antipopulist remark that he had never believed in the saying *Vox populi, vox Dei*. Well, you wouldn't take much stock in public opinion if you were a composer whose every new work had been savaged mercilessly by the press for thirty years. At the same time, he had his critical admirers, of course, but Taruskin oddly reports this by saying that he had a great success with the aristocracy and the wealthy bourgeoisie; actually, many of his supporters were musicians and music-lovers from more modest reaches of society. He would not have had such a success with wealthy patrons if he had not been backed by the members of his profession.

Taruskin says not a word about the public humiliation of Beethoven by Prince Esterhazy at the first performance of the Mass in C Major, commissioned by the prince, who, on hearing it, said, "My dear Beethoven, what have you done?" and walked out (an incident witnessed by Beethoven's colleague Johann Nepomuk Hummel).

Taruskin ignores the constant negative criticism, virulent throughout Beethoven's life, and refers only to composer Louis Spohr's protests about the Ninth Symphony, characterizing it as "the reaction of one who had known and played under Beethoven in his youth, but who could not accept the new turn the master's art was taking." As a matter of fact, what Spohr said was that the Ninth Symphony was "worse than all of the eight previous Symphonies," which does not suggest that he was objecting only to the new tack.

None of this would matter very much for an understanding of Beethoven's music if Taruskin did not reinforce his tendentious approach by a long and uninspired quotation from the score of *Der glorreiche Augenblick* ("The Glorious

Moment"), written to commemorate the Congress of Vienna, one of the only two large-scale pieces of junk that Beethoven was ever to produce (the other is the *Battle* Symphony, which he composed with Maelzel, the inventor of the metronome). Taruskin compounds this with a failure even to mention the "Prisoners' Chorus" from Beethoven's opera *Fidelio*. In a book that lays claim to being the first social history of music, this omission is hard to justify. The chorus is perhaps the most significant political statement in music of Beethoven's time, and it occurs in an opera about the wrongful imprisonment of an innocent man for political reasons by a despotic governor. At the end of the first act the jailer is persuaded to allow the prisoners to walk briefly in the sun, and they come out hesitantly from the darkness of the prison into the light of which they have been deprived. In its effective musical portrayal of the transition from hesitant fear to the dawning of hope, the chorus is an indictment of the abuses of power and a hymn to enlightened humanity.

This slanted view of Beethoven is the result of an excessively naive idea of musical patronage. Taruskin believes that a composer's music directly reflects the ideology of the class that pays for it, and that, specifically, Beethoven wrote profound and complex music because the Viennese aristocracy paid him to write works that were controversial, hard to listen to, and difficult to appreciate. He does not ask whether the rich patrons who financed Beethoven had artistic inclinations representative of their class, or whether they were mavericks with eccentric taste, a liking for art that was challenging. He does not take into account the desire of professional musicians to make music an art that could be compared to literature and painting, or the tradition of difficult or challenging music kept alive largely in German-speaking countries—in Berlin, for example by Carl Philip Emmanuel Bach, a composer revered by Mozart. In my experience, musicians and artists in general take money wherever they can get it, and look for a patron that will give them the freedom to produce the art that inspires them. They sometimes, but not always, have to compromise, but with any luck they can accomplish what they set out to do.

Following the historian Daniel Heartz, Taruskin attacks what he considers the myth of the supremacy of eighteenth-century German music by insisting that the basic style of the time was Italian. So it was—except that the Germans exploited the style with greater efficiency and more permanent effect. Mozart's operas are still the supreme Italian operas of the time, closely followed by those of Gluck (who used to be called "the German who wrote Italian music in France"). Even Vivaldi's concerti grossi, which were the model for all others, take second place to those of Handel and Bach. As for symphonies in the Italian style, Johann Christian Bach (called the "London Bach," from where he lived) provided the basic model for Mozart, and by the end of the century, the Austrians became great exponents of the style in symphony and concerto.

That is because the German-speaking composers were able to enrich the somewhat facile and simplistic Italian style with the great contrapuntal Flemish technique they continued to preserve and exercise, and of which Taruskin gives so excellent an account in his first volume. He is not interested in this historical development, however, or in the growing admiration for Johann Sebastian Bach by professional musicians of the 1780s.[3]

Taruskin believes that one can write social history by explaining the music with an account of who paid for it. This is simplistic: what is needed is an investigation of how the music functioned in society and the culture of the time, the individuals who played it, financed it, and listened to it. Above all, one must realize that society can inflect and influence the development of style, but only within limits: the musical language of the previous generations, the weight of its history, is a check on any new development, and at the same time a stimulus and inspiration to what can be accomplished in the future. Musical style is not a passive material that can be molded at will, but a system that both resists and inspires change.

At one point, Taruskin takes a step in the right direction with a solid and cogent relation of the championship of Beethoven's chamber music by the members of the Schuppanzigh quartet throughout a great part of his life; but then he draws back from any detailed view of the music that resulted except for one brief passage from the Quartet in B-flat Major, op. 130. There is no consideration of how Haydn's and Mozart's quartets were played, no discussion of the conditions of performance of Beethoven's piano sonatas, very little weight given to the relation between private and public performance, no attempt to assess whether performance conditions were adequate or whether several decades had to go by before certain works could be successfully presented to more than a small group. In short, the relation of the music to the society in which it was produced is largely abandoned in favor of generalizations about political ideology and the role of the elite.

7

Elitism is not the only villain in Taruskin's narrative. There is also German nationalism. He insists on elevating Brahms's *Triumphlied* ("Song of Triumph"), a chauvinist celebration inspired by the Franco-Prussian War, into a major work, and ignores much more significant and inspiring achievements. He ends

3. A good history of this development can be found in the article of 1801, Johann Karl Friedrich Triest, "Remarks on the Development of the Art of Music in Germany in the Eighteenth Century," *Allgemeine musikalische Zeitung* translated by Susan Gillespie, in *Haydn and His World,* edited by Elaine Sisman (Princeton: Princeton University Press, 1997).

up by treating Brahms largely through his imitation of Beethoven's C minor heroic mode. The nostalgic melancholy of Brahms that gains him the affection of so many musicians, the rhythmic experiments that won him the admiration even of Stravinsky, who originally loathed his work—all this passes unnoticed.

Taruskin even spends time on the suggestion of another musicologist that the main theme of the finale of Brahms's Symphony no. 1 conceals a quotation from a similar bass part in Sebastian Bach's cantata, the *Actus Tragicus* (the rhythm and accent of Brahms's motif are unlike Bach's). Brahms's main theme, however, openly and exactly embodies part of the famous melody of the finale of Beethoven's Ninth Symphony, recognized immediately by all, so an extra hidden citation does not seem convincing, although an unconscious reminiscence is, I suppose, a very remote possibility. But Taruskin needs this detail for a bizarre theory. He thinks that Brahms is engaged in a German nationalist conspiracy: "We have another attempt at forging a factitious link between Bach and the Viennese classics [Haydn, Mozart, and Beethoven]."

This is about as plausible as the theory that Bacon wrote Shakespeare, and the resort to coded references typical of Baconite logic is a sign that Taruskin's theory is in trouble. The best-known aspect of Beethoven's childhood, both to his contemporaries and to his later biographers, is that at the age of thirteen he played the entire *Well-Tempered Keyboard*—but Taruskin does not mention this. Nor will he say that Beethoven continued to study Bach very late in life, and even transcribed a Bach fugue for string quartet in 1814. Mozart came into contact with Bach at the latest in 1782, when he arranged ten fugues from the *Well-Tempered Keyboard* and one from the *Art of Fugue* for string trio and string quartet, and he also studied some of the Bach suites and motets. He even imitated the style of the Bach chorale prelude in *The Magic Flute*. The growing interest in Bach was natural, as just at this time a dissatisfaction with the over-simplified instrumental style derived from Italian opera began to be felt. In Germany, fugues appeared in the 1770s in the string quartets of Haydn and Florian Gassmann (an important figure banished from the history of music by Taruskin, along with the revival of baroque polyphonic technique that transformed late eighteenth-century style).

In his attempt to discredit the classical Viennese composers' evident debt to Bach, Taruskin's manner develops ominous symptoms of the paranoia of conspiratorial theory:

It was Brahms, in other words, whose music forged the link between Bach and the "Viennese classics" that has since been spuriously read back into the historical narrative, at first by German ("insider") scholars, and that has quite recently come under intense skeptical scrutiny, chiefly by Americans, the quintessential musicological outsiders.

No doubt about it: Taruskin feels threatened by those German insiders. But he mysteriously does not identify his brave Americans, forced beyond the pale. Do they belong to some lunatic fringe? In any case, the link between Bach and the "Viennese classics" (are those quotation marks really necessary?) is not spurious, but an established fact.

More serious is his misjudgment of Brahms's references to the past. No composer studied his predecessors so intensely and borrowed more from them. What he took, however, was mostly procedures. Like many other composers, he did occasionally refer to a previous composer's melody, but he generally did so in a way that is prominent and easily perceptible. Everyone recognizes the Beethoven *Hammerklavier* allusion at the opening of Brahms's opus 1, and the reference to Beethoven's Ninth in Brahms's First Symphony is impossible to miss (it is an exact quotation of one characteristic measure from Beethoven's theme, played three times in a row in case anyone misses the reference, and the character and style of the Brahms theme is clearly an imitation of the Beethoven). These are messages or manifestos. "Any ass can see that," he said, when the quotation from the Ninth was noticed. (The only "secret" allusions in Brahms are to his own or Schumann's music, intended for Robert and Clara Schumann's ears.) If he had wished improbably to assert a link with Bach, he would not have hidden it in a reference so secret and unconvincing that it took more than a century to pick up the clues.

The most interesting uses of Brahms's studies of the past are rarely quotations, but adaptations of what he gleaned from his astonishing familiarity with music of the past. The few real quotations he permitted himself are almost always either immediately recognizable or else identified by Brahms for the musicians and readers of the score—the only exceptions are very personal, quotations from his own works to be recognized by friends, and quotations from Schumann's works intended to be comprehended by the composer in his last years in the insane asylum, or later by Clara (in this case they are messages to be privately understood as a homage). The main theme of Brahms's Third Symphony, for example, quotes a modest and not very conspicuous phrase from a cadence at the end of the exposition of the first movement of Schumann's *Rhenish* Symphony: what he does adapt more blatantly in his main theme, however, is the rhythmic structure of the opening of Schumann's *Rhenish* and the harmonic structure of Schubert's G Major String Quartet, as well as transforming an interesting detail from Schubert's great C Major Quintet. None of this is a quotation.

Brahms once said that there wasn't a single song by Schubert that you couldn't learn something from, but he didn't steal Schubert's tunes or even allude to them; he adapted his ways of conceiving the relation of text and music. Brahms's study of Schubert was particularly intense, and he edited many of Schubert's works for the complete critical edition. For example, the finale of Schubert's Grand Duo for piano four hands is a rondo in Hungarian style; at the end of the movement in a coda, Schubert slows the tempo, fragments his theme into small four-note motifs, and then repeats the individual elements. Brahms's Quintet for piano and strings has a Hungarian finale with a somewhat similar melody, and we might think this an unconscious reminiscence, until Brahms also slows the tempo and repeats four-note fragments of his main theme. But he does this in the main body of the movement, not at the end, making a more powerful integration of the effect. He generally strengthened any model he was using in some way.

Taruskin, who has splendid pages in volume 1 on what he calls "emulation" as opposed to imitation, discussing the practice of the Flemish composers' borrowings from an earlier composer, each one striving to outdo the previous example, lets his preoccupation with pitch alone run away with him and privileges what he believes to be Brahms's quotation of tunes by a predecessor including an absurd theory that Brahms, over a tonic harmony at the opening of his First Symphony, is citing the four chromatic steps at the end of the first phrase of the Prelude to Wagner's *Tristan,* a motif harmonized there by a chord so radical that theorists at first refused to recognize it as legitimate. This motif occurs elsewhere in the symphony, and is generally only three chromatic steps (in the introduction to the first movement, it is simply a rising scale with chromatic and diatonic steps, a scale progression so commonplace as to make the suggestion of quotation untenable). It is also difficult to believe that Brahms would make a point—a slyly secret point to be discovered by musicologists two centuries later—of quoting Wagner in a symphony that openly displays a homage to Beethoven. Although Taruskin discusses Brahms's emulation of Bach's passacaglia form in the Haydn Variations, his concentration elsewhere on resemblance of theme and motif does less than justice to the complex relation of Brahms to tradition and music history.

Another instance of Taruskin's iconoclasm is even less judicious:[4] he claims that Debussy was anti-Semitic on the basis of his declaration that Paul Dukas's opera *Ariane et Barbebleue* "is a masterpiece, but not a French masterpiece," meaning that Dukas was Jewish. This is surely wrong: Debussy was certainly implying only that the opera was too Wagnerian, too German, to fit his ideal of French style.[5] An idolater of Wagner when he was young ("to the point of forgetting decent manners," he once remarked), he was concerned to escape

4. He oddly misses a good chance to blacken the reputation of a famous composer when he writes about Orlandus Lassus, who composed a motet on a text of his own, congratulating the archbishop of Canterbury on the number of Protestants he had burned at the stake.

5. Georges Liébert, one of the editors of the new edition of Debussy's correspondence, has assured me that there is no trace of anti-Semitism in Debussy's life.

from the influence, and, as Taruskin reports his saying, to keep the old magician Klingsor, the villain of *Parsifal,* out of his opera *Pelleas et Melisande.* Taruskin might have told us how he exorcised him: by literally quoting Klingsor's leitmotiv at the death of Melisande. And not by a partial and obscure allusion, like the dubious ones that Taruskin thinks he has uncovered in Brahms and elsewhere: there is a silence, and then all nine notes of the leitmotiv are played by the unaccompanied cellos, followed by another silence. It is Debussy's way of signaling to the Wagnerites and to himself what has been eliminated. (In any case, the question whether Debussy was anti-Semitic does not concern his music at all: it is just gossip, absolutely unconfirmed by any evidence. A consideration of his late works, now very much admired, but absent from the book—the chamber sonatas, the piano Etudes, and the ballet *Jeux*—would have been more to the point.)

Earlier in *The Oxford History,* Taruskin asks if we have the right to listen to the chorus in Bach's *St. John's Passion* where the Jews demand the death of Jesus: he hastens to say that he is only posing the question, not giving an answer, but some questions are too foolish to be asked. The proposal to censor the art of the past to hide unpleasant aspects of history puts Taruskin with one foot in the camp of those who would ban *Huckleberry Finn* from the shelves of our school libraries.

8

Starting with 1700, major developments in Western music are passed over by Taruskin without a word. Perhaps the most astonishing lapse concerns the changed role of dynamics and marks of expression in the late eighteenth century. Before then, these were largely left to the performers, and, with few exceptions, only pitch and rhythm were notated (these exceptions were generally confined to a simple opposition of piano and forte). Taruskin never considers the drastic change in the nature of composition when accents became an integral element of the written work, when a *sforzando* became as much a part of the identification of a motif as pitch. He mentions in passing that the Mannheim orchestra was famous for its crescendo, but neglects the way a musical conception was fundamentally altered when gradual changes of dynamics became an essential element of the musical structure.

Taruskin has proclaimed the opposition between score and performance, between the "literate" and the "oral," as the keystone of his account, but when the greatest revolutionary change takes place in the relation between them and so much of the performer's role is incorporated in the score, he passes it over in silence. The dethronement of pitch and rhythm as the sole significant elements of music by composers after 1750 changed the face of Western music, and saw the invention of rapidly changing and complex orchestral tone color that went beyond the simple contrasts to be found in the Baroque. Gradually more and more details of performance are specified by composers until, in twentieth-century electronic music, the performer has disappeared from the scene.

Taruskin says almost everything possible at length about what notes are played in the main theme of Haydn's *Surprise* Symphony, but never remarks on the elaborate and subtle changes of dynamics and a startling off-beat accent in the second violins more striking than some of the pitches that are his only concern. This simple concentration on pitch to the exclusion of almost everything else persists even in his examination of twentieth-century works. His detailed analysis of Anton von Webern's Variations for Piano, for example, never considers dynamics and phrasing, and these are what make the piece so poetic. (I have played this piece for years never knowing exactly what the tone row was that determines the succession of pitches until I read Taruskin's pages, and I can't say that I am now in a better position to play, or listen to, the work.)

Register and tone color are also neglected by Taruskin: the sonorities invented by Debussy that contrast and combine high and low notes are sometimes more important than the harmony, but they are not part of this history. His remarks on the last pages of Strauss's *Salome* make a good point about the gritty harmonic dissonance, but he says nothing about the soft trill in the high woodwinds, which goes on relentlessly for minutes and by its friction makes Salome's orgasm convincing.

It might appear unfair to reproach Taruskin with what is missing when he gives so much, but in a work of six large volumes that aspires to replace all other contenders for the basic university text for introductory courses in music history, one expects that some of the most important elements of the subject should not be entirely absent. With his chapter on Mozart's operas, however, we realize that this monumental history is suitable only for those who already have a deep and wide acquaintance with the subject. He has a fine description of the final scene of *Idomeneo,* but does not even touch upon the major innovations of Mozart in this work: an ensemble of a dramatic power and complexity never before attempted in the history of opera, and the unprecedented richness of orchestration (Ilia's aria in the second act, for example, is a sinfonia concertante for flute, oboe, bassoon, and horn).

When he comes to *The Abduction from the Seraglio,* Taruskin makes interesting observations about Belmonte's aria, remarking on the tone painting of the hero's sensibility, but passes over in silence the astonishingly long instrumental concerto that introduces Constanze's "Martern aller Arten," or the second-act finale quartet that Mozart was so proud of, or the exquisite serenade in exotic folk style of the hero's valet, unique in opera literature. It is perverse in a work that claims the status of social history to eliminate the political aspect of *Figaro, Don Giovanni,* and *The Magic Flute.* (Taruskin curiously affirms that Beaumarchais's Figaro plays were in no way revolutionary: maybe not, but everybody at the time thought they were, which is almost as good.)

In short, the experienced may profit from parts of Taruskin's work, but students will have to go elsewhere for the operas of Mozart, perhaps to Hermann Abert's great book on Mozart (a translation of this still-authoritative and almost century-old work would be welcome), or to Joseph Kerman's *Opera as Drama.* Since Taruskin has nothing to say about the variety of Sebastian Bach's fugues or about the *Goldberg Variations,* they will have to go to Robert Marshall, Christoph Wolff, or Lawrence Dreyfus. The absence of any proper consideration of the Beethoven string quartets means that students must refer to Joseph Kerman's well-known study, or to Lewis Lockwood's recent biography, particularly admirable for its consideration of the last Quartets, opp. 131 and 135. Taruskin's has a chapter on Beethoven's heroic style, but a better discussion of the subject can be found in Scott Burnham's *Beethoven Hero.* And a history of music that omits any consideration of *Aida* or *Parsifal* is not adequate for the inexperienced student.

In his analyses, Taruskin often tells his readers with great vivacity and accuracy what is going on, but he is rarely willing to inform them what is conventional and what is novel. In the end, his unbending refusal to generalize about the musical language of an era, to distinguish the banal from the radical, may be the secret of the liveliness of his analyses: he often writes for us without preconceptions, as if he is hearing the piece for the first time and has never heard any other music to prejudice and distract him. This gives an unparalleled freshness to much of his account, but it erases history.

Taruskin uses the word "defamiliarization" to make the excellent point about Handel's genius at thwarting our expectations that gives the music its drama. He then remarks on the way Handel makes us wait for the third voice to enter in the fugue from his Concerto Grosso, op. 6, no. 7, and adds: "Thereafter, the whole fugue consists of a game of hide-and-seek: when and where will the subject next turn up?" Indeed, but delaying the third entry after the second has followed directly on the heels of the first is standard practice, even banal: the fugues in C minor and B-flat minor from Bach's *Well-Tempered Keyboard* are two examples that spring immediately to mind, and Beethoven still keeps to this pattern in the Sonata for Piano, op. 110.

About the return of the first theme very early in the first movement of Haydn's *Surprise* Symphony, Taruskin writes:

> We seem to be back at the starting point; but this time the elided cadence (m. 43) does produce the inevitable modulation to the dominant. (And that is the purpose of the initial avoidance: to stave off the inevitable is the essence of suspense, as any dramatist knows.)

This is well put, but Taruskin sounds as if he is explaining this particular symphony, when he is simply describing one of the basic conventions of sonata and symphony. Playing the first theme again immediately after the first appearance and using it to modulate to the dominant is the most common procedure of sonata form: everybody did it almost all the time. The second appearance even has a traditional name; it is usually called the counterstatement.

What Taruskin terms "the closest technical analysis yet attempted in this book" is on the slow movement of Mozart's Symphony no. 39 in E-flat Major. He begins by quoting Donald Francis Tovey:

> The form of the whole is roughly that of a first movement [i.e., a "sonata form"] with no repeats . . . and with no development section, but with a full recapitulation and a final return to the first theme by way of coda.

Taruskin leaps immediately to comment: "But no one ever listens to music like that. Any meaningful description of the movement will have to account for what it does contain, not what it doesn't." What this misplaced attack on Tovey conceals is that a sonata form with no repeats and no development section—in other words, just an exposition and a recapitulation—is a standard form frequently used in slow movements by composers of the late eighteenth century including Beethoven and was also the standard form of the opera overture in Mozart, Rossini, and Berlioz. Mozart used it often in the string quartets and piano sonatas, although rarely in the symphonies, but the slow movement of his *Paris* Symphony displays another example. Unfortunately the form was never given a name—or, rather, the nineteenth century named it "sonatina form," a term that Tovey evidently refused to employ, perhaps because it mistakenly sounds as if it was a shorter form of the sonata, which it is not, instead of an independent form, which it was. Taruskin's presentation of Mozart's symphonic working of this standard form in the E-flat Symphony is exciting, bringing out the violent effects that Mozart could accomplish with it, but so is Tovey's, although he does not need to refer to Freudian repression. The most valuable aspect of Taruskin's pages on this movement is his riff on E. T. A. Hoffmann's perception of the increased subjectivity in Mozart's work.

9

What is missing in Taruskin's history, what, in fact, he seeks to evade throughout, can be seen in his treatment of what he himself calls "an elegant and memorable" observation of Manfred Bukofzer in his history of Baroque. Bukofzer claimed that Bach lived at a time when the old polyphonic tradition was declining, the new and simpler harmonic style was gaining, and the two "were in exact equilibrium." Bukofzer added that "this interpenetration of opposed forces has been realized only once in the history of music, and Bach is the protagonist of this unique and propitious moment." Taruskin comments:

> There was indeed a unique moment of which Bach was the protagonist. It took place, however, not during Bach's lifetime but in the nineteenth century, when the concept of impersonally declining and ascending historical "curves" was born. It was a concept born precisely out of the need to justify Bach's elevation to the legendary status he had come to enjoy as the protagonist of an unrepeatable, mythical golden age and the fountainhead of the Germanic musical "mainstream."[6] The "equilibrium" and "interpenetration" of which Bukofzer wrote, and to which he assigned such a high value, were qualities and values created not by Bach but by those who had elevated him. The history of any art, to emphasize it once again, is the concern—and the creation—of its receivers, not its producers.

Taruskin's final flourish conveniently gets rid of the intention of the artist. Very fashionable in literary circles today, such an approach absolves the historian of any responsibility to the work itself. In short, Bukofzer is writing the history of music, and Taruskin is writing the history of the reception of music. He even implies here that the history of music does not exist.

It is true that the history of music cannot be fully understood without the history of its reception, but the belief that it can be completely reduced to its reception is crass. The dismissal of Bukofzer's terms "equilibrium" and "interpenetration" is not merely dogmatic, but naive. The second volume of Bach's *Keyboard Exercises* (one of his few publications) contains an Italian Concerto and a French Overture, which showed his vital interest in the balance and synthesis of stylistic tendencies of his time. His revival of the most ancient forms of counterpoint in the *Art of Fugue* at the same time that he was absorbing and incorporating much of the new courtly style of younger composers (the so-called galant style)[7] in the *Goldberg Variations* demonstrates his ability to deal at the same time both with the less fashionable contrapuntal art and the new conceptions of harmony.

Taruskin asserts that the declining and ascending musical traditions are merely a "concept" invented by German nationalists, a kind of fiction. But it is a simple demonstrable fact that the contrapuntal art of intertwining individual

---

6. The quotation marks around "mainstream" are tendentious: the acceptance of Bach in England, Poland, and France was widespread even if it redounded to the credit of German culture. Ascribing the success of Bach only or even principally to German propaganda is a shallow and oversimplified view of the international musical world of the time.

7. See Robert L. Marshall, "Bach the Progressive," *Musical Quarterly* (1976).

lines was less and less practiced (although it continued to be taught), and that a new and simpler Italian art based on a succession of chords was more and more widespread. Is Taruskin actually trying to deny this? Bukofzer's terms call for discussion: Did the older tradition of counterpoint really balance the new harmonic fashion, or did Bach, in fact, need to resurrect it almost willfully? Were there personal factors at work in his life that took on the recent developments of style almost aggressively and asserted the importance of the past? Did it come about because the composer was imprisoned in the ambiance of an unimportant town instead of being active in the life of an important and up-to-date musical center?

Bukofzer attempted to explain what made it possible gradually to impose Bach in professional circles as a great master in the later years of the eighteenth century and reveal him to the general public in the nineteenth. We must note that Taruskin does not debate Bukofzer's point that the old contrapuntal and the new harmonic traditions were in exact equilibrium at the moment Bach appeared, but simply dismisses it: Does he think that they did not exist, or that they had no strength or influence over musical practice—or simply that music history can be written without any consideration of the prevailing musical traditions?

He produces fascinating pages on the influence of provincial Protestant theology on Bach's music, and the way it illustrates by unpleasant sounds how mankind wallows in degradation and sinfulness (pages written by Taruskin with a certain glee as he is sure that readers today will find aspects of it disagreeable and even disgusting), but he passes over the influence of musical tradition. He evidently wants to realize Carl Dahlhaus's once radical suggestion that music should be studied not according to its moment of creation, but in reference to the moment it became socially and critically significant and relevant. The study of reception, however, is only a necessary completion of the study of the historical forces that influenced its creation, not a substitute for it. His claim that the history of any art is the concern only of the receivers and not the creators is unreasonably reductionist.

10

Volumes 4 and 5 of *The Oxford History of Western Music* are devoted to the twentieth century, and are the result of formidable research, presented in the liveliest way. The movements in the history of the last century are laid out at length: neoclassicism, expressionism, atonality, futurism, symphonic jazz, minimalism, electronic music—all there, with all the gossip, the factional struggles, and the internecine warfare in the different camps. The information is well organized with the chief emphasis on music in America, and Taruskin's account is magnificently detailed. What he is unable to do, however, is give us any idea why anybody would want to write, or listen to, most of the music of the century that he treats at such length. He leaves us feeling only sympathy and admiration for a historian who would subject himself to so much ungrateful material in order that we may be better informed.

Music—even classical music—is intended to give pleasure. Without pleasure, there is no understanding. In a letter to Stephen Spender, T. S. Eliot put it with eloquence and precision:

> You don't really criticize any author to whom you have not surrendered yourself. . . . Even just the bewildering minute counts; you have to give yourself up, and then recover yourself, and the third moment is having something to say, before you have wholly forgotten both surrender and recovery. Of course the self recovered is never the same as the self before it was given.[8]

Taruskin lacks the humility to surrender. As a result, he writes polemics and not criticism.

With the work of the twentieth-century avant-garde, Taruskin makes life difficult for himself by a curious view of listening. He likes to identify other people's fallacies, but this is one of his: we may name it the fallacy of instant intelligibility. It already appears in the previous volume.

He writes well about Chopin, and even makes the excellent comparison of the brilliant last sections of the Chopin Ballades with the final virtuoso section called cabaletta of the Italian opera aria. Analyzing Chopin's Prelude, op. 28, no. 2, in A Minor, he interestingly and, in fact, bravely declares it "a deliberately, fancifully ugly or absurd utterance." This is perceptive and satisfying, and so, at first glance, is his remark about the second phrase, which, he says, "is famous for the functional undecideability of the harmony. Where it's leading is anyone's guess." Yet you can, of course, guess that it's leading to A minor if you have heard it before.[9] The first time one hears or plays this prelude may shock or puzzle, but

8. May 9, 1935. Quoted by Frank Kermode in *Pleasure and Change: The Aesthetics of Canon* (Oxford: Oxford University Press, 2004), p. 43.

9. Taruskin maintains wrongly that "there is no thwarted inevitability about the harmonic trajectory, although (and this should be taken as a caution) analysis can always be employed in hindsight to suggest the opposite." Wrongly, because analysis properly works by hindsight, not by analyzing first impressions, and because he himself knows just how Chopin makes it sound inevitable, as he remarks that "the part writing, however arbitrary the effect, is contrapuntally pristine, rendering the piece at once academically impeccable and poetically fractious." It is the part writing and not the standard tonal analysis that makes it work.

every time one listens again, it becomes more convincing. And not just because of familiarity. There are works that never convince, no matter how often they are experienced, and they fall by the wayside. But you cannot always judge a piece of music adequately by tasting it once, as if it were a soft-boiled egg.

Works of modernism notoriously require re-listening, re-reading, re-experiencing. With music, we must learn what to listen for—or, indeed, what not to listen for. After a 1964 concert in Berlin of Xenakis's music in the 1950s, the great Nadia Boulanger, who had taught so many American musicians since the 1920s, said to the composer in her usual forthright, no-nonsense manner: "Xenakis, you don't know how to develop your themes!" "What themes?" he replied reasonably.

Even more instructive is a comment made to Elliott Carter by a member of the Boston Symphony, when they played his Piano Concerto: "Mr. Carter, the trouble with your music is that if one doesn't play the dynamics you wrote, it doesn't make any sense." "I thought you're supposed to play the dynamics" was Carter's comment. What is interesting here is the sighting of a glimmer of sense on the horizon as one learns to perform an unfamiliar work.

On this subject, Taruskin makes me say exactly the opposite of what I once wrote thirty years ago by removing the beginning of a paragraph and slicing off the end as well. He would like me to maintain the ridiculous thesis that music should be unintelligible to be any good. He starts by misinterpreting what Stravinsky said about Carter's Double Concerto for Piano, Harpsichord, and Two Small Orchestras, claiming that Stravinsky only called it a masterpiece because he could not understand it. That is of course patently untrue. Then Taruskin adds:

> Charles Rosen, the pianist in the first performance of the Double Concerto, offered a secular variation of Stravinsky's piety when he wrote that "it is important for a radically new work to be understood only little by little and too late," because "that is the only proof we have of its revolutionary character." On the face of it, both Rosen's and Stravinsky's remarks are examples of a special kind of tautology known as the assumption of a false converse: if masterpieces are inscrutable, then what is inscrutable is a masterpiece; if what is revolutionary is understood too late, then what is not understood now is revolutionary.

If I replace some of the context, it is clear that my nonsense should be credited to Taruskin's ingenuity. It comes from an article that had more to say about the experience of performing new works than it did about listening,[10] and that it referred to a "myth" where Taruskin would have the reader think otherwise:

10. "One Easy Piece," *New York Review,* February 22, 1973.

The myth of the unrecognized genius is a necessary part of the public aspect of art today. It is important for a radically new work to be understood only little by little and too late: that is the only tangible proof we have of its revolutionary character. There has never, of course, been a truly neglected genius in the history of music—at least not since the time that we have any real data on the lives of composers. . . .

I am elsewhere cited with great courtesy in this six-volume monument, but it is reasonable to ask how a critic as astute as Taruskin can have misunderstood my clearly spelled out insistence that the difficulty of much contemporary work is, at least in part, a delusion fostered by tradition, since the rest of my article explained how it was generally overcome without much trouble.

I do not believe that Taruskin's twisting of my words was done in bad faith. It must be distressing, however, to write about music that has never given you the pleasure that is the prerequisite for understanding, and it is easy to grasp at straws that will allow you to think that neither the pleasure nor the understanding actually exists. Taruskin finds himself goaded by the prestige Carter's music has recently gained to write forty pages on him that are detailed without ever being illuminating, unable to explain why some find the music so eloquent and fascinating. I know of no other distinguished scholar so anxious to display not only his talents but his limitations with such panache, as if they were stigmata.

His neglect of tone color makes it difficult for him to deal not only with the range of avant-garde music in the twentieth century, but even with the more conservative strains. He says nothing about the brilliant sonorities Rachmaninov could create, the bell-like clang of his piano writing, and comments only on the fact that the melody of the slow variation of the Paganini Variations for Piano and Orchestra is the main theme inverted. He does not give a good account of the extraordinary tone colors of Stravinsky's *Rite of Spring* (and I am astonished that he does not know that the four-hand version from which he takes his examples is not an arrangement, but the original, and that the orchestration came later).

With some major composers of the second half of the century, he is at a loss. Of Pierre Boulez, the master of iridescent sonorities, he deals largely with the driest and most dogmatic work of all, the opening section of *Structures* for two pianos, because it is notoriously easy to analyze; the gorgeous sounds of *Pli selon Pli* and *Répons* are ignored. With Karl-Heinz Stockhausen, he discusses a short piano piece, but says nothing about his most famous work, *Gruppen,* for three orchestras. Taruskin's claim neither to advocate nor to denigrate the music he discusses is a hollow one: you cannot make sense of music without advocacy, and not to make sense of it is to condemn.

In the volumes of the twentieth century, there is a serious omission: American musical comedy. Gershwin gets in for the *Rhapsody in Blue* and the Concerto, but his songs are out. For most musicians, the songs are more interesting than the concert pieces, and even the score for a Fred Astaire movie, *Damsel in Distress,* would give a fairer view of his genius. Taruskin claims to write the history of "literate" music, and musical comedy was certainly written down. It's not as if he restricted himself elsewhere to highly serious work: Offenbach and Johann Strauss get in, and Gottschalk is absurdly treated at length, juxtaposed with Chopin in a foolish effort to provoke. Harold Arlen is a more interesting composer than Gottschalk, and "Stormy Weather" a much better and more important piece historically than a lot of the music Taruskin takes seriously and plows through laboriously.

Some of the twentieth century's once admired stars of high style treated by Taruskin (Roy Harris, Ernst Krenek) are already candidates for resuscitation as unlikely as some of the once celebrated figures from the middle of the eighteenth century, the great age of Hasse and Vinci, while Gershwin, Arlen, Cole Porter, and others still retain their freshness after so many decades. In addition, the arrival of the phonograph has abolished the fundamental distinction between literate and oral on which Taruskin bases his work. The improvisations of Art Tatum, Miles Davis, and Bill Evans are now preserved for examination as surely as the notated scores of Machaut and Mozart. Ignoring, as Taruskin does, all of the music of improvised but unwritten jazz recorded from Tatum to Miles Davis leaves a gaping hole in his history of the music composed in the twentieth century. Future histories will have to do justice to the total picture.

A brief final note: Taruskin continues to circulate a widespread myth that has outlived any interest it may have had, which was not much to start with. It concerns Hans Sachs's admonition at the end of *Die Meistersinger* to honor the old German musicians. This has been taken in our time as a forecast of Nazi aggression (and is so taken by Taruskin): at this point in the opera, most producers now feel obliged to make some kind of pictorial reference to Auschwitz or to SS troops, and if they don't, the critics protest. What Sachs says is that when Germany is conquered by a foreign power like the French, a continued respect for the old masters will allow German culture to survive. This seems to me patriotic, but perfectly acceptable. Protests are misplaced. When an American lecturer exhorts us to continue reading Emerson, Whitman, and Mark Twain, I do not think we should feel obliged to flash slides of Abu Ghraib and Guantánamo on the screen.

Modernism and the Cold War

M Y FRIENDS LET ME KNOW that Professor Taruskin has written an article entitled "Afterword: *Nicht blutbefleckt?*" in the *Journal of Musicology* vol. 26, no. 2 (2009), partially devoted to answering my review of his *History of Western Music.* In this answer he declares himself "as one who regards Rosen's literary output—all of it—as Cold War propaganda."

This seems sufficiently extreme and provocative to warrant a few observations. For the most part, following the recent work of a few musicologists largely hostile to most modernist style, Taruskin maintains that whatever success and prestige in music and painting American modernism has achieved is mainly due to the efforts of promotion by the CIA and the U.S. State Department in order to counter Soviet propaganda during the Cold War years.

The claim that the prestige of American modernism is basically due to the programs of the CIA and the American government is simply a warmed-up version of a French theory of some years ago that the success of American abstract expressionism was due to a conspiracy of art dealers, aided by official American propaganda. This was inspired by indignant patriotic panic at the replacement of Paris by New York for a few years as the major center of artistic innovation and interest. The principal expression of the attack was a book by Serge Guilbaut; the title is sufficiently explanatory and indicates the level of the argument as well: *How New York Stole the Idea of Modern Art: Abstract Expressionism, Freedom, and the Cold War.*

This thesis has recently become fashionable among a small group of American musicologists, and Taruskin seems determined to ride along. He acts as prosecutor, determined to corner the criminals and convict them. He writes:

> But the guilt and blood a critic like [Louis] Menand will admit into a discussion of [Jackson] Pollock is presumably only guilt over booze and fornication, and the blood shed in a fatal car crash. . . . But Pollock was an entirely knowing beneficiary of Cold War promotion, and so were John Cage, Morton Feldman, and any number of others of whom it is still conventional to say that they were far better appreciated in Europe than at home. The role of Cold War policy in their histories is part of our history, and we must report it.

It would appear that Jackson Pollock was stained with blood by having allowed his paintings to be exhibited in a show arranged by the Congress for Cultural Freedom, an organization that was afterwards revealed to have been financed by the CIA. That is the same accusation that Taruskin levels against Elliott Carter. He dates what he calls Carter's "superlative prestige" precisely from the European performance of Carter's First Quartet at the 1954 Rome festival of contemporary music, an event sponsored by the Congress for Cultural Freedom—the notorious (thanks to its subsequently disclosed CIA connections) cultural organization on the Western side of the Cold War.

Nevertheless, the most distinguished and brilliant of all the musical scholars, on whom Taruskin relies for his evidence on the subject of the effect of Cold War propaganda, Professor Anne C. Schreffler,[1] makes it clear that he is wrong on this point. In this festival, she writes, "Carter's quartet received wide exposure but mixed reviews. . . . The recording by the Walden Quartet did even more than these early performances to make the work known." In any case, before the festival, the quartet had already won the first prize in the International Competition for the Composition of String Quartets at Liège.

It is evident that the success of this quartet—which, to Carter's surprise, was soon in the repertoire of a number of ensembles in spite of its length and difficulty (at the competition at Liège, the quartet broke down trying to perform it)—was not due principally to the CIA-sponsored performance at the Rome 1954 festival of contemporary music, but to the intrinsic merit of the work. This is even grudgingly admitted by Taruskin as he writes:

> I did little else but quote rapturous comments—from Stravinsky, Wlliam Glock, Joseph Kerman, Andrew Porter Bayan Northcott, and Rosen

1. Felix Meyer and Anne C. Schreffler, eds., *Elliott Carter: A Centennial Portrait in Letters and Documents* (Woodbridhge, Suffolk, England: Boydell Press, 2008).

himself, among others—testifying to their belief in Carter's eloquence and allure (an enthusiasm that in the case of the First Quartet, among other works, I fully share, although the *Oxford History* was not the proper place for me to say so).

But he wants to claim that these responses are not "wholly innocent and spontaneous," and he does not believe that an historian should be an advocate. The repetition of quoted testimonials he boasts of, however, is not criticism, and is only a facile substitute for historical explanation. The responsibility that an historian owes his readers, particularly in a textbook for college students, is not a list of advocates, but a critical explanation how "the eloquence and allure" work.

However, the role that Taruskin has laid out for himself is simply that of a whistle blower. He finds it scandalous, as many of us do, that the financing of the Congress for Cultural Freedom by the CIA was clandestine, unavowed. . . . After the war the intellectual prestige of the Communist parties in France and Italy was very great, as they had been the principal organizations of the Resistance to Mussolini and to the German occupation of France. The intent of the CIA was to strengthen the political center-left and to restore the intellectual reputation of America with exhibitions and concerts and the literary magazines *Encounter* and *Tempo Presente* in Britain and Italy. The few performances and exhibitions arranged by the Congress for Cultural Freedom did not establish prestige, but showcased musicians and artists who had already achieved some success.

There is no evidence at all that the CIA was interested in dodecaphonic style or even in simple difficult and dissonant modernism. Taruskin says nothing about the fact that works of Samuel Barber, hardly a representative figure of the modernist school, were also played at the festival in Rome where Carter's First Quartet was introduced to a European public, including a song cycle sung by Leontine Price, and the *Capricorn* Concerto. It is not clear why Barber should not be tainted by the blood guilt smeared on the figures of Jackson Pollock and Elliott Carter. The fact that works of avant-garde music and painting attracted more attention in Europe at that time than the neo-Romantic and neoclassical styles is understandable if one remembers the European work in those fields after the war, with Pierre Boulez and Stockhausen and the still active figures of Matisse and Picasso. Nor does Taruskin even mention glancingly the U.S. State Department's important international promotion at this time of African-American jazz musicians like Louis Armstrong and others. Maybe he felt that calling attention to this would be politically incorrect, or perhaps he just wishes to imply that any prestige that attached to their work was well-deserved. . . .

In his *History,* Taruskin maintains that "Both [Carter and Rosen] were beneficiaries of the prestige machine in which both were willing partners." It is agreeable to benefit from prestige, but it is obviously wicked to receive it from a "machine." Any success whatever in the arts is always due to some kind of promotion, whether the beneficiary be the Beatles, or Jackson Pollock or Richard Taruskin. But the implication of the phrase "a willing partner" that Carter knew that the CIA was paying for the execution of his quartet is a bold-faced misrepresentation.

The appearance above of the name of William Glock among the advocates with little mention of him elsewhere reveals the essential poverty and incompetence of Taruskin's account of the success of modernism. He has made no serious attempt to explore how the music was actually promoted and who was fundamentally interested in the promotion; he simply wants to yoke modernism with an organization that is now generally considered morally deplorable.

The really efficient work to make modernism better known and acceptable came from the public radio stations in Europe, above all the BBC. Taruskin mentions only the German stations, and then simply to claim that their financing of modernist music ceased with the fall of the Berlin Wall, the end of the Cold War, and the reunification of Germany. He fails to observe that the reunification nearly bankrupted the German state, by the granting of parity to the relatively worthless East German mark and the mark of the West. Support for all forms of culture diminished, not just for modernism.

Considerable promotion for the avant-garde was also offered by the Italian radio system. The French held back, and the major representative of French modernism, Pierre Boulez, was systematically refused access to official channels in the 1950s, although he was financed as the resident composer by the German radio station at Baden-Baden—run by Heinrich Strobel, who had also engaged the greatest interpreter of the orchestral modernist repertory, Hans Rosbaud.

The most important promotion of musical modernism came, above all, from the BBC when William Glock became Comptroller of Music. He hardly needed any stimulus from Cold War ideology, as he had been for many years the editor of *Score* magazine, the foremost voice for avant-garde music in the world at the time. Upon taking over the BBC, Glock's first action was to transform the Promenade Concerts, which took place every summer in the Albert Hall, the largest concert space in London. These were largely popular concerts with Beethoven, Tchaikovsky, and Gilbert and Sullivan. Before starting his reign at the BBC, Glock said to me, "We get 3,000 people every night at the Proms, and we don't know why they come, so we are going to change the programs and see what happens." He programmed Karl-Heinz Stockhausen's *Gruppen* for three orchestras—only 2,500 people came, but that seemed like a success—and continued with unusual works like the Berlioz *Requiem,* and Mozart's unfinished opera *Zaide,* as well as standard repertory. There was a huge injection of the modernist tradition which caused an outcry in Parliament with protests at "*Gauleiter* Glock," who was inflicting subversive foreign art upon innocent concertgoers. The Prom Concerts under Glock gained the reputation for a number of years as the most distinguished and exciting music festival in the world. For chamber music, the Thursday Invitation Concerts were created as broadcasts with an invited audience that mixed adventurous recent scores with music of the past.

Glock had quickly hired Pierre Boulez as principal conductor of the BBC Symphony (along with Antal Dorati, who lasted only two years), and sent the orchestra on tour to America playing four programs of difficult twentieth-century music in two weeks in New York (a project that few orchestras could have matched at the time.) The two concerts directed by Boulez were a revelation and a critical sensation, creating on the spot his international fame as a conductor. He received a contract from Columbia Masterworks (first from the British outlet and then the American, where Goddard Lieberson had been head of artists and repertory, and who had alread done a good deal for the promotion of difficult new music); Boulez's contract gave him carte blanche for repertory and a guarantee of a recording of all his own works. He immediately chose to do a complete set of Webern, although Columbia already had one that Lieberson had authorized.

A year or so later Glock said to me "Pierre is going to break his contract with me and go to the New York Philharmonic. Do you think I should sue?"

"Would it do any good?" I asked.

"None at all," he replied. In his New York years, Boulez presented a small amount of difficult contemporary music, the largest part of it not on the main subscription concerts, but in small events in Greenwich Village. He steadfastly refused to perform his own works with the Philharmonic, claiming that there was not enough time for rehearsal. After a few years in New York he had become one of the highest paid conductors in the world, and France set about enticing him back with the promise of elaborate sound laboratories and a highly paid chamber orchestra.

Taruskin remarks with a certain undignified satisfaction that Amercan modernist composers were, and are, better known in Europe than in their native country, and explains this by the machinations of the CIA, which is absurd. All contemporary music is better known in Europe, since almost all the countries have a public radio system with some stations devoted entirely to classical music, and the musicians' unions there have enforced regulations that most of the music must be either live or recorded by the stations and strictly limited the use of commercial recordings. Many of the stations have their own orchestras. Their budget far exceeds that of any of the classical music stations in the United States.

The relative, or even absolute, lack of success in America is not due to the absence of brainwashing propaganda, but to the fact that almost all modernist art is rebarbative at first encounter and requires several experiences of it to come to terms. The lack of a public radio system in the United States that presents live performances regularly and has staff musicians means that there are many music-lovers in America who have never heard even one piece by Babbitt, Sessions, or Carter; and the possibility of hearing any piece more than once is very dim. In addition, many of the performances are likely to be inadequate of Carter's works, for example, I heard the song cycle *Syringa* on poetry by John Ashbery three times and disliked it before finding it beautiful a year or two later on a fourth hearing . . .

Taruskin begins his article with the figure of Milton Babbitt and oddly ascribes to the Cold War the formation of the Ph.D. Program in musical composition at Princeton University, where Babbitt taught. As Taruskin puts it:

> Babbitt's composing and theorizing have always been symbiotic . . . ; and for a while that symbiosis of music and analysis was powerfully institutionalized in the pioneering Princeton Ph.D. Program in composition and in its clones, the countless other degree programs that Princeton's made not just possible but necessary. . . . That Princeton degree program, inaugurated in 1962, was a major trophy of the Cold War. The call for it had come in 1958, the year after *Sputnik,* in Babbitt's celebrated, if generally misunderstood, manifesto 'Who Cares If You Listen?'

Taruskin is surely too intelligent to claim seriously that *Sputnik* was an actual cause for the creation of the musical Ph.D. program, but he places the phrase "the year after *Sputnik*" in the hope that his readers will be stupid enough to believe it.

Nevertheless, a Ph.D. in musical composition was created for reasons that Taruskin either does not know or does not wish to know, but had nothing to do with international politics. In the 1950s, American universities were rated by the number of Ph.D.s on their faculties. Graduate students in musical composition were awarded only a doctorate of music, while the Ph.D. was reserved for musicologists. This meant that when a job in a university music department for teaching harmony, counterpoint, and composition came available, it generally went to a young musicologist—and a composer, as a mere D. Music, was shut out of the job market.

Taruskin follows this by a brief disquisition on the development of the attempt to make music—composition as well as musicology—more "scientific," tracing it back to the late nineteenth century. This includes a misrepresentation of the great Austrian musicologist Guido Adler, not nearly as "scientific" as Taruskin claims, who did try to make the editing of the music of the past as reliable as the editing of classical texts of literature, and who had also an extraordinarily sensitive understanding of the stylistic development of the eighteenth century, to which we are still indebted.

This leads Taruskin to an attack, which has some justification, on the pretensions of artists to be uninfluenced by political considerations. It is true that we are all sometimes unaware of how politics impinges not only on our aesthetics, but on our view of life and morals in general as well. This inspires Taruskin to affirm: "Equally squeamish—and equally strategic—is Charles Rosen's phobic reaction to reception studies, by now the most widely practiced and uncontroversial aspect of contextualization."

This effectively confuses two issues. Contextualization studies the conditions, social and economic, of the moment in which the music was created. Reception studies, however, deal with the later history of the music, its influence and its performance. I have, on the contrary, always insisted on the importance of reception studies, merely remarking from time to time that they do not totally replace the understanding that comes from listening to the music, and are not a substitute for an assessment of the intrinsic character of the music.

Nor am I an enemy of contextualization, only of the cut-rate version that Taruskin is selling, which downgrades all serious studies by determining the ideology of a work of music or art solely and simple-mindedly by the ideology of the social class of the individual patrons who paid for the work. Since Professor Taruskin teaches at Berkeley, this would identify the ideology of his crusade against difficult modernism with the policy of a state close to bankruptcy. This kind of historical criticism based upon a facile, uncritical identification with class interest is what used to be called "vulgar Marxism," and it is astonishing to see its reappearance on the stage of postmodernist theory. It is only a way of avoiding any serious engagement with a work or a style that one happens not to like, a way of indulging one's prejudices without admitting them, a way, in fact, to give the impression of scientific objectivity—exactly what I have charged Taruskin with in his writing on the twentieth century. His hostile presentation of much of the twentieth century does not result in historical objectivity.

Taruskin was clearly psychologically troubled by the atmosphere of the Cold War, much more so, I think, than most Americans, as he writes: "I believe it is fair to say that the Cold War gave Americans a far greater scare than any of our actual wars our armies fought overseas. . . . How could anyone's psychic equilibrium remain undisturbed? (Mine was definitely unbalanced. I could never take seriously plans or promises that had to do with anything that lay more than a few days in the future.)"

For me, on the contrary, the Cold War years were a time of hope and looking forward. I got a Ph.D., made my first recordings, made my New York debut, and got a two-year Fulbright fellowship to work in Paris. The 1950s were the time when I found stronger ties to modernism, which had always interested me, but I learned some twelve-tone pieces for the first time (with great difficulty at first, but the style became rapidly easier to assimilate). But I was never a dodecaphonic fanatic, finding as Elliott Carter did, that the system was too constraining. I was certainly never aware that I was being influenced by the CIA. On one occasion, indeed, I was guilty of being promoted by the State Department. I had played a recital in New York, which received a favorable review in *Time* magazine with a two-column picture. The American Embassy in Paris, when I returned to finish my Fulbright, was so impressed by the magazine attention that I had to repeat the concert in the Embassy concert hall for an invited audience, although I had included no American music on my program.

I also admit that in 1953–54 I played concertos with the symphony orchestra of the occupying Seventh Army of the U.S. stationed in Stuttgart, all young soldiers drafted from Juilliard, Curtis, and other music schools, and we toured Germany, Austria, France, and Denmark, performing the Schumann, Beethoven no. 4, and Brahms no. 2, demonstrating to the local populace the good will of the occupying army. I even persuaded the Army radio to broadcast a performance with three members of the orchestra of the Trio Sonata from the *Musical Offering* of J. S. Bach. As far as I know, this was how I benefited from a "prestige machine" run by the U.S. government.

CHAPTER 18

Theodor Adorno:
Criticism as Cultural Nostalgia

I

No art appears as remote as music from the life and the society that produce it. Painting and sculpture reflect some aspects of the figures and objects, or at least the forms and colors that we encounter; novels and poems convey experiences and aspirations that recall, however distantly, the world that we know. The sounds of music, however, are artificial and set apart: even sung music does not give the sound of speech, and instrumental music has little to do with the noises that we come upon in our daily life, and can seem to be even more abstract than abstract painting. That is why Charles Lamb compared a piece of instrumental music to a poem made up entirely of punctuation. Nevertheless, as Diderot remarked, even though the signs of music are more ephemeral and less easily definable than those of painting or literature, their emotional impact upon our senses is even greater. We would consider it unreasonable to think that music does not, in many ways, reflect the culture and the age in which it was made.

To understand the significance of music for the musicians who created it and the society in which it was produced, is therefore a challenge to music-lovers. Perhaps no writer on music devoted more energy to this task than Theodor Wiesengrund Adorno, and the translations into English of his writings on philosophy and music and their diffusion have been multiplying in recent years, while his ideas have become widely influential in the United States and Europe.

In American, French, and Italian universities, his views are frequently cited. The admiration is rarely unmixed. Almost everyone agrees that his essay on jazz (where he attacks popular music with a snobbish contempt matched only by his ignorance of the subject) is embarrassing.[1] His difficult prose is a stumbling block (even his closest colleagues admitted that they could not always understand his writing), but it is also an attraction; it forces one to pay attention and he achieves effects with it unobtainable by a more pellucid manner.

Born in 1903 in Frankfurt into a rich and influential family, he studied piano at an early age, but he does not seem to have shown a strong ambition to become a professional musician before 1924, when he met the composer Alban Berg and heard *Wozzeck,* which fired him with enthusiasm. He went to Vienna in 1925, attached himself to the circle of Arnold Schoenberg, and studied composition with Berg and piano with Eduard Steuermann.

The little I have heard of his compositions has the curiosity value of the amateur musical works of other men of letters, and may be rated somewhere below the musical endeavors of Nietzsche or Rousseau, and above those of Ezra Pound. He also studied philosophy and, returning to Frankfurt, wrote a university thesis, largely a Marxist interpretation of Kant and Freud, called *The Concept of the Unconscious in the Transcendental Theory of Mind,* and, later, a second thesis on the aesthetics of Kierkegaard. For a while he published articles on music, chiefly in support of the Schoenberg circle, but could never obtain full-time work as a critic. At last he received a lectureship in philosophy at the University of Frankfurt in 1931, which he lost in 1933 when Hitler came into power, and he went into exile, ending up eventually at the Institute for Social Research, which had transferred from Frankfurt to Greenwich Village in New York, and provided a wartime refuge for many exiled European intellectuals. After the war he returned to his native city, and became a professor at the University of Frankfurt.

Perhaps the fundamental critical insight of Adorno was a recognition that works of art do not passively reflect the society in which they arise, but act within it, influencing and criticizing it. The critical concepts used by Adorno to clarify the way art criticizes social conditions were largely derived from Marx's reading of Hegel, above all the concept of reification, the reduction in capitalist society of, for example, a human being, a work of art, or even an idea to a material object. This reification takes place when the value of anything in itself, its use, its purpose, is obscured by its exchange value, how much it is

---

1. Some critics have excused Adorno's ignorance of popular music by pointing out that the finest jazz of the 1920s was not performed in Germany, but it is hard to believe that recordings of the great American jazz musicians were not available on the European continent.

worth when it is sold. Serious art music—what we call classical music—is characterized for Adorno by its resistance to commercialism and provides, by this refusal to conform, a criticism of the ideals of the society and culture in which it is produced. For him, the Central European tradition of serious music from Beethoven to Schoenberg was a protest against the growing reification of capitalist culture: composers imposed their often uncompromising individuality, their "subjectivity," upon the traditional language of music, even when—perhaps, indeed, above all when—the innovations were difficult for the public to accept. A balance between the objective musical tradition and the subjectivity of the composer, a balance that would allow the new works to be performed and understood, became increasingly hard to achieve, as the musical language became more complex.

The stimulus Adorno received from the Schoenberg circle was rivaled by his contact with Walter Benjamin, more than ten years older than Adorno. They were united by their left-wing political views, but it was Benjamin's thesis on the drama of the German Baroque, *Ursprung des deutschen Trauerspiels,* rejected by the University of Frankfurt, which inspired Adorno's greatest admiration. His interest in Schoenberg and Benjamin was combined in his best-known and most influential book, *Philosophy of Modern Music,* which set out to do for contemporary music what Benjamin had done for seventeenth-century German tragedy. He makes this intention explicit by a quotation, typically hermetic, from Benjamin as the opening sentence of his book:

> "The history of philosophy viewed as the science of origins is that process which, from opposing extremes and from the apparent excesses of development, permits the emergence of a configuration of an idea as a totality characterized by the possibility of a meaningful juxtaposition of such antitheses inherent in these opposing extremes." This principle, adhered to by Walter Benjamin as the basis of cognitive criticism in his treatise on the German tragedy, can also serve as the basis for a philosophically oriented consideration of new music.[2]

For Benjamin, followed by Adorno, concepts of style like "Baroque," "German tragic drama," and "musical modernism" were Ideas, the effects of which were perceptible as they were made manifest and worked out in history, but which could not be pinned down and confined by a simple dictionary definition as they developed. An outline of their trajectory in history could be found, above all, by concentrating on the extreme limits that the examples of the style could

2. *Philosophy of Modern Music,* translated by Anne G. Mitchell and Wesley V. Blomster (New York: Continuum, 2007), p. 2. Quotation from Benjamin, *Ursprung des Deutschen Trauerspiels,* in *Schriften,* ed. Theodor Adorno, vol. 1 (Frankfurt, 1955), p. 163.

attain; for Benjamin the heightened language and violent plots of the largely forgotten German Baroque dramas were the extreme examples of the Baroque theatrical style. The insistence on the extremes proposed by Benjamin was a way to avoid reducing a style to its most typical and average examples. The emphasis on the unusual and extravagant manifestations best reveals the potential of the forces at work in history.

The extremes of modern music considered by Adorno consist simply of only two: Schoenberg, along with his disciples, and Stravinsky. His treatment is asymmetrical: Schoenberg continued the central development of European art music ("Schoenberg and Progress" is the title of this part of his book) while Stravinsky was an intruder from a marginal Slavic culture trying to appropriate a past which did not belong to him ("Stravinsky and Restoration"). The book contains brilliant observations, but is skewed by this structure, which is only too obviously prejudicial. In addition, the method is essentially a misunderstanding of Benjamin. Adorno did not quote the words by Benjamin that immediately follow the sentences he presented at the opening:

> Under no circumstances can the representation of an Idea be considered as successful as long as the virtual sphere of its possible extremes has not been reviewed.

The "review" has to remain virtual, Benjamin explains, because not all the possibilities of an Idea are perfectly worked out in history; a review of the "possible extremes" implies that all the extremes, even those imperfectly realized, must be considered in order to arrive at historical truth, which is the representation of the Idea.

Adorno, however, eliminates from his review all forms of popular music, including jazz, and refuses to consider such contemporary figures as Rachmaninov and Sibelius. Hindemith is dismissed as a reactionary and Bartók given the most cursory treatment. In this way, he reduces the picture of the modern age to two isolated images, and does not even seriously consider the relations between the work of Schoenberg and that of Stravinsky. Of course, this has become much easier to assess with the distance of time, like the relations between the opposing camps of Wagner and Brahms, who now seem more alike than they did to their contemporaries, and in a moment of clarity, Adorno predicted that eventually Schoenberg and Stravinsky "will some day no longer strike the ear as so distinct from one another as they do today."

It should now be obvious that Schoenberg's move from the freedom of atonality to what Adorno called "the rigid apparatus of the twelve-tone system" was fundamentally neoclassical and conservative, an attempt to reconstruct the respectable classical forms like the sonata and the set of variations, which had become seemingly impossible with atonal expressionism, and that Stravinsky's idiosyncratic use of eighteenth-century tonal formulas in his middle period was, in fact, profoundly radical and even subversive in many of his works.

Nevertheless, in *Philosophy of Modern Music,* the relation of Schoenberg and Stravinsky is mostly represented as a struggle between good and evil. Even Schoenberg's move from the expressionist style of 1911 to 1920—in such works as *Erwartung* and *Pierrot Lunaire*—to the systematic twelve-tone system, which Adorno largely deplores, is viewed sympathetically as the tragic result of the clash between the developing musical style and the degeneration of capitalist culture. Stravinsky's work, on the other hand, is subjected to a polemical onslaught well illustrated by the section headings: Archaism, Modernism, Infantilism; Permanent Regression and Musical Form; The Psychotic Aspect; Alienation as Objectivity; Fetishism of the Means; Depersonalization; Catatonia. Remarks like "The sado-masochistic element accompanies Stravinsky's music through all its phases" sustain the polemical tone, so congenial to Adorno, who had for his youthful journalism used the pseudonym Detlev Rottweiler. Much of this reads like a parody of the only too familiar Philistine picture of the avant-garde tradition as the work of degenerate perverts.

The pejorative vocabulary is systematic, not only about Stravinsky but about other composers such as Debussy. It should be evident, for example, that Debussy put new emphasis on sonority, giving it priority over the development of motifs characteristic of the German tradition. Adorno labels Debussy's sound at once "fetishism of the material," turning it into a vice. If a composer simplifies his style for a particular work or group of works, this is immediately called either "regression" or "infantilism." The limit of this tendency is reached when Adorno ascribes Stravinsky's success in dealing with the crowd scenes in *Petrouchka* to the incapacity of the Slav to achieve subjectivity. Subjectivity, Adorno thought, was a bourgeois product, and Russia was still largely prebourgeois, or, as he circumspectly presents his cultural racism: "In essentially prebourgeois Russia, the category of the subject was not quite so firmly fitted together as in the Western countries." That explains, Adorno remarks, why "not one of the brothers Karamazov is a 'character'" and why "the lyricism of Mussorgsky is distinguished from the German Lied by the absence of any poetic subject. . . . The artist does not converge with the lyric subject."

This absurd anti-Slavic prejudice did not, however, prevent Adorno from making fairly sharp observations about Stravinsky, in, for example, the following discussion of his motifs:

In Beethoven the motives are definitive and reveal a specific identity. . . . Stravinsky's technique of archaic-musical images views the circumvention of such identity as one of its primary concerns. . . . The concept of dynamic musical form which dominates Western music from the Mannheim school down to the present Viennese school assumes [the] motif as a prerequisite in a firmly defined identity, even if it is minutely small. . . . Stravinsky's regression, reaching back beyond this, for this very reason replaces progress with repetition. . . . This lack in Stravinsky's music is, in the narrowest sense, a lack of thematic material, a lack which actually excludes the breath of form, the continuity of the process—indeed, it excludes "life" itself from his music. (p. 118)

In this clotted prose, Adorno contends that Stravinsky's motifs are not dynamic: they generate neither sequences nor the developing variation that characterize the Austro-German tradition, which he thought the only defensible musical style.

By denying that Stravinsky's motifs have identity, he does not mean that they are not striking or memorable: the "identity" of a motif here means the possibility of "drawing the consequences" from motifs through development and variation. Similarly, for Adorno, the identity of a person is not merely what he or she looks like, but the past history and the future possibilities of his or her character. In this sense, the "identity" of a theme in the classical tradition is defined by its transformations within the whole work. ("The thematic material," Adorno claims, "is of such a nature that to attempt to secure it is tantamount to varying it. It really does not in any way exist 'in itself' but only in view of the possibility of the entirety.")[3]

Adorno was right about Stravinsky's motifs: they do not have the dynamic charge of the German motif. Even the Schoenberg of the periods of atonality and the later twelve-tone system chose motifs that mimicked the generative effects of the German classical tonal tradition. (That is why Pierre Boulez was eventually to react against this conservative approach and write the manifesto emphatically entitled "Schoenberg Is Dead.") The magnificent opening phrases of Stravinsky's *Sacre du Printemps* or *Les Noces* do not, indeed, invite development, but only repetition with new shaping of the accents; and the extraordinary dynamic energy of the music comes from shifts of rhythmic weight, irregular repetition, and contrasts of texture.

These motifs, which Adorno considered dead, were an invention of genius that revolutionized music. Adorno, who understood certain aspects of Stravinsky more clearly than most of Stravinsky's disciples, could not see that his technique was in fact dynamic and generative largely because the elements were so neutral, and that they offered an escape from the academic tyranny of the only tradition that Adorno judged viable.

---

3. Adorno's claim that "with very few exceptions" this treatment by transformation of the theme starts with Beethoven is of course deeply mistaken; it is already obvious in the music of the late fifteenth century, and there are few of Beethoven's transformations that cannot be traced back to Bach and Haydn.

According to Adorno, Schoenberg's music, as a criticism of the commercialism of modern culture, deliberately but nobly sought out failure through its clear-sighted, logical, and progressive exploitation of the central classical tradition; Stravinsky pathologically betrayed this tradition. Schoenberg's reaction to Adorno's view, as we might expect, was not favorable:

> I know that he has clearly never liked my music. . . . It is disgusting, by the way, how he treats Stravinsky. I am certainly no admirer of Stravinsky, although I like a piece of his here and there very much—one should not write like that.[4]

2

For a great part of his life, Adorno worked at a book on Beethoven. He did not succeed in finishing it, but left a mass of notes, now published, along with a few articles, the most important of which are two on Beethoven's *Missa Solemnis* and on his late style. The essay on the late style—by which Adorno meant the late quartets and late sonatas as well as the *Diabelli Variations* and the Ninth Symphony—reveals both Adorno's strength and his limitations. In criticizing Beethoven's late style, he starts from the remarkably cogent observation that in the late works of Beethoven, conventional formulae and phraseology are inserted. They are full of decorative trills, cadences, and fiorituras. The convention is often made visible in unconcealed, untransformed bareness.

Adorno equates the attempt to get rid of convention with subjectivity, with the achievement of personal expression. He follows in this a well-established principle of eighteenth-century aesthetics: the conventional is arbitrary, imposed from without, and does not speak for the individual. To turn the arbitrary into the natural, to make it seem as if the language was created for the moment of writing or speaking, is the task of the poet, making the reader believe that the expressions are spontaneous, invented for the purpose at hand. Here in contrast to his view of the late style of Beethoven, in which he finds that the music has become fragmentary, he remarks on the success of the "middle Beethoven," that is, the Symphonies Three to Eight, the fourth and fifth piano concertos, *Fidelio,* and the *Waldstein* and *Appassionata* sonatas. About this period, Adorno writes:

4. In the most detailed study of Adorno's writings on music, *Adorno, Modernism and Mass Culture* (London: Kahn & Averill, 1996), a brilliant piece of work, Max Paddison quotes this from a letter to H. H. Stuckenschmidt. Paddison writes that Schoenberg "misunderstood" Adorno's critiques. I don't see how.

For to tolerate no conventions, and to recast the unavoidable ones in keeping with the urge of expression, is the first demand of every "subjectivist" procedure. In this way, the middle Beethoven absorbed the traditional trappings into his subjective dynamic by forming latent middle voices, by rhythm, tension or whatever other means, transforming them in keeping with his intention. Or—as in the first movement of the Fifth Symphony—he even developed them from convention through the uniqueness of that substance.

This accurate description of Beethoven's technique is essentially what Guido Adler, the great Viennese musicologist and contemporary of Adorno, named in a brilliant account the defining characteristic of Viennese classicism, the obbligato accompaniment.[5] With this technique, which Adler identified in Viennese works from Haydn to Mozart, the accompanying voices—what Adorno calls "the latent middle voices"—are derived from the same thematic material as the principal voice, and the accompaniment ceases to appear arbitrary or conventional, but arises organically from the basic material and conception of the work. The principal melody and the accompaniment are cut from the same cloth, and match each other.

Far from being an invention of the middle-period Beethoven, however, the thematic technique of the obbligato accompaniment is essential to Haydn from the Quartets op. 33 (1780) on for the rest of his life. Deriving all the contrapuntal voices of a piece from the principal motifs has also been basic to Baroque style, and is exemplary in the fugues of Bach, in which all the voices are theoretically equal. What the later eighteenth century demanded, however, was a hierarchy of voices, a distinction between main voice and accompanying voices, in which one voice carries the melody and the other voices are clearly subordinate. It was largely the contemporary prestige of opera that imposed this hierarchy of solo part and accompaniment everywhere in music. The mechanical and banal accompanying figures of middle-century operatic style that resulted were given new vitality by Haydn through the new intimate relation between subordinate parts and the melody.

Blinded by his reverence for Beethoven, whose work he believed could be identified with the philosophy of Hegel, Adorno hardly noticed the existence of Haydn. In one of his rare references to Haydn, he wrote (in the essay "Society"):

These moments of transcendence do not occur in Haydn, nor do we find in his work the substantiality of the human individual, the eloquence of

5. In the *Handbuch der Musikgeschichte* (Berlin: Max Hesses Verlag, 2nd ed., 1930), vol. 2, pp. 788–793.

the detail, however meagre. This gives rise to an element of constriction, even of narrow-mindedness in Haydn, despite all the grandeur. The functional interconnections present throughout Haydn's music give an impression of competence, active life and suchlike categories, which ominously call to mind the rising bourgeoisie.

The last clause is an illustration of Adorno's attempt to unite art and society with a facile metaphor.[6] "Constriction" is an accurate if ungenerous way of describing Haydn's economy, but Adorno's lack of sympathy is evident in his disappointment that Haydn does not sound more like Beethoven.

Neglecting the tradition of Viennese classicism, Adorno misinterprets the role of convention in middle-period Beethoven. The conventions in the music that Beethoven wrote at this time of his life were often as naked as they became in the late works: they are paradoxically masked only by being magnified. The tritest possible cadence at the end of the Fifth Symphony, which would have been given two or (at most) eight bars by Mozart, takes fifty bars here. The most traditional way of returning to the main key at a recapitulation is subjected to an extraordinary inflation in the *Waldstein* Sonata, op. 53. Adorno's perceptive observation about the conventional formulae in the late style is illuminating, but he fails to understand that Beethoven had become by then simply more laconic, more economical. Adorno, however, wishes to characterize the late style as revealing a despair at no longer being able to achieve a synthesis of objectivity and subjectivity rather than a growing impatience with the facile low-level methods of synthesis and a sustained attempt to incorporate the most disparate and opposing elements within a single structure.

As an example of Beethoven's late use of the conventional, Adorno offers the Sonata in A-flat Major, op. 110: "The first theme . . . has an ingenuously simple sixteenth-note accompaniment which the middle style would hardly have tolerated." Unfortunately Adorno's admirers often treasure the worst aspects of his work. Inspired by this claim, Adorno's most eminent disciple, Edward W. Said, calls the accompaniment of this theme "a student-like, almost clumsy repetitive figure."[7] (It is, however, very similar to the opening accompaniment in Mozart's Rondo in A Minor, his most sophisticated and perhaps his greatest work for piano.)

---

6. Carl Dahlhaus wrote about Adorno's attempts to unite musical analysis and sociology, "The verbal analogies perform the function of hiding a gap which the arguments could not close." Quoted by Max Paddison, "Immanent Critique or Musical Stocktaking," in *Adorno: A Critical Reader,* edited by Nigel Gibson and Andrew Ruben (Oxford: Blackwell, 2002) p. 223.

7. Edward W. Said, "Adorno as Lateness Itself," in Gibson and Ruben, *Adorno,* p. 198.

It is untrue that Beethoven's middle style would not have tolerated so simple an accompanying figure: there are many examples of equally simple accompaniment in the years from 1800 to 1810,[8] but the problem lies not so much in the untenability of Adorno's generalization as in his failure to read the significance of the passage. As he himself says elsewhere, the meaning of any detail of a work of this kind has to be read with respect to the whole structure, but he fails to ask how the simplicity of the accompaniment in bars 5 to 12 operates in the movement.[9]

What Adorno sees as discontinuity in the late style is, in fact, a more powerful integration on a larger scale, one that can reconcile the most brutal contrasts. What causes him to misrepresent the character of the late work is his too easy identification of convention with objectivity and original expression with subjectivity. This relegates the conventional to the inexpressive, but the musical conventions have in fact an expressive charge of their own, and the art of the composer lies in knowing how to release that charge with the greatest effect. Adorno perceives the importance of the conventions in the work of elderly artists like Beethoven and Goethe, but he does not see the power of the most banal aspects of the musical and poetic languages, and he is hamstrung by the Romantic view that genius consists chiefly in breaking the rules.

This is manifest in a particularly absurd note for his Beethoven study (in "Music and Concept"):

> The works of great composers are mere caricatures of what they would have done had they been allowed. One should not assume any pre-established harmony between the artist and his time, inseparable as the two may be. . . . [Mozart's] music is a sustained attempt to outwit convention. In piano pieces such as the B minor Adagio, the Minuet in D major; in the "Dissonance Quartet"; in passages of *Don Giovanni* and heaven knows where else, traces of the dissonance he intended can be discerned. His harmony is not so much an expression of his nature as an effort of "tact." Only Beethoven dared to compose as he wanted: that, too, is a part of his uniqueness.

---

8. The tritest of all accompaniment figures, the so-called Alberti bass, is found in the first movement of the Sonata in E-flat Major, op. 31 no. 3, starting at bar 46 of the first movement, sustained for seven bars, and repeated unvaried. Many other instances of simple accompaniments can be adduced, particularly the type in which one chord is just repeated over and over unchanged, a technique to which Beethoven was addicted throughout his life.

9. It precedes a very elaborate accompanying figure which sweeps up and down the keyboard and that later combines with the opening bars. When the lyrical phrase with its simple accompaniment finally returns, it becomes the occasion for the only radical and dramatic modulation in the movement.

To explain the genius of an artist, we tend to concentrate on the more purple passages, the most outrageous and complex moments, the aspects that shocked contemporaries and that they found unacceptable. This is particularly egregious when dealing with Mozart, although it apparently works a bit better with Beethoven. Part of the greatness of Mozart is that he handled the conventional better than any of his contemporaries. It is, of course, possible that he might have liked to experiment more than he did. One will distort Mozart by taking him out of history, however, if one argues that he unwillingly invested the simplest cadences with extraordinary grace, that his tact is not as much a part of his nature as his more radical impulses, and that the exquisite sonority of the spacing of his music is less essential than the occasional indulgence in dissonant chromatic harmony.

The most spectacular critical failure of Adorno's Beethoven studies is the essay "Alienated Masterpiece: The Missa Solemnis." In an attempt to play the part of the little boy who saw that the emperor had no clothes, he claims that this work "remains enigmatically incomprehensible" and "offers no justification for the admiration accorded it."[10] The Mass is indeed difficult to appreciate and to perform (the two are connected), more difficult perhaps than any other late work of Beethoven, but, as Georg Christoph Lichtenberg once remarked about literary critics, when a book meets a head and there is a hollow sound, it is not always the fault of the book.

No other essay of Adorno is so riddled with unsupportable assertions. He writes: "Who after all can sing a passage from it the way one can sing a passage from any of the symphonies or from *Fidelio*?" I can. Comparing Beethoven's Kyrie with Bach's, he claims that in Beethoven, "there are complexes almost without melodic profile which delineate the harmony and avoid expression with a gesture of monumentality." Only the chorale parts at the opening, however, are solidly monumental; the solo voices, which start a few seconds after the chorus, have clearly defined motifs that are deeply expressive renderings of the text (*Kyrie eleison* means "Lord have mercy"). In this way, Beethoven solved a problem of church music that had beset composers for almost a century: the church wanted a setting of the opening Kyrie to be a celebration, while the aesthetic of most composers of the late Enlightenment called for a music that expressed the sense of the words. In Beethoven, the chorus with brass and strings largely affirms the dignity and the serious character of the rite; while the

10. Theodor W. Adorno, *Essays on Music,* edited by Richard Leppert (Berkeley: University of California Press, 2002), p. 569. This massive tome (over seven hundred pages) is the finest introduction to Adorno's musical thought, and the extensive commentary of Leppert is judicious, sympathetic, and invaluable. It will be indispensable for the study of Adorno for many years to come.

solo voices and the solo wind instruments give the prayer a personal and individual sense.

The most revealing point made by Adorno—revealing of his prejudice, not of the character of Beethoven's mass—is that the Et resurrexit of the Credo "is not endowed with the pathos which is raised to an extreme pitch in the analogous passage in Bach." Beethoven's setting of the resurrection is one of the most astonishing moments of the work. It is, indeed, laconic—only six bars long—and is one of the rare moments in the work where the text is set without instruments a cappella; it begins with a dramatic and sudden forte and a vigorous rhythm after the exhausted pianissimo ending of the depiction of the burial of Christ. The emphasis is on the first word *et* with a pause after it: "AND—he was resurrected on the third day according to scripture." The harmony recalls the medieval Lydian mode. Then the outburst of joy begins with "And he ascended into the heavens," with the scales that sweep to the highest register *sempre più forte*.

Adorno insists repeatedly on the archaic character of parts of the Mass, but the archaism is ostentatious only at two points, the Incarnation and the Resurrection. For a rational age, these were the two basic mysteries of faith, and Beethoven set them unforgettably into relief. The Incarnation is represented by bare and austere two-part counterpoint with the harmony of what sounds like the ancient Dorian mode, and the Resurrection by the supposedly medieval sound of voices alone. Adorno's comparison with the Bach setting makes little sense. The B Minor Mass was never performed during Bach's lifetime; nor was it for a century after his death (except for an execution of one movement by his son Phillip Emmanuel in Berlin), and it is unlikely that Beethoven knew it. The tradition he was working with was the settings of the text of the mass by the Haydns (Joseph and his brother Michael), Mozart, Cherubini, and other contemporaries.[11] As for Bach's treatment of the Resurrection, the music was not originally composed for that purpose at all but was an arrangement of an earlier piece from a cantata, and "pathos" is an odd word to describe it. It requires an act of will on the part of a critic as intelligent as Adorno to fail to recognize the power of Beethoven's representation and to miss its significance; it amounts to a refusal to listen.

Adorno's most serious charge against the *Missa Solemnis* is the creative lack of thematic development. The motifs are often simply restated after their first presentation, remaining identical. This is very perceptive of Adorno, and largely

11. In an excellent article on Adorno and Beethoven's Missa Solemnis, Paolo Isotta has persuasively maintained the influence of Haydn's "Creation" Mass on Beethoven's. ("Alcune Osservazioni sulla Forma della Missa Solemnis di Beethoven nota Antiadorniana," *Rivista Internazionale di Musica Sacra*, vol. 3, no. 3 (1982).

true, although he exaggerates the point (there is, in fact, considerable motivic development). But he does not ask why this is so, because he refuses to acknowledge what Beethoven is up to. Beethoven was clearly determined on an unprecedented setting of the text in which every syllable would receive a musical interpretation, from the descent of the dove of the holy spirit in the Benedictus, as the solo violin and two flutes descend from the heights, to the vision at the end of the Credo of the eternal life to come *(Et vitam venturi saeculi amen)* as the parallel scales of the orchestra rise from the depths and, continuously accelerating, disappear in the distance of the highest register. Adorno relays the cheap joke that Beethoven keeps repeating the word "credo" like one trying to convince himself that he believes; but for Beethoven, each clause of the Credo is, in fact, a further act of faith. That is why he gives such extraordinary importance throughout to the word *et:* "AND I believe" is the background significance of every phrase.

For his project, Beethoven needed not the neutral motifs that were malleable and so useful in symphony and sonata, but motifs that would be in every case a sufficient and definitive expression of the particular phrase of the text. That is why, for example, the beautiful cadence used to set "Give us peace" *(Dona nobis pacem)* at bars 212–215 is repeated so often without alteration: it is, in the most important sense, perfectly adequate. The casting of this section of the Mass as a pastoral is original, as are the interruptions of the tumult of war, which turn the prayer into a cry of desperation, and they give a musical meaning to the conception of peace.

Nevertheless, Adorno had a particular strategy in mind. For his view of the history of music and society, he needed the Mass to be a failure—and not only the Mass, but the whole late style of Beethoven, which he nevertheless revered. In what seems like a forecast of the movement to come of deconstruction in criticism, it is the greatness of an artist's failure that awakens Adorno's imagination. In order to understand the seduction of Adorno's view, I quote the following passage:

> The late Beethoven's demand for truth rejects the illusory appearance of the unity of subjective and objective, a concept practically at one with the classicist ideal. A polarization results. Unity transcends into the fragmentary. In the last quartets this takes place by means of the rough, unmediated juxtaposition of callow aphoristic motifs and polyphonic complexes. The gap between both becomes obvious and makes the possibility of aesthetic harmony into the aesthetic content of the work; makes failure in a highest sense a measure of success.

This is eloquent and moving. It is also largely false. Contrary to what he says, the juxtaposition of disparate material begins very early in Beethoven, reaching an early fulfillment in the piano sonatas, op. 31. In the *Tempest* Sonata, op. 31, no. 2, for example, within the space of a few seconds Beethoven forces together a slow mysterious arpeggio and a dramatic short allegro phrase. The contrasts of the late style are perhaps more difficult to accept at first hearing but a close listening reveals a powerful interaction.

The claim that "unity transcends into the fragmentary" is a fine example of Adorno's style: the fragmentary suggests failure, the transcendence a failure that has become a nobler success. But the claim cannot be seriously defended. No quartet has ever given a more obvious impression of greater unity than Beethoven's op. 131 in C-sharp Minor, and for most musicians even the abrupt changes of mood and character in the Quartet in B-flat Major, op. 130 (Beethoven's favorite quartet, he once said), have an extraordinary effect and become increasingly justified with repeated listening. Adorno's characterization of late Beethoven as fragmentary comes down in the end to nothing but a more grandiose way of saying how abrupt and disconcerting the late Beethoven can be.[12]

The failure is not Beethoven's, but Adorno's. Samuel Schonbaum once demonstrated that each biographer of Shakespeare saw him as resembling the biographer: Lytton Strachey's Shakespeare at the end of his career was bored with life and bored with literature, and Oscar Wilde saw a dramatist interested in elegant young men. Adorno wanted a Beethoven that resembled him. The most autobiographical of his books, *Minima Moralia,* is subtitled "Reflections from Damaged Life." Adorno's view of the world and of culture has been beautifully characterized by Edward Said, who puts his finger directly on what was essential:

> Adorno is very much a late figure because so much of what he does militates ferociously against his own time. Although he wrote a great deal in many fields, he attacked the major advances in all of them, functioning instead like an enormous shower of sulfuric acid poured over the lot. . . . It is the Zeitgeist that Adorno really loathed and that all his writing struggled mightily to insult.

His condemnation of his time, easy enough to understand and justify, did not, however, lead Adorno to support any movement to improve or alleviate the deplorable cultural conditions that were steadily worsening. His hatred was

---

12. Adorno's claim has induced Edward Said, in his conversations with Daniel Barenboim, *Parallels and Paradoxes* (New York: Pantheon, 2002), to give the last sonata (in C minor, op. 111) as an example of the fragmentary in late Beethoven: "Some of the pieces, like the last sonata, are unfinished; it's only two movements." Many musicians would consider the second movement the greatest and most satisfying finale of a piano sonata ever written. It is difficult to decide which is more astonishing: Said's ludicrous statement or Barenboim's failure to protest.

poured into his criticism, not into possibilities of action. The sad last days of his life were colored by this refusal of practical engagement. When the student revolts of 1968 reached the University of Frankfurt, Adorno evinced no sympathy for the students, and was seen shaking hands with the stocky chief of police who brutally put down the rebellion. The students organized a Bacchanalian dance around Adorno in the lecture room. He fled and died of a heart attack not long after.

Adorno's contempt for contemporary society fueled his passion, and in a time of troubles, could be welcome; it strikes a responsive chord. It was brightly colored by the relentlessly polemical tone and the use of pejorative terms to express ordinary developments as if they were a failure of ethics. If Stravinsky uses tonality in an original way, that is called "mutilated tonality." Beethoven's increasing interest in fugue and his renewed study of Bach are pretentiously described by Adorno as if they were the acts of a desperate man:

> The composer experiments with strict style because formal bourgeois freedom is not sufficient as a stylization principle. The composition unremittingly controls whatever is to be filled out by the subject under such externally dictated stylization principles.

Under Adorno's hands, many of the terms so frequently repeated begin to lose a great part of their meaning. He himself makes a fetish of "fetishism," as well as of "bourgeois," "subjectivity," "regressive," "infantile," and other words, which tend to become vacuous when applied so mechanically and so uncritically. I do not know what he means by "the withering of harmony" in late Beethoven, and I do not believe that it could be an adequate description of any phenomenon that I would recognize.

With all their defects, Adorno's polemics are invigorating at a time when traditional culture seems in trouble. In addition, his sharp intelligence led him to confront important issues in the arts and culture that other critics refused to face—changes in reading and listening habits, the increasing difficulty of modern art, the influence of commercial interests in artistic distribution. His intelligence, nevertheless, was derivative rather than original. One important influence on Adorno is not mentioned by his admirers because it is no longer intellectually respectable: the Oswald Spengler of the once-famous *Decline of the West*. Like Spengler, he preferred intuition to empirical research, and theory to empirical description. This gave his work a unique character. He combined brilliant insights into the phenomena of culture with an essentially fraudulent manipulation of terms to hide the inadequate relation of his theory to historical detail.

His view of modern culture arises from the natural despair of one who lived through the terrible inflation in the Germany of the 1920s, which ruined so many upper-middle-class families. His attack on commercial interests betrayed him into an idealization of the past: a wonderful time when subjectivity and objectivity were balanced, when listening was not regressive. In our time, he argued in "On the Fetish-Character in Music and the Regression of Listening,"

> Contemporary listening . . . has regressed, arrested at the infantile stage. Not only do the listening subjects lose, along with freedom of choice and responsibility, the capacity for conscious perception of music, which was from time immemorial confined to a narrow group, but they stubbornly reject the possibility of such perception.

This account of the present age implies that there was a time when things were much better, but Adorno is almost never precise about what life was like before the rot set in.

Once, however, he gives us a glimpse of the better world of the past. It is in the fragments entitled *Minima Moralia,* his best-written work. Many of its frequent aphorisms, the heritage of a great German tradition, are excellent, although a few sputter like damp firecrackers. In any case, at one point his prose rises to a truly poetic evocation of the Golden Age, a world whose disappearance is a cause of poignant regret. What was this world whose disappearance could inspire in Adorno such profound and ironic nostalgia?

> Rampant technology eliminates luxury, but not by declaring privilege a human right; rather, it does so by both raising the general standard of living and cutting off the possibility of fulfillment. The express train that in three nights and two days hurtles across the continent is a miracle, but traveling in it has nothing of the faded splendor of the train bleu. What made up the voluptuousness of travel, beginning with the goodbye-waving through the open window, the solicitude of amiable accepters of tips, the ceremonial of mealtimes, the constant feeling of receiving favors that take nothing from anyone else, has passed away, together with the elegant people who were wont to promenade along the platforms before the departure, and who will by now be sought in vain even in the foyers of the most prestigious hotels. That the steps of railway carriages have to be retracted intimates to the passenger of even the most expensive express that he must obey the company's terse regulations like a prisoner. Certainly, the company gives him the exactly calculated value of his fare, but this includes nothing that research has not proved an average demand. Who, aware of such conditions, could depart on impulse on a voyage with his mistress as once from Paris to Nice?

CHAPTER 19

Resuscitating Opera:
Alessandro Scarlatti

I T SHOULD BE a cause for rejoicing that much of our ignorance of the history of music is permanent, irrevocable. In economic and social history, a statistical sampling or a well-established general trend can sometimes stand in for a large number of missing specific facts: we do not need to know the details of every market transaction, every marriage contract. In the history of music, as of any other art, nothing can supply the absence of the individual work. Knowledge of the work itself is not simply one of the prerequisites of research in music history, but the goal. Economic history does not exist until the data are grouped and generalized: for music history, generalization is either a second best, or an intermediate step on the road that starts with the work and returns to it with greater understanding.

The history of music begins to collapse under the strain of too many works. Understanding a work of music is not quite synonymous with enjoying it, but it demands imagining someone else's enjoyment, and seeing why this is, or once was, possible. Any generalization is based on this necessary effort of appreciation. No music historian, therefore, can build on his predecessor's labors with anything like the confidence, however limited, of the historian of science. Each advance in any branch of history may demand a tiresome reexamination of each piece of detailed evidence, but in the history of an art it also leads to a renewed concentration on the individual work, a reappreciation. Too much evidence, and the process would grind to a halt.

For this reason, the historian of, say, eighteenth-century music tended to rely blindly on nineteenth-century values to select his evidence for him and, in short, to determine his field of study. He concentrated above all not on what was done in the eighteenth century, but on what later generations thought was important out of all the things that were done. This old-fashioned attitude could be justified persuasively enough: history is what is remembered. Mozart was remembered and his elder and once-famous contemporary Wagenseil, who wrote some fine works, was forgotten; Mozart remains a living force in the history of music until this day, while Wagenseil must be disinterred each time in order to reenter history. I have been told, to my surprise, that Wagenseil continued to be performed occasionally in Vienna during the early decades of the nineteenth century, twenty and thirty years after his death in 1777. That proves only that one can be both performed and forgotten. (In fact, it still happens today. Many works are played simply because the conductor once learned the score and the parts are easily available, and no one—neither public nor orchestra—pays the slightest notice, except for the critic who reports the event.)

A wave of historicism in the twentieth century and an ever-growing uncertainty of values threaten the comfort and stability of musicology. What ought to count, it is now felt, is not what later generations thought great, but what contemporaries judged significant. Since this formula would eliminate now-acknowledged masterpieces like Bach's *Passion According to Saint Matthew,* which (as far as we know) passed unregarded and unappreciated by Bach's contemporaries, it has to be enlarged to include everything that contemporaries or their posterity judged significant. That opens the floodgates. Since hardly an opera was ever produced or a piano sonata published that did not have the respect of someone besides the composer, the study of music ceases to be concerned only with masterpieces (why should it be?) and becomes genuinely democratic and tolerant. Works of music, like their composers, are children of God and He loves them all.

Happily, therefore, many thousands of works have disappeared beyond recall. On hearing that a manuscript of Byzantine chant, which had never been transcribed or photographed, had been destroyed, a friend who works in that field exclaimed with relief: "Thank God! One less to deal with." It is not the unimportant and the trivial that have gone forever. Major works, unquestionably among the finest of their time, have been totally annihilated. This is, above all, the case with operas, almost none of which were published before the end of the eighteenth century. Few people needed or wanted a full score and the orchestral parts of an opera, and even during the nineteenth century it was usual for an opera company to pay for a handwritten copy: manuscript copies, indeed, were easily obtained, and there were copying bureaus in several Italian cities and elsewhere.

In the eighteenth century, manuscript copies were naturally even more wide-spread than in the nineteenth. Bach's *Well-Tempered Keyboard,* for example, was known and played by many musicians including Mozart and Beethoven long before it was published. Copying music was a menial but not a degrading task: Rousseau preferred to make his living by it. An opera that was performed only a few times (and in an age of frequent and revolutionary changes of musical style, many operas became old-fashioned almost before being staged) had a good chance of vanishing completely, leaving nothing behind except the libretto, if that, and the bill for the scenery and costumes. Of the more than a dozen operas by Monteverdi, the first master of the form, only the earliest one (*Orfeo* of 1609) and two late ones (*Il Ritorno di Ulisse* of 1641 and *L'Incoronazione di Poppea* of 1642) have come down to us. What he did in the intervening thirty years was never published and the manuscripts were destroyed during his lifetime.

The greatest composer of opera at the beginning of the eighteenth century is generally agreed to be Alessandro Scarlatti. So far this reputation has been based largely on hearsay, on the word of a few scholars who have actually seen a score. Scarlatti wrote more than a hundred operas between 1679 and 1721: the music for less than half of these has survived, sometimes only in fragmentary form. Until 1974, only two of these operas had been completely published, neither in a satisfactory edition.

For the study of the history of music, the most important event of the 1970s has been the start of a complete critical edition of Alessandro Scarlatti's operas, under the direction of Donald Jay Grout, with the help of Joscelyn Godwin and H. Colin Slim. What graduate students in music today know about their subject comes largely from Grout's excellent one-volume general history. After his recent retirement from Cornell, he has devoted himself passionately to the operas of Alessandro Scarlatti. The first volume came out in 1974, and four more have been issued to date. Professor Grout told me that around another two dozen operas are salvageable, enough of their music having come down to us to warrant publication. Perhaps someone will then commence work on a complete edition of the five hundred or so cantatas of Scarlatti that are still extant today.

Serious opera *(opera seria)* between Monteverdi and Mozart has had a bad press, while the importance of comic opera *(opera buffa)* has been more generally recognized. Opera seria, in its time the most prestigious form of music, is the most neglected today, the least performed and perhaps the least understood. It is obviously unfair to judge the opera seria from 1660 to 1760 by the dramatic standards which we would apply to most plays and most other operas, but this very unfairness requires some comment. The operas of Monteverdi, both *Orfeo* and *L'Incoronazione di Poppea,* treat classical mythology and classical history in a Baroque style with some plausibility and great dignity. Later, Mozart could meet Beaumarchais's plays and even Molière's with a dramatic conception fully their equal, as Verdi could deal with the plays of Victor Hugo and Shakespeare. In early eighteenth-century opera in France, however, the influence of the tragedies of Racine was palpable, but more as a reproach than an inspiration. In Italy (and Germany, where the opera was largely Italian in language and even in style), the conception of drama in opera was even more constrained.

Racine's plays and the eighteenth-century French opera librettos that imitated them, however distantly, reached out of their court atmosphere not only to the mythological world of Greek tragedy, but also to the political world of ancient Rome and, by implication, of modern Europe. The Italian librettos (even—or perhaps above all—those of Metastasio, the greatest of the early eighteenth-century Italian poets, and master and tyrant of the libretto form) stay almost entirely within a completely artificial court ideal, heavily influenced by the antiquated pastoral of the Renaissance; the politics rarely rises above court intrigue and then only when some kind of dynastic consideration is involved.

An example is the medieval male-chauvinist tale of Griselda, the patient wife who never wavered in the respect, obedience, and love she owed her husband, even when he beat her, took away her children, and repudiated her publicly. In its original form, it has a grisly emblematic power. In the libretto by the court poet at Vienna, Apostolo Zeno, set by Scarlatti among many others, it is degraded into a series of public humiliations for the low-born wife of King Gualtiero, so that his rebellious nobles would be persuaded by her virtue that she was worthy to reign and, above all, that the son she bore Gualtiero was a worthy heir.

Another opera by Scarlatti, *Marco Attilio Regolo*, has a subject that would have been most apt for a heroic drama of Corneille: a Roman general, captured by the Carthaginians, is sent by them on his word of honor back to Rome to arrange peace; instead he urges war and returns voluntarily to Carthage alone to be put to death. For most of the opera this subject is pushed aside: the Roman general has a wife and a daughter captured with him; the commander of the Spartans, allies to the Carthaginians, loves the daughter; the Carthaginian general loves the mother, and he repudiates his fiancée, the princess of Sicily, who loves him although she has only seen his picture; and she disguises herself as a man to plan revenge—what kind of revenge is unclear. (A later libretto by Metastasio on the same subject restored the basic heroic theme, but dissipated most of its energy.)

It is easy enough to make fun of any form of drama, and opera is particularly subject to absurdity. But nineteenth-century opera—hero and villain exchanged long ago as infants in the cradle, the hunchback with the beautiful daughter, the dragon-killer—has a fairy-tale charm: it is disfigured mostly by its obeisance to the moral pieties, as when John of Leyden in Meyerbeer's *Le Prophète* gives up his revolution because he loves his mother. Early eighteenth-century opera seria repudiates comparison with any other form of literature except court pastoral—and that in an insipid form, with all the Renaissance idealism and bold speculation of the pastorals of Sidney and Tasso drained out of the genre: even the erotic casuistry of the early seventeenth-century pastoral is coarsened and cheapened.

The politics of romantic nineteenth-century opera has some force in, say, *William Tell, Les Huguenots, Don Carlos,* and *The Sicilian Vespers;* but, with few exceptions, the sole political interest of opera seria is that of the alliance by marriage of ruling families. Will the princess disguised as a shepherd win the love of the prince disguised as his best friend? No doubt marriage between two ruling houses was the façade behind which some of the important political developments actually took place in the seventeenth and even the eighteenth centuries, but the pastoral conventions of opera seria are a façade for a façade—in so far as they retain any significance at all.

The original ideals of opera had been jettisoned by 1700. The invention of opera in the late sixteenth and early seventeenth centuries came about, at least to some extent, as an attempt to recreate Greek tragedy. We are almost as ignorant today as then about music in classical Greece, but one thing was known: Greek tragedy was chanted and sung. By the end of the seventeenth century, however, the model of Greek tragedy had been largely abandoned (although it was never wholly forgotten, merely pushed into the background of consciousness as an inconvenience: it came to the fore again by the 1760s with the operas of Gluck). Opera seria became a specialized, artificial form that had little to do with the drama of its own time or of any other.

The narrowness of the world of opera seria arose from its dependence on court and singer. The dependence on court patronage was inevitable because of expense. Opera has almost always been a losing proposition, needing huge, even extravagant subsidies. Put on a concert of avant-garde chamber music and you will lose only a few thousand dollars, and perhaps break even. Produce the most popular opera (say, *La Bohème*) and there is a dead certainty that the loss will run into tens of thousands—perhaps hundreds of thousands if you do it on the scale of the Paris Opéra. Those losses are invariably paid for out of the taxpayer's pocket, directly or indirectly. In the seventeenth and eighteenth centuries, the court was often directly concerned in the production of opera. There were public opera houses, too, but they also generally required aristocratic patronage. Popular singers commanded high fees, scenery was lavish, scenic effects (traditionally including earthquakes, a bear, etc.) expensive. The influence of the patron's taste on both subject matter and form in the opera was as inescapable as the influence of advertising on television programs.

The tyranny of the singer has always been the glory and the misery of Italian opera. The early eighteenth century was the age of the castrato. In Rome, where for a time women were not allowed to appear on the stage, all the parts of an opera would often be sung by eunuchs. Musical forms became standardized to permit individual vocal display: duets are infrequent, trios and quartets rare. The basic form is a three-part aria in ABA form called the da capo aria: the third part is a literal repetition of the first part—literal, except for improvised embellishments added by the singer, generally very lavishly. From 1700 to 1740 almost all arias in opera seria take this form. The technique of embellishment was then among the most elaborate and most powerful that Western music has known before the coming of jazz. The return of the first part was a real test, both of the singer's vocal technique and of his or her ability to improvise expressive ornamentation. The early eighteenth century concentrated most of the power of expression in the ornamentation—written out in instrumental works by Johann Sebastian Bach and Couperin, or improvised in those of Handel and Alessandro Scarlatti.

The only other musical texture admitted by opera seria, with rare exceptions, was that rapid, barely sung, largely spoken form called recitative. Dry recitative—recitativo secco—is the main form, the harmonies provided by a keyboard and a bass instrument. Accompanied recitative is a more expressive version, the harmonies now provided by the orchestra. An intermediate form of the seventeenth century, the arioso, expressively sung but with a speaking quality and a free musical structure, was abandoned. The chorus of the early essays in opera was dropped in Italy (although retained in France): any chorus was provided briefly by the five or six principals singing together. Without arioso and chorus, and with only a rare ensemble, opera was reduced to two textures: recitative, barely distinguishable from speech; and aria, formal and elaborate.

This division now determined the dramatic form: action took place in recitative, sentiment was expressed in aria. No attempt was made to combine formal music and action; occasionally there was an interesting harmonic change or—even more rarely—a broken phrase and an expressive turn or two in the recitative. This was not a love-match between drama and music, but a marriage of convenience, each party going its separate way. The librettist was, of course, interested in the recitatives (one could easily understand the words there and he often put his most interesting poetry into them), but hardly anyone else was. It is true that recitatives were often not as dull as they were said to be, but the musical interest is always at its lowest point.[1] People often talked or played chess during the recitatives, and stopped only to listen to the arias.

The century's disdain for the recitatives of opera seria is shown by the contemporary manuscript copies: many of them omit all the recitatives. Some of these manuscripts were selections of airs for private or semiprivate performance. They also omit orchestral introductions and the few ensemble pieces. Others, however, have the complete opera with all the orchestral detail minus the recitatives. As late as the 1770s, Niccolò Jommelli's beautiful *Olimpiade* was published in full score but without the secco recitatives—a pity, because Jommelli's settings of dry recitative were far less perfunctory than those of most other composers. A production based on this score would have meant hiring someone to rewrite the recitatives—not a daunting prospect, evidently. (The score cannot have been intended for private performance, as it is very elaborate, and one of the arias uses a double orchestra.) It was obviously not worth engraving recitatives when a local musician could recompose them more cheaply.

One exception to this general musical indifference to recitativo secco needs to be noted. The recitatives of comic scenes are often included with the arias in manuscripts for home performance. For Scarlatti's *Eraclea* of 1700, only the comic recitatives survive, although the formal music of the arias is otherwise complete. In comic scenes the arias and recitatives are much more closely integrated, and it was, indeed, only in comic opera that the eighteenth century was to find a way to unite dramatic action and music. The first experiments in this seem to have been made by Galuppi in the 1740s, and it was Mozart who finally achieved the synthesis. What probably saved comic opera was that it never seemed an important enough genre to become official government music with a large subsidy. It was therefore forced to depend on the rendering of a lively and realistic action in music instead of on expensive singers and scenery.

The exclusive alternation and opposition of recitative and aria turns opera seria into a string of situations that create pretexts for emotional outburst and vocal display; the two are largely synonymous—that is the strength of the style, as no period has ever better understood the emotional effect of virtuosity. (The instrumental virtuosity of the Romantic era—of Chopin and Liszt—is in many ways a re-creation of this traditional operatic technique.) After each outpouring of sentiment, the singer generally left the stage (so he or she could be recalled by applause, I presume) even if the aria had been a declaration of love or a plea for mercy which would imply some hopes of an answer.

---

1. Many composers, of course, took great care over the dry recitatives, but the musical form is only that of a local response to the text—an interesting harmonic or melodic detail. There was never a possibility of creating a larger musical form with it, or even—and this must be emphasized—of integrating it within a larger form.

In the finest works of the period, above all those of Alessandro Scarlatti and Handel, there is much great music. The librettos often contain some lovely poetry and some shrewd and neat juggling with the conventions of the genre. Metastasio is a far more elegant versifier than any other librettist: he makes even da Ponte and Boito look coarse, not to mention Wagner and most of the hacks who wrote for Rossini and Verdi. (Scarlatti died before Metastasio's period of fame, and Handel rarely set his texts.) If one's level of expectation is not too high, one can find a certain dramatic coherence in the best operas. It is not only that one needs different standards to appreciate opera seria, however, but lower ones—at least if it is judged as drama. These works for the stage, therefore, stand apart from the great achievements of Monteverdi and Mozart which came before and after them. Some of the music in them is as sublime as any ever written, but a revival will, I think, always seem quaint, always remain an archaeological enterprise.

The reason for this is that a string of great arias does not make a great drama. The finest operas of this period are, one must admit, more than a mere string of arias—but only a little more. The structure of the genre prevented it from being much more than that. There were many complicated rules about which type of aria should follow another—rules more often obeyed than broken: each principal singer had to have a certain number of arias of different types, and less important singers had to have an allotted number, too, placed so as not to take away from the grand effect made by the stars. The classification of aria types was very complicated: it appears to have been an important consideration to librettist and composer, although it is more than a little puzzling today.

Any attempt to find psychological portraiture in these works is most often wishful thinking on the part of the critic. The kind of aria written was largely tailored to the needs and whims of the original cast. This gives the illusion of consistency of character to the music written for each role, but it is only a consistency of musical type. When the cast changed (or when a principal singer changed his mind about the style he liked), new arias had to be written, often by another composer to new words—frequently enough the new aria fit badly into the plot.[2] It must, in fact, have been exceedingly rare for two productions of an opera to have exactly the same music: singers were accustomed to sing an effective aria they had learned from an earlier work in any other opera they were appearing in.

2. In an interesting essay on Vivaldi's *Griselda,* John Walter Hill has shown that the recitatives were sometimes changed to accommodate the new arias. The changes in the arias were made, according to the librettist Goldoni, to fit the developing vocal style of the prima donna, but Hill claims reasonably that dramatic effectiveness played a role in the revision as well. *Journal of the American Musicological Society* 31, no. 1 (1978).

Late in the century, Mozart was obliged to make minor revisions for the second production of *Don Giovanni,* when it was done in Vienna. His changes, however, leave the large-scale structure mostly intact. The trouble with early eighteenth-century opera is that there is no large-scale structure that could be damaged. This was, in a way, an advantage: the effect of revision and rewriting was minimal—unless the revisions were particularly absurd. As a result, there is no musical shape to the opera as a whole: the libretto has some shape but there is nothing in the music to correspond to it; the structural principle of the music is essentially one damn aria after another. The succession of arias was governed largely by contrast—what musical life there is in the form is discontinuous, from moment to moment. Only Handel seems to have succeeded sporadically in creating groups of arias that hang together as a larger complex, and there is no consistency about his procedure.[3]

The creation of a large form in opera does not exist between Monteverdi and Mozart. It was not beyond the grasp of the contemporary composer when he was given a variety of textures to build with. Bach created a large-scale form in *The Passion According to St. Matthew* with such a variety: besides aria and recitative, he had arioso, chorus in concerto grosso form, and chorale. Handel had a similar success in oratorio with similar means. Most of these means were forbidden to the Italian opera from 1700 to 1770. Earlier, Monteverdi had the freedom of texture that was lost afterward, turned into a rigid succession. The development of the ensemble and the large finale (a long succession of ensembles at the end of an act) in comic opera gave Mozart, by the 1780s, the possibility of constructing a total form, and restored integrity to opera.[4]

Edward J. Dent has written:

> Scarlatti, indeed, is the founder of that musical language which has served the classical composers for the expression of their thoughts down to the close of the Viennese period. Thematic development, balance of melodic phrase, chromatic harmony—all the devices which the seventeenth century had tentatively introduced, are by him woven into a smooth and supple texture, which reached its perfection in one who, although he never knew his true master, was yet his best pupil, Mozart.[5]

3. See Grout, *A Short History of Opera,* 2nd ed. (New York: Columbia University Press, 1965), p. 161. His account is deeply skeptical, and he remarks on some insignificant examples of tonal consistency in operas of Keiser and Purcell.

4. The unexplored possibilities of the earlier part of the century may be glimpsed in the rare ensembles in Scarlatti, or in the duet "Padre/Sposo" from Marco Attilio Regolo (misprinted "Sposa" in the score).

5. *Grove's Dictionary of Music and Musicians,* 5th ed., vol. 7, p. 452.

This is the kind of nonsense that sometimes masquerades as the history of music. In fact, Scarlatti had far less to do with later stylistic developments than his younger rivals, composers of early eighteenth-century Italian opera like Lotti and Porpora. Dent's book on Scarlatti is the only one in English, so passages like this still get quoted. It represents a standard device: in order to establish the importance of a little-known figure, he is made the ancestor of someone that we all know—a kind of reverse pedigree established through the grandchildren. Only in this way, it appears, can he truly enter history.

In a trivial sense, of course, Dent is right: history is a continuum, and anything that happened in 1700 is necessarily the ancestor of all that happened in 1780. The facile and widespread view that Dent represents, however, is the history of music as an endless relay race in which the great composers hand the torch on to each other across the ages while the minor figures play their indispensable role of tending the flame, keeping it alive. But in so far as the history of music is the history of what is "great" (however that is defined or determined), it is discontinuous, a history of ruptures and breaks. The traditional view, which attempts to integrate these discontinuities into a grand movement of history—little waves ruffling the surface of the great sea of time—is generally harmless. In the case of a wonderful but—until now—inaccessible figure like Alessandro Scarlatti, it is insidious. To appreciate both Scarlatti's greatness and his subsequent extraordinary eclipse, we need to understand that he was a dead end.

Even Dent's larger considerations are misleading: the seventeenth century did not introduce, tentatively or otherwise, "thematic development, balance of melodic phrase, chromatic harmony"—all this existed since at least the fifteenth century, and the use of these devices in the eighteenth century is radically different from their use in the seventeenth. But it is perhaps a pity to belabor a writer like Dent for the kind of foolishness we have all been guilty of: he had the enthusiasm that distinguishes the better British musicologist, and many of his observations on Scarlatti are very fine.

For the nonspecialist, assessing Scarlatti's place in the history of opera has been made much easier by Howard Brown's facsimile printing of fifty manuscript copies of Italian operas from 1640 to 1770. I should think that, except for the works of Handel and Pergolesi, fewer than two dozen operas from this period have been previously printed complete: the easily available material has therefore suddenly been tripled. Few of Brown's choices are opera buffa: the concentration is upon opera seria. The fifty operas have been chosen from the works of forty-five composers. We get no adequate idea of any one composer, although a good view of the general activity in Italy and Germany. An important composer like Niccolò Jommelli is represented by two operas; another had been published by the great German scholar Hermann Abert in 1907. Unfortunately all three now available works are from the 1760s. Since Jommelli was already writing operas in the late 1730s, it would be interesting to see something of the early work. At what point did he acquire the extraordinary style of the operas written for the court at Stuttgart: brilliant, serious, even grim, without charm, and with an intense development of short motifs comparable to the instrumental music of Carl Philipp Emanuel Bach?

Looking over several of the drearily tuneful works in this series gives one a foretaste of the scholarship of the twenty-second century, when musicologists will dredge through piles of Broadway musicals, discovering some kind of musical invention only in rare figures like Gershwin and Arlen. The average libretto of the Broadway show, too, is no more absurd or incoherent and not always less pretentious than those of opera seria.

Brown's publication has not resolved for me the mystery of Johann Adolf Hasse's immense and long-lasting reputation: the opera he prints, *Siroe*, of 1733, seems to me to have the same easily singable, easily forgettable style that I know from the only other example printed some years ago, *Arminio*. Those historians who are as puzzled as I am explain it by Hasse's durable marriage to the most famous soprano of the time, which gave him the prestige of years of brilliant performance, but that is surely insufficient to account for his glory. Brown calls *Siroe* "a superb example of Hasse's music when the composer was first at the height of his powers." Perhaps the secret is that the music is both vigorous and facile. It stimulates mildly without shock. It is a pleasure to turn from it to the comic opera of Galuppi that Brown prints, *La Diavolessa*.

In general, Brown's choice of operas is impeccable: every one of his composers deserved to be present, although some of them need a larger scale; a new series is planned, and perhaps the gaps will be filled. Everyone interested in eighteenth-century music should be deeply grateful for the ones already printed.

The operas by the contemporaries and successors of Scarlatti in this series demonstrate the justice of Grout's observation,[6] very different from Dent's assessment:

> His [Scarlatti's] fate, like Bach's, was to be outmoded before his death, "a great man—forgotten by his own generation." His influence, except on Handel and Hasse, was only partial and indirect. His own happy combination of strength and sweetness, of passion and humor, was not to be heard again in music until the time of Mozart.

Scarlatti is indeed sometimes like Mozart, but the relation, as Grout implies, is not historical, but an affinity of type—just as Ingres thought rightly enough

6. In *Short History of Opera*, p. 180.

that Mozart was like Raphael. Scarlatti's actual influence was small: to the names of Handel and Hasse, we should perhaps add Vivaldi. The influence on Hasse is difficult to define; perhaps Grout put him in because he is known to have studied with Scarlatti. But the young Hasse arrived in Naples only a year or so before Scarlatti died in 1725: the association was not long, and the little of Hasse's music that I know seems to come straight from the style of those rival composers who were popular when the old Scarlatti was already neglected.

The operatic style of Handel is in great part a direct expansion of Scarlatti's: what Handel missed of the older composer's delicacy and wit, he made up for by an unparalleled rhythmic energy, a sense of mass, and a flair for dramatic effect. Neither he nor Vivaldi often accepted the stereotypes developed by the younger contemporaries of Scarlatti—Antonio Lotti, Leonardo Vinci, Antonio Porpora (samples of whose work are now at last available in Brown's set). These stereotypes—short symmetrical phrase grouping, simple popular tunes, easily perceptible formal symmetries—carried the seed of the future: if anything led to Viennese classicism (not all that directly in this case either), it was this largely uninspiring music, and not the subtle, aristocratic, reactionary art of Alessandro Scarlatti.

Between the style of Handel, as it came from Scarlatti, Purcell, and others, and Mozart, there is a break. It was not until the 1780s, when Mozart's musical language was already fully formed, that he could take account of Handel's achievement. From those years may be dated the reentry of Handel and Bach into the mainstream of musical influence. They have never needed rediscovery since. Alessandro Scarlatti lacked that good fortune. The time has probably passed when he could be a vital musical influence, but with Grout's beautiful new edition he is now a permanent acquisition for musicians and students.

The present revival of interest in opera seria is no doubt part of that new conservative movement that hopes to revive French nineteenth-century academic painting, the Victorian potboiler novel, the salon music of Gottschalk. The rehabilitation of opera seria is helped and discredited by the strange alliance of two comic figures, the antiquarian and the opera buff.

Neither is necessarily interested in music: the opera buff may be interested mostly in sopranos, old recordings of coloratura arias, and operas that no one has heard of; the antiquarian in ancient instruments and obsolete styles of performance. They are like those adolescents in Britain who watch trains or copy down automobile license numbers, and they have the same relation to music that those do to transportation.

The opera buff knows interesting things like what year Mme Callas lost weight, and how long Selma Kurz could sing a high E at the end of "Caro nome" in *Rigoletto* (she would go back stage, walk up a flight of stairs, and reappear on the balcony of Rigoletto's house on the stage still singing the note).

Some opera buffs would rather hear a performance of Auber's *Gustave III ou le Bal Masqué* than Verdi's masterpiece on the same subject, *Un Ballo in Maschera*. The antiquarian knows that early instruments were very different from modern ones and generally played out of tune, and that is the way he likes to hear Handel played; he knows that eighteenth-century singers often ruined their arias by overembellishment and outraged the composers, and he would be thrilled to hear someone sing that way today. He complains when he cannot hear a keyboard instrument accompanying a Haydn symphony, although Haydn's contemporaries complained when they could hear it. He has his patches of ignorance: he is certain that all of Scarlatti's sonatas are for the harpsichord and thinks that choral music in the Renaissance was always a cappella (or, alternatively, never a cappella—the ignorance remaining constant while the sophistication changes). They are both rank materialists; they equate a work of music with its performance and would not understand the profundity of Mark Twain's "Wagner is better than he sounds."

The renewed attention given to opera seria provides a field day for these two: their interests are generally opposed, but now they have joined hands. To some extent, anyone will sympathize with the camp taste for this absurd genre. Opera seria glorified the singer; its chief interest (like that of *Lucia di Lammermoor* a century later) was dazzling vocal display used to express a heartbreaking situation; hardly anybody has ever heard or seen one of these works; the music has until recently been difficult to access; a large part of the research on the subject consists delightfully of gossip about the lives of the castrati and the prime donne; and almost every aspect of the style of performance is not only obsolete, but in some cases impossible to reconstruct.

There is often a lack of frankness about the special pleading for old performance practice and old instruments. It goes largely unmentioned that the style of vocal ornament used from 1700 to 1750 is unsuited to anything except a small hall (and opera houses were often then quite tiny), but anyone who has ever heard the delicate French ornaments in a Rameau opera bawled over the orchestra in the present vastness of the Paris Opéra will never forget it. We are not often told that we do not know how some of those old instruments really sounded, particularly the keyboard instruments—it is naive to imagine their sonority has not altered in two centuries—and that we are still not exactly sure how others were played. An "authentic" performance of a Scarlatti opera— even if there were such a thing—is not even going to be approached in this life. The antiquarian and the opera buff have stopped short of insisting on a return to the castrato, but that is only because they think they have no chance of getting away with it.

If we are to capture even a part of the heritage of Scarlatti for the general musical public, then it must be taken out of the hands of these people, and restored to musicians. We also need modest views. One sentence in the preface of Joscelyn Godwin's wholly admirable edition of *Marco Attilio Regolo* makes me uneasy: "Any producer of the opera should aim at the greatest possible splendor and display. 'Modern' sets make a sad background to this extravagant poetry and elevated music." Mr. Godwin is right, but I hope nobody listens to him. Even if anyone could afford to pay for it (and anyone eventually means the taxpayer), I do not see why this discreditable and discredited genre should be resuscitated. No doubt Scarlatti's music would gain by being heard in something like its original context, but (as I have tried to explain above) the gain is too small to be worth the cost. The music can stand without such props.

The problem, indeed, is that the music is so good that it is only worth doing superlatively well. I am tolerably entertained when Dittersdorf, or Henselt, or Vivaldi, or Praetorius are given a moderately good performance. It is the inadequacies in a performance of Mozart, or Josquin, or Beethoven, or Debussy that are unbearable. A full opera of Scarlatti is beyond our reach: we need singers with several years of experience in the style, and a great deal of experimentation in performance, before we can envisage a large-scale attempt. The editors' advice on performance practice is very wise in these volumes. Applied to make music and not antique reproductions, their recommendations are indispensable to any attempt to perform these works. Perhaps a concert performance of an act or even a complete opera would be workable: if audiences can take to Berlioz's *Béatrice et Bénédict* in concert, they might accept two hours of Scarlatti.

Grout's beautiful words about the operatic music of Scarlatti's great contemporary Rameau should be recalled here:

> Today it stands as a classic example of great music forgotten because it cannot be detached from a dead operatic style—for Rameau's opera cannot be revived as a living art without reviving the age of Louis XV. Yet by means of the requisite knowledge and imagination, one can in some measure learn to hear and see it as it lived in Paris under the ancien régime and thereby alone arrive at a just estimate of its greatness.[7]

This is as true of Scarlatti and equally tragic. The new edition gives us the requisite knowledge and the opportunity to use our imagination. The music transcends its time, as a glance at the scores will show. The genre for which it was written is dead. Rightly and permanently dead. It remains to be seen whether some of the music may be made to live again after all.

---

7. *Short History of Opera*, p. 173.

CHAPTER 20

Operatic Paradoxes:
The Ridiculous and Sublime

I

The most prestigious of musical forms, opera is also traditionally the most absurd, the most irrational. No musical dictionary could ever deal adequately with the nonsense of opera. It is true that other forms of musical activity—or of life in general—are equally shot through with absurdity: ridiculous jokes about violists and equally ridiculous but true stories about deranged conductors are a sufficient testimony. Nevertheless, in orchestral life competent violists are the rule rather than the exception, and rational conductors may be discovered, while a certain extravagant absurdity is inseparable from opera, and even helps to define it.

Opera ought not to be reasonable, and this expectation of essential lunacy governs the genre and regulates the behavior of everybody concerned with it. A soprano who does not give herself the comic airs of a prima donna betrays her public; an operatic director who does not add some irrelevant and distracting piece of stage business will be viewed with suspicion and probably sets his career in jeopardy. I remember a performance of Verdi's *Il Trovatore* in Naples, in which the tenor, unprepossessing musically as well as physically, finished a performance of "Di quella pira" by stepping forward to the front of the stage, facing his audience with a bold stare, and, after a deep breath, bellowing the unauthorized but

A review of *The Grove History of Opera* and of *The Queen's Throat* by Wayne Koestenbaum.

frequently sung high C for no less than half a minute, to his own evident satisfaction and the delight of the public. This is a central aspect of operatic life with
which *The New Grove Dictionary of Opera* does not attempt to deal, but it was an
incredible moment that almost everybody had come to hear, and this wonderfully unmusical feat rejoiced their hearts. It was what opera was all about.

Certainly the most useful of all reference books on its subject to date, *Grove's
Opera,* will give us the plots of all the operas about which one could be reasonably curious, but it will not tell us which Tosca, when throwing herself to her
death off the Castel Sant'Angelo, bounced back above the battlements from the
trampoline hidden beneath; or who was the first tenor in *Lohengrin* to ask
"When does the next swan leave?"; or which famous two-hundred-pound
soprano has prudently written into her contract that no director can make her
move or gesture if she doesn't want to—and she generally doesn't (one director,
Nicholas Joel, solved the problem that he felt this presented in San Francisco
by having almost the entire production of *Ernani* take place in a dim pen-
umbra in which one could only vaguely perceive the principal singers). *Grove's
Opera* will list the cast for the premiere of *Salome,* but will not divulge which
great soprano made it clear that she wore no underclothes during the Dance of
the Seven Veils. Yet these are important issues in the economy of opera, and
they help us to see why comparisons of the stars of opera with the great actors
and actresses of the legitimate stage always seem oddly out of place, as if opera
were not really a serious dramatic art; opera singers, however, are very like
movie stars—at least, that is how they behave, how they are promoted, and
how we think of them, even if they rarely look like movie stars.

The articles on individual operas are the glory of *Grove's Opera:* no other
dictionary of music has ever given so full an account of the libretto scene by
scene, along with some details of each work's conception and initial productions. There is, understandably, much less musical information than we found
in the parent *New Grove:* I am not sure whether editor and subeditors of the
Grove's Opera consciously decided that opera buffs are less interested in music
than the readers of the twenty-volume general work, but if so, they were probably right. Technical terms are largely avoided. Some of the writers, however,
take pleasure in telling us what key different parts of the opera are in. This is,
I believe, a British trait, and the opera volumes seem much less influenced by
transatlantic musicology than the heavily Americanized general work.

Perhaps the British are proud of knowing what key a piece is in, a gift not
granted to all scholars. In the article on Richard Strauss's *Elektra,* David
Murray writes: "The key declines to a curdled B flat minor, however, and the
tempo to a dim, sluggish pulse, as [Elektra] calls upon her father." "Her sister
pleads her own tearful despair, in mellifluous E flat." "Electra agrees that a
sacrifice is justly required—at once the music pulls itself together in stark C

minor." "Brother and sister embrace, speechless; the music churns for a long time before reaching haven in soft, glowing A-flat." It is evident from a phrase or two in his other articles on Strauss that Murray has a genuine feeling for what large-scale key structure can effect, but he seems to have been constrained here to hold this understanding in check, and supply only picturesque detail.

Most of the articles on individual composers are, like the articles on individual operas, strong and very satisfactory if rarely original or provocative, but the general articles are, sadly, more uneven. Aria, for example, has four authors (with help parenthetically indicated from three more). The first part, on the seventeenth century, is an antique relic by Jack Westrup preserved from the earlier dictionary. The eighteenth century, however, is treated with up-to-date brilliance by Marita P. McClymonds, who provides a clear and useful summary of all the different aria forms and a wonderful fund of information in an elaborate and readable essay. On the nineteenth century, Julian Budden is more perfunctory: although the aria forms of Rossini, Bellini, Verdi, and Meyerbeer are as conventional as the eighteenth-century patterns, if not more so, we are given little help toward comprehending them. We could all use that help: in Roger Parker's otherwise splendid article on Verdi, he writes:

> [Verdi] was occasionally encouraged by the dramatic situation to construct lyric movements of extreme formal simplicity. The final section of the Aida-Radames duet (*Aida* Act IV) is a most telling example. This passage, first sung by Aida, is repeated literally by Radames and then repeated again by both characters in unison.

This is, however, not an original construction of Verdi, but a return to an exceedingly common pattern for the cabaletta (or final section) of a duet, found many times in Bellini and others. It is not the extreme formal simplicity which is particularly remarkable here, as that is rather the rule than the exception in cabalettas, but the intensity of Verdi's melody, and the use of a slow lyrical cabaletta in place of the usual brilliant coloratura. (In his article on Verdi, Parker actually describes the nineteenth-century aria with greater detail and accuracy than the article on Aria does.)

We might have expected more care in an article as important as Aria for a dictionary of opera. There are, however, many fine and many extraordinary general entries, and I enjoyed Piero Weiss on Opera Buffa and Will Crutchfield on Ornamentation. The latter is full of good things, but I would have liked some indication of how ornamentation changed between Mozart and Rossini, and above all between Rossini and Bellini. Certain ornamental practices continue beyond their usefulness or their relevance; the study of performance practice needs to become more critical, and take account of the difficulty that performers and singers have in adapting themselves to changes of style, and we must guard against the fallacy of thinking that if a certain musical practice (like adding Rossinian ornaments) did not die out, it was therefore appropriate.

The entries on singers (and there are thousands of them) are less useful than they might have been because of the refusal of the editors to include even a selected discography. Occasionally a record is mentioned in the text, but there is no systematic policy; this is like writing about a composer with only an incidental and passing mention of any of his works. (A propos, the entry on *Der Rosenkavalier* praises the Schwartzkopf-Karajan recording, but passes in silence over the great early set with Lotte Lehmann, Elisabeth Schumann, and Richard Mayr, which is musically more distinguished, and famous as one of the milestones of opera recording.) The entries on singers are largely uncritical, but they will come in handy if you want to settle a bet about, say, where Rosa Ponselle was born.

The entries on historians of opera are almost equally uninformative unless the writer has been dead for more than a century. We are told, for example, something about the ideas of Francesco Algarotti, who was much admired by Frederick the Great and by Lady Mary Montagu. About Hermann Abert, however, we learn only that he wrote important books on Mozart and Gluck, but not why they were important, and the bibliography of his writings lists his editing of operas by Gluck and Jomelli, but fails to mention his edition of *The Marriage of Figaro,* although his preface to that is one of the finest things ever written about the opera, with a brilliant discussion of the structure of Mozart's finales. We are told that Joseph Kerman wrote a provocative book about opera, but not why it was provocative: perhaps one of the editors of the dictionary would have enjoyed reading it, and could have added one or two sentences about the nature and tendencies of Kerman's thought. As it stands, the dictionary lumps together a few dozen original thinkers and many hundreds of professional hacks in a gray uniformity.

Cross-references are capricious: the entry for Nietzsche quotes some of the things he had to say about *Carmen,* but the account of that opera does not refer us to it; nor does it list Nietzsche in the bibliography. On the other hand, the article on *Don Giovanni* informs us that Kierkegaard derived his ideas on that opera from the music rather than the libretto, but it does not tell us what those ideas were. Furthermore, it does not give us a cross-reference to Kierkegaard, presumably because there is no article on Kierkegaard.

The gaping void at the heart of *The New Grove Dictionary of Opera* is the absence of an article on Singing. The editor-in-chief, Stanley Sadie, puts a brave face on this, remarking in the preface that the twenty-volume *New Grove Dictionary of Music* had no article on "Music." I am told that committing the first crime makes the next ones easier. In place of a proper article on "Singing" there is an enormous bibliography. You may well imagine that a simple list of books that takes up sixty pages of small print contains a lot of junk alongside the few interesting and important items; and since the list is absolutely uncritical, no commentary or guidance is offered.

The result is that the history of singing is badly represented in *Grove's Opera,* in spite of a large number of articles on particular aspects of the subject. One example may show what is missing: there is no entry for *spianato,* a particular style of vocal production in which the voice floats evenly and expressively over the accompaniment. This is a term used in a well-known letter of Mozart to his father, written when he was rehearsing *Idomeneo,* when the superannuated tenor who sang the title role complained about the great quartet (which was Mozart's favorite number in the opera) that he could not *spianare la voce*—that is, show off the evenness and beauty of his voice. Mozart was indignant: that was not the proper way to sing in an ensemble, which had to be executed *parlando*—that is, with a speaking style. *Spianato,* a term also used by Chopin and by Saint-Saens as well as by nineteenth-century writers on vocalism, is to be contrasted not only with the speaking style, but also with the *fioriture,* or virtuoso passagework. An operatic term like *spianato* needed by Mozart and Chopin should not have been omitted. This would not have escaped the editors of *Grove's Opera* if they had tried to represent the history of singing in a general way: a reaction away from Rossinian coloratura had a momentary success in the 1820s with Bellini, and profoundly influenced future vocal styles, including Wagner's.

With all its deficiencies—and what enterprise of this magnitude would not have as many—the new dictionary is a remarkable achievement; it gives pleasure as well as enlightenment. What it mainly lacks is a sense of history: the nonarticle on singing is symptomatic. Even the entry entitled "Opera" has only a thin sense of historical development. Perhaps a sense of reality would be a better term for what is missing, as the lack of any responsible discography indicates. The world of opera, as it must face today's economic problems, depends on recordings. In the dictionary, opera comes out as a respectable but abstract genre, the various facets of which are treated as if they were synchronic. It must be admitted that a dictionary is forced to classify, to assume fixed meanings where there is very often nothing but a wavering series of associations that changes with every decade. Nevertheless, it is regrettable that the extravagant reality of opera does not break in more often.

2

Opera is clearly a disreputable or droll form throughout most of its history—from the eighteenth century, when members of the audience played cards or chess during the recitatives, to the nineteenth, when enormously fat sopranos impersonated heroines in the final stages of tuberculosis, and to the twentieth, when Rhine maidens who had to appear as if swimming under water were sometimes suspended upside down by mistake, or when famous nearsighted tenors have peered anxiously about the stage trying to find the heroine.

The ideal of opera, the way it attains a vision of the sublime, cannot be disengaged from its grossly physical side, and this interdependence is realized intensely in the poet Wayne Koestenbaum's personal celebration of homosexuality and opera. The discovery of his own homosexuality and of his obsession with opera are so inextricably tangled together that it is not always clear which he is writing about. Half autobiography, half essay or fragmentary meditation on the mythical figure of the diva, this book might seem at first sight to tell us less about opera in general and more about Wayne Koestenbaum, whose photograph boyishly solicits our gaze from the inner back flyleaf. In fact, *The Queen's Throat* obliquely and sometimes even directly engages some aspects of the history of opera that are often passed over too lightly.

The camp taste for opera, the homosexual cult of the diva, is very much a product of our century, like the gay interest in the ballet. In the eighteenth and nineteenth centuries, ballet attracted the interest principally of the heterosexual male. It was fashionable to have a ballet dancer as a mistress, and the male dancer received relatively little attention before the arrival of Diaghilev early in the twentieth century, when Nijinsky and, later, Massine became stars whose fame rivaled and even surpassed that of Pavlova. Opera, it is true, was sexually more ambiguous from the beginning, particularly in the early eighteenth century when almost all the heroic male roles were written either for castrato or for female soprano, but—as far as I can gather from very limited reading—the castrato attracted much more sexual interest from women than from men. Although the last role written for the castrato voice was in Meyerbeer's *The Crusader in Egypt* of 1821, heroic male roles for women's voices continued to be written for a few years more, above all the Romeo of Bellini's *I Capuletti ed i Montecchi*.

If there was no specific homosexual interest in ballet or opera at that time, that is because there was no specific homosexual society or culture. In the Old Testament, the Sodomites may have been considered a race apart, but from the Renaissance to the late nineteenth century, homosexuality was a vice open to everybody, sometimes harshly repressed, sometimes tolerated or ignored, but never presented as an exclusive way of life. In sixteenth-century Florence, for example, Niccolò Machiavelli wrote amusingly and maliciously of his friends cruising for boys by the River Arno, but they all seemed to be ready as well for encounters with women at other moments. His contemporary Pietro Aretino, in that stylish masterpiece of pornography *The Conversations (I Raggionamenti)*, constructs an elaborate and improbable scene in which an abbot dallies with a girl with one hand and a boy with the other while simultaneously screwing a nun and being sodomized by a novice priest (all their simultaneous cries of delight skillfully orchestrated by the author). Very little precedence is given here to either straight or queer sex, although heterosexuality understandably takes up most of the space in these dialogues. From the sixteenth to the eighteenth centuries, homosexuality is treated generally either as an overflow of sexual vitality or as an extra delight in sin and evil. At the end of the seventeenth century, the Earl of Rochester, undoubtedly heterosexual, writes of buggering his page when there is nothing better at hand: we need not take this as autobiographical, but as a commonplace of the libertine poetry of the time.

No doubt there were always those who preferred their own sex, like the satiric poet Boisrobert at the court of Louis XIII of France, but he is amiably described by the gossip-writer Tallemant des Réaux as an eccentric, not as a member of a special sect. There was always a certain contempt and pity for a man who could not perform properly with a woman, and Alexander Pope's remark to Joseph Spence that both of the famous essayists Addison and Steele were "hermaphrodites" (that is, homosexuals) is an example of eighteenth-century homophobia ("I am sorry to say so," Pope added, "and there are not twelve people in the world that I would say it to at all"—a statement that wonderfully dispenses tolerance, sympathy, hypocrisy, and malice in equal parts). The use of a word like "hermaphrodite" reveals that the possibility of setting homosexuals apart almost as a separate race was always latent. Nevertheless, homosexuality was generally conceived, not as a propensity, but as an addiction: evil, disgusting, interesting, amusing, or even idealistic, depending upon the viewpoint.

Not until the later nineteenth century does homosexuality have a cultural ideology of its own, mocked by Gilbert and Sullivan in *Patience,* and exploding into scandal in 1889 with the affair of the Cleveland Street brothel, and then the trial of Oscar Wilde. The homosexual as a being apart, alienated from normal society and identifiable by the connoisseur's eyes through the subtle traces of effeminacy in his anatomy and his comportment, is introduced with a brilliant fanfare at the opening of Proust's fourth volume, *Sodome et Gomorrhe.* For the first time, we have a gay culture and a gay society.

In his meditation on the diva, Koestenbaum writes:

> By the twentieth century, homosexuality already meant more than just sex acts or desires shared by bodies of the same gender. It implied a milieu and a personality, flamboyant, narcissistic, self-divided, grandiose, excessive, and devoted to decor. These stereotypes have shaped behavior, and have been reinforced by gay people when they have made the transition from enduring their preference, to choosing it.

These stereotypes, however, were certainly reinforced by constraint as well as by choice, and the milieu and personality are only one kind of fictional mask out of many possibilities. What, after all, has the opera queen to do with the mustachioed clones in blue jeans, the leather and motorcycle freaks, the yearning subscribers to pedophile magazines, the marine who longs for a blow job from a transvestite, the happily married businessman who needs a regular escape from straight sex, the pale graduate student dreaming about freshmen in his lonely bed, or even the cultured yuppie lawyer who keeps house with a young musician? Like opera itself, the opera queen is a remarkably artificial, specialized creation.

In his chapter on the "codes of diva conduct," Koestenbaum calls up the monumental figure of Mae West:

> Legend has it that Frank O'Hara called Mae West the inventor of "small-town faggot psychology." Mae West was not an opera singer, but she thought like one. She pontificated: "Personality is the most important thing to an actress's success. You can sing like Flagstad or dance like Pavlova or act like Bernhardt, but if you haven't personality you will never be a real star."

Unfortunately, Koestenbaum never pursues Mae West's implicit comparison of herself to the diva, and does not call up the equally illuminating camp adulation of Bette Davis.

In an age which had already formed an anorexic ideal of woman with a boyish figure and no hips, Mae West displayed a generous mass of pulchritude. This mass, however, was held in check, never allowed to overflow its boundaries. Firmly corsetted with the strength of armor plate, with never a hair or a sequin out of place, Mae West was as stately as a battleship. The flesh never asserted its grossness; she appeared at her most typical in a tableau vivant of the Statue of Liberty. She was an abstract of female sexuality: no one afraid of real physical contact with a woman was made in the least nervous by Mae West. Her famous sexual innuendoes were at once provocative and innocent, never disquieting. She offered no passion, only invitation, and rarely expressed any emotion beyond mild amusement. Someone once said that she was the greatest female impersonator of all time.

The grossness of the real world entered the picture only with the men that surrounded her. As the camera panned out over the audience that applauded her singing, it revealed, not a crowd of handsome young males or even the muscle-men that so frequently surrounded her in real life off the screen, but an ordinary collection of middle-aged and elderly lechers, their faces transfigured with admiration. As a lion tamer in *I'm No Angel,* she opens a large trunk of equipment, and we see, pasted to the inside of the lid, the snapshots of her many one-night stands, balding, unattractive traveling-salesman types. The contrast brought out her glamour, and the tension between the tawdry surroundings and her idealized corseted shape was always a source of comedy. She played an artificial, forever unalterable, vision of sex, plunged into the reality of everyday life.

The diva, like Mae West, presents an erotic charge with no sexual threat. The erotic interest is in the voice; sensuality pours from her throat. Even if she is physically attractive—which may happen, although rarely—that is irrelevant to the opera queen. On the contrary, the intrusion of the physical spectacle of an unattractive diva actually makes the erotic purity of the vocal line more manifest, more palpable.

In *Now, Voyager,* the most powerful as well as the trashiest of her important films, Bette Davis plays a dumpy, overweight, neurotic Boston virgin. Emboldened by psychiatrist Claude Rains, she goes on a cruise, falls in love, and, like Maria Callas, at once loses all her unwanted pounds. However, the man she wants is unattainable (for complex and not very interesting reasons), and she has to renounce sex for the rest of her life and sacrifice herself by raising the daughter he has had with another woman. Unlike Mae West, Bette Davis presents the disorderly reality of sexual desire, but like the homosexual, either she is frustrated, or society takes revenge on her for her wicked libido. Her sexual menace is neutralized in *Jezebel,* where only if she nurses the sick can she offset the sexual depravity of appearing in a red dress at a ball where the girls with a normal sex drive wore white.

Both Mae West and Bette Davis play outsiders who flaunt the differences of their sexuality from the norms that society tries to impose, and they do so as flamboyantly as any opera queen. The homosexual finds release from his inner tensions in the violence of Bette Davis's expression of feminine rage, and he identifies with her frustrations. The coarseness of Mae West's verbal comedy, combined with the way her appearance both represents and distances an erotic invitation at the same time, allows the homosexual to approach female sexuality without fear of aggression. The cult of the diva offers him similar and even greater freedom. The opera queen may admire tenors, but like Koestenbaum, it is only sopranos that he idolizes. The diva helps him escape the shame with which society has characterized his inadequate response to the female anatomy. At last he can find genuine passion for a woman, not merely as a mother or as a nanny, but as an erotic object, for the sexuality embodied—or disembodied—in her voice.

For this purpose, the physical absurdity of opera is crucial, an absurdity that the finest of stage directors and the most graceful of singers can mitigate but can never entirely dispel. A small number of famous sopranos are indeed attractive, generally the ones who sing the lighter parts, but few of them look appealing with their mouths wide open. However, the spectacle of Tristan and Isolde trying to embrace, but too fat to get their arms conveniently about each other, does not lessen the emotional power of the love duet for the opera buff, or for that suborder of the opera buff, the opera queen. The voice, not the physical frame in which it is merely lodged, is the center of excitement. Perhaps this is why a certain element of bad taste is essential for the opera queen: a preference for *Lucia di Lammermoor* over *Norma,* or even an eager tolerance of the second-rate soprano (Koestenbaum has written poems to Anna Moffo), allows homosexual pathos more space, more room to expand.

The figure of Maria Callas is central to the mythology of the opera queen, and Koestenbaum devotes a whole chapter to her:

> We love Callas because she revised her body. In three years she dropped from 210 pounds to 144, and changed from ugly duckling to glamour queen. Bodies can't always be altered, but Callas's self-revision, like a sex change, makes us believe in the power of wish.

He writes well about her faults and her self-discipline. He does not sufficiently acknowledge her purely musical intelligence, or remark about what two conductors have told me—that she had an uncanny ability to take account of the orchestra and alter the timbre of her notes according to the accompanying harmony. But, then, *The New Grove Dictionary of Opera* does not tell us that either. I heard Callas sing in public only twice, and she was still fat: her worst vocal problems were not yet troublesome, her stage presence was dramatic, and her weight did not matter. The work was *Norma* at the Rome Opera, and it was the only time I have ever gone to the same opera twice in one week. With all her faults, she revealed Bellini with all his faults as a great composer.

At one point, Koestenbaum reaches a profound observation that transcends both Callas and her relation to the homosexual fan. It applies, however, beyond the limited range that he intended:

> When we value Callas for creating a revolution in operatic performance practice, for singing neglected Bellini and Donizetti operas as if they were tragic vehicles of undiminished power, we are valuing her for opening up the opera box, the closed space of a genre that never seemed to let us in or to let our meanings out. And yet, ironically, her revitalizations of dismissed bel canto operas only emphasized opera's moribund nature.

Anachronism was one aspect of opera that long ago opened it to gay appropriation; opera seemed campy and therefore available to gay audiences only when it became clear that it was an outdated art form, sung in foreign languages, with confused, implausible plots. Opera's apparent distance from contemporary life made it a refuge for gays, who were creations of modern sexual systems, and yet whom society could not acknowledge or accommodate. Opera is not very real. But gayness has never been admitted into the precincts of reality. And so gays may seek out art that does not respect the genuine.

Superficially, Maria Callas took away opera's campiness by making it believable and vivid. And yet by importing truth into opera, an art of the false, she gave the gay fan a dissonance to match his own. Bestowing verisimilitude on Lucia or Norma or Elvira, Callas perforated the operagoer's complacency; her voice and her presence, arsenals of depth, when brought to bear on music that had become superficial, upset the audience's sense of perspective. Though it seems sacrilegious to call Callas's musically compelling creations camp, she performed the same kind of reversal that camp induces: she shattered the codes that separate dead from living works of art. Callas "camped" *Lucia* not by mocking it (Lucia is too easy to mock) but by taking it seriously. Resuscitating *Lucia,* Callas challenged our belief that history's movement is linear, that there is a difference between past and present, and that modern reality is real.

The last phrase comes too easily, but it is true that there is a distance between opera and modern life, and that this distance imposes a form of alienation on the spectator. This alienation, however, is inseparable from opera since its invention; it was at first intended, after all, as the revival of sung Greek classical tragedy. It was always distant from modern life, critics always complained about its confused, implausible plots, and in eighteenth-century London and Vienna—and often in Paris as well—it was generally sung in a foreign language unintelligible to the public. It was not opera that had become so dated, so artificial that it could bring gays a "matching dissonance," an analogue in music for their supposedly artificial, unnatural lives. Opera has always been artificial, and great artists have performed the miracle of making it seem natural. It was the construction of "gay consciousness," the fiction of a "gay community" that created from their lives a metaphor for opera and a public that believed it could recognize itself in these masterpieces from the past.

The extraordinary aptness of the new alliance came from opera's imposition of an eroticism of the most powerful nature, but an eroticism in which the body strangely counted for almost nothing. In most cultures, the erotic has always been a source of shame, the body a source of disgust—perhaps most of all for the homosexual who has had to outface shame and disgust so often and from so many. Through his worship of the diva, the homosexual discovered what seems to be a way of sexually rejoining the heterosexual community—in its way, as much a fiction or an illusion as the gay community. It is the erotic power of music, which achieves its most obvious effects in opera, that presents the listeners with both a momentary release from anxiety and a transient sense of ecstasy.

Of all the arts, music works most directly on the nerves, seemingly unfiltered through a system of meaning. In the opera, music does not come to us through the words: the words arrive through the music and sometimes give it greater force: in most operas, the force of love. Provided that the staging does not distract or force itself too insistently upon our unwilling consciousness, the music benefits from the bright contrast with the dumpy, sweaty bodies that are producing it—it is like sex without shame or physical awkwardness or postcoital sadness, not as good as the real thing, of course, but still a great consolation.

This is the side of opera from which *The New Grove Dictionary of Opera* modestly averts its eyes. There is no article on Eroticism and Opera. Why not? There is one on Milwaukee. This is why the entry on *Tristan und Isolde,* except for the banal observation that the love duet ends with coitus interruptus, does not face the sexual implications of the score, or the way it is almost always Isolde who is on top, so to speak—playing the man's role, when she stands with the sword raised over Tristan's wounded body as her narrative recalls in the first act, or seizes the only too obvious symbol of the torch in the second act to brandish it and bring on the catastrophe. It is also why there is no article on Kierkegaard, who wrote more explicitly than anyone before him on the erotic nature of music, and who understood the character of Mozart's art better than most of the critics who came after. The basis of opera speciously appears to be an opposition between the ideal purity of the music and the gritty reality needed to produce it, the silly costumes, the ridiculous plots, the embarrassing decor: but the music hides within itself a reality fully as abrasive, equally physical.

CHAPTER 21

Lost Chords and the
Golden Age of Pianism

Pｅｒｆｏｒｍａｎｃｅ ｐｒａｃｔｉｃｅ is a wonderfully speculative branch of musicology with an eminently practical side: it discovers how the music of the past was played and helps us to perform it today. The discipline began in the nineteenth century with the study of late medieval and Reniassance vocal polyphony, making it possible to hear again the now canonical works from Josquin des Prez to Palestrina and Orlandus Lassus. Of course, we have almost no idea how this music actually sounded in the late fifteenth and sixteenth centuries. Later, research went into the performance of the seventeenth- and early eighteenth-century Baroque tradition; and much more material is available for this period. Not all of it is a useful guide for performance today: as we know from contemporary authors like Saint-Evremond, only the first ten minutes of an opera were played with the instruments in tune after which cacophony set in. Much Baroque practice is still the subject of controversy, like the use of uneven (or dotted) rhythms, called *notes inègales,* which can result, massively and relentlessly applied, in what Pierre Boulez has called "an infernal boogie-woogie." With some reluctance, musicology has recently been persuaded to acknowledge that we are not sure of many aspects of

Originally written in 2008 as a review of *After the Golden Age: Romantic Pianism and Modern Performance,* by Kenneth Hamilton.

the way Mozart, Beethoven, and Schumann were played; and now we have reached the early twentieth century, and at last we are in a territory more easily mapped out.

After the Golden Age is a melancholy title for a jolly and entertaining book about performance on the piano for about a century, from 1830 to sometime in the 1940s, from the beginning of Franz Liszt's career to the death of Ignacy Paderewski and the success of Vladimir Horowitz. At the opening of his book, Kenneth Hamilton acknowledges that the conception of a golden age is a dubious one, but by a dozen pages later he has reconciled himself to treating its existence as a fact, and paints a remarkable picture of late nineteenth- and early twentieth-century pianism. The book is full of interesting detail and funny stories, and written with undisguised passion.

The passion is not one of nostalgia, for Hamilton is too young to have heard most of the pianists he writes about, but rather one of indignation for the abandonment of a great tradition. He was, he says, inspired by "the sheer routine and funereal boredom of some piano recitals I have attended (and no doubt given)." There may be more formality about piano recitals today than a century and a half ago, but great playing when it is found ought not to be boring. The belief that the average piano recital was more interesting in the 1890s than now is a delusion. Bernard Shaw, a music critic in those days, claimed that after a week of listening to pianists, he liked to go to a dentist and have his teeth drilled by a steady hand.

Hamilton admirably sums up a good deal of recent research, some of it his own, on the development of the piano recital after its invention by Liszt in the 1830s, and includes much fascinating and amusing detail on the mixed concerts with singers and other musicians, and the insistence of audiences that the keyboard virtuoso improvise. Most of the evenings in the middle of the nineteenth century were filled with popular arrangements, generally of operatic selections, but over the decades they became more and more deadly serious, ending with the enormous recitals of Anton Rubinstein, who played eight Beethoven sonatas on one program.

Chiefly, however, Hamilton is occupied with certain performance practices that have fallen into disuse: arpeggiation (playing the notes of a chord one after the other instead of together), improvising a little prelude to introduce the new key before each piece on a program, freedom of tempo, and, above all, what he calls "dislocation" or "asynchronization"—playing the melody note in the right hand later than the bass note in the left. This last was called "limping" by Josef Hofmann, the pianist considered by many (including Sergei Rachmaninov and Vladimir Horowitz) the greatest of the twentieth century. Rachmaninov qualified his judgment in a letter, saying that Hofmann is the greatest pianist when he is in the mood, otherwise you wouldn't recognize him (and added acidly that some people thought Horowitz might eventually be as good, but that up to now he was just able to play octaves, but since he had married the daughter of the greatest conductor, Arturo Toscanini, perhaps he would improve). Hofmann described "limping" as the worst habit a pianist can develop, but employed it sparingly himself for special effect.

Hamilton is a convincing partisan of all these, and a few other devices, and gives a fine account of the widespread use, in so far as it is possible from the sources available, early recordings, piano rolls for mechanical pianos, and critical accounts. He appreciates the limitations and defects of all these sources, but misses one important problem presented by the principal one, early recordings. They are almost all only a little over four minutes in length (the most that could be accommodated on 78 revolutions per minute shellac discs until the coming of the use of vinyl in the early 1950s); multiple record albums began to be issued in the 1930s, but most of the pianists Hamilton is interested in were already dead by then. This means that none of the great pianists before 1930 are represented on vinyl by serious long works, but largely by their most popular encores, short pieces they had played hundreds of times on concert tours. In my opinion, some of the flamboyant freedom and even trickery that one finds on these recordings may be due to boredom, or to an attempt to find something new to dazzle the public in the last informal minutes of a recital. On one occasion early in twentieth-century Vienna, three pianists performed Chopin's "Black-Key Etude" in the same week, the first playing the famous octaves at the end brilliantly as written, the next playing them *glissando,* and the third topping that by *glissando* with the two hands in contrary motion (it hurts my fingers just to think about this athletic feat, which can be painful).

When I was very young, I heard only three of the great figures from early in the twentieth century: Josef Lhevinne (mentioned only once in passing by Hamilton, but who had a wrist that could play octaves with the rapidity of a machine gun); Moriz Rosenthal, with whom I studied from 1939 until his death six years later; and Josef Hofmann, whose recitals I heard almost every year from when I was four years old till his death when I was fifteen. However, Lhevinne suffered from lapses of memory in his old age, and he would often improvise his way back into pieces until he picked up the thread again. Rosenthal had almost ceased to play in public when I knew him, and I never heard him perform those works for which he had been most famous: the *Réminiscenses de Don Juan de Mozart* by Liszt (with whom he had studied), the Schumann *Phantasie,* or the Paganini-Brahms Variations, which Brahms had asked him to perform. As a very young man, Rosenthal had played that *Don Giovanni* fantasy in a hall in Vienna with tables where one could drink beer;

Brahms was seated in the audience with his back to the stage, and Rosenthal was determined to make him turn around; coming to the big chromatic scale in thirds in the right hand, he played chromatic thirds up and down the keyboard in both hands and Brahms afterward urged him to perform the Paganini Variations—a good tactical move on Brahms's part, as the work is Brahms's manifest challenge to the opposing school of Liszt, whose Paganini etudes were his first great musical shock success. Brahms had previously gained one Liszt student for this work, Karl Tausig, but Rosenthal was the new great Liszt prodigy. Rosenthal's spectacular spur-of-the-moment improvised revision of his master's work is the kind of technical exploit cherished by Hamilton.

Both Rosenthal and Hofmann did record the great B Minor Sonata of Chopin in the 1930s, but neither of them allowed the record to be issued, considering them unworthy to represent their art; both were, nevertheless, published after their deaths. Hofmann authorized no recording after 1925, although when very young, he had made the first recording on a piano. Selections from some of Hofmann's public concerts were later recorded, but not the great performances I heard in Carnegie Hall of the *Réminiscences de Don Juan* (Hofmann is said to have remarked on leaving the stage, "That is the first time I played the piece the way it should be") or of the Chopin B Minor Sonata (about which Rachmaninov, who was in the audience, remarked, "Another piece I must strike from my repertoire"). Hofmann, as Rachmaninov observed, was not always "in the mood" and the records I have heard of his live performances for students at the Curtis Institute in Philadelphia do not show his playing when he was really serious. One live recording made in Carnegie Hall in 1945, however, gives an idea of what he could do at his best; Chopin's C Minor Nocturne, a truly inspired and exquisite performance. Otherwise, an imperfect idea of his great mastery and huge range of tone color must be looked for in the 1925 Brunswick recordings.

Hamilton thinks that Hofmann sounds more "modern" than his contemporaries because he rarely employed "dislocation" or "limping" (not a recommendation in Hamilton's eyes), but that is not the whole story. Hofmann's rhythmic freedom made great effect because it was rare, with a sudden rubato appearing in an almost metronomic exactness, as in his Brunswick discs of Scarlatti, the Brahms arrangement of a Gluck gavotte, and Hofmann's most famous encore, the "Magic Fire Music" from *Die Walkuere*. In that series, the superb recording of Liszt's Second Hungarian Rhapsody, in fact, the rhythmic regularity is shockingly out of style, since Liszt marks the opening *a capriccio* (meaning with rhythmic freedom), and Hofmann's basic beats are pretty much exact, with rhythmic nuances delicately introduced only in very small details. (This basic regularity of the long beats, indeed, is the classic theory of how rubato should be executed, so defined by Chopin and already even by Mozart, realizable in practice only with difficulty, however.) The result here, however inauthentic, is that the first movement of the Second Rhapsody now has a nobility not often found, while the expressive phrasing is achieved not by capricious rhythmic fantasy but by the control and balance of tone.

Hamilton is right to deplore the complete disappearance of these stylistic devices (he does not seem to know that they have been revived for the last twenty years, first largely by pianists who have studied in Vienna and more recently by young Italians). The loss of any useful expressive technique must always be regretted. Nevertheless, the usefulness of a device is sometimes unclear. Take arpeggiation, for example. Hamilton would like the opening chord of Beethoven's G Major Concerto arpeggiated (and he has Czerny's authority for this, not as authoritative as he would like to believe, since some of Czerny's tempo recommendations for Beethoven's piano sonatas are ludicrous—his suggestion of a fast allegro for the Allegretto finale of op. 31, no. 1, excited the derision of Anton Schindler, on whom one cannot rely either, since he forged some pages of Beethoven's conversation book). It is true that pianists in the early 1800s would strum a little prelude before beginning a piece, like tennis players bouncing the ball before serving, and Hamilton suggests that the solo piano opening would have struck the audience then as an improvised introduction and not as the real beginning of the concerto, and this effect would be increased by an arpeggio, typically used for preludes. But no audience today is going to imagine that the pianist is just preluding while silence has descended on the hall and the conductor is waiting: an arpeggio will strike most of those who know the piece as only stylistic high jinks. If the effect of a prelude was intended by Beethoven, it will no longer work. (Dwelling with an arpeggio on the more intense chord of the second beat of the third measure would make greater expressive sense.) There is another musical difficulty: the orchestra enters at the sixth bar with a phrase that begins by an imitation of the pianist's opening, and the orchestral musicians cannot stagger their notes one after the other, but have to play precisely together. In the end, of course, there can be no firm objection to an opening arpeggio, but I am not happy to have the pianist tamper with the extraordinary lyric simplicity of the initial chord, found nowhere else in concerto literature, as it would lessen the effectiveness of the increasing tension as the phrase proceeds. The moments of unpretentious lyricism in Beethoven are an aspect of his work that Czerny never understood, and I suspect he thought up the arpeggio to add a little more emphatic grandeur to such an eccentrically modest way of beginning a concerto.

There is a curious indication in the first version of one of Liszt's Petrarch sonnets (no. 120): *quasi arpeggiando.* "Almost arpeggiating"? What can that mean? Surely, it must signify striking notes apart but so close together that one hardly notices that they are not simultaneous, but with a discreet guitar-like effect. Hamilton is right to say that the spreading of a chord by an arpeggio was sometimes slow and expressive, and sometimes light and quick. Since Brahms used to arpeggiate all his chords (the effect annoyed some of his contemporaries), that probably means that when a direction to arpeggiate is actually written by Brahms into the text, it should be set in relief and rendered expressively.

Hamilton's book is not a neutral, disinterested picture of the style of the past, but a plea for its revival. No device is closer to his heart than dislocation (he finds "limping" a more pejorative term, but "dislocation" does not sound much more attractive). We have a lot of evidence for the use of dislocation by many pianists from the end of the nineteenth century, if not by all, or only rarely by others. The ideology for it was defined by the great Viennese teacher Theodore Leschetizky (his pupils included Ignaz Friedman, Paderewski, and Artur Schnabel); for him, playing the bass note in the left hand before the melody in the right enhances the beauty of the melody note, as it vibrates more vividly in sympathy with the already sounding overtones or harmonics of the bass. There is no question that the vibrant relation of treble to bass is an important aspect of the attraction of piano sonority, and it is magnified by dislocation, which also increases the fluidity of the acoustic effect and reduces the hard-edged percussive nature of piano tone.

So attached to dislocation, Hamilton would like to extend its widespread use earlier than the late nineteenth century, to Chopin and the youthful years of Liszt (when he was still playing the piano in public). He writes: "I am in the business here of tracing the arpeggiated, asynchronized singing tone back to Sigismond Thalberg [a great pianist of the 1840s] *and his predecessors*" (p. 162) (my italics). As I said above, there is evidence for Chopin's using a rubato in which the right hand is independent of the regular beats of the left. However, the purpose of Chopin's rubato is more expressive phrasing, and it has absolutely nothing to do with Leschetizky's justification for making a more beautiful sound. The origin of Chopin's rubato technique is an ornament described by eighteenth-century theorists for varying the return of a melody and making it more dramatic; it was basically a transference to the keyboard of the vocal or operatic effect of a singer overcome by emotion, and able to produce a note only after a theatrically significant respiration. The practice may have originated in seventeenth-century French harpsichord style, where it was also an imitation of vocal ornament. Rubato is expressively and decisively emphatic, while dislocation at its best is most often a way of caressing the musical line, a delicious softening of the melodic contour.

There may, however, be a remote historic relation of rubato to the later technique of dislocation, as Mozart wrote from Italy to his father that the Italians were very astonished to hear him play rubato, so the practice may have become essentially Central European or Viennese by the 1770s. Like Chopin, Mozart uses it only for the return of a melody (but in his case, does not just direct rubato but writes it into the text, and must have also produced it spontaneously in performance).[1] The most beautiful examples in Mozart can be found in the slow movement of the Sonata in C Minor and, above all, in the Rondo in A Minor. In the latter, at the return of the theme in bars 86 and 87, every melody note is delayed a sixteenth note. It should be obvious that this must be played as if the pianist were improvising the delayed rhythm, and it is not only affecting, but passionately so. Some of Hamilton's descriptions of dislocation from recorded performances are really only examples of the old rubato (the term rubato later took on the different meaning of a general freedom of tempo, but for Mozart and still often for Chopin, it implied a relatively strict tempo in the left hand). Hamilton's failure to distinguish between dislocation and the classical rubato which lasted way into the nineteenth century is troubling.

The only convincing evidence for the use of true dislocation as early as 1850 adduced by Hamilton is *The Art of Singing on the Piano* of 1853–64 written by Thalberg, and it is double-edged. Thalberg calls a constant and exaggerated delay of the melody note "ridiculous and tasteless," and cautiously approves its employment only in a slow tempo, and then "particularly at the beginning of each bar or at the beginning of each section of the melody. . . . however only with an imperceptible delay" (p. 160). This does, indeed, imply that a mechanical use of the technique had already appeared by midcentury, but it was disgusting to connoisseurs, and Thalberg's recommended use only at the beginnings of bars or sections is, in fact, closer to the older, more expressive delay of the melody note as an emphatic effect or rubato. Nevertheless, the recommendation that it be imperceptible foreshadows the later effect of fluidity, but the advice is far from the relentless employment that we find in the pianists who imitated Paderewski.

Although Hamilton remarks that pupils do not always copy their teachers' style, he feels that Liszt mist have "limped," too, because several of his pupils did so. He relies on witnesses to Liszt's playing who are not always trustworthy, such as Alexander Siloti, who claimed that the dead Liszt visited him in visions to suggest corrections in his works, which often made them easier to play. Rosenthal's use of dislocation is unlikely to derive from Liszt, but from his

---

1. Chopin uses the term rubato once at the beginning of a mazurka, but it is still essentially an expressive variant, not a means to arrive at a prettier sound.

having resided for most of his life after the age of fifteen in Vienna, musical center of dislocation. (He would never tell me what lessons with Liszt were like, except to say that it was difficult to get him to leave the café and return to the studio.) In any case, his employment of dislocation was never insensitive or systematic; many of the delayed melody notes are examples of dramatically expressive rubato.

In Hamilton's desire that dislocation become the default position for pianism (to use the egregious computer language now fashionable with musicologists), he becomes disingenuous. He asks: "What caused the moderating of the obsession with the singing tone? Why did pianists' priorities shift?" (p. 177) Many pianists in the age that Hamilton regrets were famous for banging unmercifully at the keyboard, above all including Paderewski, and, yes, even Liszt. There has never been any shift, and an obsession with a cantabile is as great as it ever was. A singing tone may be achieved in different ways, and dislocation is not the only viable technique. It is hard to believe that Hamilton's discussion of the singing tone of pianism of the past never mentions Solomon or Arturo Benedetti Michelangeli, merely glances in passing at Artur Schnabel only because he was a Leschetizky pupil, without a word about his mastery of cantabile, or Walter Gieseking, the stupidest great pianist I ever heard, but incapable of laying his hands on a keyboard without producing a beautiful sound. Hamilton feels that "limping" was abandoned because pianists wished to sound more modern and hard-edged. But it was never universally accepted, and approval was often halfhearted and mitigated.

He never asks what the basic disadvantages of dislocation might be, or why a pianist like Hofmann used it so rarely, sometimes to set off a short section of lyric tenderness and lower dynamic level. A singing melody is achieved, as Hamilton knows but does not emphasize, mainly by weighting the different elements of a chord so that the harmonics of the notes vibrate with an intensity that reinforces the soprano line. Dislocation privileges the soprano line above all others, sets the bass in relief, and tends to leave all the inner voices in the shadow. Hofmann took great pleasure at making inner voices audible.[2] Since he was interested in much more than the melody, dislocation would only have been a nuisance to him. Hamilton quotes Claudio Arrau's sneering remarks about Hofmann's delight in polyphonic emphasis (Arrau, a fine pianist with enormous vigor and passion for a few years when young, became wise,

---

2. Interestingly enough, that is the way Chopin composed. The first manuscript of some pieces like the Etude, op. 25, no. 1, does not reveal the polyphonic complexity, but in the later versions we see that extra beams have been added to the inner tenor and alto voices, a direction to the performer to bring them out. Hofmann was only rethinking the music the way a composer would.

philosophic, and stodgy when older, and jealous of his colleagues.) Dislocation can make possible a pretty sound, but it tends to be the same kind of sound and leads to monotony. Pianists who were concerned to master a great range of tone color, like Rachmaninov and Hofmann, tended to resist it. Above all, the growing desire in the twentieth century to master orchestral color on the keyboard gradually led to the disappearance of dislocation, although, as I have said, it is making an occasionally useful comeback.

What most piano teachers mean by a beautiful tone is centered on bringing out the melody, and always setting the melody in high relief is characteristic of Viennese piano style. Ferrucio Busoni, ideologically more Viennese than Italian, once said that "any melody worth playing should be played *mezzo forte*"; in the end, this leads to the typical conservatory performance of a Bach fugue with the opening motif played louder than all the other voices each time it appears. Most theories about beautiful piano tone try to impose the same kind of sound on every style from Bach to Debussy.

Dislocation has a peculiar status among discoveries of the past that are candidates for resuscitation. Some devices are essential: *notes inégales* (dotted rhythms) are essential to most of Couperin (although preferably not applied with a heavy hand); playing notes before a rest for less than their full written value was the rule throughout the eighteenth century, as Charles Mackerras has pointed out, and it gives the music of Mozart, Haydn, and Beethoven a lightness of texture and clarity; much of Beethoven, Chopin, Schumann, and Liszt makes no sense without a supple rhythmic freedom in the details of shaping of phrases in slow tempos and even, if somewhat less so, in fast movements. "Limping," however, was never considered absolutely essential to musical meaning by any wide consensus at any time, even in the late nineteenth century. Its devotees did not counsel its use by amateurs. It may make a lovely, delicate, and vibrant sound that can be replaced, even if with somewhat different effect, by expert weighting of tone color. An admirable expressive device, it was not meant to be smeared over the whole range of musical forms. It was a luxury item, like the icing on a cake, bearable only when applied by a light-handed pastry-cook.

The great problem with performance practice studies is fetishism. I remember the discovery in Baroque studies of hairpin dynamics (swelling and diminishing on each note), and for a short while every orchestral piece of Bach collapsed into a series of woozy notes like short owl hoots. When it was remarked that Haydn had conducted his symphonies from the keyboard, recordings began to mess up Haydn's wonderfully bare two-part counterpoint with loudly miked-up percussive crashes from a harpsichord. I think that Hamilton at a piano recital leans back wearily in despair when he hears a pianist play with hands always synchronized. I am delighted if I hear an occasional and imaginative use of dislocation, but cringe when it is applied in bar after bar and phrase after phrase. *After the Golden Age* is a delightful and instructive book, and I hope it will make pianism more various, not more homogenized. But the Golden Age is a mirage.

Part Five

CLASSICAL MODERNISM:
PAST AND PRESENT

CHAPTER 22

Montaigne: Philosophy as Process

I

Montaigne remarked that when someone dwelt on the language, the style, of his *Essays,* "I would prefer that he shut up" (j'aimerois mieux qu'il s'en teust).[1] It was, above all, the objective content of which he was proud, more material and denser, he says, than in other writers. But, as he observes at once, his meaning is not always straightforward. To his essay "Considerations on Cicero," published in 1580, he added the following passage many years later:

> Neither my anecdotes nor my quotations are always employed simply as examples, for authority, or for ornament. I do not consider them only for the use that I make of them. They often carry, off the subject under discussion [hors de mon propos], the seed of a richer and more daring matter, and they resonate obliquely [à gauche] with a more delicate tone, both for me who do not wish to express at this point anything further, and for those who recognize my manner.

Originally written in 2008 on *Les Essais,* by Michel de Montaigne, edited by Jean Balsamo, Michel Magnien, and Catherine Magnin Simon.

1. There is an excellent modern translation by Donald M. Frame, Everyman's Library (2003), which I highly recommend. I have, however, preferred to alter my quotations to bring out different aspects of Montaigne.

Ny elles [mes histoires], ny mes allegations ne servent pas toujours simplement d'exemple, d'"authorité ou ornemment. Je ne les regarde pas seulement par l'usage que j'en tire. Elles portent souvent, hors de mon propos, le semance d'une matiere plus riche et plus hardie, et sonnent a gauche un ton plus delicat, et pour moi qui n'en veus exprimer davantage, et pour ceux qui recontreront mon air.

This open invitation to read between the lines is followed by a condemnation of style for style's sake, but it nevertheless implies that the manner of presentation required stylistic virtuosity.

"I speak to the paper the way I speak to the first man I meet," Montaigne claimed; and the popular and easy familiarity of his style in the *Essays* was a radical novelty in serious writing about philosophy, morals, history, and politics. He could, of course, combine this simplicity, when he wanted, with all the resources of classical Latin rhetoric on which he had been raised as a child in the Périgord. (His ambitious father hired servants for the children who spoke only Latin, and little Michel never heard a word of French before he went to school.) He did not invent the essay, of course, but he was, indeed, the first to use the term to describe a short, informal prose discussion meant to instruct, stimulate, and entertain; his book became a model for almost every writer after him who attempted the form.

Born in 1533, Montaigne was the younger son of Pierre Eyquem, a recently ennobled, wealthy merchant of Bordeaux, who had immense respect for classical studies. Montaigne's maternal grandfather came from a Spanish family, supposedly Jewish converts to Christianity, who in 1497 joined other members of the family who had already settled in Toulouse. His paternal great-grandfather acquired the Château of Montaigne, in Périgord, not far from Bordeaux. Trained as a lawyer, Montaigne became a magistrate in Bordeaux during a period of violent religious conflict between Protestants and Catholics, with terrible atrocities on both sides. He began writing in the 1570s when the death of his closest friend, Étienne de La Boétie, made him wish to retire from public life; but the melancholy of solitude engendered such monstrous fantasies, he said, that he began writing them down to demonstrate their folly to himself. In fact, he started by modeling his writing on the moral reflections of the classical prose he loved best, Plutarch and Seneca, but soon his work took a new and radical turn.

It became an intimate and frank self-examination. Not an autobiography—the events of his life were too insignificant, he thought—but an account of his "fantasies," his imagination, his whims, his ideas. This sounds modest, but it quickly became one of the most ambitious projects in the history of literature, and he claimed to be the first ever to attempt it. His idea of philosophy was not of an effort to reach the truth, but an investigation of the way the mind worked, fallibly, capriciously, and unpredictably. He studied himself:

> I propose an unimportant life without luster, it makes no difference. We can attach the whole of moral philosophy as easily to a common and private life as to a life of richer matter: each man carries the entire form of the human condition.

> Je propose une vie basse et sans lustre, c'est tout un. On attache aussi bien toute la philosophie morale à une vie populaire et privée que à une vie de plus riche estoffe: chaque homme porte la forme entiere de l'humaine condition.

The originality of his approach was his conviction that nothing was too trivial to be examined, that the way the mind acted was dependent not so much on logic as on physical health (he made little distinction between body and mind), on the social environment, on minor distractions like sudden noises, on one's dislike of the sound of a voice, on the disruption of a long-cherished habit, or on one's occupations (he claimed to get his most interesting ideas while riding a horse, when it was inconvenient to write them down).

He could be very grand about the project of studying himself:

> We only know about two or three writers among the ancients [i.e., classical Greeks and Romans] who took this path, and we cannot say if their way was like mine, since we know only their names. No one since has tread in their tracks. It is a thorny enterprise, more so than it seems, to follow a pace as vagabond as that of our mind; to penetrate the opaque depths of our internal folds, to choose and fix so many minute appearances of its agitations. . . . It is many years since I have had myself as the target of my thoughts, that I investigate and study only myself, and, if I study something else, I immediately apply it to myself, or, to put it better, within myself.

> Nous n'avons nouvelles que de deus ou trois antiens qui aient battu ce chemin, et si ne pouvons dire si c'est du tout en pareille maniere a cettecy, n'en conoissant que les noms. C'est un' espineuse entreprinse, et plus qu'il ne semble, suivre un' allure si vagabonde que celle de nostre esprit, de penetrer les profondeurs opaques de ses replis internes; de choisir et arreter tant de menus airs de ses agitations. . . . Il y a plusieurs annees que je n'ay que moi pour visee a mes pensees, que je ne contrerolle et estudie que moy; et, si j'estudie autre chose, c'est pour soudein le coucher sur moi, ou en moy, pour mieux dire.

That is why, he says amusingly, he can write about matters that he does not understand, because it is not these matters themselves but his ignorance of them that is his real subject.

Slightly restrained by the limits of decency (not too restrained, in fact), Montaigne reveals more about himself than anyone else I know of in the history of literature. He tells us that women were disappointed by the small size of his penis (particularly when compared with the monstrous members in the graffiti that children scrawled on palace walls); he admits to gobbling his food so fast sometimes that he bites his tongue and his fingers (forks were only recently introduced in Europe and not immediately very popular). He admits his virtues as well; it would be foolish not to, he claims.

Most radical of all is his sense of the instability of the mind and, indeed, of the universe. "The world is a perennial motion," he wrote:

> Everything in it moves without cease: the earth, the rocks of the Caucasus, the pyramids of Egypt, with the general movement of the whole and with their own individual movement. Even constancy itself is nothing else than a more languishing movement. . . . I do not portray being; I portray passing; not a passage of one age to another, or, as the people say, from seven years to seven years, but from day to day, from minute to minute. . . . [These essays are] an examination of diverse and changeable events and irresolute fancies, and—when it so happens—contradictory: either I am a different myself, or I seize the matter from other circumstances and considerations.

> Le monde n'est qu'une branloire perenne. Toutes choses y branlent sans cesse: la terre, les rochers du Caucase, les pyramides d'Aegypte, et du branle public et du leur. La constance mesme n'est autre chose qu'un branle plus languissant. . . . Je ne peints pas l'estre. Je peins le passage: non un passage de l'aage en autre, ou, comme dict le peuple, de sept en sept ans. Mais de jour en jour, de minute en minute. . . . C'est un contrerolle de divers et muables accidens et d'imaginations irresoluës, et quand il y eschet, contraires: soit que je sois autre moymesmes, soit que je saisisse les subjects par autres circonstances et sonsiderations.

Montaigne did not completely withdraw from public life after the death of La Boétie: he became mayor of Bordeaux for a short time, and aided the Catholic king, Henri III, in his negotiations with the heir to the throne, the leader of the Protestants, Henri of Navarre, later Henri IV. His last years before his death in 1592 were taken up with a large-scale revision of the *Essays*.

Two books of *Essays* were published in 1580, and a third book followed in 1588 with the first two books heavily rewritten and considerably enlarged. His own copy of this expanded edition (called the Bordeaux Copy) has revisions in his hand throughout, with indications of inserts that are sometimes many pages in length. The posthumous edition of 1595, overseen by his disciple Marie de Gournay, incorporated these changes with relative fidelity. Most twentieth-century editions are based on the Bordeaux Copy, and it is traditional to indicate the variants—what was printed in 1580, what was added and rewritten in 1588, and what was altered in the Bordeaux Copy.

The book was an immediate success: his neighbors in Périgord, however, thought it was a joke to see him published, and at first he had to pay locally for the printing, but afterward, he boasted, publishers elsewhere in France paid him. The *Essays* have remained a success for more than four centuries; few books of that age both can be so moving and still make one laugh aloud. Their influence over the centuries has been immense: Shakespeare and other Jacobean dramatists borrowed from them; Pascal called him "incomparable," and at least a third of the long opening section of his *Pensées* on religion are directly inspired by Montaigne. ("What I find in Montaigne, I find in myself," he is supposed to have said, and that is true for so many readers of the *Essays*.) The influence continued with Voltaire. Even Rousseau, who disliked him (it must have been disconcerting to find someone else who could write so frankly and honestly about himself without shame), borrowed Montaigne's views on primitive societies. Later, Emerson, Nietzsche, Gide, and many others would profit by his example.

2

A new modern edition was perhaps worth attempting. It is now known that there was another copy of the 1588 edition annotated in Montaigne's own hand; this copy has disappeared, but was used for the 1595 posthumous printing by his disciple Marie de Gournay, and this revision, different in many minor details, has more authority than was granted it by previous editors. Two policy decisions were made with the new one-volume edition in the large series of classics published by Gallimard called the Pléiade. The first decision was to eliminate the paragraphing added by almost all modern editors for readability, and the second was not to indicate on the page of text what came from the first version of 1580, or the new version of 1588, or was added in the margins or between the lines of the Bordeaux Copy, indications that had become standard for all twentieth-century editions. The variants are relegated to the back of the book.

The rationale for the latter decision is that the division of the text into three distinct layers, 1580, 1588, and post-1588, gives a false impression, since the revision must have been fairly continuous over the years. The version chosen is largely that of the posthumous edition of 1595, and variants are now signaled by tiny letters in the text. One has to turn to the back pages where the variants are reproduced in a way that renders them almost totally unreadable. Slight crossings-out in Montaigne's handwriting are listed pell-mell with major revisions, and these are often explicated simply (and not always accurately) as being "the next 17 lines from the Bordeaux Copy," and then we have to return to the main text and count seventeen lines after having located the tiny letter that marks the beginning of the variant.

This is a pity. The variant readings of no other author are so enchanting to read and so essential for an understanding of his thought. The major changes in Montaigne's outlook are more intelligible when one knows where and how each passage first appeared. Above all, the realization that an idea is an after-thought changes its character and often enhances its effect. Perhaps the most sublime phrase of the book is a famous manuscript addition to the essay on friendship. In the tribute to Étienne de La Boétie, whom he knew for only three years, the greatest emotional experience of his life, Montaigne origi-nally wrote: "If you ask me why I loved him, I could not give an answer." A decade later, he added: "Parce que c'était lui; parce que c'était moi" ("Because it was him, because it was me"). Identifying the variants as one reads can give us the feeling that Montaigne himself is reading over our shoulder with comments.

At one point in the third volume, he almost invites the reader to compare versions. He claims, with only a little truth, that he adds to his book but does not correct; he did revise, although most of the changes are, indeed, additions—because once an author has published, or, as he put it in 1588, "has mortgaged his work to the world, it seems to me that he has no further right to it." Second, he is not sure that his revisions are any better than the original, and insists that the changes do not invalidate the original.

> My book is always a unity. Except that when a new edition is published, so that the buyer does not go away completely empty-handed, I make sure of attaching something. . . . They are only additions, and do not condemn the original version. . . . I do not trust my thoughts more because they are second or third, instead of first. Or present or past. Often we correct our-selves as stupidly as we correct others. My first publication was in 1580. After a long stretch of time, I have become older, but certainly not an inch wiser. Me now and me then are two, but which is better I could not say at all. It would be great to be old if we always progressed toward improve-ment. It is like a movement of a tottering drunkard, vertiginous, shape-less, like reeds moved fortuitously by the wind's will.
>
> Mon livre est toujours un. Sauf qu'a mesure qu'on se met a le renouveller, afin qu'on l'achetur ne s'en aille les mains du tout vuides, je me done loy d'y attacher. . . . Ce ne sont que surpois, qui ne condamnent pouint la premiere forme. . . . Je ne me deffie guiere moins de mes fantasies pour estre secondes ou tierces que premieres. Ou presentes que passées. Nous

nous corrigeons aussi sottement souvent come nous corrigeons les autres. Mes premeieres publications furent l'an 1580. Depuis d'un long traict de temps je suis envieilli, mais assagi je ne le suis certes pas d'un pouce. Moi asture et moi tantost somes bien deus; mais quand meillur, je n'en puis rien dire. Il seroit beau estre vieil si nous ne marchions que vers l'amandement. C'est un mouvemant d'yvrouigne titubant, vertigineux, informe, ou des joncs que l'air manie casuellement selon soy.

3

Much critical effort has been expended on trying to determine the outlines of Montaigne's philosophy.[2] This is not absolutely futile: he was at the start largely influenced by the Stoic school of Seneca, then showed more sympathy for the Epicureans. However, he is likely a few pages later to contradict any position he takes, but without explicitly rejecting it. It is rarely a final position that interests him, but the movement of thought—how one arrives at a conclusion, rather than where. Sometimes the idea he arrives at is incompatible with the starting point, just as the ideas of the Stoics are incompatible with the ideas of the Epicureans; but it is the trajectory that is fascinating. Poets and historians meant more to him than philosophers, he said, and his style reveals the stamp of poetry, as we saw above when he illustrates the unstable movement of reality with the astonishing image of the rocks of the Caucasus and the pyramids of Egypt.

On a few points Montaigne never wavered: most important of all was his hatred of cruelty. On this he based his condemnation of the use of torture in judicial proceedings, and his attack on the horrifying Spanish destruction of Mexican civilization (he interestingly assumed that it was still young, and that we, the representatives of an old dying culture, had destroyed it before it could mature). Along with his insistence that women should receive the same education as men, his refusal to accept the existence of witchcraft has given him the reputation, at least partially deserved, of being a precursor of Enlightenment thought. Hundreds of witches were burned at the stake during his time.

Just what Montaigne derived from his reading has an ambiguous status. He mocks writers who quote frequently from the classics, although this was certainly his own obsessive practice. But he boasts of deforming his citations to fit their new contexts:

2. The new Pléiade edition gives a valuable account of the most recent research in a hundred pages of endnotes.

I hide my thefts and disguise them. [Pedantic writers] parade them and are proud of them. . . . Like horse thieves, I paint the tail and the mane.

Je desrobe mes larcins, et les desguise. Ceux-cy les mette en parade et en compte. . . . Comme ceux qui desrobent les chevaux, je leur peins le crin et la queuë.

He later canceled the picturesque reference to horse thieves. However, he boasts elsewhere of concealing his borrowings from the classics, since it amused him to be attacked by those who did not realize when he was citing some famous authority—so that, as he says, the critics who mock him are really "thumbing their noses" at Plutarch or Seneca without knowing it.

At his most characteristic, Montaigne does not use his quotations or his anecdotes as authority, but only as steps in a movement of thought that leads elsewhere—and the conclusion itself is rarely a place of rest. In "On Cripples," for example, he takes up the antique belief that sexual intercourse is most enjoyable with a cripple:

Apropos or not apropos, it doesn't matter, there is a popular Italian proverb that says that he who has not slept with a lame woman does not know the perfect sweetness of Venus. Chance or some particular event put this saying into common use, and it is said of males as well as females

A propos ou hors de propos, il n'importe, on dict en Italie, en commun proverbe, que celuy-la ne cognoit pas Venus en sa parfaite douceur qui n'a couché avec la boiteuse. La fortune, ou quelque particulier accident, lont mis il y a long temps ce mot en la bouche du peuple; et se dict des masles comme des femelles

Montaigne speculates on the reason for this belief: perhaps the eccentric movement of the lame person gives a new taste or pleasure to the action, he suggests, but quickly adds that he has just learned that ancient philosophy gives a different reason (he got this from the pseudo-Aristotle of *The Problems*): since the thighs and the calves of the lame do not get enough nourishment, the genital parts are fuller and more vigorous. This leads Montaigne to the first of double conclusions:

What can we not reason about at this price? . . . Do not these examples prove what I said at the beginning that our speculations about the cause often anticipate the effect, and have the range of their jurisdiction so infinite that they judge and act in the inane itself and in non-being?

Dequoy ne pouvons nous raisonner à ce pris là? . . . Ces exemples servent-ils pas à ce que je disois au commencement: que nos raisons anticipent souvent l'effect, et ont l'estendue de leur jurisdiction si infinie, qu'elles jugent et s'exercent en l'inanité mesme et au non estre?

The second conclusion, however, turns around full circle:

> For, simply by the authority of the old and public saying, in the past I made myself believe that I received more pleasure from a woman because she was not straight, and counted that as one of her attractions.
>
> Car, par la seule authorité de l'usage ancien et publique de ce mot, je me suis autrefois faict a croire avoir receu plus de plaisir d'une de ce qu'elle n'estoit pas droicte, et mis cela en recepte de ses graces

It is evident that neither the proverb nor the various steps of reasoning nor even the conclusions have a permanent value for Montaigne. It is the voyage that counts; it leads from ancient and popular authority through empty speculation to the final, ironic, and basically worthless rehabilitation of the proverbial view, and it demonstrates the weakness of rational thought as it is generally practiced.

This is the essential set piece in the chapter that questions the belief in witchcraft, and demonstrates how the mind (including Montaigne's own mind) will reason with vacuous ingenuity. Contemporaries of Montaigne complained that he flitted from one subject to another, but he insisted that it all hangs together if you know how to read it. The opening words of this discussion, "Apropos or not apropos, it doesn't matter," are a signal that we must reconstruct the reason for ourselves.

Fundamental to Montaigne is the conclusion that casts doubt upon itself, and this reveals him at his most profound. The first chapter of the third book deals with the still relevant problem of living in a society so corrupt that we cannot behave decently. At the opening he launches into a catalog of the vices that foreshadows the "Préface" to Baudelaire's *Les Fleurs du Mal*:

> Our being is cemented with pathological qualities: ambition, jealousy, envy, vengeance, superstition, despair, lodge within us so naturally that the image can be recognized in animals: indeed, and cruelty, so unnatural a vice: since, in the middle of compassion, we feel within us an indefinable bittersweet prick of malignant delight at seeing someone else suffer, and children feel it.
>
> Nostre estre est simenté de qualitez maladives; l'ambition, le jalousie, l'envie, la vengeance, la supoerstition, le desespoir, logent en nous d'une si naturelle possession que l'image s'en reconnaoist aussi aux bestes: car, au milieu de la compassion, nous sentons au dedans je ne sçay quelle aigredouce poincte de volupté maligne à voir souffrir autruy; et les enfans le sentient.

This poetic description of cruelty is immediately followed by political reflections inspired by an age torn apart by religious strife:

If you remove the seeds of these qualities in man, you would destroy the fundamental conditions of our life. Similarly, in every political state, there are necessary offices not only abject but even vicious. . . . If they become excusable, in so far as we need them and common necessity obscures their true quality, let these parts be played by more vigorous and less cowardly citizens, who sacrifice their honor and their conscience like those men of the past sacrificed their lives to save their country. Those of us who are weaker, let us play easier and less hazardous roles. The public good demands that one lie, betray, and massacre: let us resign this commission to those who are more obedient and more supple than we are.

Desquelles qualitez qui osteroit les semences en l'homme, destruiroit les fondamentalles conditions de nostre vie. De mesme, en toute police, il y a des offices necessaires, non seulement abjects, mais encore vitieux. . . . S'ils deviennent excusables, d'autant qu'ils nous font besoing et que la necessité commune efface leur vraye qualité, il faut laisser jouer cette partie aux citoyens plus vigoureux et moins craintifs qui sacrifient leur honneur et leur conscience, comme ces autres anciens sacrifierent leur vie pour le salut de leur pays; nous autres, plus foibles, prenons des rolles et plus aisez et moins hazardeux. Le bien public requiert qu'on trahisse et qu'on mente et qu'on massacre; resignons cette commission à gens plus obeissons et plus sousples.

The word "massacre" was added as the political situation worsened after 1588. Montaigne may seem almost passively to accept crimes of state. Leave it to others—that is his personal solution. Behind this acquiescence, however, there is a protest: the last words "more supple" strike with greater force if one reflects that it is difficult to be more supple than Montaigne, but the coarseness of the irony reaffirms the contempt that is naked in the previous clauses. The comparison of those heroes of the past who "sacrificed their lives to save their country" with their modern counterparts who "sacrifice their honor and their conscience" may, I suspect, have been remembered by Edward Gibbon in one of the most extraordinary works of English polemics, *A Vindication of Some Passages in the Fifteenth and Sixteenth Chapters of the History of the Decline and Fall of the Roman Empire,* when he attacked the claim that an ecclesiastical historian had the right to cover up the defects of the early Christian church. He wrote: "The historian must indeed be generous, who will conceal, by his own disgrace, that of his country, or of his religion." The irony and the contempt are similar.

In Montaigne, clearly, the ironic contempt is both a private response and at the same time a public act—a published act; indeed, one of the few acts that a single and helpless man could have carried out in a period of civil war and religious conflict. However, the irony is more complex. It is also directed paradoxically against virtue and honesty: the very words "fearful," "easy," "less hazardous," and "weaker" cumulatively undermine the position of decency. The attempt to balance the utility of treason, murder, and vice with the feeble and cowardly exercise of virtue is intended to be deeply unsatisfactory and inconclusive. The result is a devastating indictment of the political order. Montaigne was a conservative who believed that one should never attempt to change the religion or the government of a country, but he was in no way the dupe either of religion or of politics. (Firmly a Catholic, he was imprisoned by the extremist Catholic League, and had to be released by Catherine de Médici.) Montaigne wrote that he was willing to stand by his principles up to the point where his opponents would burn down his house, but no further.

Trying to define Montaigne's religious position has always entailed controversy. The nineteenth-century belief that he was secretly a skeptical freethinker describes unfairly someone who said "I was born a Roman Catholic and I shall die a Roman Catholic" and insisted on practicing the Catholic rites at home in a predominantly Protestant neighborhood. Nevertheless (given the present academic fashion of imposing on students a devout and impeccably orthodox Catholic Montaigne), we might reflect on the passage that opens this review. An author who is unwilling to express himself completely and expects the happy few (the readers who understand his manner or "air") to guess at his oblique resonances "à gauche" is not likely to hold the most respectable opinions.

Sainte-Beuve's summary observation that Montaigne would have been a very good Catholic if he had been a Christian was a cogent formula. It is unsatisfactory, but helps to explain his importance for Pascal: Pascal did not need Montaigne to find out how to argue with his enemies; he already knew that better than any writer in history, as he demonstrated in the crushing, unanswerable and definitive attack he mounted on the Jesuits in his *Provincial Letters*. What he learned from Montaigne was how to argue with himself, to discover within himself that incredulity has an attraction as powerful as faith—an impeccably orthodox Montaigne would have been of little use to him. The power and the originality of Pascal's *Pensées* are indebted to his recognizing the seduction of disbelief and indifference.

4

Montaigne may have thought himself an orthodox Catholic, but he had little faith in the power of prayer (he could only remember one, anyway, the *Paternoster*), and he did not share in the Mariolatry popular at that time. Absolutely unacceptable to the Church, indeed, was his essay on repentance, a virtue he found extremely dubious: it is rarely sincere, he thought, and not very useful even then (he was asked by the clergy to change this, but he never did).

Even his friends were shocked by the outspoken essay on sex called "On Some Verses of Virgil," first published in 1588, and they suggested he remove it. Instead, he considerably enlarged it in the years that followed. He wrote it, he said, so that women would not leave his book lying around publicly in their salons, but would keep it for a more private room. In fact, his discussion takes its point of departure from the fact that sexual intercourse cannot be discussed openly in polite society:

> What has the genital action done to men, an action so necessary and just, that we dare not speak of it without shame and we exclude it from serious and respectable conversation? We can bravely pronounce the words: kill, rob, betray; and this we only dare to mumble between our teeth. Should we say that the less we exhale the words, the more we have the right to magnify the thought?
>
> Qu'a faict l'action genitale aux hommes, si naturelle, si necessaire et si juste, pour n'en oser parler sans vergongne et pour l'exclurre des propos serieux et reglez? Nous prononçons hardiment: tuer, desrober, trahir; et cela, nous n'oserions qu'entre les dents? Est-ce à dire que moins nous en exhalons en parole, d'autant nous avons loy d'en grossir la pensée?

He then added later in the Bordeaux Copy:

> For it is good that the words the most rarely used, the least written and the most kept silent, are the best known and the most generally recognized. No age and no way of life ignores them, no more than bread. They are imprinted in everyone without being expressed, either audibly or by image.
>
> Car il est bon que les mots qui sont le moins en usage, moins escris et mieus teus, sont les mieus sceus et plus generalement conus. Nul eage, nulles meurs l'ignorent non plus que le pain.

The essay is his farewell to sex, now that he has become old.[3] He still, he says, "remembers its power and its merits; there are some remnants of emotion and heat after the fever." He was, in fact, fifty-five years old, but he was already

3. This is emphasized by Jean Starobinski in his beautiful little volume *Montaigne en movement,* rev. ed. (Paris: Gallimard, 1993), which has the most persuasive and moving treatment of Montaigne's friendship with Étienne de La Boétie, and a brilliant discussion of Montaigne's elaborate criticism of the medical science of his time. (Montaigne asserted that when a doctor prescribed a medicine, he waited until he recovered from his illness so he could survive the medicine.)

experiencing the sense of old age. In another essay, he describes what the advancing years have done to him: among other things "I can no longer make children when standing up" (Je ne peux plus faire des enfans debout) (perhaps that was considered a proof of virility in his time).

He returns consistently to the sexual difficulties of old age. "Nature should have been content to have made old age wretched without making it ridiculous as well." He mocks the elaborate rituals of sex and courtship in society (after all, "it is just a way of emptying our vessels"). Then, some passages later, he reverses himself: when one reaches his age, he says, and it is hard to get it up even three times a week, these rituals are useful in the end, and allow a more leisurely pace (besides, women were not always pleased with him, he says, because he went at it too quickly).

The greatest distress concerning his age arises from his conviction that an old man making love to a young woman destroys the balance necessary to love:

> It is a business that needs relation and correspondence: the other pleasures we receive can be rewarded in different ways; but this one has to be paid in the same money. . . . There is no generosity in one who receives pleasure where he gives none. . . . If women can only gratify us by pity, I should rather not live at all, than live by accepting alms.

> Or c'est un commerce qui a besoin de relation et de corresponadance: les autres plaisirs que nous recevons se peuvent recognoistre par recompenses de nature diverse; mais cettuy-cy ne se paye que de mesme espece de mon-noye. Or cil n'a rien de genereux qui peut recevoir plaisir où il ne donne point. . . . Si elles ne nous peuvent faire du bien par pitié, j'ayme bien plus cher ne vivre point, que de vivre d'aumosne.

After 1588, he added, "I find more pleasure just seeing the proper and sweet mingling of two young beauties, or just imagining it, than taking part myself in a sad and shapeless mélange" (Je treuve plus de volupte a sulement voir le juste et dous meslange de deux junes beautes ou a le sulement considerer par fantasie, qu'a faire moimesmes le secont d'un meslange triste et informe).

He does not shrink from contradiction even on this point. He dismisses the suggestion that he have sex with a woman of his own age as a "foolish and insipid proposition."

The acceptance here of voyeurism and even of a masturbation fantasy reveals the most extraordinary aspect of this long essay: the refusal to treat sex as in any way sinful or obscene. It is true that in an earlier essay on friendship, he endorses the contemporary disapproval of homosexuality—however, not because it is unnatural or even physically repugnant, but only because it lacks the reciprocity and equality necessary to friendship as to love. For Montaigne, homosexuality could only exist between an older man and a very young one. A relation between two men of the same age seems not to have been conceivable for him (perhaps that came from his reading of pederasty in the Greek classics). In "On Some Verses of Virgil," on the other hand, Socrates' openly erotic relations with young men are treated with consistent sympathy, observing how powerful the sexual urge can be in old age.

A view of adultery as completely natural is developed at length. (Montaigne himself, who married somewhat late in life, kept his marriage vows much to his own surprise—"I gave more than I promised or expected.") At one point he astonishingly addresses all his male readers directly: "All of you have cuckolded somebody"—and that logically means that it will eventually happen to you. In the East Indies, he reports, a married woman is expected to be chaste, but is allowed to abandon herself to any man who gives her an elephant. This essay best reveals an essential trait of Montaigne: he had almost no sense of guilt—regret, often enough, of course, but not guilt or remorse. It is no wonder that he thought repentance more of a nuisance than a virtue.

"On Some Verses of Virgil" is not only a nostalgic and frank discussion of sex, but also a collection of misogynist anecdotes and jokes, banalities of medieval and classical traditions, largely to establish that it is absurd to force women to live by the rules fashioned by men, and to require them to pretend to believe that they are not interested in sex, when they are in fact even more lascivious than men—having so much less to occupy them. But when, on the last page, he writes, "I say that male and female are cast in the same mold; except for education and custom, there is little difference [je dis que les masles et femelles sont jettez en mesme moule: sauf l'institution et l'usage, la différence n'y est pas grande]," the declaration gains power from the mass of the preceding misogyny. It is not compromised by it, nor does it erase it. They coexist happily. And the idea is reinforced by a further concluding commonplace:

> It is easier to accuse one sex than to excuse the other: As we say: the pot calls the kettle black. [More literally, the poker mocks the shovel.]
>
> Il est bien plus aisé d'accuser l'un sexe, que d'excuser l'autre. C'est ce qu'on dict: Le fourgon se moque de la poele.

This declaration is more persuasive than the fashionable and generally insipid feminism of many of Montaigne's contemporaries, precisely because it follows hard upon the lively vigor of the popular medieval tradition.

The coexistence of opposites and the refusal of a logical synthesis are essential to Montaigne. After 1588, he added without further explanation the cryptic remark: "Perhaps I have a personal reason to speak only half my thought, to speak confusedly and discordantly." When this is not acknowledged, we lose the vivacity and the abundant sense of life that makes him so close to the readers of his own and later times. A famous and shocking sentence on the last page of his book is sometimes tortured by critics to remove the discord it creates. The final essay, "Of Experience," ends with a plea for an acceptance of the world as it is given us for "a life that conforms to the common and human model, but without miracle and without extravagance."

It is the ultimate message of Montaigne, and entails a frontal attack on the extremist religious factions that were tearing apart his society. He mounts a sustained and comic protest against the religious moralist of great austerity, who believes

> that pleasure is a bestial quality, unworthy of the philosopher. The only pleasure he takes from the enjoyment of a beautiful young wife is the pleasure of being conscious of doing something according to the rules. Like putting on his boots for a necessary ride on horseback.

> Que volupté est qualité brutale, indigne que le sage la gouste: le sul plaisir qu'il tire de la jouisaance d'une belle june espouse, que c'est le plaisir de sa comscience de faire un'action selon l'ordre, come de chausser ses bottes pour une utille chevauché.

After this satiric picture of the ascetic life, Montaigne prudently separates out the truly devout from "the childish mob of ordinary men like ourselves," setting apart "those venerable souls raised by their fervor of piety and religion to a constant and conscientious meditation on divine matters." (After 1588 he expanded this description of the saintly life, writing that it "disdained all necessary commodities, fluid and ambiguous, to concentrate on the eternal nourishment of Christian desires.") In 1588, the section had been rounded off simply: "This is a privileged study."

After that, in the Bordeaux Copy, he added the famous provocative sentence:

> Between you and me, these are things I have always seen of singular accord: supercelestial opinions and subterranean behavior.

> Entre nous, ce sont choses que j'aye tousjours veües de singulier accord: les opinions supercelestes et les meurs soubsterraines

Scholars who would prefer an orthodox Montaigne have assured us that, of course, he is not talking here about those venerable souls to whose religious ardor he has just paid such eloquent tribute, and that it is a misunderstanding to apply it to them.

This attempt to resolve the contradiction pays no attention to two important details of the text. Montaigne exempts no one. The first detail is an interesting variant: in the Bordeaux Copy, Montaigne originally crossed out the word "subterranean," and then wrote it back in. He understood that it would shock and lead to a reading that critics would deplore, and he decided that he would risk or even welcome the provocation. Second, the opening words "between you and me" signal that what follows will be found unacceptable to many, taking the reader who is on his side into his confidence. M. A. Screech interpreted "Entre nous" to mean "among us" (i.e., ordinary men like ourselves);[4] so separating the condemned from the fully devout and saintly (an interpretation that delighted the conservative taste of Marc Fumaroli), but in citing the text, Screech misquoted a significant detail, failing to notice the comma after "Entre nous," which makes it clearly an introductory warning that something a bit risky is about to be advanced, and makes the attempt to edulcorate Montaigne improbable. And the whole train of thought is vigorously reinforced a few sentences later:

> They want to get outside themselves and escape from humanity. It's madness: instead of transforming themselves into angels, they transform themselves into beasts. . . . And on the highest throne in the world, we are only seated on our ass.

> Ils veulent se mettre hors d'eux et eschapper à l'homme. C'est folie: au lieu de se transformer en anges, ils se transforment en bestes. . . . Et au plus eslevé throne du monde si ne somes assis que sur nostre cul.

The contradictions do not cancel each other, and may not be resolved. Montaigne submits, but does not capitulate, to religious and social authority. A few sentences later, he closes the book of essays with a few verses by Horace in praise of the pagan life addressed to Apollo. He must have expected those readers who "recognize his air" to draw their conclusions.

The editors of the Pléiade edition in an excellent introduction claim that Montaigne subjects everything to critical examination except for matters of religious faith. This is not quite accurate, although Montaigne does avoid undisguised religious controversy. Starobinski more perceptively points out that the only place where Montaigne professes his acceptance of all Catholic doctrine (instead of picking and choosing as he confessed he did when young) is followed immediately by his remarking how many contradictory beliefs have been held in the past and how many things we once believed that are now seen to be nothing but fables—taking away with one hand what he has just given with the other. Starobinski has a beautiful phrase for this procedure: "soumission désabusée" (submission without illusions). Montaigne certainly allows more than a hint of his reserves to appear.

He gloried in the contradictions, but he does not display them as such. His oppositions reflect the tensions of his age. His method was, by revealing the casual, hidden workings of the mind, to show how the profound is mixed with the trivial, the corporeal with the spiritual, the capricious with the reasonable. In so doing, he revealed what he saw as the disintegration of his society.

4. M. A. Screech, *Montaigne and Melancholy* (London: Penguin Books, 1991), pp. 134–135.

CHAPTER 23

La Fontaine:
The Ethical Power of Style

I

On the second of May, 1684, La Fontaine, now aged sixty-two, was admitted
to the Académie Française, taking the seat of the Prime Minister Colbert, who
had died the year before. Colbert had been ill-disposed toward the poet for a
long time, and was the principal agent many years before in the arrest and
imprisonment of La Fontaine's patron, Nicolas Fouquet. For more than six
months, Louis XIV refused to ratify La Fontaine's election. When the ceremony of admission finally took place, the speech of welcome was made by the
abbé de La Chambre, director of the Académie, who remarked that his own
profession as a priest made it impossible for him to read La Fontaine's fables
properly in order to give him the praise that was his due. "To tell you the truth,
Monsieur," he added:

> We needed a good subject to soften the bitterness of a separation as painful
> for us as that of M. Colbert, whom you succeed. . . . You should, Monsieur,
> forget this less than anyone, as I have the right to tell you with all the
> authority that my task gives me (a task that Fate, never more blind than
> now, has imposed on me, far from my wishes, and which would better
> suit anyone else in a reception like this one), you should, I say, Monsieur,
> remember without cease the one whose place you occupy, in order

Originally written in 1997 as a review of *Le Poète et le Roi: Jean de La Fontaine en son siècle*,
by Marc Fumaroli.

perfectly to fulfill your duties and to satisfy the obligations that you indispensably contract by taking your part in this assembly, on this day that you enter into our society.

La Chambre further informed the new member that his unique function would now be to work for the glory of the King, to have "no other purpose than the eternity of his name." In his answer of acceptance, La Fontaine skated very rapidly over his predecessor's virtues. The famous architect and writer of fairy tales, Charles Perrault, reported that La Fontaine's speech was witty and pleasing, but that "he read it badly and with a rapidity absolutely unsuited to an oration." La Chambre's harangue was printed by the Académie, but the abbé took the unprecedented step of refusing to reprint the speech of the poet that followed his.

Marc Fumaroli has written a fine and perceptive account of La Fontaine. He remarks on the difficulty for a modern reader of appreciating a poet who was neither persecuted as a *poète maudit* (which would satisfy the leftist critic) nor given genuine official status (and so gratify the right wing). Official recognition, when it came, was only grudging. In Fumaroli's judgment, La Fontaine was the greatest French lyric poet of the seventeenth century, the grand century of French classicism. While this estimate would not be contested by most readers of La Fontaine, it might appear at first sight an odd one. La Fontaine worked principally in genres that are not in the least lyric: he is famous only for his fables and his *contes,* a didactic genre and a burlesque versifying of off-color stories. Very few of his poems are specifically lyrical in character, and those few are not among his most typical. It is clear, however, that the power of La Fontaine's lyricism depends on its displacement into the most surprising contexts.

The Poet and the King is the title of Fumaroli's study, and it is almost as much about Louis XIV as about La Fontaine: the absolutist politics and the consequent attempt to enforce an official style by the King and his ministers are continuously present throughout the book. Fumaroli's distaste for the King is as evident as his admiration of the poet, and he treats Louis XIV with unmitigated ferocity. He repeats Saint-Simon's anecdote of the King's reaction to the possibility that the young Duchess of Burgundy (the wife of his grandson) might not be able to conceive again after a miscarriage caused by the King's forcing her to travel:

> What of it? . . . What do I care? Doesn't she have a son already? Thank God, she's hurt, since she was going to be, and I will no longer be constrained in my travels and in everything I want to do by the ideas of doctors and the reasoning of matrons.

And he quotes the extraordinary letter to Louis written by Fénelon, archbishop of Cambrai and author of the novel *Telemachus:*

You were born, Sire, with an honest and equitable heart, but those by whom you were educated gave you for a science of ruling nothing but suspicion, jealousy, an avoidance of virtue, the fear of all exceptional merit, a taste for men who are supple and servile, disdainful pride, and an attention to your own interests alone. For about thirty years your principal ministers have weakened and reversed all the ancient maxims of state in order to strengthen your authority to the limit. . . . They have made your name odious and the whole French nation insupportable to all your neighbors.

Fumaroli's study is a meditation on the plight of the artist under such a ruler during the imposition of an absolutist, centralized political regime.

The fall of Fouquet is the central event of Fumaroli's book. At the death of his prime minister, Cardinal Mazarin, Louis XIV was twenty-two years old, and anxious to take power into his own hands. The superintendent of finances, Nicolas Fouquet, who hoped to become the new prime minister, had recently built for himself a magnificent chateau at Vaux-le-Vicomte near Paris. On the seventeenth of August, 1661, he gave a party there for the entire court of such sumptuous splendor that it was talked about for decades. Nineteen days later, he was arrested and accused of embezzlement and treason.

His trial aroused no little indignation. Fouquet was a popular and impressive figure: after a period under Mazarin of considerable unrest and rebellion called the Fronde (a reaction to the unprecedentedly ruthless absolutist policies of Cardinal Richelieu, the previous minister), Fouquet had succeeded in negotiating peace with the different factions, showing a tolerance and a generosity that was not always to the taste of other members of the central government. He was a patron of the arts on a scale that had perhaps not been seen since the death of Francis I. After his arrest, Louis XIV immediately employed all the artists who had constructed and decorated Vaux-le-Vicomte to build Versailles for him.

There is no question that Fouquet's wealth had been acquired by methods that were strictly criminal: these methods were also widespread, commonplace, and expected. The prime minister, Mazarin, had himself built up a vast fortune by pillaging the state, and he encouraged those who worked for him to do the same. The problem for the young King was to reform the finances and, at the same time, salvage the reputation of Mazarin, to whom he had been deeply attached. Fouquet made an excellent scapegoat.

The King ordered Colbert to seize all the documents at Fouquet's residence in order to prevent the accused from demonstrating the implication of Mazarin in the corrupt financial dealings of the state. The trial was universally considered a mockery. Judges thought too favorable to Fouquet were quickly replaced. Even so, the trial court still refused to pronounce the death sentence desired by Louis, and decreed only permanent exile. Brutally, Louis changed the sentence to perpetual imprisonment.

The disappearance of Fouquet from the political scene meant a return to the universally hated absolutist policies of Richelieu: this time, however, the King wished to exercise the power himself rather than through a prime minister. It is probable that Louis could not abide a popular figure like Fouquet, considerably more cultured than himself, but in any case, the former superintendent of finances would have been a dangerous figure. He had connections in all parts of French society, many of his advisers were Protestant, and he had a marked tolerance for all varieties of philosophical thought. He stood clearly for a liberalism that Louis wished to destroy.

For La Fontaine, the arrest of Fouquet was a disaster. He had been protected and generously supported by the superintendent, and he remained loyal to him for decades, helping in his defense, and writing with considerable eloquence a plea for a pardon or more generous treatment. Many of Fouquet's friends were arrested; others hastily and prudently left town, among them La Fontaine. His uncle had been closely connected to Fouquet, and La Fontaine accompanied him on a trip to the Limousin. The *Letters from the Limousin,* written by the poet to his wife, are a masterpiece of conversational charm and wit. For the years that followed, La Fontaine had to rely upon support from groups unconnected with the central government's administration of grants for writers and artists. He found his friends among Jansenists, who were largely in opposition to the religious policies of the court, among Protestants, and even among the libertine and homosexual circle of the Duc de Vendôme—although in both religion and sexual character, he himself was perfectly conventional: an unenthusiastic and untroubled Catholic and a heterosexual philanderer, without ostentation in either respect.

The royal cultural policy supported only the noblest literary genres—tragedy and the heroic ode—and even Louis's weakness for the comedy of Molière shifted to an interest in the more prestigious and costly operas of Lully with librettos by Quinault. Panegyrics of the King were preferred and even demanded. The basic role of literature in the eyes of the court was that of an official propaganda machine. Fumaroli emphasizes the contrast with the much greater variety of literature favored by Fouquet, who encouraged satire and lyric poetry as well as the grander genres, and he looks with regret upon the destruction of this liberal policy by the more rigid official line taken by Louis's ministers upon his accession to power.

One must agree with Fumaroli that the generous freedom of Fouquet's support of the arts was preferable to the persistent attempt under Louis to direct all artistic work, insofar as possible, into unqualified glorification of the royal person. Nevertheless, if the variety of artistic style was admirable before Fouquet's arrest, and was considerably narrower afterward, most of the literature favored by Fouquet does not bear comparison with the great achievements by which the century of Louis is still remembered today. The finest works came later: the tragedies of Racine, the satires of Boileau, the fables of La Fontaine. For all French schoolchildren, these works are still the basis of French classicism. In recognizing this, Fumaroli is forced to claim that the principal achievements of the time, even the tragedies of Racine, were created against the ideals of the King's cultural policy, although this opposition is hidden under the surface of the works. This is close to a statement, curious in a writer as conservative as Fumaroli, that great art is subversive of official values, a cliché dear to left-wing critics, although no less true for being a cliché.

2

With La Fontaine's *Fables,* we do not have to burrow far under the surface to recognize a discreet opposition to the grandeur of style and the servile obedience wanted by the court, an opposition never openly expressed but evident on every page.[1] It is an opposition all the more striking in view of the moments of the *Fables* which realize the ideal of the sublime so essential to seventeenth-century aesthetics. In any case, the opposition is already inherent in La Fontaine's choice of genre. The fable was always considered a minor form without pretensions. It has an important classical history starting with Aesop, but it never had the prestige of the ode or the epic forms. Fumaroli remarks on the contempt for the genre of the fable in the period following the accession of Louis XIV to power, and he deploys a formidable erudition in an attempt to demonstrate that its earlier prestige, particularly among humanists of the Italian Renaissance, was greater than is sometimes thought, but the evidence he brings actually tends to demonstrate the contrary.[2] However, he decisively proves that La

---

1. The opening fable of book 1 ("The Grasshopper and the Ant") is throughout in seven-syllable lines with one three-syllable verse.

> La cigale ayant chanté
> Tout l'été

This is like a manifesto against the grand style patronized by the court. No one at that time wrote poetry in verses with an odd number of syllables, and this was certainly a gesture of independence.

2. He writes that Leonardo Abstemio in 1495 "combats the prejudice of the ignorant, for whom the animal fable is a poor genre," and he cites Le Maistre de Sacy's preface to his fables of 1647 which says "that this sort of fable has little cause to pass for a low and puerile form since people believed in the past that Aesop was inspired by God." These quotations are largely defensive, and demonstrate that only a small minority respected the animal fable as a grand genre.

Fontaine was indebted to Italian sources as well as to the classical and the Renaissance French versions of Aesop and the Latin fables of Phaedrus.

The superiority of La Fontaine as a fabulist to all of his predecessors—and successors, for that matter—is impossible to demonstrate in translation. It is often said about poetry that it cannot be appreciated in translation, but this applies much more to some poets than to others. Baudelaire and even Racine, for example, come through in English much better than La Fontaine. The most famous translation of the *Fables* into English is by one of the greatest poets of this century, Marianne Moore, and it is a disaster both for La Fontaine and for Moore. Her translation is, in a way, a tour de force: she rendered every one of La Fontaine's lines of irregular length with all the rhymes in the same place and exactly the same number of syllables. She was inspired to undertake this unfortunate project by W. H. Auden, who observed that Moore's prosody was based, not on accent as in standard English verse, but idiosyncratically on counting the number of syllables per line, as in French; she also wrote wonderful animal poems, like "The Frigate Pelican" and "The Pangolin," and she had a profound feeling for moral observation. She was apparently the ideal translator of La Fontaine. What was missing was one part of the poet's craft, which no one regrets when reading Moore's original poems (its lack may even be part of her charm), but was essential for La Fontaine. In a famous essay, "Lord Tennyson's Scissors," R. P. Blackmur recalled Tennyson's boast that he knew the "quantity" of every word in the English language except "scissors." No twentieth-century poet could make this claim, wrote Blackmur, except for W. B. Yeats, T. S. Eliot, Ezra Pound, and W. H. Auden. This suggests that the genius of the greatest poets is less intellectual than physical, like being good at throwing a forward pass or playing a violin strictly in tune.

English verse is regulated ostensibly by accent or emphasis, and not by quantity—that is, not by the weight of the vowel sounds, which make a syllable long or short; in English, quantity is regulated only by the ear of the poet. Eliot's sensibility for quantity gives his weakest poems a melodious balance that is missing in even the finest poems of, for example, William Carlos Williams. (Perhaps only John Ashbery today possesses this sense of quantity.)

In French verse, the line is principally ordered by the number of syllables, but vowel sounds have greater impact than in English poetry. That is because all syllables in French have, at least theoretically (and most of the time in practice as well), equal emphasis until the last syllable, which receives a slight accent. All French words are invariably accented on the last syllable unless the last syllable is an unaccented *e,* which is not pronounced except by speakers from the south of France; when words are grouped together in phrases, only the final syllable of the last word is accented. (For example, in the case of "Louis XIV," the word "Louis" used alone would be accented on the second syllable; but when the words are pronounced together, the only accent is on the last syllable of "quatorze.") In addition, most consonants are not pronounced with English force. When I was taught French in high school, our class was told to light a candle: if one pronounced a *p* (as in "petit pois") in front of the candle, the flame was not supposed to flicker as it did when we pronounced an English *p* (I should think that a German *p* would blow out the candle).

This makes vowels play a role in French poetry which might seem wildly extravagant even to foreigners who speak French well. Most American and English students have a hard time understanding why Alfred de Musset literally fainted with ecstasy at the Comédie Française when he heard the line in Racine's *Phèdre:*

La fille de Minos et de Pasiphaé.

No doubt the idea that Phaedra's parents were a god who now rules over Hell and a woman who had an amorous passion for a bull and gave birth to a monster has something to do with the dramatic force of the line, but its power for Musset came from the sonority, the way the tight vowels of "fille" and "Minos" move into the open double sound at the end, along with the symmetrical echo of "a-i" at the beginning by "a-i-a-é" in the last word.

La Fontaine was the greatest master of this kind of aural patterning in French before Victor Hugo, and he is subtler and more elegant than Hugo. Paul Valéry handled it almost as well, but he was a much less interesting poet in almost every other way. Marianne Moore's translation finds no equivalent and no substitute for this play of sound. It is, however, precisely by this play that La Fontaine became the greatest lyric poet of his time. It was essential to his achievement that the lyricism was never constant, but intermittent. In the middle of the narrative, the virtuoso patterns of sound suddenly set into relief a sentiment, a detail of landscape, or a simple action. In English, the following observation about a rabbit has nothing special:

After having grazed, trotted, done all his turns,
Jack Rabbit returns to his subterranean dwelling.

In French, however, the play of echoes and the symmetry of the sound arrangements are enchanting for the ear:

Après qu'il eut brouté, trotté, fait tous ses tours,
Janot Lapin retourne aux souterrains séjours

where "Janot" and "séjour" balance each other as a kind of mirror symmetry, "souterrains" mirrors the phonemes of "retourne," and the "ou" of "brouté" keeps echoing through the two lines as "tours" finds itself again in "retourne."

There are other aspects to the pattern, but the most essential is the way the staccato rhythm of the first line, imitating the movement of the rabbit, opens out into the long sonority of the second.

This sense of almost pure sound is not a modern critic's anachronistic aberration. Starting earlier in the seventeenth century with François de Malherbe, who more or less established many of the principles of high classical French prosody, some writers became abnormally sensitive to effects of pure sound. This has been famously documented: Malherbe's copy of the works of a contemporary poet, Philippe Desportes, was annotated with disagreeable comments about unpleasant sound effects, as well as other faults. Desportes had written "Comparable à ma flamme" (comparable to my flame), and Malherbe maliciously set down in the margin "PARABLAMAFLA." The most often quoted lines by Malherbe, from an elegy on the death of a young girl, reveal the pure balance of sound in a mirror image:

> Et Rose, elle a vécu ce que vivent les Roses,
> L'espace d'un matin

> And Rose, she lived the life of a rose,
> The space of one morning

where the end echoes the beginning, and the consonants of "vécu" mirror those of "que vivent." La Fontaine's virtuosity, however, was even more varied and more supple than Malherbe's.

Fumaroli unfortunately does not discuss La Fontaine's prosody or technique in any detail, but he calls attention frequently to the mastery of a great variety of tones that one finds in the work of La Fontaine, and correctly ascribes this to the profound influence of the Latin poet Horace. The observation needs to be carried further. Other poets have mastered a variety of tones, styles, and genres: in John Donne and Victor Hugo, to give only two examples, we find the amorous lyric, satire, invective, conversational verse, philosophical meditation, and classical eloquence. What sets La Fontaine and Horace apart from almost all other poets is that the different tones are not in separate poems, and they are in no way contrasted or opposed within the single poem; both poets glide from one tone or style to another, and the transitions are almost imperceptible. The *Fables* mingle comedy and eloquence, mock epic and satire, personal lyric and witty conversation; and all these tones belong to the same world and coexist happily without the slightest sense of incongruity.[3] In a period when

3. The only important essay on La Fontaine that Fumaroli seems not to know is Leo Spitzer's brilliant "The Art of Transition in La Fontaine." Spitzer, however, deals only with

the separation of high and low genres was consistently affirmed, this was a major stylistic triumph that was also a challenge to classical principles.

3

It was seen very early on that the *Fables* presented an image of contemporary society. La Fontaine transformed the little moral apologues that were the basis of the genre into a critical view of his world. Fumaroli treats this aspect with great elegance and more good sense than most critics. In the late nineteenth century, Hippolyte Adolphe Taine published a brilliant essay on La Fontaine in which he dogmatically ascribed a single social and political meaning to almost every detail, as if there were a hidden code to be broken: the lion, for example, with all his cruelty and his arbitrary will, and with his dependence on servile flatterers, was always to be understood as Louis XIV. Fumaroli steers a course between this rigid extreme and a purely aesthetic interpretation of the kind best found in Paul Valéry's essay on La Fontaine's poem *Adonis*. Perhaps the most interesting aspect of Fumaroli's book depends on an interpretation, supple and tactful, of the social criticism evident enough in the *Fables,* as he raises the problem of the awkward position of a poet faced with political acts of obvious injustice.

The question of what political engagement is to be expected of a poet is discussed with great intelligence by Fumaroli, and if his answer is not completely satisfying, it is unlikely that any answer will be. He treats with disdain Jean-Paul Sartre's absurd condemnation of Baudelaire's refusal after his early youth to take a political position. Other critics have interpreted the fables as a disguised attempt to attack the prime minister, Colbert, in order to avenge Fouquet, and Fumaroli remarks acidly that this would make La Fontaine "not an amiable madman, but an idiot." Most of the important writers in the last half of the seventeenth century made no public protest against the most outrageous acts of the King and his ministers, although private dismay was widespread.

It is true, as Fumaroli points out, that after a century of devastating religious conflict and the decades of political turmoil of the Fronde, the French public was exhausted and the legitimacy of Louis XIV's reign appeared to be the only guarantee of peace. The return of absolutist policy may have been a hard price to pay, but open resistance was no longer practical. The fundamental distinction that Fumaroli wants us to accept is between the "politics of the politicians"

---

the transitions from one subject to another and does not discuss the transitions from one style or genre to another that are even more remarkable, and which give La Fontaine his unique position in French poetry.

and the "politics of poetry": the latter preserves the integrity of language and the truths that it embodies against a politics that distorts language and truth in the interests of power. He writes:

> Poetry has no need to be politically engaged in order to be political. On the contrary, when it is politically engaged it ceases to be at the same time politics and poetry, the politics of poetry. If all great poetry is political, we can say precisely that it is so by definition, since it seeks for the City a foundation in the truth of the heart, wagered and rewon by the integrity of language.

We ought not to dismiss this statement merely because the large generalities and oversimple grandeur of style suggest the empty formulas of so much French philosophical writing that derives from Alain, whose influence on the writers of the 1930s is still unfortunately discernible today. Fumaroli is raising a legitimate and difficult point.

There is, indeed, a process by which a totalitarian regime—and even a dishonest democratic government as well—corrupts language, and making a stand against the corruption of language is an aspect of the literary profession that cannot be dismissed. In addition, expecting a poet to make a public protest against every injustice is a waste of his, and our, time. Yet Fumaroli still leaves us with a sense that he is at least partially evading the issue. He has every right to do this, since there is no way that the general questions he raises can be directly faced with success, but the position of La Fontaine in the society of his time brings out aspects that Fumaroli prefers to leave at least partially in the shadow. What he has written is cogent, but not quite adequate.

The greatest political crime of the reign of Louis XIV is often acknowledged to be the Revocation of the Edict of Nantes in 1685. This edict, proclaimed under Henri IV at the end of the sixteenth century, granted religious toleration to the large Protestant minority. Louis XIV's intent to destroy any form of opposition led to the persecution of the Jansenist sect, resolutely Catholic but opposed to that part of the Church hierarchy subservient to Rome; and he consistently tried to reduce the Protestant force in his kingdom. Protestants were paid to convert, and at first it looked easy, but the resistance of a large number irritated the King.

The terms of the Revocation provide a perfect example of corruption of language: The government proclaimed the Edict of Nantes was no longer valid, because there were no Protestants left in France. Of course, those who were still around had a choice: they could convert or they could leave the kingdom. Many of them chose to leave, and they improved the textile industry in England with their skills, managerial abilities, and investment in much the same way that German refugees from Hitler created American musicology and inspired

American research in physics. La Fontaine's patron, Mme. de la Sablière, had been Protestant (she converted to Catholicism in 1680 when she shut herself despairingly in a convent after being abandoned by her lover); some of her children refused to convert and left the country.

La Fontaine's attitude to religion had always been one of benign detachment. He received a religious education at the Oratory, but it is admitted that he spent the time reading a novel while his teacher studied Saint Augustine. Religious controversy excites him only to mockery. Nor is he much impressed by religious ritual. Describing his voyage to Limousin with his uncle he writes:

> We had to wait for three hours, and to keep from being bored, or to be even more bored (I don't really know which one I should say), heard the parish mass. Procession, holy water, instruction, nothing was missing. By good fortune, the curate was ignorant and there was no sermon.

He does not seem to have taken religion very seriously until the end of his life, although Pascal's superbly comic attacks on the Jesuits inspired him to transform some of Pascal's prose into witty verse.

What was La Fontaine's reaction to the Revocation of the Edict of Nantes, a political crime which touched many of the people closest to him? In public, he had a poem printed in 1687 in which he praised the King for the Revocation:

> He wishes to conquer Error: the work advances,
> It is done; and the fruit of his many successes
> Is that the Truth reigns through out France,
> And France throughout the universe.

In private, at the same time, his reaction was somewhat different from this extravagantly groveling panegyric: in a poem that remained in manuscript (but we must remember that what he wrote was widely circulated among a large circle), he set down enthusiastic praise of Pierre Bayle, a Protestant whose brilliant journalism provided the most controversial and influential plea for religious tolerance at that time.[4] "He wishes to please men of wit, and he pleases them," observed La Fontaine, and praised his literary style and his honest language. "If he can find the occasion for a stinging and satirical remark, he seizes it, God knows, like a clever and adroit man. As a child of Calvin, he would decide about everything if he dared, since he has the taste for it along with the learning."

This was still a period of religious agitation: James II was about to be thrown out of England for his adherence to the Catholic faith. The Revocation was by

---

4. He later published the first part of the poem, but not the lines on Bayle.

no means universally welcome to all Catholics: the Pope, in particular, astonishingly refused to approve it, which outraged the French government. In a verse letter to his English friends, La Fontaine reported a joke making the rounds ("and it's a good joke," he added) that it would promote peace if the Pope became a Catholic and James II of England became a Huguenot. His praise of Bayle (neglected by Fumaroli) was written in the year following Bayle's publication of a virulent and sardonic attack on the Revocation. Not even privately does La Fontaine condemn the Revocation (that would certainly have been imprudent, even if he had wanted to) but he made it clear enough that he himself was not governed by the spirit of intolerance that had produced it.

This discrepancy between public and private statement is not one that is easy for us to assess, and we may think, in fact, that we are not called upon to pass judgement. Some kind of estimate is hard to avoid, however, just as it is difficult to remain neutral about the attitude of the German artists to the Third Reich. Nevertheless, no simple criterion exists to help us distinguish clearly among Furtwängler, who accepted an official post under Hitler, but used his prestige to try to mitigate the Nazi racial policy, von Karajan, who joined the Nazi party twice, the second time to make sure that his adherence would be noticed, and Gieseking, who was ideologically a perfectly satisfied, if stupid, Nazi. As we go centuries back in time, the difficulties of assessment are compounded.

If we feel, and with some justice, that La Fontaine's compromises are at least mildly deplorable, Montaigne may help us clarify the matter, and Fumaroli has called attention to the importance of Montaigne for La Fontaine, as for almost every other writer of the seventeenth century in France. The relation of the individual citizen to public crimes was a subject for Montaigne's meditation, and he gives an answer to the dilemma that naturally arises, which not only has the merit of being as subtle and ambiguous as the problem demands, but also confronts its own ambiguity:

> The public good requires betrayals, lies, and massacres; let us leave that to people who are more obedient and more supple.

Montaigne may seem almost passively to accept crimes of state. Leave it to others—that is his personal solution.[5]

La Fontaine's favorite philosopher was Plato, and one of his friends reported that the margins of his copy of Plato were filled with comments that went directly into the *Fables*. Since we have lost this volume, we cannot know just how Plato inspired him, and he rarely mentions Plato. The debt to Montaigne was certainly equally great. In one of his most brilliant comments, Fumaroli

5. For a detailed account of this passage of Montaigne, see my essay on Montaigne, pp. 303–318.

writes that La Fontaine made a synthesis of Montaigne and Ariosto. He does not expand on this at any length, but the suggestion comes close to describing the essential achievement of La Fontaine.[6] The *Orlando Furioso* of Ariosto was, for more than two centuries, considered the most civilized and urbane of all European poems. Most educated people in France, England, and Germany had even read it in the original Italian. An epic of the adventures of the knights of Charlemagne with all its mythical elements, the sorcerers, magic rings, hippogriffs, and travels to the moon, it gives the most revealing picture of Renaissance society and its ideals. The greatness lies in Ariosto's supple and melodious prosody, an unbelievably varied and malleable syntax, and a continuous and ambiguous irony. The reader is never sure how seriously or how playfully one is meant to take the story, but it never falls into parody or satire. When Angelica, the heroine, assures the Saracen who loves her, Sacripante, that she is still a virgin even though she has already been kidnapped by other knights half a dozen times, Ariosto does not deny it, but he finds the opportunity to draw a commonplace moral with delicacy and tact, and observes:

> Perhaps this was true, but nevertheless not credible
> To one who was master of his senses;
> But it seemed easily possible to him
> Who was lost in a much graver error.

6. La Fontaine's knowledge of Italian literature was as great as his reading in French and Latin: he admired Boccaccio, Tasso, and Machiavelli, and borrowed from Aretino (it would not have been politic to admit an admiration for the latter, as he was best known for pornography, but he was the greatest prose stylist of the Italian sixteenth century). Keeping this in mind, we can clear up an enigma that has puzzled scholars: in the Epistle to Huet, where La Fontaine details the poets he admired among the Ancients and the Moderns, he alludes—without naming him—to a "poet whom I took in the past for my master. He was going to spoil me. In the end, thank heaven, Horace happily opened my eyes. The author had some good things, some of the best, and France admired the turn and the cadence of his verse. Who would not have esteemed them? I was ravished by them, but whoever followed his style was lost. His overabundance of wit displayed too many beautiful things."

He adds in a note that "some authors of that time affected antitheses, and the sort of thoughts that one calls concetti. That immediately followed Malherbe." Who was this author? There have been many unsatisfactory suggestions, including Malherbe, which is absurd since La Fontaine revered him to the end of his life. It has been assumed that the author is French, since La Fontaine writes that he was admired in France, but in fact that should suggest a foreigner. Internationally the most famous and most influential European poet of the early seventeenth century, Marino Marini, lived in France, where he was called the Chevalier Marin, and his longest and best-known work, *Adonis,* was dedicated to Louis XIII. His florid Baroque style and use of concetti fit La Fontaine's characterization perfectly.

That which man sees, Love makes it invisible to him,
And he is made to see the invisible by Love.
This was believed; and misery can habitually
Give easy credence to that which is desired.

Ariosto's cynical detachment treats his characters with tact and sympathy. La Fontaine pictures his animals in his fables, as well as the humans and the gods, with the same ironic distance. He draws his morals with similar grace and detachment, if often more brutally:

The loss of a husband does not go without sighs.
One makes a lot of noise,
And then one consoles oneself.
Sadness flies away on the wings of time.

(In French that last line has an exquisite equilibrium:

Sur les ailes du Temps la Tristesse s'envole

as the sound and meaning of "sur les ailes" is echoed by "s'envole," and the dentals—the consonants pronounced with the tip of the tongue against the teeth—of "du Temps" reappear in "Tristesse": a trite cynical comment is transformed into a delicate lyric moment.)

It is in his treatment of the traditional morals of the fables that La Fontaine's kinship with Montaigne is most obvious. Montaigne, too, is indebted to the banalities of classical philosophy and literature, to the Latin and Greek authors that he loved to cite. Much of his own thought has so little originality that his right to the title of philosopher is sometimes contested. In the passage I quoted, the belief that crimes are sometimes necessary for the good of the state was commonplace enough after Machiavelli, and even before. What is original in Montaigne is the strange path he takes to arrive at the idea. In his work, the movement of concepts is the center of interest, and his presentation of that movement is unique in philosophical literature.

The morals of Aesop are not in themselves interesting today, and they were almost equally unimpressive in the seventeenth century, although people still had a taste for serious epigrams. What holds our attention in La Fontaine is how he arrives at the final banal significance. Often enough, the traditional moral tag is partially contradicted or undercut by La Fontaine's sophisticated recasting of the story, its significance radically altered, just as Montaigne warns us that his quotations from classical authors do not have direct relevance to what he appears to be talking about, "but they often carry, beyond the subject in question [hors de mon propos], the seeds of a richer and more daring substance, and they ring obliquely [à gauche] with a more delicate tone both for myself who have no desire to express anything further and for those who understand my tune." Montaigne invites us to read between the lines (and that is why respectable scholarly efforts today to turn him into a more conservative thinker are so unconvincing). The informally civilized tone of La Fontaine's rewriting of the old moral tales, the details from contemporary life in which he dresses them, allow him to present a critical view of his society that rivals Ariosto. His real model was much grander, however: the poet to whom he most often alludes, circumspectly and with apparent modesty, is Homer.

The epic poem is the traditional vehicle of the sublime: in its mythical adventures it represents the ideals of the society from which it comes. From the Renaissance to the French Revolution, French poets aspired to write a great epic. Almost no one succeeded, not even Ronsard in the sixteenth century: many poets in the seventeenth made fools of themselves by their attempts. The most powerful man in the French Academy for many decades of the seventeenth century, Jean Chapelain, found himself a laughingstock when he published his pitiful effort. Only by the poet's standing outside the traditional sublime could something like the grand epic be reached at that time. There are only two triumphs of this kind in France: Agrippa d'Aubigné's *Les Tragiques,* a virulent Protestant polemic against the persecution of the Huguenots, and La Fontaine's *Fables.*

Starting with miniature poems in a genre without pretensions at the greatest distance from the standard noble style, La Fontaine made his ambitions clear:

> Sometimes I oppose, by a double image
> Vice and virtue, foolishness and good sense,
> > The Lambs to the violent wolves,
> The Fly to the Ant: making of this work
> An ample comedy in a hundred different acts
> > Of which the scene is the universe.
> Men, Gods, Animals, all play some role here,
> Jupiter like anyone else. . . .

This is from the opening of the fifth book of fables. In the epilogue to the eleventh book (the end of the second collection he published) his claims are even grander:

> It is thus that my Muse, on the banks of a pure stream,
> Translated into the language of Gods
> Everything that is said under the heavens
> By so many beings borrowing the voice of nature.
> Interpreter of different peoples,
> I made them serve as actors in my work;
> For everything speaks in the universe

> There is nothing that does not have its language
> More eloquent in their place than in my verse.

The moral tags are no longer the center of gravity in La Fontaine's fables, as they are in Aesop's; that has shifted to the eloquence of the universe from which he can distill these banal little moral phrases, and when they leave his hands, they have been transformed by his experience of the society and the culture he was representing.

"The Oak and the Reed," the traditional fable of the tree that stood fast against the storm and was uprooted and the reed that bent and survived, is often called La Fontaine's most perfect achievement. He placed it significantly at the end of his first book. The moral does not survive his treatment intact, and in this fable he does not even draw it; he ends the poem without comment. In the classical version, the oak is stiff and is destroyed by his refusal to be as supple as the reed. In the Middle Ages, the apologue was given a Christian turn: the oak is sinfully proud, and the reed acts with humility. Neither of these moral lessons keeps its integrity in La Fontaine. In his version the oak is proud, but the reed is far from properly humble.

The fable begins in mock-epic style. The oak is comic in his grand bluster, a parody of eloquence:

> While my head, similar to the Caucasus,
> Not content with stopping the rays of the sun,
> Defies the effort of the storm.

(This is funnier in French, as the pile-up of oversonorous vowels makes the oak sound like a brass band:

> Cependant que mon front, au Caucase pareil,
> Non content d'arrêter les rayons du soleil
> Brave l'effort de la tempête.)

The lines are both a blasphemy and a crime of state: the oak stops the sun's rays, a divine power and also the power of Louis the Sun King, as he liked to be known.

The reed is obviously from a lower social class than the aristocratic oak, and he has a different style, conversational and impertinent:

> Your compassion, responded the shrub,
> Springs from a good nature, but do not worry.
> The winds are less fearsome to me than to you.
> I bend and do not break.

> Vostre compassion, luy répondit l'Arbuste,
> Part d'un bon naturel; mais quittez ce soucy.
> Les vents me sont moins qu'à vous redoutables.
> Je plie, et ne romps pas. . . .

Even the sound of the reed lacks the power of the oak's boasting. The vowels are less sonorous, the rhythm much more short-winded. There is, however, no opposition between the two styles. The last line of the oak is neutral enough to mediate between the mock-heroic and the informal:

> Nature seems to me to have been very unjust to you.

The little scene between persons of two classes is presented as a unity, and the dialogue in turn is fused with the narrative that follows as the wind rises:

> I bend and do not break. You, until now,
> Against their terrifying blows
> Have resisted without bowing.
> But wait for the end. As he was saying these words,
> From the edge of the horizon rises with fury
> The most terrible of the children
> That the North had borne until then in its loins.

The narrative is in a new style, genuine epic and no longer mock-epic. There is also no opposition, as the new manner moves without any break from the reed's impudent warning.

The end is famous, one of the great tragic effects in French classical verse:

> The wind redoubles its efforts
> And did so well that it uproots
> The one whose head was neighbor to the sky
> And whose feet touched the empire of the dead.

> Le vent redouble ses efforts
> Et fait si bien qu'il déracine
> Celui de qui la tete aù ciel était voisine
> Et don't les pieds touchaient à l'empire des morts.

The shift of style is unprecedented. No one had ever used the modest genre of the fable for such grand effects (the last two lines are, in fact, lifted directly from Virgil's *Aeneid,* but their grandeur is equaled and even magnified in the fable).

There is no moral stated. Nor could there be, since the oak has astonishingly become the hero of the poem. It should be noted here that La Fontaine's experience of the tragic fall of Fouquet probably made the effect possible. We must not take too literal a reading, since La Fontaine would never have made Fouquet ridiculously vainglorious as he does the oak at the opening; he retained his affection for him over the years. But the oak presents himself as a possible patron to the reed. It is perhaps this that justifies the impertinence of the reed. Far from protecting the artists he supported, Fouquet ended by putting all of them in danger:

> Still if you were born in the shelter of the leaves
> With which I cover the vicinity,
> You would not have so much to suffer:
> I would defend you from the storm;
> But you are born most often
> On the humid borders of the Kingdoms of the wind.

The last of these lines is famously exquisite.

> Encore si vous naissiez à l'abri du feuillage
> Dont je couvre le voisinage
> Vous n'auriez pas tant à souffrir:
> Je vous défendrais de l'orage;
> Mais vous naissez le plus souvent
> Sur les humides bords des Royaumes du vent.

The destruction of the oak is due to his foolish pride, but he is still the superior figure who has earned the right to the true epic style. Like Fouquet, the oak challenges royalty: he blocks the rays of the sun, and even the winds that he defies have their kingdoms. In this poem, the downfall of his patron gave the work of La Fontaine a power that the lyric poets patronized by Fouquet had never been able to achieve. It is because the lyricism is intermittent, as elsewhere in La Fontaine, appearing suddenly in the context of simple narrative and satirical comedy, that it has a force that always takes the reader by surprise.

The oak may be the tragic hero, but his fate is presented without pity and without sentimentality. La Fontaine reflects the difficult realities of his society uncompromisingly. What many French children like about the *Fables* is exactly what Jean-Jacques Rousseau thought made them unfit for pedagogy: their frequent cruelty, their heartlessness. Unlike any other fabulist, La Fontaine was too clear-sighted to be moral. The *Fables* are not immoral like the *Contes* (which are charmingly so and with only a rare touch of pornography); they are amoral, realistic. It is the harshness of so many of his miniature scenes that helps to give the whole work its seriousness and depth and vindicates his ambitious claims, which lend it an epic dimension. The realistic brutality he cultivated opens the first book, although with a certain gaiety, when the grasshopper, who spent the summer singing, begs the ant, who worked all those months, for a little food:

You sang: I'm happy to hear that.
Well, you can dance now.

It was obvious enough to Rousseau that this did not teach children the virtues of frugality, but the bitterness of experience.

4

On one matter should I like to take strong issue with Fumaroli's biography: the so-called "conversion" of La Fontaine in his last years. At the age of seventy-one, the poet repented his past libertinism and became devout. Fumaroli ascribes this radical change to the influence of Fénelon, archbishop of Cambrai, and an elegant writer inclined to mysticism. There is no question about La Fontaine's contacts with Fénelon, but no evidence of any influence, and I do not think we need an intellectual inspiration for the conversion.

In December 1692, the young abbé Poujet went to see the old poet intending to reform his dissolute way of life. La Fontaine had been ill and was extremely receptive. "I have just been reading the Bible," he said, "and it really is a very good book." What he could not understand about religion, he added, was eternal damnation, particularly of infants. You don't have to understand it, the abbé told him, just accept it. After several visits, the abbé determined that he was properly reformed (or converted), but first he had to condemn publicly the indecent stories in verse he had written and that were so popular. The old man appeared not to comprehend why, and the abbé insisted that they corrupted the readers. With what the abbé took to be genuine naiveté, La Fontaine protested that they had done him no harm when he wrote them.

Fumaroli thinks the twenty-five-year-old abbé Pouget intelligent, but he seems to me to have been a very ordinary ecclesiastical official of limited understanding. The appearance of naiveté and absentminded simplicity in the seventy-year-old La Fontaine was a kind of mythical persona or mask that he had both created and allowed to be imposed on him over the years—not without a certain malice, as Fumaroli himself remarks early in his book. The young abbé took it seriously, and so did La Fontaine's housekeeper: "God would never have the courage to damn him," she told the abbé when he was too insistent. She also said, "Stop tormenting him; he's much more stupid than wicked."

This personality was useful to La Fontaine; it not only kept him out of trouble, but it also gave him the detachment from society necessary for his unsystematic critical outlook. (In 1778, Lichtenberg wrote in one of the notebooks where he jotted down anything that came into his head: "Just as the vilest and most vicious actions demand intelligence and talent, the accomplishment of the greatest acts demands a certain apathy that one calls, at other times, stupidity.") In the end, the abbé won out: the poet made a public and humiliating condemnation of his stories, and he burned a comedy he had just written. He spent the last two years of his life translating the Psalms. After his death, it was discovered that he wore a hairshirt and had been flagellating himself.

A conversion or reform of this sort in old age was commonplace during the sixteenth, seventeenth, and even eighteenth centuries. (When it did not take place, relatives and friends sometimes claimed that it had in order to save the reputation of the loved one.) There was considerable doubt among the educated classes about the truth of revelation—but then, one could never be sure. Perhaps there was a hell and even a purgatory, after all. If the Church was right, and one reformed in time, preferably not too near the end, one had a chance of making at least purgatory. We do not know exactly what La Fontaine's religious convictions were before his reform, or how strongly they were held, and it is possible that he did not know himself, but he was obviously intent on carrying out his conversion as well and as sincerely as possible. Pascal had observed that if an unbeliever went through all the motions and behaved as if he had faith, he might end up with true belief: it is likely that the hairshirt and the flagellation were not simply penance for La Fontaine, but a way of life that would enforce belief, and allow his faith to become deeply rooted in the habits of the body and the daily routine.

Pascal's wager—if you bet on religion, you might gain eternal and infinite bliss, but if you bet on the truth of atheism and win, the reward would be only a limited amount of pleasure in this world and then nothingness, so the huge eventual compensation makes religion the more rational side on which to lay one's stakes—is often taken as an original, eccentric, and somewhat discreditable invention of a mathematician. In fact, it was at that time the average educated attitude to life in this world and the next. The usual approach was to get as much material pleasure as one could from the particular sins which interested one most, and then reform before it was too late. It was understood as a matter of course that the conversion had to be sincere, wholehearted, and passionate. La Fontaine did what was expected of him and what was necessary for him to receive the blessing of his church. Whether he was ever convinced by the arguments that his erotic tales were harmful is not clear, but the Church demanded obedience without understanding and he complied.

About a year after his conversion, and shortly before the end of his life, he wrote in a letter to his closest friend: "I would die of boredom if I had to stop writing verse."

CHAPTER 24

The Anatomy Lesson: Melancholy
and the Invention of Boredom

I

Long ago, when reading a lengthy, serious, and technical book was considered an agreeable and even entertaining way of passing the time, Richard Burton's *The Anatomy of Melancholy* was a best seller. This was a curious fate for a superannuated medical treatise written in the early seventeenth century not by a doctor, but by a reclusive clergyman and scholar at the University of Oxford who set out to write on melancholy and made it the occasion to take up much else as well. During his lifetime the book went through six editions. From 1621 to 1651 it grew considerably in bulk, starting at 353,369 words and finally attaining 516,384 (a seventh edition with no revisions was published in 1660 shortly before Burton's death). It was not reprinted during the eighteenth century, but there must have been many copies still available from the previous century. Samuel Johnson told Boswell that it was "the only book that ever took him out of bed two hours sooner than he wished to rise."

In the early nineteenth century, the Romantic movement made this tract into literature. Charles Lamb, Samuel Taylor Coleridge, and John Keats were all, among many others, fascinated by the work, and in one of Keats's letters there is even a very elaborate, admiring, and funny pastiche of Burton. Coleridge is said to have pronounced it "one of the most entertaining books in the language."[1]

1. His copy, which he must certainly have annotated in the margins as he did with most of what he read, has been lost, so we only have his opinion as reported in conversation. See

It became indeed a classic: forty-eight editions were published in the nineteenth century.

Interest then subsided. In standard histories of English literature, of course, Burton always retained a grand place, but the twentieth century saw few reprints, although many libraries were, and still are, well stocked with the editions of the nineteenth century. Recently, however, there has been an important revival. A six-volume critical edition has appeared, containing all the many thousands of variants of the work as it appeared in the seventeenth century, with the last three volumes an extensive (although by no means exhaustive) commentary. At the same time, the French have suddenly decided after almost four centuries to translate the book, in two chunky volumes, with an introduction by Jean Starobinski, the world's leading authority on the relations of literature and medicine, as well as on much else.

To call *The Anatomy of Melancholy* a medical treatise, as I have done, is misleading, in part because Burton uses the subject as an excuse to introduce whatever takes his fancy, but principally because melancholy was not so much a disease as a basic component of civilization. It defined a type of personality, but technically the condition of Melancholy was a physical imbalance created by an unwelcome preponderance of one of the four humors that regulated the body, in this case the invasion into the blood of the humor of black bile. When Burton wrote, the theory of the humors, which had dominated medicine since classical Greece, was about to be demolished, its foundation subverted by William Harvey's demonstration in 1628 of the circulation of the blood and the fundamental revision in our ideas of the human physical constitution. The theory of the humors continued, nevertheless, to dominate medical practice tenaciously (in spite of the fact that there was no empirical evidence for the existence of black bile in the blood) and it is central to Burton's view of human nature.

However, the theoretical confusion was already striking. In a book on the history of the treatment of melancholy,[2] published in 1960, Starobinski remarks:

> We can easily understand that the persistence of the word melancholy—preserved by medical language since the fifth century BC—is only a witness to the taste for verbal continuity. . . . But we should not be duped by the similitude of words: under the continuity of the word melancholy, the indicated facts varied considerably. From the moment in the distant past when persistent fear and a sadness could be identified, the diagnosis appeared certain. To the eyes of modern science, there was a confusion of

---

Coleridge on the Seventeenth Century, edited by Roberta Florence Brinkley (Chapel Hill, N.C.: Duke University Press, 1955), p. 432.

2. *Histoire du traitement de la mélancolie des origines à 1900* (Basel: J. R. Geigy, 1960), p. 9.

endogenic depression, reactive depression, schizophrenia, neuroses of anxiety, paranoia, etc.

Burton himself acknowledges the disparate variety and complexity of the theory:

Who can sufficiently speake of these symptoms, or prescribe rules to comprehend them? . . . If you will describe melancholy, describe a phantasticall conceipt, a corrupt imagination, vaine thoughts and different, which who can doe? The foure and twenty letters [of the alphabet] make no more variety of words in divers languages, then melancholy conceipts produce diversity of symptoms in severall persons. They are irregular, obscure, various, so infinite, Proteus himselfe is not so divers, you may as well make the Moone a new coat, as a true character of a melancholy man; as soone finde the motion of a bird in the aire, as the heart of a man, a melancholy man.

He then lists some of the symptoms mentioned by his sources, including headache, dropsy, gallstones, epilepsy, gout, hemorrhoids, etc.

The confusion was apparent already by the second century AD, when different varieties of melancholy were distinguished by the physician Galen. It could, he wrote, be localized in the brain, generalized over the whole system through the blood, or centered in the digestive organs—a division followed by Burton. It would seem as if melancholy could be used to account for any form of physical disorder except accidents and non-self-inflicted wounds. Nevertheless, the fragility of the conception was becoming more troublesome and hastening toward its collapse, when Burton decided to celebrate it with an encyclopedic account.

At least in intention, *The Anatomy of Melancholy* is not a work of original thought. Burton's ambition was enormously bookish: to present everything that had ever been thought or written about melancholy. It is an anthology, or, better, a compendium. He himself called it a "Cento" (a patchwork garment, or a composition formed by joining scraps from other books): "I have wronged no Authors, but given every man his owne." Like a bee, he says, he has gathered honey out of many flowers: "'Tis all mine and none mine. . . . The method onely is myne owne."[3] Burton claimed that he would have written the book in Latin if the publisher had been willing to accept that, but this may be disingenuous: his delight in writing his native language is evident. He does, however, include a lot of quotations in Latin, to such an extent that he himself characterizes his book as a Maceronicon, a macaronic medley of languages. Much of the Latin was

3. All quotations from the prefatory "Democritus to the Reader," p. 11.

translated for the reader, and this gave Burton the advantage of a popular author and the dignity of a scholar.

Since he includes more or less uncritically everything he read on the subject (and the work grew as he continued his reading), he cannot avoid contradictions or evident absurdities. In the section "Bad Diet a Cause," his various sources condemn beef, pork, goat, venison, horse, hare, rabbit, most fowl, and all fish. "Milke, and all that comes of milke, as Butter and Cheese, Curds, &c. increase melancholy." One authority "utterly forbids all manner of fruits, as Peares, Apples, Plummes, Cherries, Strawberries, Nuts, Medlers, Serves [sorbs, the fruit of the service tree], &c." He does not always reconcile absurdities, but merely observes them, most often without comment. His aim was not to set in order, but simply to set down, and the disorder, it would seem, filled him with legitimate satisfaction.

Paradoxically, Burton holds this millennia-old, crumbling theoretical edifice together by expanding it so that melancholy becomes at times synonymous with any form of madness: "Folly, Melancholy, Madnesse, are but one disease." The disease, moreover, is the universal human condition:

> And who is not a Foole, who is free from Melancholy? Who is not touched more or lesse in habit or disposition? . . . And who is not sick, or ill-disposed, in whom doth not passion, anger, envie, discontent, fear & sorrow raigne?

This comes, of course, from Burton's reading of sermons and also of Montaigne, for whom the vices were the essential constituents of society that held it together.

That Burton knew that his expansion of the idea of melancholy was improper is evident. That he nevertheless rejoiced in his impropriety is clear from what follows close upon the above observations:

> So that take Melancholy in what sense you will, properly or improperly, in disposition or habit, for pleasure or for paine, dotage, discontent, feare, sorrow, madnesse, for part, or all, truly, or metaphorically, 'tis all one. Laughter it selfe is madnes according to Solomon, & as S. Paul hath it, worldly sorrow brings death. The hearts of the sons of man are evill, & madnes is in their hearts while they live, Eccl. 9. 3.

2

The equation of melancholy and madness was not an idea exceptional or unacceptable in its time. In *The Harleian Miscellany,* a once-popular collection of sixteenth- and seventeenth-century historical documents edited by Samuel

Johnson, we find an account of a young Frenchman, converted from Catholicism to Protestantism, who decided to change to Judaism. This apostasy was a capital crime, and he was strangled and burned at the stake in Geneva in 1632. He was unsuccessfully defended by a distinguished theologian, Paul Ferry, who urged a treatment of mildness and patience, and wrote:

> I make no doubt that his illness proceeds from a black and deep melancholy, to which I always perceived he was very much inclined. . . . You know, Gentlemen, that there is a sort of melancholy . . . which is neither a crime, nor a divine punishment, but a great misfortune . . . there being so many reasons to believe that [his madness] proceeds from the disorder of the brain, and from melancholy.[4]

Melancholy furnished an early form of the insanity defense.

The almost unlimited expansion of the significance and field of action of melancholy is carried out by Burton with enjoyment:

> This Melancholy extends it selfe not to men onely, but even to vegetals and sensibles [i.e. animals]. I speake not of those creatures which are Saturnine, Melancholy by nature, as Lead, and such like Minerals, or those Plants, Rue, Cypresse. . . .

This is metaphor run riot, and it even caused Burton to be tempted into the delights of anecdote, which he resisted:

> Of all other, dogges are most subject to this malady, in so much that some hold they dreame as men doe, and through violence of Melancholy, runne mad; I could relate many stories of dogges, that have died for griefe, and pined away for losse of their Masters, but they are common in every Author.

The final expansion is to the melancholy of whole nations and societies: "Kingdomes, Provinces, and Politicke Bodies are likewise sensible and subject to this disease." But Burton takes this idea from a late sixteenth-century Savoyard writer on politics, Jean Botero, and it was obviously congenial to the period. The metaphorical play with ideas, extending a word beyond its proper sphere, was part of Burton's contemporary culture, essential to the writing of sermons. Applying the idea of melancholy to the whole of society, however, permits Burton in his satirical preface to launch an indictment of contemporary civilization as mad, sick, melancholy, and foolish, and stimulates him to construct a Utopia: "a poeticall commonwealth of mine owne, in which I will freely domineere, build Cities, make Lawes, Statutes, as I list my selfe. And why may I not?" The charm of his Utopia depends on his awareness that it is unrealistic, "to

---

4. *The Harleian Miscellany* (London: John White, 1809), vol. 3, pp. 215–216.

be wished for, rather than effected," in spite of all his reasonable and practical proposals for the reform of education, economy, and politics.

His Utopia would not, however, please today's ecologists. Virgin nature was anathema to him:

> I will have no boggs, fennes, marishes, vast woods, deserts, heaths, commons, but all inclosed; (yet not depopulated, and therefore take heed you mistake mee not). . . . I will not have a barren acre in all my Territories.

This shows that it may be as dangerous to leave the control of the world up to a scholarly Oxford clergyman as in the hands of a Texas oil man.

Melancholy, however, is not only an infirmity, but also a character trait that confers extraordinary prestige. When La Fontaine wrote of the somber pleasure of a melancholy heart ("Jusqu'au sombre plaisir d'un coeur mélancolique"), he implied that this pleasure is not granted to everyone, but only to the moral and aesthetic connoisseur. In the most popular and accepted image, the melancholic is the man of exceptional sensibility, difficult to rouse to action, but abnormally receptive. Suffering from partial paralysis of the will, he does not act without reflection and out of habit, but must force himself into action. Melancholy is also an almost irresistible pleasure, a continual temptation that, yielded to without prudence or restraint, leads to the mortal sin of despair. Escaping from the routine of ordinary behavior, the melancholic has pretensions to superiority.

These pretensions are validated by a long tradition that can be dated back to Aristotle or at least to a pseudo-Aristotle, as the book *Problems,* in which the main discussion of melancholy is to be found, is no longer ascribed to Aristotle. The opening is forthright:

> Why is it that all men who have become outstanding in philosophy, statesmanship, poetry or the arts are melancholic, and some to such an extent that they are infected by the diseases arising from black bile, as the story of Heracles among the heroes tells?

The long discussion that follows does not give either a convincing or coherent answer to this question, but compares melancholy to wine that changes the nature of those who become inebriated so that they behave in ways they would reject when sober. However, Empedocles, Socrates, and Plato are cited as eminent melancholics, and our pseudo-Aristotle adds, "The same is true of most of those who have handled poetry"; he concludes grandly that "all melancholy persons are abnormal, not owing to disease but by nature."[5]

5. Quoted from the Loeb Library translation, Aristotle, Problems, *Books XXII–XXXVIII,* translated by W. S. Hett (Cambridge, Mass.: Harvard University Press, 1965), pp. 156–157 and p. 169.

For the artists of the Renaissance and the Enlightenment, this tradition provided a model for the anxiety and eccentricity of such geniuses as Josquin des Prez, Montaigne, La Fontaine, Michelangelo, Goya, Beethoven, and a host of major and minor figures. It was a tradition that produced innumerable illustrative works of literature and art, of which the most famous are Shakespeare's *Hamlet* and the engraving of Dürer, *Melancolia* I, in which the emblematic figure of Melancholia implies the complex relations among wisdom, poetic inspiration, genius, and depression. The tradition lasted, even after the theory of humors had been finally discredited, until the *poètes maudits* of the late nineteenth century. In this way, melancholy became for centuries a stimulus to the imagination and an inspiration.

3

The first part of the seventeenth century was, for Samuel Johnson when he compiled his dictionary, the moment when the English language reached its ideal state. One would have thought that he would have preferred the clarity that was achieved a half century later in the prose of Dryden and Swift, but he was evidently conquered by the Baroque exuberance of the time of Burton. In the seventeenth century English prose came into its own, and reached the distinction previously held only by verse. With the exception of William Tyndale's translation of the *Old Testament* (which seventy years later became the basis of the King James Version), English prose in the sixteenth century has nothing to set by the side of the contemporary power, variety, and subtlety in France of Rabelais, Calvin, or Montaigne. English prose remained a somewhat awkward, provincial mode of expression. At the very end of the sixteenth century, however, prose suddenly took on a new vigor in the prose sections of the plays of Shakespeare, Middleton and Dekker, and in Richard Hooker's *Of the Laws of Ecclesiastical Polity* of 1594.

Unfortunately, much of the magnificent eloquence of the early seventeenth century lacks a considerable readership today, even in academic circles, perhaps because it deals largely with religious matters in sermons, tracts, and prayers.[6] The prose of Thomas Browne and John Donne still finds a few readers, and Lancelot Andrewes was taken up by T. S. Eliot. But Thomas Adams, so much

---

6. French eloquence of the seventeenth century is comparatively tame; even the most famous figures—Bossuet and Bourdaloue—have little of the verve of their English counterparts, and were unable to enliven the decorum of high style with the vigor of the low. The greatest master of French prose of the time, Blaise Pascal, had little use for the extravagant manner.

admired by Coleridge and Lamb that he was compared to Shakespeare, is almost forgotten, Richard Hooker is read only by specialists in the history of religion, Thomas Fuller recalled only for a few quaint details, and Jeremy Taylor, previously revered, is now neglected, as his suavity does not recommend itself to modern taste.

I offer two brief quotations to show the tradition in which Burton worked, both typical of their authors and the age, the first from Thomas Fuller's *Good Thoughts in Worse Times* (a sequel of 1647 during the Civil War to his *Good Thoughts in Bad Times* of 1645):

> Living in a country village, where a burial was a rarity, I never thought of death, it was so seldom presented unto me. Coming to London, where there is plenty of funerals (so that coffins crowd one another, and corpses in the grave jostle for elbow room), I slight and neglect death, because grown an object so constant and common.
>
> How foul is my stomach to turn all food into bad humors? Funerals neither few nor frequent, work effectually upon me. London is a library of mortality. Volumes of all sorts and sizes, rich, poor, infants, children, youth, men, old men, daily die; I see there is more required to make a good scholar, than only the having of many books: Lord be thou my schoolmaster, and teach me to number my days, that I may apply my heart unto wisdom.[7]

This combines a low, familiar manner with high style; a gnomic phrase announces with a new rhythm the metaphor of the library, worked out and accelerated with a complete listing of the ages of man; and the biblical style of the Psalms grandly rounds it off. There is a wealth of physical detail. English prose of earlier ages was rarely this complex, but here the variety of tone is employed with great ease.

Thomas Adams was habitually more sensational:

> Satan therefore shapes his Temptations in the lineaments of an Harlot: as most fit and powerfull, to worke upon mans affections. Certaine it is, that all delighted vice is a spiritual adultery. The covetous man couples his heart to his gold. The Gallant is incontinent with his pride. The corrupt Officer fornicates with bribery. The Usurer sets continuall kisses on the cheeke of his security. The heart is set, where the hate should be. And every such sinner spends his spirits, to breed and see the issue of his desires.[8]

7. From *Good Thoughts* [etc.] (London: Pickering, 1841), pp. 78–79.

8. From *In God's Name: Examples of Preaching in England,* 1534–1662, edited by John Chandos (Bobbs-Merrill, 1971), pp. 194–195.

This is from a sermon of around 1613, printed in 1629 in *The Fatall Banket, Works*. (In the phrase "spends his spirit," the meaning of spirit is semen, as in Shakespeare's "Th'expence of spirit in a waste of shame.") With this passage, not only is an idea—a conceit—given the physical immediacy of an image, but the figure of speech is detailed in such a way that it loses its metaphorical nature and starts to seem literal. Language is manipulated to increase the feeling of presence.

Chronologically, Burton falls between Adams and Fuller, and he has their picturesque variety, immediacy, and addictive looseness of construction. He, too, was a clergyman, although denied the position which would have allowed him to give sermons; he was, in fact, somewhat aggrieved about this, and took out his resentment in a satirical attack on the verbal extravagance of contemporary preachers, but he is himself no less extravagant, and generally more profuse. He makes, indeed, a virtuoso display of profusion and verbosity, and in his hands they became literary virtues.

One "Subsection" of *The Anatomy* is concerned with the "Discontents, Cares, Miseries, etc." that can cause melancholy. Toward the end of this understandably lengthy chapter, Burton lists the inconveniences of the various professions, and continues:

I can shew no state of life to give content. The like you may say of all ages: children live in a perpetuall slavery, still under that tyrannicall government of Masters: young men, and of riper yeares, subject to labour, and a thousand cares of the world; to trechery, falshood and cosenage,

—Incedit per ignes,
Suppositos cineri doloso,

["He walks on fire hidden by treacherous ashes," Horace, *Odes,* book 2, ode 1]

[the] old are full of aches in their bones, cramps and convulsions, silicernia [funeral meats], dull of hearing, weak sighted, hoary, wrinkled, harsh, so much altered as that they cannot know their owne face in a glasse, a burden to themselves and others after 70. years, all is sorrow (as David hath it) they doe not live but linger. If they be sound they feare diseases; if sicke, weary of their lives: Non est vivere, sed valere vita [Life is not just living, but living in health]. One complaines of want, a second of servitude, another of a secret or incurable disease: of some deformity of body, of some losse, danger, death of friends, shipwrack, persecution, imprisonment, . . . ingratitude, unkindnesse, scoffes, flouts, unfortunate marriage, single life, too many children, no children, false servants, unhappy children, barrennesse, banishment, oppression, frustrate hopes, and ill successe, &c.

The et cetera (or &c.) (one of Burton's favorite words) is a sign of exhaustion; inspiration has momentarily given out. The list, which appears to speed up as it proceeds with extraordinary drive, is not compiled systematically but by association: wrinkled and weak-sighted evoke a mirror; loss and danger suggest the death of friends and shipwreck. This is not a logical depiction of the misery of life and old age, but a description written by a melancholic, not a reasoned display of possibilities, but a license to the mind to allow reminiscences and associations to come flooding in unimpeded. Burton does not strain to impose order, but almost passively allows the experiences of life and reading to present themselves in a succession imposed by the elements themselves, by the words and their associative meanings; at times this makes Burton read like a thesaurus. The above passage is followed by a cascade of literary reminiscences:

> Our hearts faile us, as Davids did Psal. 40. 12. for innumerable troubles that compassed him; and we are ready to confesse with Hezekiah, Isay 58.17. behold for felicity I had bitter griefe: to weepe with Heraclitus, to curse the day of our birth, with Jeremy 20. 14. and our starres with Job: to hold the axiome of Silenus, better never to have beene borne, & the best next of all, to die quickly, or if wee must live, to abandon the world, as Timon did, creepe into caves and holes, as our Anchorites; cast all into the Sea, as Crates Thebanus; or as Theombrotas Ambrociato's 400 auditors, precipitate our selves to bee rid of these miseries.[9]

This is truly a patchwork filled with a profound and moving, if bibliographical, sentiment. For Burton, books give us access to our most intimate feelings.

In an impressive essay on the relation of Burton to Hooker's moderate Anglicanism, the poet Geoffrey Hill suggests that "the nature of the true discourse of the mind seems to me to be the central issue of *The Anatomy of Melancholy*." (On religion, Burton tended to show a rigid intolerance, above all of Roman Catholics, whom he placed below Turks, Jews, and atheists.) It was the nature of his subject, Melancholy, that allowed Burton to construct a style that studied and followed the movement of the mind in its least constrained form, liberating associations as his sentences change pace, hurtle forward, and swerve so often in the middle of an argument. That freedom was the melancholic's prerogative, and for this reason Burton was so anxious to extend it by identifying melancholy with madness in general.

9. The commentary of the Oxford edition, vol. 4, p. 313, tells us that a certain Cleombrotus of Ambracia, cited by both Cicero and Saint Augustine, "was so consumed for the better life on reading Plato's *Phaedo* that he threw himself into the sea," but we are not told anything about the four hundred auditors.

5

Although writing mainly from the medical point of view, Burton generally holds the balance between the pains and the delights of melancholy. A long introductory poem entitled "The Authors Abstract of Melancholy. Dialogue" (the last word written in Greek) alternates two refrains through twelve stanzas: "Naught so sweet as melancholy" and "Naught so sad (sour, damned, harsh, fierce) as melancholy." When he composed his treatise, however, the meaning of the word had shrunk so that the delights of melancholy had begun to outweigh the misery. It had become fashionable. According to the *Oxford English Dictionary*, "In the Elizabethan period and subsequently, the affectation of 'melancholy' was a favorite pose among those who made claim to superior refinement." The anguish of melancholy was often set aside and it began to recede into the background.

After Burton, as the grand established medical synthesis of the concept of melancholy broke apart, the pejorative content was largely replaced by other, more limited terms. In medical jargon melancholy retained its old meaning until 1800 and beyond, but in general speech by the eighteenth century the term, in fact, had lost much of its force and became genteel. Part of its old, more serious meaning, however, was taken over by the concept of boredom, or ennui (the French word always had a charge of greater anguish than the English, and still has the double meaning of pain as well as boredom). Interestingly, in England the French seemed initially to be regarded as specialists of the subject of boredom: according to the *OED*, the word "bore" does not exist in English before the 1760s, and several of the quotations from that period call it "French bore," as if the French were better at boring, or being bored than anyone else, or else as if they had invented the idea.

Perhaps they did, at least in its novel and almost transcendent aspect: the first example that one finds in which the experience of being bored is given its full weight is a famous, laconic, and beautiful sentence in Pascal:

> J'ai dit souvent que tout le malheur des hommes vient d'une seule chose, qui est de ne savoir pas demeurer en repos dans une chambre.
> I have often said that all man's unhappiness came from one thing, that is, not to know how to remain quietly in a room.

His source is in fact Montaigne, who remarked that the agitation of the hunt is more pleasurable than the kill, but the elaborate development that follows in Pascal on the essential role of distraction in our society has a power and an intensity that was new. From then on, the concept of boredom or ennui gradually gathered to itself and brought into focus some of the more sinister cultural aspects of melancholy. Tedium, boredom, and ennui became one of the great literary subjects after 1700, particularly in France.

In the eighteenth century the virtuoso descriptions of ennui that occur in the correspondence of Madame du Deffand with Horace Walpole were never surpassed. Old and blind, the mistress of perhaps the most important salon in Paris, in love with a distinguished literary British noble twenty years her junior (who was embarrassed by her love, terrified that it made him look ridiculous, but anxious to keep the affection of a woman so powerful and so witty whom he sincerely admired), she wrote to Walpole at least once a week for twenty years in an accomplished prose that had few equals at that time. In a letter of October 20, 1766, she describes one of her salon evenings:

> J'admirais hier au soir la nombreuse compagnie qui était chez moi; hommes et femmes me paraissaient des machines à ressorts, qui allaient, venaient, parlaient, riaient, sans penser, sans réfléchir, sans sentir; chacun jouait son rôle par habitude: Madame la Duchesse d'Aiguillon crevait de rire, Mme de Forcalquier dédaignait tout, Mme de la Vallière jabotait sur tout. Les hommes ne jouaient pas de meilleurs rôles, et moi j'étais abîmée dans les réflexions les plus noires; je pensais que j'avais passé ma vie dans les illusions; que je m'étais creusé moi-même tous les abîmes dans lesquels j'étais tombée; que tous mes jugements avaient été faux et té méraires, et toujours trop précipités; et qu'enfin je n'avais parfaitement connu personne; que je n'en avais pas été connue non plus, et que peut-être je ne me connaissais pas moi-même.

> Yesterday evening I admired the numerous guests who were at my house; men and women like machines with springs who came and went, spoke and laughed, without thinking, without reflecting, without feeling; each one played his role through habit: Madame the Duchess of Aiguillon burst with laughter, Mme De Forcalquier showed her disdain for everything, Mme de la Vallière jabbered about everything. The men were no better, and as for myself, I was buried in the blackest reflections ; I thought that I had passed my life in illusions; that I had hollowed out for myself all the abysses into which I had fallen; that all my judgments were false and rash and always too precipitate; and finally that I had never really known anyone, that I had never been known, and that perhaps I did not know myself.

This is the experience of boredom at its greatest depth, when society has lost all human significance and all actions are mechanical and predictable, and when personal identity ceases to have any meaning. "We are fully alive, and we experience the void" (On est tout en vie, et on éprouve le néant) was Mme du Deffand's most anguished expression of ennui. For other eighteenth-century authors, ennui could be a weapon: "I amuse myself by boring you," Diderot wrote with his usual verve.

I do not know of so profound an expression of boredom before this date, although Jean Starobinski in *Histoire du traitement de la mélancolie des origines à 1900* cites some lines of Seneca that come close, and that certainly were known to writers of the late Renaissance. I do not think we can claim that no one was bored between the second century AD of Seneca and 1700, but the complexity of the concept of melancholy inhibited the development of a simple vocabulary for the specific expression of profound *ennui* that the Enlightenment fostered. In English, as we have seen, the word "boredom" is a very late arrival, the older "tedium" never signified anything more than being irritated by excessive repetition, and it took a long time for "ennui" to appropriate so much of the power of melancholy. (Perhaps, too, the society of the eighteenth century was more like the sophisticated imperial court of Nero than anything the Middle Ages had to offer.)

Coincident with the revival of interest in Burton at the beginning of the nineteenth century, an affectation of melancholy became fashionable in France and England for young men and women. The word had become sentimentalized, a term for a vague sadness. By contrast, ennui took on a new power in France, and gradually reconstructed and acquired much of the significance that melancholy had had a hundred years before. Like melancholy, boredom became a stimulus, an escape from routine, and it is fundamental to the nineteenth-century novel. Mme Bovary reaches her tragic end simply because she was bored with her provincial life and timid husband, and boredom is the mainspring of action for the heroes of the other novels of modern life by Flaubert, for Frédéric in *L'Éducation Sentimentale* and the eponymous heroes of *Bouvard et Pécuchet,* as well as for Benjamin Constant's hero of *Adolphe,* Tolstoy's *Anna Karenina,* Stephen Dedalus in *Ulysses,* and the principals of too many other narratives to list here. It provided the basis for a critical view of the social order. The positive image of this concept is given perhaps only and remarkably by the hero of Stendhal's *La Chartreuse de Parme,* the seventeen-year-old archbishop who finds happiness at last in the solitude of prison, but his acceptance of loneliness shows up the superficiality of the ideals by which everyone else in the novel must live.

Boredom now offered the characteristic alienation from society once provided by melancholy. The word took on a grand meaning, not just a void of interest or a sophisticated indifference, but a dissatisfaction with the world, with civilization. Alfred de Musset wrote about the death of Byron:

> Lorsque le grand Byron allait quitter Ravenne
> Et chercher sur les mers quelque plage lointaine
> Où finir en héros son immortel ennui. . . .

> When great Byron was leaving Ravenna
> To search the seas for some distant beach
> Where he could heroically end his immortal ennui

Burton, perhaps not disingenuously, had claimed that he wrote his book both to cure himself of melancholy (giving the patient some activity was a very popular cure) and to aid those who suffered from melancholy. But above all he warns those of his public who are inclined to the malady that it was dangerous to read a description of the symptoms. For the unhappy few, melancholy could be irresistible.

After the nineteenth century, the large streams of melancholy and ennui split into the complex delta of all the various mental diseases: neurosis, manic depression, bipolar disorder, and so forth. Almost two and a half millennia of melancholy contribute to the development of psychiatry and psychosomatic medicine.[10] Melancholy had, indeed, been a fruitful way of studying the mind.

10. For a brilliant account of the fruitful and illogical ambiguity of the theoretical foundations of psychosomatic medicine, see Jean Starobinski, *La Relation critique* (Paris: Gallimard, 1970), pp. 214–237.

CHAPTER 25

Mallarmé and the
Transfiguration of Poetry

> Yes, my dear poet, to conceive literature and for it to have a reason must
> lead to this "lofty symphony" that no one perhaps will ever write; but it
> has haunted even the least aware and its principal features mark, subtly
> or vulgarly, every written work. Music in the proper sense, which we
> must pillage, plagiarize, if our own, unspoken, is insufficient, suggests
> such a poem.
>
> —MALLARMÉ, LETTER TO PAUL VALÉRY, MAY 5, 1891

On Thursday, February 27, 1890, in the salon of Berthe Morisot in
Paris, Stéphane Mallarmé gave a lecture on his recently deceased friend,
the poet Villiers de l'Isle-Adam. "A man accustomed to dream comes here to
speak of another, who is dead," he began. In the first row sat Edgar Degas, an
admirer of Mallarmé (whose masterly photograph of Mallarmé and Renoir was
one of the most beautiful exhibits at the Musée d'Orsay in last year's com-
memoration of the centenary of Mallarmé's death). After a few minutes Degas
left precipitously, holding his head in his hands, and crying, "I do not understand, I do not understand."

Most essays on Mallarmé begin with the difficulty of understanding him,
and this review will be no exception. That is, in fact, how Bertrand Marchal
opens the introduction to his splendid new edition of Mallarmé's complete
works, of which the first volume of two has just been published. He quotes at
once Mallarmé's ferocious answer in 1896, in his article "Le Mystère dans les
lettres," to an attack on the difficult style of modern poetry by the young
Marcel Proust:

> I prefer, faced with aggression, to retort that my contemporaries do not
> know how to read—except in the newspaper; it certainly provides the
> advantage of not interrupting the chorus of preoccupations.

A review (1999) of *Oeuvres complètes,* vol. 1, by Stéphane Mallarmé, edited by Bertrand
Marchal (Paris: Bibliothèque de la Pléiade/Gallimard).

Proust, who was eventually to become an admirer, had written three years before that Mallarmé had not much talent but he was a brilliant talker. "How unfortunate that so gifted a man should become insane every time he takes up the pen."

To be considered mad by one's contemporaries is common enough in the history of nineteenth-century art, but the obscuring fog lifts with time as the public learns new ways of reading, looking, and listening. In Mallarmé's case, however, if the lapse of a century has brought some comprehension and greater sympathy, most of his finest work remains today still unapproachable, or at least largely incomprehensible, not only to the general public, but even to the university-educated reader—even, in fact, to a good part of that curious, tiny, and still-dwindling public passionately interested in verse.

Nevertheless, this seemingly unreadable author has acquired immense prestige and is accepted without question as one of the greatest of French poets. He is rivaled in the latter half of the nineteenth century only by Baudelaire, Rimbaud, Verlaine, Laforgue, and the elderly Victor Hugo. The new edition is the second attempt to present his work in the Pléiade library, which aims to make available the important classics of world literature. The amount of the actual poetry proper—that is, the serious pieces of verse—is so small as to be unique for a major poet. This first volume of more than 1,500 pages starts with the poems that Mallarmé himself collected, a section of only forty-two pages. To this are added seventeen pages of verse he did not collect, twenty pages of poems in prose, and the twenty pages of his extraordinary typographical experiment *Un Coup de dés jamais n'abolira le hasard* (A throw of the dice will never abolish chance).

This astonishingly modest body of work of less than one hundred pages must be eked out with seventy pages of verse written before Mallarmé was twenty years old, and 120 pages of versified amusements—in particular rhymed addresses on postcards with which Mallarmé liked to puzzle the post office. To this are added a selection of letters concerning poetry, what remains of a few unfinished works, almost a hundred pages of earlier versions of the published poems, and over 300 pages of transcriptions of manuscript notes and sketches, as well as a further 350 pages of explanatory notes and variant readings. The rest of the prose works are reserved for a second volume. However, the line between his poetry and prose is hard to draw. Many of the critical articles and the journalism have a poetic quality equal to the verse, and the prose can be as difficult as the poetry—often, in fact, considerably more difficult.

The less than fifty pages of serious verse, however, remain the center of Mallarmé's achievement, along with *Un Coup de dés*. It is only in the presentation of this small nucleus that the new edition can be faulted, and the blame is largely the publisher's parsimony. Printing a sonnet with eleven lines on one page, and with the last three lines to be discovered overleaf, is a disgusting procedure when dealing with any poet. In the case of Mallarmé, who spent a lifetime considering the aspect of a page and for whom the white spaces around a poem were as important as the printed characters, we must call this a betrayal. It is a particularly foolish economy if one considers that beginning each poem of Mallarmé properly on a new page would have added only about twenty pages to a volume of 1,610 pages; and the trivial increase in expense could have been made up easily by printing the prose poems in the second volume—which will be done anyway.

I can see that Mallarmé's own preference for a full blank leaf recto and verso between each poem would make excessive demands on modern publishing, but it is not too much to ask that some thought be given to the design of a page, at least with the small number of major poems. And with *Un Coup de dés,* although the large format demanded by the poet for arranging his words with different typefaces on the page like a constellation was not possible within the format of the series, we could have been spared the thoughtless insertion of little numbers and letters indicating variant readings and explanatory notes in the back of the book, a form of vandalism more or less equivalent to printing the names of the characters over their heads in the reproduction of a group or family portrait by Titian.

The appearance of the poem on the page was essential for Mallarmé's aesthetic: he felt that the poem must be read as an object detached from the life of the author, separated from the society and culture in which it arose, and even independent of the world in which it existed, as if it had its being outside history. His poems may be said to detach themselves partially from the literary tradition that made them possible—at least they appeal over the head of that tradition to manifest themselves as part of the language itself, but a language purified of the ordinary slipshod meanings it has in life, cleansed of the daily need simply to communicate. "To give a purer sense to the words of the tribe" is perhaps the most often quoted line of Mallarmé ("Donner un sens plus pur aux mots de la tribu," from the sonnet on Edgar Poe; "To purify the dialect of the tribe" is T. S. Eliot's inspired version in "Little Gidding" from the *Four Quartets*). We learn from the new edition that Mallarmé first wrote "To give too pure a sense" ("trop pur"). The original version is more provocative (and I am not sure that the change was not made principally because Mallarmé wanted to add an extra "u" sound to supplement "pur" and "tribu").

It may seem strange that the supremacy, the privileged status, of a poet should remain absolutely unchallenged when access to his work is largely denied to the largest part of his potential audience; the hermetic character of his poetry seals it off from most readers. The endurance of his prestige rests on two factors: on the passion that his work arouses in those who are determined to read him and to make sense of the poems, and on the professional importance of his achievement for the poets that succeeded him. It is not only French poetry that was radically altered by his example (his influence was crucial for Paul Valéry, René Char, Paul Eluard, Paul Claudel, Yves Bonnefoy, and many others). He was decisive in the creation of the modernist tradition in German and American poetry: his example was basic for Stefan George and Rainer Maria Rilke and remained powerful with Paul Celan, and his use of language was the model for Walter Benjamin and, I think, an important influence on Martin Heidegger's style. In America, his work was essential for the generations that included T. S. Eliot, Wallace Stevens, and Hart Crane, and it has lasted until John Ashbery. Across the numbers of his imitators, he influenced even those who never read him. He was a liberating force.

To understand the nature of that liberation, it may be useful to start with the hatred he aroused. With the exception of Baudelaire, no poet of the past two centuries has been so fiercely execrated, and the horror inspired by Baudelaire is, on the surface at least, more easily explained by the defiantly immoral subject matter of his work. With Mallarmé, the subject matter was not so obviously objectionable—at least the fiercest attacks were launched mostly by critics who had no idea what the subject matter of most of the poems was, largely because they had not been able to figure it out. It is difficult to credit the lunacy of some of these attacks. One journalist, Max Nordau, who wrote a book called *Degeneration* in 1894 in which he famously attacked almost all forms of modern art—Wagner, Strauss, Manet, and whatever—inspiring a vigorous reply by George Bernard Shaw, found Mallarmé particularly obnoxious: he accused him of fostering a deplorable taste for the Pre-Raphaelites, and (oddly enough for a poet who had lost his religious faith) of spreading Neo-Catholicism, and wrote:

> Let us add as well, in order to be complete, that one notices in Mallarmé "the long pointed ears of a satyr." R. Hartmann, Frigerio and Lombroso have, after Darwin (who first emphasized the simian character of this particularity), determined the atavistic and degenerative significance of the pavilions of the ear which are abnormally long and pointed, and proved that one meets them frequently above all with criminals and the insane.

In a lecture that Mallarmé gave at Oxford, "Music and Letters," he commented on Nordau's attacks on modern art in general with a certain mildness and his usual elliptical complexity:

This vulgarizer has observed a fact. Nature does not engender an immediate and complete genius, which would correspond to a type of man and would not be any one man in particular; but practically, occultly, touches with an innocent thumb a certain faculty and almost abolishes it in the one to whom she proposes a contrary munificence; here these are pious arts or maternal actions that ask for a clairvoyance not lacking in tenderness from critic and judge. Let us continue: What happens? Deriving force from his privation, the crippled chosen one [infirme élu] grows toward his plenary intentions, and he leaves after him, of course, like a numberless waste product, his brothers, case histories medically labeled or election bulletins once the vote is over. The error of the pamphleteer in question is to have treated everything like a waste product. Thus the subtle arcana of physiology and of destiny, ought not to stray into the hands, too coarse to handle them, of an excellent foreman or of an upright adjuster—who stops in mid-path and behold! with the addition of some instinctive foresight, he would have understood, in time, the poor and holy natural processes and he would not have written his book.

This anticipates the theory of overcompensation of the Austrian psychiatrist Alfred Adler: it is from his weakness, from what he lacks, what is incomplete within himself, that the original genius draws the force that gives such power to his remaining faculties. This passage also affirms the Romantic notion of the source of genius in infirmity, of originality as a form of sickness. It is here, too, that Mallarmé faces the inconvenient side of avant-garde style, the minor artists who can only imitate the weakness that inspired the innovations. Bad conservative art comes from a mechanical imitation of the conventional; the failure of so much modern art comes from an inability to distinguish the infirmity of the innovator from his strength. After Mallarmé, a considerable amount of bad poetry appeared that was as hermetic and as forbidding as his masterly creations. He was, as I have said, a liberating force, but he loosed on the world a good deal of deplorable verse while he made possible some of the greatest achievements of modern poetry, including his own.

The infirmity of Mallarmé that gave him his genius was his despair. In spite of his desire to keep poetry detached from the life of the poet, this despair was both personal and metaphysical. His loss of religious faith was traumatic. He had no secular faith in science or history to compensate for it; like the greatest of Italian nineteenth-century poets, Giacomo Leopardi, he was persuaded of the emptiness, the total insignificance of human life: the universe was void of meaning. The more personal trauma was his life as a high school English teacher in a small Rhône valley town, Tournon, that he found ugly and unpleasant. He cannot have been an inspiring teacher; the students were rowdy and threw chalk at him. It was at Tournon that he began his most famous poems, "Hérodiade" and "The Afternoon of a Faun." On his transfer to Paris, his situation was more cheerful, made agreeable above all through his friends and disciples who were fascinated by his theories of language and of aesthetics. What he said about Villiers de l'Isle-Adam was equally true about himself: "His life—I find nothing that corresponds to this term: truly and in the ordinary sense, did he live?" His poems mostly circulated privately. The few that were published in reviews created at one and the same time a growing hostility and admiration.

Paul Valéry, whose encounter with Mallarmé's poetry transformed his view of literature and of life, eloquently reflected on the hostility that his master provoked.

> In this strange work, a sort of absolute, there dwelt a magic power. Merely by existing, it acted as a charm and as a sword. With one stroke it divided all the people from those human beings who knew how to read. Its appearance of an enigma instantly irritated the vital nervous center of literary understanding. It seemed immediately, infallibly, to strike at the most sensitive of cultivated consciousness, to overstimulate the center itself where there exists, and is contained, some prodigious charge of self-esteem, and where resides that which cannot suffer not to understand. What happened is that the moment one laid eyes on it, this work without peer hit on, and grappled with, the fundamental convention of ordinary language: You would not read me if you had not already understood me.[1]

It is true that the intolerant protest against difficult art was as philistine and as morally disgraceful in Mallarmé's time as it is today, and it is also true that not being able to understand can be the excuse for a childish tantrum. I knew a five-year-old boy who bit a foreign babysitter on the leg because he could not grasp what she was saying to him. However, Valéry's account stops short of a satisfactory explanation. Few sane people experience an uncontrollable resentment at not being able to comprehend what is beyond their technical competence, like differential equations or the more complicated formulas of quantum theory. Nor is there any inevitable shame in an inability to share someone else's taste or artistic preferences. The problem with Mallarmé, as with so many innovators, lay on a deeper level. Reading him, many critics sensed that they were on the verge of understanding, trembling on the edge of comprehension— worse, they had a suspicion that what they were reading was very good. One anonymous critic wrote in 1876, after quoting a large extract from the opening of "The Afternoon of a Faun":

1. Paul Valéry, *Oeuvres,* vol. 1 (Paris: Gallimard, 1957), p. 638.

What is terrible in the case of Monsieur Mallarmé is that, in reading these absolutely incomprehensible verses, one senses a sort of music which is an incontestable witness to a poetic temperament and a refined nature.

Is Monsieur Mallarmé in good faith? Does he want to replace poetry which says something with a new poetry, like Manet in painting, which limits itself to giving an impression? One must believe it in the interest of Monsieur Mallarmé?[2]

We can only marvel at a critical intelligence that can find the exquisite beginning of "The Afternoon of a Faun" absolutely incomprehensible and yet recognize the kinship of the poet to the friend he so much admired and who painted his portrait.

Mallarmé himself always denied, surely with at least a touch of irony, that his poems were difficult. He once said to the poet Henri de Régnier, speaking about a friend: "He's a charming boy, but why does he explain my verses? That would tend to make one believe they were obscure."[3] Nevertheless, he was partly in earnest: read properly, he felt, his poetry gave at least a satisfactory surface meaning at once. In "The Mystery in Literature," his answer to Proust's attack on obscurity, he claimed:

> Every piece of writing, on the outside of its treasure, must—out of respect for those from whom, after all, it borrows the language, for a different purpose—present with the words a meaning, even if an unimportant one: there is an advantage to turning away the idler, who is charmed that nothing here concerns him at first sight.

The idler is the one who scans a poem as if he were reading a newspaper, without the passion and the good will that enables a reader to abandon himself completely to the work. The exterior meaning to be given the idler as a sop to protect the treasure inside was not, however, always successful in Mallarmé's case in appeasing that casual reader's incipient anxiety. Mallarmé's ambition did not allow him too easy a surrender to the idler's susceptibilities. All too often in his work, the exterior meaning appeared to be only a provocation, a way of implying that there was a hidden sense. As Valéry remarked, the reader of Mallarmé is required to do much of the work for himself.

A sonnet published in 1887, not, perhaps, one of my favorites but a fine and relatively simple example of the poet's method at an extreme point, opens enigmatically:

2. In *Mallarmé,* edited by Bertrand Marchal (Paris: Collection Mémoire de la critique/Presses de l'Université de Paris-Sorbonne, 1998), p. 52.

3. Quoted by Paul Bénichou in *Selon Mallarmé* (Paris: Gallimard, 1995), p. 18.

Victorieusement fui le suicide beau
Tison de gloire, sang par écume, or, tempête!

Victoriously fled the beautiful suicide
Burning brand of glory, blood through foam, gold, tempest!

The word "sunset" is unspoken, but it is represented by image and metaphor. In a splendid blaze of color, the sun voluntarily annihilates itself each evening.[4] The meaning comes only a little further to the surface with the second quatrain:

Quoi! De tout cet éclat pas même le lambeau
S'attarde, il est minuit?

Well! of all that brilliance not even the shred
Lingers, it is midnight?

This way of describing by suggestion has an importance for the poem that exceeds the idea of the sunset. Withholding the referential meaning concentrates attention initially upon the technique of representation: the poem refuses to allow the reader to substitute immediately the concept for the description. To understand, we must return over and over again to the lines. Mallarmé fixes the attention of the reader where it properly belongs—on the words of the poem, the assonance, the rhythm, the juxtaposition of images, the emotional associations of burning brand, glory, blood, foam, suicide. He forces the reader to pause at each point in the attempt to understand the relations of one image to another in the strange collection, and this allows, as he himself put it, the different facets of the words to reflect off each other. Some wit once said that Mallarmé was a poet so difficult that only foreigners could understand him. There is this much truth in this: foreigners do not read paragraphs or even whole sentences; they read word by word. That is how these poems are to be

---

4. The first lines of the original version of this sonnet are no clearer, and they are less successful:

Toujours plus souriant au désastre plus beau,
Soupirs de sang, or meurtrier, pâmoison, fête!

With ever greater smiles at the more beautiful disaster
Sighs of blood, murderous gold, fainting away, festival!

However, the second quatrain is slightly more explicit:

Quoi! De tout ce coucher pas même un cher lambeau
Ne reste, il est minuit?

Well! of all this setting not even a dear shred
Remains, it is midnight.

read, not only to be understood, but even to be appreciated. And they cannot be understood without being appreciated.

This stands the classical way of reading poetry on its head. In general, first we take in the text visually, and we understand it almost as we take it in, and afterward we find it interesting or beautiful. With the modernist tradition of poetry, which is more or less founded by Mallarmé, understanding is temporarily postponed until we have savored and enjoyed the poetic art: image, metaphor, assonance, rhythm, rhyme, alliteration, and the connotations of the words that count for more in poetry than the referential meaning. All these aspects of language have traditionally played a role in poetry that displaces in importance what may be considered the message—that is, any meaning that can be translated into prose. Those who read paying little attention to these other aspects and seek only for the message have always and inevitably misunderstood the poetry and even failed to grasp the message. Temporarily blocking access to the message was only Mallarmé's drastic way of avoiding misunderstanding. That is why he insisted he was not obscure, or even difficult.

In a letter to the English essayist Edmund Gosse he made this point emphatically. He quoted from Gosse's article on his poetry a sentence which, he said, had a "diamond clairvoyance": Gosse wrote, "His desire was to use words in such harmonious combination as will induce in the reader a mood or a condition *which is not mentioned in the text,* but was nevertheless paramount in the poet's mind at the moment of composition" (italics added by Mallarmé to Gosse's text). Mallarmé commented gratefully:

It's all there. I make Music, and I name by this not only that music that one can draw from the euphonious bringing together of words,—that is an initial condition that goes without saying: but also that music which goes beyond and is magically produced by certain dispositions of speech [parole], where this remains only in the state of a means of material communication with the reader like the keys of a piano. Truly, between the lines and above the gaze this takes place, in all its purity, without the intervention of gut strings or of pistons as in the orchestra, which is already industrial; but it's the same thing as the orchestra, only literary and silent. Poets in all ages have never done anything else, and it's amusing today, that is all, to become aware of it. I only quibble with you over obscurity: no, my dear poet, except by clumsiness or awkwardness, I am not obscure the moment one reads me in order to seek what I have set forth above, or the manifestation of an art which makes use—let us say incidentally, I know the profound cause—of language: and I become obscure, of course! if one makes a mistake and thinks one is opening a newspaper.

The art of reading Mallarmé requires us to realize that the enigmatic surface of his poetry does not cover or hide a secret; and we cannot discard the surface once the treasure has been unearthed. The solution to the enigma is on the surface, which itself becomes the treasure as our experience of it grows.

Modernism in the other arts closely parallels the development effected by Mallarmé in poetry. Painting became harder to read at first glance. In a classical painting we recognize the objects portrayed at once, and then we admire the way they have been represented, the construction, the play of colors, the expressive lines. In a cubist painting, on the other hand, it is often hard to identify what object is represented until we have admired the painted surface. Already in Manet, sections of the canvas can appear to us obtrusively first as a pattern of brush strokes before we can grasp what they represent—and it was in this aspect of the picture that Manet sometimes took the greatest pride.[5] In much of James Joyce's *Ulysses,* it is often difficult to figure out the plot before we have enjoyed the author's stylistic virtuosity; in the hospital sequence, for example, we can only realize what is going on if we appreciate the series of parodies that ranges through the entire history of English literature.

Music inspired Mallarmé, as it did so many of the Romantics, because the role of the message in it, of what Mallarmé called "material communication," is so substantially reduced. Before modernism, however, the emotion or sentiment represented by the music was evident at once; after this initial response, music lovers could turn to a perception of the art with which this emotion was conveyed, the ingenuity of the representation and the abstract beauty of the melodic lines. With Schoenberg and Webern, however, and with Stravinsky (starting with *The Rite of Spring*), we must generally begin with a dispassionate understanding of the art and an appreciation of the technique in order to comprehend the emotional content; for those who succeed, the sentiment is perceived at last with an intensity rare in music that allows a more facile comprehension. (That is why some critics still find Schoenberg's music to have no feeling, while his admirers find it, on the contrary, often embarrassingly overcharged with emotion.)

In those works of the modernist movement considered difficult or hermetic, in short, the content is partially withheld from us until we have understood the

5. The catalog of an exhibition called *A Painter's Poet: Stéphane Mallarmé and His Impressionist Circle,* held at Hunter College, New York, from February 16 to March 20, 1999, has several essays on Mallarmé and some texts by him which show his appreciation of this aspect of Manet's work and reveal his remarkable critical sense of the painting of his time. His contempt for the academic style is found in his splendid characterization of it: "insignificant and at the same time terrifyingly meticulous."

technique; the delayed perception then arrives with greater power. As Valéry remarked about his discovery of Mallarmé's work:

> He raised the condition of the reader, and with an admirable intelligence of real glory he chose in the world a small number of special amateurs who, once having tasted could no longer suffer impure poems, which could be understood at once and with-out resistance. Everything seemed naive and slack after they had read him.[6]

But Valéry's invocation of a small elite is profoundly misleading and reflects his own intellectual aloofness; there is no reason to think that Mallarmé, Joyce, Webern, and other modernists would not have welcomed the admiration of thousands; but they wanted admiration on their own terms, and had to be satisfied with a grudging popularity, much of it only posthumous.

Mallarmé's observation is profound: "Poets in all times have never done anything else, and it is amusing, today, that is all, to become aware of it." It is now understood more clearly how much modernism has altered our view of the art of the past. Mallarmé was right: poets have always used all the different aspects of language that transcend the conveying of information, that have a value of their own independent of "material communication." Some twentieth-century critics have since read Racine, Shakespeare, and other writers as if they were modernist poets, as if the surface of their work was enigmatic, and with the most skillful of these critics, it is evident that they were often justified in doing so. Poets have indeed written to some extent as Mallarmé did, and many readers of the past did, in fact, perceive this even if they were not fully aware of it. The modernist poet forced his readers, on pain of being lost in bewilderment, to become conscious of what has always been present in literature. Twentieth-century music has changed our understanding of Mozart and Beethoven. What we now hear was, of course, always there.

The extent to which the way to an understanding of content has necessarily been through a love and appreciation of the significance of technique, and a familiarity with it, can be shown by an article written in 1796 by the influential music critic Johann Friedrich Reichardt on Handel and Bach. They were both praised for their astonishing harmonic and contrapuntal mastery. But what Bach, in particular, lacked was

> a deep feeling for expression. If both these men had had more knowledge of man, of language, and of poetry, and if they had been bold enough to cast off all idle fashions and conventions, they would have become our

6. Paul Valéry, *Variété Ouvres I* (Paris: Gallimard [La Pléiade], 1957), p. 639.

highest ideals of art, and every great genius who today is not satisfied with equalling them would have had to overthrow our entire tonal system in order to clear a new field for himself.[7]

The sentiment in Bach's music, which seems so intense to us today (and was already so understood by the generation that followed Reichardt), went unperceived by a critic who was dazzled by the technique but thought it excessive. Admission to the sentiment in Bach's music required a familiarity with his style and a joyful acceptance of his complexity; like Mallarmé's poetry, the elaborate and hermetic technique originally barred even the educated academic listener from the emotion implicit in almost every work, the physical passion of his lines. The reputation of Bach was made by the composers who studied him, from Mozart and Beethoven through Chopin until the present. The prestige of Mallarmé was created largely by the poets who were inspired by him.

Far from being merely a virtuoso play with the elements of language, as many of his contemporaries believed (including those who admired him as well as those who were frightened by him), his mature poetry has a tragic cast that has become more visible with time.[8] His work is only in part a reaction to the deterioration of language in journalism and public life. It is fundamentally a despairing protest against ordinary life, made void by the irrelevance of all religious faith, by the corruption of general culture, by the gradual decline of the prestige of art except as a commodity. The greatest of his poems are about death, absence, empty rooms, and unfulfilled ambitions. His most famous sonnet opens:

> Le vierge, le vivace et le bel aujourd'hui
> Va-t-il nous déchirer avec un coup d'aile ivre
> Ce lac dur oublié que hante sous le givre
> Le transparent glacier des vols qui n'ont pas fui!

> The virgin, vivacious and beautiful today
> Will it tear us with a drunken blow of the wing
> This hard forgotten lake haunted under the frost
> By the transparent glacier of flights which have not flown!

7. Quoted in Hans T. David and Arthur Mendel, ed., *The Bach Reader* (New York: Norton, 1966), p. 455. It is interesting that the distress of a conservative critic overwhelmed by technical mastery foreshadowed the overthrow of the tonal system that would not be attempted for another century; the destructive momentum of modernism was already in embryo.

8. The best account of this aspect of the work is Yves Bonnefoy's introduction to Mallarmé, *Poèmes* (Paris: Gallimard, 1992), where he shows how Mallarmé moved from the cold celebration of sterility in "Hérodiade" to the erotic ambiguity of "The Afternoon of a Faun," which receives its final form only when sexual desire is renounced by the faun to be reconstituted as a purely poetic ideal in words.

The "today" of that breathtaking first line is everyday life, and the vain hope is that it will break the winter ice in which a magnificent swan has been trapped, surrendering himself to the "resplendent ennui of sterile winter." But as we read the poem, the second line implies at first that it is we who are rent by the eternally recurrent present, and the ambiguity makes us its victims.

> Un cygne d'autrefois se souvient que c'est lui
> Magnifique mais qui sans espoir se délivre
> Pour n'avoir pas chanté la région où vivre
> Quand du stérile hiver a resplendi l'ennui.

> A swan from the past remembers that it was he
> Magnificent but without hope surrenders himself
> For not having sung the region where life can be
> When the ennui of sterile winter has become resplendent.

The swan (the poet as we know from tradition) is trapped because in the past he has not sung of the region in which life can be. For Mallarmé that region was not the present, but the ideal world of poetry, which transforms language from a means of conveying a message into an object which is beautiful in itself and which exists only for itself. Poetry, however, cannot change the ever-returning present, and it does not, in fact, as the poet knew, create a world that can be lived in. The beautiful today whose existence was denied by the swan will not free it from the ice. In the last lines, the swan has become a phantom, immobilized in the cold dream of contempt ("Il s'immobilise au songe froid de mépris"). No one has ever expressed with greater power than Mallarmé the illusion of nineteenth-century aestheticism, and no image of the despair of ordinary daily life has ever surpassed the astonishing opening lines of this sonnet.

The poem that Mallarmé originally entitled "An allegorical sonnet of himself" is the description of an empty room. It ends with the image of the mirror facing the open window, in which the septet, the constellation of the Pleiades, the seven muses, has moved into sight at the open window. Mallarmé wanted to use only two rhyming sounds in this poem, one "or" (gold), the other "ix": for the fourteen lines of a sonnet, one needs therefore eight and six rhymes. There are few words in French that rhyme with "ix": onyx, Phénix, Styx, nixe, and fixe. Mallarmé was delighted, to invent a new one—*ptyx:*

> Sur les crédences, au salon vide: nul ptyx,
> Aboli bibelot d'inanité sonore

> On the sideboards, in the empty salon: no ptyx,
> Abolished trinket of sonorous inanity

Mallarmé said he hoped that *ptyx* had no meaning in any language so that he could create one (it does, in fact, mean "fold" in Greek). To some it has seemed evident that a ptyx is a seashell, a common decorative object for a salon, and it is more than adequately described as sonorous inanity, since one can hold it to one's ear and listen to the nonexistent sea. (In the original version of the poem, "abolished trinket" was "strange vessel" [insolite vaisseau]).

The ptyx is the allegorical figure of the poem itself. It is only an empty sound for it has no meaning in ordinary French; it is purely imaginative, but it comes into being by the logic of the poem's structure; it is abolished (although it has never existed, it is no longer there), yet it takes on a meaning from the action of the poetry, by the will of the poet—who is also not there, because the room is empty and the master of the house is gone, but his symbolic image scintillates in the oblivion of the mirror.

> encor
> Que, dans l'oubli fermé par le cadre, se fixe
> De scintillations sitôt le septuor.

> while
> In the closed forgetfulness of the frame, is set
> So soon the scintillating septet.

The poetry of absence was not, in spite of all the intricate ways that these words reflect each other like distorting mirrors, a trivial game. It was an expression of Mallarmé's despair. In the first stanza the void of the room is forcefully illuminated by this despair:

> L'Angoisse, ce minuit, soutient, lampadophore,
> Maint rêve vespéral?

> Anguish, this midnight, bears like a lampholder
> Many a twilight dream?

The faun, in "The Afternoon of a Faun," renounces the fulfillment of sexual desire for its perpetuation by the poetic imagination. All of the late work of Mallarmé reenacts that renunciation, and the sonnet in "yx" is its emblem. Out of emptiness and absence he created a poetry of extraordinary intensity.

Nevertheless, he knew that, in one sense, art was a game of chance, although a deeply serious one. "Every thought emits a throw of the dice," he wrote in the typographical poetic images of *Un Coup de Dés*. The way the game must be played is compared to the movement of a constellation: "watching, doubting, rolling, glittering and meditating before stopping at some final point which consecrates it." A throw of the dice will never abolish chance, he claimed:

> Never
> Even when thrown in eternal circumstances from the bottom of
>   a shipwreck

Postscript

How to read a poem, according to Mallarmé:

Reading—
  This practice—
  Apply, according to the page, your ingenuousness to the white which inaugurates it, forgetful even of the title which would speak too loud: and, when, in a break (the smallest break, disseminated), chance, vanquished word by word, is lined up, the white returns inexorably, previously arbitrary, now positive, to conclude that nothing lies beyond and to authenticate the silence.
  —From "Le Mystère dans les lettres"

CHAPTER 26

Hofmannsthal and Radical Modernism

I

From the eighteenth to the twentieth centuries, many young men and women would go through a spell of writing lyric poetry in late adolescence, abandoning the practice forever when they reached the age of reason around twenty-one years old. However, those who failed to persist beyond this cut-off date never achieved great fame as poets, with two remarkable exceptions at the end of the nineteenth century: Arthur Rimbaud, who composed some of the most memorable verse of his time from the age of fourteen to twenty-one between 1868 and 1875, after which he abandoned literature for the rest of his life; and Hugo von Hofmannsthal, who dazzled Viennese literary society with a series of lyric poems published under the pseudonym of Loris, written from the age of sixteen to twenty-four (1890 to 1898), at which point he permanently renounced lyric poetry, with a few insignificant and incidental exceptions. He did not completely quit literature, however, but remained a major figure in the cultural life of Vienna as a brilliant critic and a dramatist, with an international fame chiefly due to his opera librettos for Richard Strauss. A recent selection of his work, *The Whole Difference,* offers new and old translations, including a few pages of verse, two plays, one act of the libretto of *Der Rosenkavalier,* and a number of essays. The poetry of both Rimbaud and Hofmannsthal is now

A review of *The Whole Difference* by Hugo von Hofmannsthal.

permanently in the literary canon today, represented in bulk by every anthology of nineteenth-century French or German poetry.

They were very different. Arthur Rimbaud was a scruffy boy from a poor family in a small town in the north of France, generally dressed in rags, rarely washed, and was known above all for his flamboyant misbehavior in public and his homosexual liaison with the somewhat older poet Paul Verlaine. The elegant son of a wealthy banker, with two Jewish grandparents in his recently ennobled family, Hugo von Hofmannsthal was educated at the most fashionable and elite high school of Vienna. They had much in common, nevertheless. Classical studies, to begin with. When he was fourteen, Rimbaud, who won first prize in school for every subject except mathematics, displayed an extraordinary talent for writing Latin verse, as well as a mastery of the traditional styles of French poetry (one must acknowledge the high standard of classical studies in French high schools even in provincial small towns.) Hofmannsthal concentrated on Greek, and his most impressive early works in this field were translations and free adaptations of Sophocles and Euripides.

Rimbaud's ambition was above all to leave the suffocating provincial atmosphere of Charleville and to become part of the literary life of the capital. Arriving penniless in Paris, he astonished the members of the most advanced literary circle with his imitation of their work, sometimes mocking as well as serious. His poetry soon displayed an expansive vocabulary, far beyond the range of the usual literary lexicon. Later he would claim that poetry will have to be written in a new language, and the works of the last years of his literary activity have had an international influence on later poets second to none. As Rimbaud's fame continued to grow after his death, he was triumphantly hailed by the surrealists as their precursor (but for the surrealists, violating the decorum of language was as much a a game as an expression of anxiety). Rimbaud redefined the nature of poetic meaning. "Before Rimbaud, poetry had to make sense," Paul Valéry remarked, when the late work was finally made known, and predicted that they would erect monuments to him. "Poetry is not a form of communication," Valéry wrote later, when discussing the great symbolist period. A provocative observation, of course,—but when one has received a telegram and understood its message, one can throw away the telegram, which no longer has much value; but when one has grasped the sense of a poem, its interest is far from exhausted and has sometimes only begun. Rimbaud initiated the modernist attempt to isolate the intensely poetic effect from the effort to communicate information and make sense. In his last works, Rimbaud went farther than anyone else before him in dislocating the translatable content of the poetry from its total impact. Rimbaud's reputation was absolutely secure by the 1920s, and his influence has continued unabated, not only throughout French poetry, but also in American poetry from Hart Crane to John Ashbery.

Hofmannsthal was able very early to publish his poems and essays pseud-onymously in literary magazines. When he turned up one day in the most important literary meeting-place in Vienna, the Café Greinsteidel, he had already built up a formidable reputation. Established writers like Arthur Schnitzler and Hermann Bahr were astonished that this sixteen-year-old in short pants was the author of poems and essays they had presumed to be by a much older man. Artur Schnitzler, the most admired Austrian dramatist of the time, wrote about a reading by the young Hofmannsthal of some of his work: "We had never heard verses of such perfection, such faultless plasticity, such musical feeling, from any living being, nor had we thought them possible since Goethe." Certainly, it must have been difficult to live to up to that kind of reputation. It is true that the greatest influence from German literature on the lyric poetry of Hofmannsthal was Goethe, generally as dangerous a model as Shakespeare, leading in most cases to disaster. As for more recent writing, however, his work showed his experience of French symbolism. The editor of the anthology, *The Whole Difference,* remarks "that the German poet Stefan George sought him out at the Griensteidl, trying to add another disciple to his circle of devotees, all of whom worshiped at the altar of symbolism. But George found the young Hofmannsthal already knew the work of Swinburne and Pater, Baudelaire and Mallarmé." In fact, he sent the teenager bouquets of flowers at his high school, to the indignation of Hofmannsthal's father.

At that time, the new French poetry dominated the work of the avant-garde in German lands, and both Rainer Maria Rilke and George even wrote some poetry in French of varying quality. Many years later, toward the end of his life, Hofmannsthal appreciatively characterized the poetic revolution in France of the late nineteenth century as the most radical change of style in French literature for three hundred years, and wrote:

> The secret life of language on which the most intimate vitality of the nation depends, readied itself for defense. The old battle led in the 16th century by the Pléiade—the battle for a free syntax, for sharper and more complexly significant metaphors, for a merger with the music of the time—, we see this renewed at the end of the 19th century. Mallarmé is the great doctrinaire leader of this movement (but his doctrine is like his poetry, consummated in suggestion, and in it reigns the elimina-tion of precision, of pragmatic connections, and the effect is all the greater and more durable). However, before Mallarmé go Baudelaire and Rimbaud, with the majestic stream and secret polyphony of the one and the savage violation of conventions of the other; with both of them there is a movement of poetry into the kingdom of music that makes them brothers to Mallarmé. For he was almost as much musician as poet:

in composition, it is hard to discover any distinction between him and Debussy.

2

During the very few years that he wrote lyric poetry, Hofmannsthal was possessed by the idea of death. While never abandoning a traditional classical prosody, he progressed from a Romantic subjectivity to a more objective presentation, in which the full significance of the details of powerful emotional suggestion are left to the readers to work out. His most famous poem is "The Ballade of the Outer Life" (I offer a coarsely literal translation, as the one in the anthology is inaccurate, and it is impossible to capture the subtle play of sound in these verses along with the graceful swing of the popular folk ballad rhythm):

BALLADE DES ÄUSSEREN LEBENS

Und Kinder wachsen auf mit tiefen Augen,
Die von nichts wissen, wachsen auf und sterben,
Und alle Menschen gehen ihre Wege.

Und süße Früchte warden aus den herben
Und fallen nachts wie tote Vögel nieder
Und liegen wenig Tage und verderben.

Und immer weht der Wind, und immer wieder
Vernehmen wir und redden viele Worte
Und spüren Lust und Müdigkeit der Glieder.

Und Straßen laufen durch das Gras, und Orte
Sind da und dort, voll Fackeln, Bäumen, Teichen,
Und drohende, und totenhaft verdorte . . .

Wozu sind diese aufgebaut? Und gleichen
Einander nie? Und sind unzählig viele?
Was wechselt Lachen, Weinen und Erbleichen?

Was frommt das alles uns und diese Spiele,
Die wir doch groß und ewig einsam sind
Und wandernd nimmer suchen irgend Ziele?

Was frommts, dergleichen viel gesehen haben?
Und dennoch sagt der viel, der »Abend« sagt,
Ein Wort, daraus Tiefsinn und Trauer rinnt

Wie schwerer Honig aus den hohlen Waben.

THE BALLADE OF THE OUTER LIFE

And children grow up with deep eyes,
That know of nothing, grow up and die,
And all men go their ways.

And sweet fruits come from the acrid
And fall down in the night like dead birds
And lie for some days and rot.

And the wind always blows, and always again
We perceive and speak many words
And our limbs sense pleasure and fatigue.

And streets run through the grass, and places
Are here and there, full of torches, trees, ditches,
And menacing and deadly dry up.

Why are these built? And never resemble
Each other? And are so many, countless?
What changes laughter to weeping and to dying away?

What use is all that to us and these games,
We who are great and yet always lonely
And wandering never to seek any goal?

What use to those who have seen so much?
And nevertheless he says much who says "evening,"
A word from which deep meaning and grief run out

Like heavy honey from the hollow combs.

It should be said that the last lines cannot work properly in English, because "evening" is a word too clipped and without enough resonance to bear all the significance of grief that Hofmannsthal gives it, while the German "Abend" works much better, with a grand opening vowel and the rhythm of a sigh. It is evident that salvation from the fatal conventionality of the outer life for the young Hofmannsthal lies in the secret inherent power of language. Mallarmé once remarked that the French word for day, "jour," has a full open sonority, ideal for its meaning, while a German poet is saddled with the terrible sound of "Tag" (pronounced Tak). Of course, German poets from Novalis to Richard Wagner have been inspired to do a lot with the impressive sonority of "Nacht," while the sounds of "night" and "nuit" have some intensity, but no glamor.

In the ballad, the menacing, banal insignificance of the outer life dominated by death is only narrowly redeemed for the poet by the affective resonance of the word. The meaning of grief he reads into the word *Abend* is, of course, not the usual or principal sense of "evening" in any language, but only the connotation of "Abend," and it is curiously isolated in the poem from any experience of everyday life. When Hofmannsthal was sixteen, he boasted in a poem that "for most people words are only small change, but for me they are the source of imagery, and I own what I perceive." The secular mysticism of a semireligious value ascribed to language, literature, and art should be familiar to us from the Romantic tradition of the early nineteenth century, but the despair of ordinary life has attained here a new exasperation.

The "Ballad" was written when Hofmannsthal was twenty-one. "Travel Song," three years later, is less self-indulgent, evoking an alpine landscape with a brutal and powerful contrast:

REISELIED

Wasser stürzt, uns zu verschlingen,
Rollt der Fels, uns zu erschlagen,
Kommen schon auf starken Schwingen
Vögel her, uns fortzutragen.

Aber unten liegt ein Land,
Früchte spiegelnd ohne Ende
In den alterslosen Seen.

Marmorstirn und Brunnenrand
Steight aus blumigem Gelände,
Und die leichten Winde when.

Water crashes down, to devour us,
The cliffs rumble, to destroy us,
Birds on strong wings already
Come to carry us away

But below lies a land,
Fruits mirrored without end
In ageless lakes

Marble front and spring banks
Rise from the flowering countryside
And the light winds blow

The style is impersonal but dramatic, and it is one of his last lyric poems, although he continued to write verse in plays and librettos. His faith in the redeeming power of language did not last.

3

Rimbaud never explained his abandonment of literature (he did not need to, he had had no popular success during his short productive years, almost nothing had been printed, and he was without money). But Hofmannsthal famously did, in 1901, with a short prose work, *A Letter,* that was soon recognized as a fundamental document of modernism. It casts light on the dazzling achievement and the renunciation of poetry by both Rimbaud and Hofmannsthal and on the tumultuous history of modernism

It is not a treatise but a short narrative, that has no parallel elsewhere in literature, as far as I can see. It presents itself as a letter written three centuries before 1902, sent to the philosopher Francis Bacon in 1603 by a young English aristocrat, Lord Philip Chandos, explaining how he gradually became aware that he would never be able to write anything in the future. Generally called "The Chandos Letter," it became Hofmannsthal's most important work, rivaled only by the libretto of *Der Rosenkavalier.*

A Letter is a detailed account of the progress of the developing sense of alienation that informs so many significant examples of the expressionist anguish that was one important aspect of modernist style, and which led consequently to the rejection by writers and artists of the most conventional and respectable forms of expression or communication. It is all the more persuasive as it is not couched as a theoretical exposition, but as a work of historical fiction. It begins with an account of the young Lord Chandos's early grandiose literary ambition, an encyclopedic work:

> In those days I, in a state of continuous intoxication, conceived the whole
> of existence as one great unit: the spiritual and physical worlds seemed to
> form no contrast, as little as did courtly and bestial conduct, art and bar-
> barism, solitude and society; in everything I felt the presence of Nature,
> in the aberrations of insanity as much as in the utmost refinement of the
> Spanish ceremonial; in the boorishness of young peasants no less than in
> the most delicate of allegories, and in all expressions of Nature I felt
> myself.

His faith in language gradually wanes, and he writes "I have completely lost the ability to think or speak of anything coherently." This loss begins with a distaste for familiar abstract words, like spirit, soul or body. . . . The abstract terms of which the tongue must avail itself as a matter of course to voice a judgment—these terms crumbled in my mouth like moldy fungus.

Ordinary observations of everyday matters became incomprehensible:

Single words floated around me; they congealed into eyes, which stared at me and into which I was forced to stare back—whirlpools which gave me vertigo and, reeling incessantly, led into the void.

Chandos continues to lead his social life, and, in the midst of his anguish, there are "gay and stimulating moments," but of a strange character:

Once again words desert me. For it is, indeed, something entirely unnamed, even barely nameable which, at such moments, reveals itself to me, filling like a vessel any casual object of my daily surroundings with an overflowing flood of higher life . . . A pitcher, a harrow abandoned in a field, a dog in the sun, a neglected cemetery, a cripple, a peasant's hut—all these can become the vessel of my revelation. Each of these objects and a thousand others similar, over which the eye glides with a natural indifference, can suddenly, at any moment (which I am utterly powerless to evoke), assume for me a character so exalted and moving that words seem too poor to describe it.

The most astonishing moment of *The Letter* follows hard upon this. Chandos had given an order to spread rat poison in his dairy cellars, and goes riding in the country:

there suddenly loomed up before me the vision of the cellar resounding with the death struggle of a mob of rats. I felt everything within me: the cool musty air of the cellar filled with the sweet and pungent reek of poison, and the yelling of the death cries breaking against the moldering walls; the vain convulsions of those convoluted bodies as they tear about in confusion and despair . . . But why seek again for words which I have forsworn? You remember, my friend, the wonderful description of Livy of the hours preceding the destruction of Alba Longa when the crowds stray aimlessly through the streets which they are to see no more . . . I carried this vision within me, and the vision of burning Carthage, too; but there was more, something more divine, more bestial, and it was the Present, the fullest most exalted Present . . .

Forgive this description, but do not think it was pity I felt. For if you did, my example would have been poorly chosen. It was far more and far less than pity; an immense sympathy, a flowing over into these creatures, or a feeling that an aura of life and death, of dreams and wakefulness, had flowed for a moment into them—but whence? For what had it to do with pity, or with any comprehensible concatenation of human thought when, on another evening, on finding beneath a nut tree a half-filled pitcher and the water in it, darkened by the shadow of the tree, and a beetle swimming on the surface from shore to shore—when this combination of trifles sent through me such a shudder at the presence of the Infinite, a shudder running from the roots of my hair to the marrow of my heels . . . As soon as this strange enchantment falls from me, I find myself confused; wherein this harmony transcending me and the entire world consisted, and how it made itself known to me, I could present in sensible words as little as I could say anything precise about the inner movements of my intestines or a congestion of my blood.

The key point in this rendering of an inexpressible feeling of unity with the world outside is the extraordinary phrase: "there was something more divine, more bestial, and it was the Present, the exalted Present." At the moment of feeling intensely at one with other creatures or with objects, we abandon all calculations of the future, rid the mind of all contamination with memories of the past, and concentrate on the single moment at hand. This experience can be understood oddly either as mystical or as aesthetic. In "The Dry Salvages" from *The Four Quartets,* T. S. Eliot makes almost exactly the same point:

> Man's curiosity searches past and future:
> And clings to that dimension. But to apprehend
> The point of intersection of the timeless
> With time, is an occupation for the saint—
> No occupation either, but something given
> And taken, in a lifetime's death in love,
> Ardour and selflessness and self-surrender.
> For most of us, there is only the unattended
> Moment, the moment in and out of time,
> The distraction fit, lost in a shaft of sunlight,
> The wild thyme unseen, or the winter lightening
> Or the waterfall, or music heard so deeply
> That it is not heard at all, but you are the music
> While the music lasts. These are only hints and guesses.

There are all the elements of Hofmannsthal's predicament, the odd collection of natural objects observed by chance that stimulates a mystical sense of the present ("the intersection of the timeless with time") and annihilates the trivial daily obsession with past and future, and that ends up for most of us only as a fragile and transient aesthetic experience, the impossibility of a full rational explanation, and the intensity that appears in a moment of distraction.

Hofmannsthal found his greatest poetic eloquence in this odd prose fiction that affirms the impossibility of using language for the purpose of conveying the deepest emotional experiences. For him this was not a paradox, but a truth essential to the nature of language. Lyric poetry is properly the expression of the most personal and individual thoughts and feelings. But Hofmannsthal would claim later: "The individual is inexpressible. What is expressed already slips into generality, and is no longer individual in the strictest sense. Language and individuality are opposed." Language is social not personal; words must be understood by others, an idiolect is a non-sense. There are no special words to convey what I alone have experienced. What is most individual, most deeply personal, is therefore perverted and ruined by being put into words.

Chandos concludes *A Letter* with a prevision of future stylistic fireworks:

> The language in which I might be able not only to write but think is neither Latin nor English, neither Italian nor Spanish, but a language none of whose words is known to me, a language in which mute things speak to me and wherein I may one day have to justify myself before an unknown judge.

The effort to invent a language more individual and less bound by social convention was not in the future but was taking place during Hofmannsthal's lifetime, and in all the arts. The sense of the inadequacy of both the spoken and the literary language swept throughout Europe in the latter half of the nineteenth century and gave rise to a suspicion of any form of artistic convention. *A Letter* is a witness to a widespread, enduring movement.

Three decades after the Chandos Letter, Samuel Beckett could still write:[1]

> It is indeed getting more and more difficult, even pointless for me to write in formal English. And more and more my language appears to me like a veil which one has to tear apart in order to get at those things (or the nothingness) lying behind it. Grammar and style! To me they seem to have become as irrelevant as a Biedermeier bathing suit or the imperturbability of a gentleman. A mask! It is to be hoped the time will come, thank God, in some circles it already has, when language is best used when most efficiently abused. . . . Or is literature alone to be left behind on that old, foul road long ago abandoned by music and painting? Is there something paralysingly sacred contained within the unnature of the word that does not belong to the elements of the other arts?

---

1. From a letter of Samuel Beckett, quoted by Gabriel Josipovici, in a review of *The Letters of Samuel Beckett,* vol. 1, 1929–1940, in *The Times Literary Supplement,* March 13, 2009, p. 3.

4

Hofmannsthal himself held back from radical modernism, but it was not for lack of sympathy as his remarks in the 1920s on Rimbaud and Mallarmé show, but he could not bring himself to go as far as they had ventured. His social philosophy became very conservative, although his conservative views had basically an aesthetic cast; he was buried, at his request, costumed as a Franciscan friar. Nevertheless, as editor of a literary magazine, he was the first to publish a major essay by Walter Benjamin, who aroused his enthusiasm. Perhaps the extraordinary facility and intuitive grace for traditional prosody that so impressed his contemporaries when he was only seventeen made it impossible for him to venture into the rough experimentation that accompanied modernism, and he drew back from the steps he had already tentatively taken in that direction. His long relation with Richard Strauss is significant. Their first collaboration was *Electra,* Hofmannsthal's most successful radical essay at avant-garde expressionism, and with this work Strauss, too, went further in the employment of modernist dissonance than any other composer before him. At its English premiere under Thomas Beecham, the most important London critic, Ernest Newman, declared that Strauss may have been a great composer but that the new opera was both unintelligible and vulgar, provoking a splendid protest from George Bernard Shaw. From then on, Strauss's work was considerably more conservative.

However, Hofmannsthal's most important article on the visual arts is a passionate description written in 1901 of an exhibition of the most radical avant-garde art of the time by a then little known painter, Vincent Van Gogh. Both Van Gogh and his friend Gauguin had gone beyond the impressionists and even beyond Cézanne in their rejection of the academic conventions of painting. Hofmannsthal's account demonstrates the relation of the Chandos Letter to the new artistic developments of the time. On stepping into the exhibition, Hofmannsthal was, indeed, at first taken aback by the pictures:

> At first sight they seemed to me harsh and disturbing, quite raw, quite odd, I had first to adjust in order to see the first ones as pictures, as a unity—then, however, then I saw them all as such, each one, and all together, and Nature in them, and the human spiritual power that Nature had formed, and tree and bush and field and slope, and something further, something behind what was painted, the essential thing, the indescribably fateful thing,—, I saw the whole, so that I lost the sense of myself in these images, and came back powerfully and was lost again.

In this fourth *Letter from a Returning Voyager,*[2] written in 1901, the year of the Chandos Letter, Hofmannsthal suggests that Van Gogh had found a pictorial

---

2. Not contained in *The Whole Difference.*

language capable of rendering the extraordinary sense of the unity of one's consciousness with the mute inanimate world. The new visual language had found a way to allow the mute to speak. As he continues, the naming of the objects portrayed in the exhibition recalls the collection of images in *A Letter*,— the pitcher, the harrow, the dog in the sun, the neglected cemetery are replaced by a pitcher, a pan, a chair, a wall. Hofmannsthal proceeds to identify the difference between this new style of painting and the tradition that preceded it:

> Shall I tell you about the colors? There is an unbelievably intense blue that keeps recurring, a green like molten emeralds, a yellow that is practically orange. But what are colors, if the inner life of objects does not break forth from them! And this inner life was there, tree and stone and wall and tunnel exuded their innermost and simultaneously flung it at me; but not the sensuous quality and the harmony of their beautiful life which in the past, from old pictures, sometimes flowed at me like a magical atmosphere. No, only the full weight of their existence, the raging, incredible staring wonder of their existence attacked my soul. How can I convey to you that here every being—*a being* of every tree, every yellow strip or green field, every fence, every hollow tunnel in the stone hill, a being of the pewter pitcher, the earthenware pan, the coarse chair,—rose up to me as if newborn out of the frightful chaos of non-life, out of the abyss of non-being. . . .

He experienced the paintings as an assault, flung at him, and puts his finger on a major element of Van Gogh's originality: the absence of the harmony, sensuousness, and magical atmosphere of traditional painting, now replaced by a feeling of sheer physical weight conveyed by the often unremitting intensity of the colors. The initial impact of seeing a painting by Van Gogh sometimes makes us very briefly, for a second or two, more aware of the shapes of the colors on the canvas than of the nature of the objects represented. The coercive intensity of the color patterns on the surface have initially the upper hand, and the absence of academic trompe l'oeil make the artist's sense of the represented objects all the more real and powerful in the end, the paint on the canvas becoming not an illusion of the scene but a physical, palpable substitute for it. Many of Van Gogh's works shocked contemporary observers by his painting objects the wrong hues, using color for purely emotional effect.

The remaking of the conventional language of painting continued with Matisse and the other Fauves. The information given about the details of the objects and figures represented is scaled down to bring the raw emotional effect to the fore. I do not think that anyone would comprehend at once that Matisse's great painting, *French Window at Collioure* (at the Musée Nationale d'Art Moderne in Paris), represents an open window. We first see four strips of color,—blue, black, blue, green—almost as abstract as a Barnett Newman;

without having seen the title, we would need some minutes of contemplation to decipher the scene.

The modernist movement was extraordinary in the brutality of its rejection of the reigning artistic conventions, in its dissatisfaction with the basic language of all the arts. Every new style has always opposed what it considered the outdated style it wished to replace, but the violence of the rejections from 1850 to 1920 may be unique in the history of culture. It would seem as if Rimbaud and Mallarmé in the end found it physically repellent to write the kind of verse of the great Romantic generation of Hugo, Vigny, and Musset. After 1850, painters like Courbet, Degas, Monet, and Manet became quickly famous, and they all hoped that their paintings would eventually end up in the Louvre, but, in spite of their virtuosity, consistently refused ever to make the slightest compromise, to paint a single picture that would have been bought by the Ministry of Fine Arts. They achieved effects of realistic representation unknown before their work, above all in the rendering of light, but insisted on producing canvases that emphasized the distance between a painting and the reality represented, and that called constant attention to the physical surface of paint. Poets from Mallarmé to Ezra Pound and T. S. Eliot also wrote verse that often showed an unbridgeable distance both from the spoken language of everyday life and from the traditional and conventional literary language, except for Eliot's ironic deployment of popular and learned speech in the Prufrock volume:

> Sweeney shifts from ham to ham
> Stirring the water in his bath
> The masters of the subtle school
> Are controversial, polymath

The accepted languages of art were attacked in different ways, and initial comprehension was made tougher for the public. The first abstract paintings of Kandinsky began as landscapes, which get harder to read, and it is difficult to distinguish the last landscapes from the first abstracts. Cubism and surrealism are inventions of pictorial language that proved deliberately puzzling. In music, the assault on the conventions of the previous two hundred years by Debussy, Schoenberg, Stravinsky, and others were initially scandalous, and they had the clear intention of devising a style free of old conventions. When Schoenberg began the songs of *Pierrot Lunaire,* he wrote in his diary that he had at last achieved something "new and animal," and we are reminded of Hofmannsthal's "divine and bestial Present." There was a glorious sense of anarchy and improvisation in all the arts for a few short decades with the invention of each new style, which accompanied, and was stimulated by, a despairing anguish—a ferociously pessimistic and contemptuous view of everyday life, eventually intensified by the killing of twelve million men in the war.

In short, the visual arts followed the same loosening of the immediately communicative aspect of language that we find in the last works of Rimbaud. The remaking of language by Mallarmé was equally radical. He wrote in a letter about one poem, "If this sonnet has a meaning—and if it doesn't, I would console myself with the large dose of poetry it displays." And this was about an earlier version that would become considerably more opaque—and more poetic—with revision. That is what Hofmannsthal meant by saying that with Mallarmé and his predecessors, poetry had "joined the kingdom of music." Music was traditionally considered an imitative art, but it was generally admitted that what it imitates is often exceptionally difficult to put into words. Literary experiments ventured still further with the surrealists and with Gertrude Stein, although the limits of modernist experiments with language are probably reached with James Joyce's *Ulysses* and, above all, *Finnegan's Wake,* written in a macaronic amalgam of all the languages that Joyce knew well. The latter is, surprisingly, readable, but only for adventurous spirits, although Joyce's recordings of parts of it are intelligible and beautiful enough to give a pleasure like that of listening to music.

In one respect, the renunciations of Rimbaud and Hofmannsthal have an emblematic character for early radical modernism. Creating an artistic language that dispensed with convention and allowed totally individualistic expression was essentially an impossible undertaking (as Hofmannsthal claimed), although for a few years it produced a great heritage. In most cases, the freewheeling energy of the movement lasted only a few years. The T. S. Eliot of *The Waste Land* turned into the poet of the *Four Quartets.* The atonal style of Schoenberg's initial revolution (the years of *Pierrot Lunaire, Erwartung,* and the Five Pieces for Orchestra) soon developed into the highly organized twelve-tone technique in which he could write in classical forms like the sonata. During the years from 1907 to 1917, Matisse produced nothing but imaginative masterpieces; in the years that followed, the masterpieces may still be found but more rarely and now along side a large number of odalisques lolling in well-upholstered armchairs.

Stravinsky followed the few years of *Petrouchka, The Rite of Spring,* and *Les Noces* with a turn to neoclassicism: he continued for many more decades to produce some of his finest music, but the energetic panache of the first years had evaporated. Picasso's art took a similar turn after cubism, and Kandinsky's savage early abstracts became more orderly and hard-edged. Webern's complex early atonal style was reduced to insistently regular rhythms and lean textures. Even with Joyce, *Finnegan's Wake* was a far more systematc project than *Ulysses.* In all these cases, the initial impulse could not be sustained.

As for Hofmannsthal, who fully understood the roots of the stylistic revolutions of his time, but remained aloof after a few tentative moves, Walter Benjamin remarked about him soon after his death:

> Hofmannsthal turned his back on the task which emerges in his Lord Chandos Letter. His loss of speech was a kind of punishment for this. Perhaps the language that escaped Hofmannsthal was the very language that was given to Kafka around the same time. For Kafka took on the task which Hofmannsthal had failed morally, and therefore also poetically, to fulfill.

CHAPTER 27

The Private Obsessions
of Wystan Auden

I

At the age of thirty-one, Wystan Hugh Auden, the major British poet between A. E. Houseman and Philip Larkin (with a range of styles, techniques, forms, and themes far greater than either), left England to settle in New York for the rest of his life until a year before his death. Other poets of the twentieth century had chosen life abroad, notably T. S. Eliot and Ezra Pound, but they quit their native land early in their twenties at the beginning of their careers. When Auden went into a self-imposed exile in 1939, he had already achieved a firmly established and distinguished position as poet and essayist. His literary executor (and editor of the critical edition), Edward Mendelson, has remarked,[1] "No English poet since Byron achieved fame as quickly as Auden did." This new volume of the critical edition of his complete works *(Prose, vol. 3)* contains the prose writings from 1949 to 1955 that followed after Auden's first ten years in America.

Auden's transplantation was the subject of much controversy. Some English men of letters meanly resented his safe residence in America that spared him the experience of the German bombardment of Britain. In his *Memoirs,*

Originally written in 2008 as a review of W. H. Auden, *Prose, vol. 3, 1949–1955,* edited by Edward Mendelson (2008), and *Randall Jarrell on W. H. Auden,* edited by Stephen Burt, (2005).

1. W. H. Auden, *Selected Poems,* ed. Edward Mendelson, expanded 2nd ed. (New York: 2007), p. xx.

Kingsley Amis reports a conversation with the novelist Anthony Powell on the occasion of the report of Auden's death in 1973.[2]

> He looked up from his newspaper and said, "No more Auden," adding when I looked blank, "W. H. Auden is dead."
>
> "Oh," I said. "Well. Quite a blow," or some similar banality.
>
> "I'm *delighted* that *shit* has gone," said Tony with an emphasis and in a tone of detestation that made me jump slightly. "It should have happened years ago." Feeling perhaps some elucidation might be called for, he went on not much more mildly, "Scuttling off to America in 1939 with his boyfriend like a . . . like a . . ."
>
> I have forgotten what it was that Auden had scuttled off like but I never knew Tony before or since to show the kind or intensity of emotion he showed then.

The resentment of Auden's departure seems to have lasted for decades.

The change of residence was accompanied in Auden's work by radical changes in manner and theme (a more sociable and relaxed style and a loss of political fervor), and they also created controversy. That these changes were due principally to his leaving Britain is dubious: poets like everyone else naturally alter with time. W. B. Yeats gained new power and economy in his last years, but there is generally a loss of audacity when poets grow older, as in Wordsworth's descent from the powerful and imaginative landscape poetry and autobiography of his early years to the dull sonnets in favor of capital punishment. What is curious, however, about the new American Auden is the intensity of the disappointment of his greatest admirers, including as fine a poet as Thom Gunn, who never ceased to admire his mastery and his wit.

The most cogent witness to the general evaluation of later Auden is the posthumously published series of lectures given in 1952 by Randall Jarrell, in many ways, the finest critic of contemporary poetry America has ever had. This was a fierce onslaught on the recent work of the poet who may have influenced Jarrell more than any other ("I think Jarrell is in love with me" was Auden's amused [and justified] comment on hearing of the lectures). What is most interesting about this critical attack is that Jarrell was at once ferocious and generous. His consternation at some of the changes in Auden's work since he settled in America (the stylistic mannerisms, the ethical posing) did not prevent him from expressing the most eloquent admiration for much of it. About the magnificent poem "Under Sirius," he writes that on reading it, "the rest of us poets feel 'Well, back to our greeting cards,'" and remarks that Auden "has a more extraordinary command of language than almost anyone else alive" (p. 71).

2. P. 150.

This third volume of Auden's collected prose has a somewhat more academic tone than the first two, as Auden was now often invited to lecture at American universities. Brilliant, quirky, fascinating, and original, the long study of sea imagery called *The Enchafed Flood* is the finest example of this academic style; it is subtitled *The Romantic Iconography of the Sea,* but it roams from Dante and Shakespeare to Wordsworth, Gerard Manley Hopkins, Ibsen, and much else, and then to Melville's *Moby Dick* (the final pages becoming something of a detailed graduate seminar on the last book). There is also a great deal of fashionable journalism for magazines like *Vogue* and the *New Yorker,* most of it entertaining and delightful, along with serious lectures on religion and history.

2

The gathering helps us to understand why many of Auden's greatest admirers were distressed at the turn his career had taken and its new outlook. As Montaigne remarked, "Everyone says foolish things: the mistake is to say them seriously," and I have no intention of simply picking out some of the foolishness that occasionally turns up in the midst of Auden's brilliance. But I have found it a good rule of thumb in understanding the limitations and the character of a fine critic to consider the occasional absurdity defended by an even greater absurdity, as this indicates the concealed presence of an obsessive trait so fundamental that it escapes the writer's rational control. A simple and very brief example can be found in T. S. Eliot's Norton Lectures, *The Use of Poetry and the Use of Criticism,* where he wants to assert that a poet ought not to be an original thinker, and the disturbing example of Goethe naturally presents itself. He writes:

> Of Goethe perhaps it is truer to say that he dabbled in both philosophy and poetry and made no great success of either;

This is so evidently absurd about the most successful German author of all time, that Eliot attempts to justify it, and finishes the sentence with an even more foolish qualification:

> his true role was that of the man of the world and sage—a La Rochefoucauld, a La Bruyère, a Vauvenargues.

La Rochefoucauld? Far from dabbling at different things, he did only one thing better than anyone else: writing the most renowned modern collection of maxims. Eliot's belief that original thought is irrelevant to the practice of poetry was so profoundly and obscurely important to him that all his critical intelligence deserted him in trying to demonstrate it.

A similar process is at work in two articles by Auden, both of them, however, interesting and sharply observed. The first ("Huck and Oliver") is a fascinating contrast of two books about a young boy, Charles Dickens's *Oliver Twist* and Mark Twain's *Huckleberry Finn*—the passive hero compared to the active. On the latter book, Auden considers at length what is surely its most powerful moment: when Huck Finn, helping the slave, Jim, escape from being sold down the river, reflects that in Sunday school he would have been taught "that people that acts as I'd been acting about that nigger goes to everlasting fire." He tries to pray, but cannot because God knows that he will not give up his sin. He writes a letter revealing Jim's whereabouts to his owner, and says that "I felt good and all washed clean of sin for the first time I had ever felt so in my life . . ." Then he remembers how kind Jim had been to him, that he was Jim's only friend, and tears up the letter. Here is Auden's account of this passage:

> When I first read *Huckleberry Finn* as a boy, I took Huck's decision as being a sudden realisation, although he had grown up in a slave-owning community, that slavery was wrong. Therefore I completely failed to understand one of the most wonderful passages in the book, where Huck wrestled with his conscience. Here are two phrases. He says:
>
> > I was trying to make my mouth say I would do the right thing and the clean thing, and go and write to that nigger's owner and tell where he was, but deep down inside I knowed it was a lie, and He knowed it. You can't pray a lie—I found that out.
>
> He decides that he will save Jim. He says:
>
> > I will go to work and steal Jim out of slavery again, and if I could think up anything worse, I would do that, too; because as long as I was in, and in for good, I might as well go the whole hog.
>
> When I first read the book I took this to be abolitionist satire on Mark Twain's part. It is not that at all. What Huck does is a pure act of moral improvisation. What he decides tells him nothing about what he would do on other occasions, or what other people should do on other occasions, and here we come to a very profound difference between American and European culture. I believe that all Europeans, whatever their political opinions, whatever their religious creed, do believe in a doctrine of natural law of some kind. That is to say there are certain things about human nature, and about man as a historical creature, not only as a natural creature, which are eternally true. . . . It is very hard for an American to believe that there is nothing in human nature that will not change. . . .
>
> For that very reason you might say that America is a country of amateurs. Here is Huck who makes an essentially amateur moral decision.

Except for the observation that the chapter is not abolitionist satire, it is hard to imagine a greater misunderstanding. This great moment is only incidentally about slavery, but it is above all about religion. Auden does not quote the climactic moment of decision when Huck tears up the letter:

> It was a close place. I took [that paper] up, and held it in my hand. I was a trembling, because I'd got to decide, forever, betwixt two things, and I knowed it. I studied a minute, sort of holding my breath, and then says to myself;
> "All right, then I'll *go* to hell"—and tore it up.
> It was awful thoughts, and awful words, but they was said. And I let them stay said; and never thought no more about reforming. I shoved the whole thing out of my head; and said I would take up wickedness again, which was in my line, being brung up to it, and the other warn't.

It is with those words "All right then, I'll *go* to hell" that Huck becomes the greatest hero in American literature, rivaled only by Captain Ahab.

For most of Twain's life, he timidly protested against what he considered the hypocritical ethics of respectability and piety: this chapter was his most courageous act. Auden was right to realize that *Huckleberry Finn* was not an abolitionist tract, and Twain had known households in which the slaves were treated decently and sometimes even affectionately, but selling a slave down the river, uprooting him from the society he knew, his friends and family, to send him to hard labor was an unpardonable act, and it reappears as such in other works like *Pudd'nhead Wilson*. Twain himself described his book as the struggle between "natural instincts" and a "corrupt conscience"—a conscience corrupted by a repressive society and its religion—and the natural instincts win at last.

Having returned to the Anglican faith in 1940, which he had left at the age of thirteen, Auden preferred not to notice that this moment of *Huckleberry Finn* represents Mark Twain's indictment of the official religion of that part of American society he knew best. The early Auden who challenged authority readily has been replaced by one who does not recognize a challenge. His contrast of European and American attitudes on moral decisions is unconvincing because it is partly a smoke screen to hide his ambiguous take on Twain's aggressive stand, and he even claims that what Huck "decides tells him nothing about what he should do on other occasions," overlooking Huck's clear affirmation that this decision will change his life forever. In fact, a few paragraphs later, Auden even quotes the last lines of *Huckleberry Finn* that confirm how completely Huck was affected by his decision: "I reckon I got to light out for the Territory ahead of the rest, because Aunt Sally she's going to adopt me and sivilise me. And I can't stand it. I been there before."

Auden's religious sense was profound, and an account in a letter of a mystical experience he had just before going to America is eloquent. His joining the Anglican Communion was, however, as much a public as a private act; I think he chose it over the Roman Catholic Church, which he found aesthetically more attractive, because becoming an Anglican again was less flashy, and, above all, it established a nostalgic connection with his earlier years in Britain while he lived as an alien in America. The Anglican faith was also a way of ordering his life without panache, like his absolutely strict rules for drinking alcohol even in America: never before 5 o'clock on weekdays, 12 o'clock on Sundays,—the popular British pub hours of respectable Englishmen. However, when the Anglican Church modernized its liturgy, removing the sense of tradition Auden needed, he switched to the Greek Orthodox Church. (I asked him if he understood the liturgy, he cheerfully replied, "Not a word!"—which was surely an exaggeration, but perhaps he did not comprehend, or need to comprehend, every word that was read out during the services.)

3

Another article, published in 1950 in *Partisan Review* on a new biography of Oscar Wilde, is even more personally revealing about the changes in Auden's outlook during the 1940s and '50s. The title of the review is openly hostile, "A Playboy of the Western World, Saint Oscar, the Hominterm Martyr."[3] Clearly, the more flamboyant aspects of the 1940s movement for gay rights got on Auden's nerves. He himself never concealed his homosexuality, but never asserted it—which would, in any case, have been unwise at that time for him as an emigrant living in America. Above all, he was always discreet about his private life, although never flaunting his discretion. Homosexuality is glanced at obliquely in his published work, although there is one long salaciously detailed pornographic poem, "The Platonic Blow," which he never published and only acknowledged privately in conversation.

The review of Wilde's biography is brilliantly written and deliberately provocative. For Auden, Wilde was not by nature an artist:

> Wilde is the classic case of a man who is completely dominated by the desire to be loved for himself alone. The artist does not want to be accepted by others, he wants to accept his experience of life which he cannot do until he has translated his welter of impressions into an order; the public approval he desires is not for himself but for his works, to reassure him that the sense he believes he has made of experience is indeed sense and not a self-delusion. (p. 185)

---

3. The editor remarks (p. xxvi) that "the subtitle of the review was meant to annoy Auden's acquaintances who thought of homosexuality in terms of its outcast social status rather than as a variety of love with the same temptations and rewards as any other."

There are perhaps a few grains of truth in this, but not much more, and something has gone seriously wrong when, a few lines later, Auden adds: "Further, a person with a need to be loved universally is frequently homosexual." (Of course, no effort is made to justify or qualify any of these generalizations.)

Auden considers few of Wilde's books to be worth reading, and finds *The Importance of Being Earnest* "the one work of Wilde's upon the excellence of which we can all agree" (p. 187). This does, indeed, represent a critical consensus, but the significance of much of Wilde's writing depends on more than the flawlessness of any given work. Unsatisfactory plays like *An Ideal Husband* and *A Woman of No Importance* contain splendid pages. *De Profundis* (the letter from Wilde in prison to "Bosie" [Lord Alfred Douglas]) and *Salome,* for example, make painfully embarrassing reading, drenched the one in self-pity and the other in absurdly bad taste, and are yet compelling—and they remain important with all their imperfection precisely because they embarrass and disturb while commanding our attention.

In his introduction (p. 26), Edward Mendelson quotes a remarkable passage from the review concerning the libel suit against Bosie's father, the Marquis of Queensberry and the ensuing trials that put Wilde in prison at hard labor and permanently ruined his career:

> Nothing is clearer in the history of the three trials than his unconscious desire that the truth should come out. This desire was not caused by guilt in the conventional sense but by the wish to be loved as he really was. One suspects that his secret day-dream was of a verdict of guilty being brought in whereupon Judge, Jury and public would rise to their feet, crown him with flowers and say: "We ought, of course, to send you to gaol, Mr. Wilde, but we all love you so much that in this case we are delighted to make an exception."

The sharp insight into Wilde's character that opens this paragraph is set in a false light by the facetious tone, which suggests that Wilde got what was coming to him (true enough legally, but irrelevant to any estimate we would make today of either his character or literary stature.)

Just after reading Auden's jaunty account of Wilde, I came upon Hugo von Hofmannsthal's extraordinary article "Sebastian Melmoth" (Wilde's pseudonym on leaving prison), written in 1905 shortly after Wilde's death in a shabby Parisian hotel. It begins as a protest against the banal journalistic contrast between the brilliant early career of Wilde and the scandalous trials followed by the sordid prison years and death, and maintains that the terrible fate was there from the beginning. Hofmannsthal took Wilde seriously (no doubt easier to do for the taste of 1905 than 1950). Wilde was no aesthete like Walter Pater, Hofmannsthal wrote, and continued:

An aesthete is, by nature, steeped in propriety. Oscar Wilde, however, was a figure of impropriety, tragic impropriety. His aestheticism was like a cramp. . . . He kept challenging life unceasingly. He insulted reality. And he sensed life lying in wait in order to spring upon him out of the darkness. . . .

That is why it must have been deeply moving to have seen Oscar Wilde at one moment of his life. I mean the moment when he (over whom no one but his fate had any power)—against the pleading of his friends and almost to the horror of his enemies—turned and denounced Queensberry. For then the mask of Bacchus with its full, beautifully curved lips must have been transformed in an unforgettable manner into the mask of the seeing-blind Oedipus or the raging Ajax. . . . We must not make life more banal than it is, nor turn our eyes away so as not to behold this band when for once it can be seen on a brow. . . .

Painting this image of Wilde as a tragic figure immediately after his death, Hofmannsthal was as aware as Auden of the frivolity and superficiality of much of Wilde's work, and it inspired a concluding meditation on Wilde and the unity of experience:

There are tragic elements in superficial things and silliness in the tragic. There is something suffocatingly sinister in what we call pleasure. There is lyricism in the dress of a whore and something commonplace about the emotions of a lyric poet. . . . No one thing can be excluded, none considered too insignificant to become a very great power. . . . Everything is part of the dance. . . . In the words of the [medieval Persian] poet Jalal-ud-din Rumi, he who knows the power of the dance does not fear death. For he knows that love kills.

Hofmannsthal knew that Wilde destroyed his career and his life because he wanted to be loved, not by everyone, but only by "Bosie." Hofmannsthal was not homosexual, but he was not made uneasy by homosexuality (in spite of having been propositioned when he was sixteen by the great Gerrman poet Stefan George, who embarrassed him by sending bouquets of flowers to him at his high school). His more generous estimate of Wilde's tragic life and his belief that the origins of the final disaster lay early in Wilde's career find confirmation in a sentence from a letter of Wilde written many years before the Queensberry trial: "Sometimes I think that the artistic life is a long and lovely suicide, and am not sorry that it is so."[4]

4. Quoted by Richard Ellman in the introduction to his anthology of Wilde's prose, *The Critic as Artist*, p. xvii.

Auden, however, underestimates the power of Wilde's cynicism (called by Hofmannsthal "a cynicism near to torture"), and must have felt the idolization of Wilde's ostentatious camp as a menace. His view of Wilde as a playboy has some justification, but even Wilde's frequently nonsensical playfulness often conceals an attack on established moral and social values. To take the least provocative example, after the two young women in *The Importance of Being Earnest* quarrel with the men, they spy on them from a distance, and one says, "They're eating muffins," and the other replies, "That looks like repentance." This is delicate, but it is a send-up of the serious moral attitudes of the time, and in the end such details accumulate and are corrosive. Hofmannsthal was right to say: "he insulted reality."

At the end of his article, Auden sums up his approach, and one phrase betrays a crucial misunderstanding of Wilde:

> The tough and pessimistic Greek who identified pleasure and happiness knew that pleasure depends upon power. . . . But Wilde, like anyone who has been exposed to the culture of Christendom, knew, however unconsciously, that pleasure and happiness are distinct. And that happiness does not depend upon power but upon love.

The last sentence makes a profound point, essential to Auden's thinking after 1940. Unfortunately for Auden, Wilde was not a bit unconscious of the distinction between pleasure and happiness, and was opposed to everything that Auden is saying here. The most insolent and shocking of Wilde's "Maxims for the Young" at the end of *The Portrait of Dorian Gray* is:

> *Live for pleasure alone. Nothing ages like happiness.*

4

The dependence of sexual pleasure on power, violence, and domination preoccupied Auden throughout his later years. He once maintained at a dinner party that the only sexual act that did not entail domination was a blow job, and he appeared to be very astonished when the other guests assured him that in many cultures, including the American, the one who gave the blow job was often considered, not only inferior, but degraded and humiliated.

Soon after he arrived in America, Auden fell in love with a young American poet, Chester Kallman. The relationship became permanent and lasted until Auden's death in 1973. As Edward Mendelson observes,[5] it was treated by Auden

5. Auden, *Selected Poems,* ed. Mendelson, p. xxiii.

as a marriage. Nevertheless, I understand that Kallman refused to have sexual relations with Auden after a very short time, and did not live with him in New York, staying in Athens for half of each year, and they were always together only in vacation months in Austria and Italy. Mendelson (*Selected Poems*, p. xxii) describes "the chastened personal intensity of Auden's poems in his first years in America" as "a sign of two newly discovered commitments"—to the Anglican Communion and to Kallman. It is true that from then on in Auden's writing, with few exceptions, love as Eros is repressed, and appears mainly as Agape—or what the King James Version chastely calls "charity." The "chastened" and, indeed, chaste poems like "In Praise of Limestone" written in 1948 are moving, but the lyrics of 1934 to 1958 are breathtaking. There was a loss of energy.

He held Eros at arm's length, and even the passion of his religious writing is distanced. Mendelson is justified to claim the sequence of the church hours, "Horae Canonicae," to "be the one twentieth-century poetic work whose greatness exceeds its fame" (p. xxix). Perhaps the most striking of these is "Nones": the ninth church hour, which is 3 o'clock in the afternoon, the time of the crucifixion. It is, indeed, about the crucifixion, and a great poem, but, as Jarrell remarked in praising it, "this is a crucifixion with no Christ, no cross, no Jerusalem" (Jarrell p. 76). The physical immediacy of Auden's earlier poetry is absent now, as it is from the prose as well, but "Nones" is deeply moving in part for what it leaves out, and marks a return in many ways to the poet's earlier style.

I do not want to be guilty of the cardinal sin of biographical criticism, and appear to claim that the changes in Auden's work were specifically caused by the changes in his life. To an author as intensely immersed in his writing as Auden was, the work is not secondary and the life, primary. Changes in philosophical and aesthetic outlook must have had power over his life, and radically influenced even his daily routine and all his personal and social activity. Work and life were parallel.

Prose, volume 3, is wonderfully edited, like all the many editions of Auden supervised by Edward Mendelson (a sole regret is the absence of a proper index—there is only an inadequate one of titles). Most of the articles will delight any reader with their wit, charm, and elegance. I have spent so much space on only two, because in their singularity they illuminate the new aspects of Auden's career that disconcerted so many of his admirers, and they suggest the presence of forces in his artistic and personal psyche that were beyond the reach of his extraordinary intelligence. In place of the further detailed praise that the book merits, I offer a brilliant short paragraph of almost unwilling tribute by Jarrell, Auden's sharpest critic and his greatest fan, a paragraph with a virtuoso's magnificently absurd mixed metaphor at the end that must have been intended as a submissive homage to the inspiration that Auden offered (p. 73):

Another of Auden's virtues is his great capacity for growth or change—he is as incapable as a chameleon of keeping the same surface for any great length of time. It is rather queer and pathetic to mention as a virtue this capacity for change, in the case of a man who changed away from his best poetry, got steadily worse, for many years, but he *has* begun to get better again, and is *not* laid away in that graveyard of poets, My Own Style, going on like a repeating decimal until the day someone drives a stake through his heart.

Part Six

FINAL CADENCE,
UNRESOLVED

CHAPTER 28

Old Wisdom and Newfangled Theory:
Two One-Way Streets to Disaster

I

There are basically two ways to kill a tradition. The first is a stiff-necked adherence to established practices, rejecting any adjustment for the changes in outlook and new ideals that naturally come to pass in time, an adherence that transforms and exhibits the works of the past as a collection of fossils; this approach rests on a belief that works of art or of general culture are fixed objects, forever unalterable, and incapable of development in time. The second way is a process of radical modernization that takes no account of history and brings the tradition up to date while ignoring the social and artistic ideals that made possible its creation and development, setting aside the history of its reception, and regarding the tradition as if it were just created today or, at best yesterday,—"making it relevant" is generally the commercial—or ideological—excuse for this approach. (The neutralizing interaction of these two opposing tendencies has so far warded off the final verdict of death for our inheritance of the past.)

We waver between these two extremes: either a belief that the works of earlier centuries must be understood and performed only in ways that would have been familiar to a public contemporary with their production, that a Mozart concerto should be played as Mozart would have played it, that the novels of Dickens must be interpreted as the readers of the serial magazines in which the novels first appeared would have accepted them;—or, alternatively, a denial of any sense that the past is still alive in the works handed down to us, an insistence that we must reshape the past into an image of the modern world, rejecting or discounting whatever we find unsympathetic or alien and difficult to accept. The latter project entails a novel approach to education: instead of studying history, we teach the monuments of the past to conform to our culture, educating them to understand and accept our point of view. That way we no longer need to learn anything about history, but the monuments of the past become smarter and more up to date.

Both the gain and the loss when works are transported either to another culture or to another era are equally obvious. For example, American television sitcoms are often artistically improved when they are shown on European public channels, uninterrupted by frequently irritating commercials; but they are also at some points less effective, as the script writers of the shows have learned to place a climax or a punch line just before the commercial, which acts like a pause (or fermata in a musical score) to underline the break, and allows the spectator a moment to breathe as well as to get a can of beer. In similar fashion, Dickens would place a suspenseful moment of his novels just before the end of each serial installment; the effectiveness of these moments was considerably diminished when the novel was finally printed between hard covers. (Recent editors of Dickens have indicated the serial structure of these novels, calling upon readers to use their imaginations and pretend that they were reading from the original magazine installments.)

I think we must conclude that the ideal form of works of art is always at least partially distorted both by the conditions of their initial presentation and production and by their transference to new eras, new venues, or new media. We are not always aware of the damage done to productions of culture by the social conditions in which they were made and later by the new conditions that arise in the ages that inherit them. When we watch the DVD of a blockbuster spectacle film on a small TV screen, we unconsciously imagine it as if viewing it in a large theater. I think that if going to the movies for the large-screen experience ever dies out (not an improbable speculation, as the economy of the cinema seems nowadays to be declining), no one will ever again make films like *Ben Hur, King Kong,* or *Superman* as they do not suit the small screen, and then the public of the future will no longer be able to visualize how these monsters of earlier times, although perhaps still available on DVD players, were intended to be seen.

Few members of the musical public today know that if we wish to experience Schubert's song cycles as Schubert's contemporaries would have heard them, we must imagine them as being sung to a few friends. At a party of ten people for Elliott Carter's one hundredth birthday in December 2008, I heard four songs he had just written on his birthday (still composing at the height of his inspiration) on poems by Louis Zukofsky for soprano and clarinet magnificently performed by Lucy Shelton and Charles Neidich, and I realized that no performance in a larger hall could be as moving as hearing the work in a small space with friends,—just as, on the other hand, spectacular and amusing kitsch like *Casablanca* can never carry the conviction of its brilliant foolishness on the small TV screen at home that it does in a crowded theater.

Something like that has already taken place with a good deal of the music of the past: for example, only two of Beethoven's thirty-two piano sonatas were played in Vienna in public during his lifetime; the others were heard only by a dozen or so music-lovers at a semiprivate musicale or played for oneself by an amateur or professional. Most music-lovers think of Beethoven sonatas as having always been intended for public consumption. It is true that his sonatas may have blossomed and even gained in power, come into their own, in fact, when the piano recital in large halls was invented by Franz Liszt, although, indeed, certain aspects of the music were inevitably weakened and even lost in the more spacious venue. Nevertheless, these sonatas were the greatest influence on the development and constitution of the serious piano recital that eventually replaced the first piano recitals, largely made up of opera arrangements and fantasies, improvisations and popular salon music. Several of the Beethoven sonatas, of course, incorporated elements of the brilliant public style of the concerto, as had, indeed, some of Mozart's piano sonatas (the finale of the B-flat Major Sonata, K. 333, is a rondo which imitates the contrast between solo sections and orchestral textures and boasts a full-fledged cadenza). Most of Beethoven's sonatas, however, betray at many points the character of the private occasions where they were normally performed. As for the concerto-like brilliance of sonatas like the C Major, op. 2, no. 3, or the *Waldstein,* we should reflect that public virtuosity has a peculiar and individual savor when realized in an intimate setting.

Unlike Beethoven's sonatas, but like his own song cycles, Schubert's piano sonatas were not of a nature to inspire the need for public performance for a long time. Sviatoslav Richter's comprehension of this special intimate nature can explain his interpretation of some of the late sonatas. His very slow tempo in the first movement of the last sonata in B-flat Major (marked only *Molto moderato*) excited the derision of Alfred Brendel. As I remember, Richter takes almost half an hour for this movement alone, with three more still to go. Brendel was right in thinking the tempo incorrect or inauthentic, but he also appeared not to feel that the intimacy of the work was also essential to its authenticity, and contented himself with a large-scale rendition. The movement is indeed of grand dimensions, but the paradox of Schubert's style here is the astonishing quantity of dynamic indications of pianissimo and even *ppp*, broken most memorably just before the repeat of the exposition by a single fierce and unexpectedly brutal playing as loudly as possible of the trill of the principal motif, heard so far only very softly (a repeat that Brendel refused to perform, perhaps because the unprepared violence is awkward in a large hall, although paradoxically more convincing in an intimate setting). Richter was an extraordinarily intelligent musician: whenever there was a significant detail in the score, it was always signaled by a reaction in his interpretation, not always, perhaps, the reaction that one would have liked, but no matter. For a recital in a large hall, he played the last Schubert sonata on a darkened stage, with a single small lamp near the keyboard, and the piano completely closed. The lowered light, the muffled sonority, and the exceedingly slow tempo increased the sense of intimacy, forcing listeners to concentrate to hear details. Even on Richter's recording of this piece, I find that he was impressively able to sustain the long line of the piece at the unnaturally reduced pace. However, when he employed the same tactic with the G Major Sonata, where Schubert himself does not control the line so intensely, the effect was intolerable, as we often waited impatiently for the next note.

In short, there are innovative ways of interpreting the past, and they can be magnificent even when wrong, but only if there is an awareness and at least a mitigated respect for the original historical conditions. There are also ways, of course, that are simply dead wrong. We have reasonably objective criteria of judgment, socially and professionally established, but no definitive ones. Some interpretations are persuasive and may seem almost ideal, but every one always contains the roots of a misconception or casts the shadow of a significant aspect overlooked.

2

Preserving a tradition creates fundamental problems even in the visual arts: putting a painting or a sculpture in a museum is an easy way to start, but it is only a first step. Making sure the painting does not deteriorate is more difficult. Age and climate take their toll: even the contact of light is destructive. Allowing access to the work, given the continuous overloading of major public collections, is another difficulty. Hanging and lighting the picture so that it is seen to advantage is not simple. When The Museum of Modern Art in New York reopened its doors a few years ago, two excellent paintings of Mark Rothko were placed in a large room with works by other artists. A slightly smaller room in the Philips Gallery of Washington containing nothing but four paintings by Rothko makes him appear a more impressive artist, as the power of his work comes through best only with restriction and concentration.

Even greater is the problem of recreating the conditions in which the work was originally intended to be seen, still more dubious the belief that this is always possible, or even always desirable. Many years ago, several Caravaggio altarpieces from the dimly lit chapels in Italian churches were exhibited in a show in Paris, and many details became easily visible and effective for the first time since Caravaggio himself displayed the recently finished works in his studio before sending them on for installation in a chapel. Naturally, something was lost as well when they were ripped from their ecclesiastical context.

Keeping a book in print, or at least on the shelves of a library, is but a first step to preserving literature. Ensuring that it remains intelligible even to an educated reader is a more complex task. Indeed, simply defining what it means for a novel or a poem to be understood is an ambiguous and roundabout process as well. Do we need to know not only the meaning of the words but something of the social conditions that gave the words their connotation when they were written? Preserving architecture of past ages from the erosions of time and weather, and from the alterations and often misguided restorations of later cultures may also raise unexpected difficulties. In any case, the presence of books in a library, pictures on the walls of a museum, offers at least the possibility of access, the promise or hope of future understanding. But with the works of the dance, music, and the theater, preservation is more complex as they partly depend on a living and unbroken tradition of performance. For the recent past, there are, of course, recordings of music, videos, and films of dance and drama. But these are only token performances: film is both an independent art and a reproductive process, like etching and mezzo tint, and each of these can appear as a fully artistic medium only under certain conditions—when the medium becomes, in fact, partially or wholly independent of the original which is being reproduced. But the film of a ballet is only an inferior substitute for the real thing, and no recording of music has the immediacy of playing the piece oneself, or of a live performance either in a concert hall or in private among friends. The recording of music often imposes the misleading implication that the performance is somehow definitive, or typical of its time, or even that the recorded performer always played it that way. As for the filming of a play or ballet in the theater, that is at best a document, unsatisfactory almost by definition. The physical presence of the body of the dancer is more essential to the art than the actual presence of the instrumentalist or even the singer.

A revival of a ballet generally requires more than just a film of the original for guidance, needing at least the continuous presence of one authority who worked on or in the original staging. When I was ten years old, I saw Stravinsky's *Petrouchka,* and the choreographer Mikael Fokine came out at the end and took a bow. I remember that Massine, Danilova, and Franklin were the soloists. I thought it was one of the grandest things I had ever seen and came back every year for the next few years to see it again, but I was always a little disappointed afterward, and when I met one of the dancers in the troupe of the Ballets Russes de Monte Carlo, she assured me that after Fokine's departure the year after I saw the work for the first time, the staging had been gradually falling apart: the solo parts were still fine (scenes 2 and 3), but the crowd movements of scenes 1 and 4, once sensationally controlled by Fokine, were now a chaotic free-for-all.

Restaging or reconceiving a famous ballet by a new choreographer is rarely satisfactory when the original choreographer and the composer had worked together. Even the controversial original choreography of Nijinsky for *Le Sacre du Printemps* in 1913 was more satisfactory in the attempted restoration at the Paris Opera of some two decades ago than any more recent version that I have seen. (I did not find Maurice Béjart's equal opportunity version an improvement even though he had two virgins for sacrifice at the end, one male as well as female.) The extraordinarily poetic opening pages of the work, the musical image of the Russian spring night, were originally heard in the darkened hall with the curtain down; the curtain rose only with the barbaric accents of the dance that follows. Unlike the illumination of a concert hall, the lights in a dance theater or opera house are dramatically darkened if the work begins when the curtain is down, and the effect of these first few minutes was greater than any concert performance or subsequent choreography. It has now become unthinkable for choreographers or opera directors to allow the curtain to remain lowered for more than a few seconds or to shirk inventing some action on the stage, relevant or irrelevant to the music, during every overture or intermezzo; they assume that it is their duty to make their presence felt at every moment. The opening music of the spring night in *Le Sacre du Printemps,* however, should be heard in the dark.

A continuous performing tradition may be indispensable for theater, dance, and music, but if the tradition is pedantically faithful, frozen, it becomes academic rote and loses its vital energy. Restaging the choreography of the recent past, of Georges Balanchine and Anthony Tudor, for example, demands the suppleness to accommodate the styles of the individual dancers who replace the ones that influenced the choreography when the ballets were created. And when an uninterrupted performance tradition exists for a long time, the gradual changes in style over the decades and centuries is usually imperceptible to the heirs of the tradition, unaware of the inevitable deterioration. When I first went to Vienna in 1953, I was surprised by the belief of the Viennese musicians that they were still playing Mozart and Beethoven exactly as they had been performed from 1780 to 1827 (the delusion that the Vienna Philharmonic of those sad postwar years played in tune and with admirable ensemble was per-haps even more astonishing).

3

By a paradox, the two ways of killing a tradition—absolute reproductive fidelity to an imagined original (indefinable with full precision) and ruthless unhis-torical modernization—are not independent, but each often leads directly to the other. One of the radically innovative interpretive musicians of our time was Glenn Gould, but his most impressive interpretations, as well as his most perverse, were often inspired by the contemporary movement for historically authentic performance. In any case, Gould was always well aware of the his-torical ambiance of the works he played. I knew him slightly and found him always courteous and charming, and he once invited me to listen to an unedited tape from his forthcoming Mozart sonata records: the first movement of the Sonata in F Major, K. 332. (It was a curious experience, as he preferred his tapes played back very loud, and one could hear him clearly singing on the tape; since he also sang along with the tape, the effect was doubly vocal.) His Mozart recordings were deliberately among his most willful, and very eccentrically he executed the opening theme staccato except for its last appearance. When I asked him why he played the theme legato this time, he grinned and replied disarmingly, "Well, I thought I should do it right once." (Mozart actually wrote this phrase with detached two-note slurs.) Many of Gould's performances were right and sublime, others were wrong and both interesting and stimulating, and some were wrong and simply awful: I like to think that it was only the first and second of these categories that gave him his celebrity.

The very elderly and supremely distinguished art historian Walter Friedländer once returned a paper to a student at the Institute of Fine Arts of New York University with the laconic remark that it was not good. The student asked Friedländer to tell him where it was wrong so he could correct it, and Friedländer replied sadly, "It wasn't even wrong." No doubt it has always been better to be right than wrong, and clearly better to be wrong than uninteresting or trivial. But in today's climate, being provocatively wrong is often far better than being right with no matter how great a success.

Richard Taruskin maintained with some justification that the brisk tempos adopted for eighteenth-century music in the mid-twentieth century were simply the result of a modernist aesthetic that sought to rid music of its patina of sentimental nineteenth-century subjectivity. Nevertheless, Sir Charles Mackerras pointed out to me that the metronome marks given by J. N. Hummel and Carl Czerny to their arrangements of Mozart symphonies for piano four hands show that most of the tempos in use a decade after Mozart's death were indeed brisker than those adopted in our time—with the interesting exception of finales, which tended to be slower. I can offer an explanation for this anomaly. From the 1780s through a good part of the nineteenth century, audiences applauded after every movement. During Haydn's lifetime, indeed, it was often the slow movements that were received with such enthusiasm that they had to be repeated. Today, concerts have become more solemn, and applause is discouraged until the end of each symphony. Conductors, therefore, now feel that they must whip up some popular acclaim at the end by making the finales more exciting than they need be. In fact, the relaxed mood of many eighteenth-century finales is rarely given its due. In any case, a more up-to-date or modernist approach succeeded in restoring many of the original tempos, which had considerably slowed during the nineteenth century. A religious silence was then finally imposed on the performance of long works in which all the movements hung together and were supposed to be executed without pause. But this was not always an advantage. Moriz Rosenthal claimed that the brilliant virtuoso triumphal march of the second movement of the Schumann Fantasy in C Major should properly be greeted with applause, while a fine performance of the lyrical slow finale should elicit a long silence.

The change from private or semiprivate performance to public did not take place without painful adjustments. Beethoven wanted the seven movements of his great Quartet in C-sharp Minor, op. 131, played *attacca*—that is, with no pause between the movements. The members of the Schuppanzigh Quartet, who played all his quartets, received this direction with consternation. How would listeners be able to applaud? How could they signify that they wanted to hear a movement again?[1] Beethoven's contemporaries had not yet elaborated a format for an adequate performance of this work or of many others; this still took several decades to develop. We can see however, that the important distinction is not just between public and private performance, but between different kinds of public format—and private, as well. At what point of history will a work receive its ideal interpretation? Is that moment, indeed, ever reached, or do we not always need a perpetual negotiation between past and present exigencies, to preserve the past and accommodate the present?

Nevertheless, until we reflect carefully, we generally think now that classical music consists of works meant to be performed in public, preferably a public of hundreds or even of thousands. As we have seen when discussing the sonatas of Schubert, it is not often realized that until well beyond the middle of the

---

1. I am indebted to John Gingerich's paper, "Aignaz Schuppanzigh and the Classical Culture of Listening," given at the Philadelphia American Musicological Society meeting in 2009, for this information.

nineteenth century very little music was intended to be experienced in that fashion. Most music was played at home, for oneself or for a few friends,—or, on exceptional occasions, at a private musicale for a dozen or two invited guests, that is, an event for which tickets were not sold.

Public performance radically changes the way music is heard and, indeed, the way it is played. We can see how works can become misunderstood through the conviction that all music is public by the idiotic program notes that now inevitably accompany almost any performance of Bach's *Art of Fugue,* as a whole or in part, and perpetuate the early twentieth-century legend that this work is abstract thought, written for no specified instruments. This is non-sense, as it was intended like another educational work, the *Well-Tempered Klavier,* for two hands at a keyboard (this was well understood throughout the nineteenth century)—what keyboard was, indeed, not spelled out for either collection because they are works intended to be played at home on whatever keyboard you owned—clavichord, harpsichord, small portable organ or early pianoforte (in his last years Bach was a supporter of Silbermann's manufacture of pianos, and even helped to sell them). Bach had the four-part counterpoint of the Art of the Fugue printed on four staves as that made it easier to study—and even to perform at that time for any competent keyboard player, as most could then read proficiently from score. The manuscript, however, was written on two staves and looks no different from *The Well-Tempered Klavier* (in proper English, *The Well-Tempered Keyboard*) or, indeed, any later piano piece. In the *Art of Fugue,* the only number not conveniently realizable by two hands (a three-voice fugue that, when held up to a mirror, produced an equally valid composition) was arranged for two instruments by the composer, with a fourth voice added to the original three voices, so that one of the players would not be oddly playing with only one hand.

For performance today, the question is simply how to make this great music interesting and effective for a public, a question that would have made no sense to the composer because there was no social or commercial institution at the time in which it could have been performed publicly. The *Art of Fugue* was intended to teach you how to write different kinds of fugues, something that is properly learned only by playing all the parts oneself. Performance by several instruments may perhaps be a good answer for public performance today, as varying the sonority may stimulate interest, or at least reduce the monotony, but it considerably distorts the original texture of the work. Although I recorded the work on the piano and played many of the pieces in public, I have consistently refused to play the entire work in concert, as I neither want to perform or hear at one sitting sixteen fugues all in D minor on the same theme executed with an unvaried instrumental timbre. Of course, a few fugues played for oneself every day for a week can be not only an instructive but an inspiring experience. An arrangement for several instruments, however, would have been unthinkable during the composer's lifetime, as many of the fugues are written in what was called "antique style," an *alla breve* texture that was never used at that time for anything except choral music or a solo keyboard. Concerted fugal style, like the last movement of the Brandenburg Concerto no. 5, on the other hand, was a different matter altogether. That is why a performance of the antique style six-voice ricercar from Bach's *Musical Offering* on six early eighteenth-century Baroque instruments is no more authentic or correct than the idiosyncratic but beautifully original arrangement by Anton von Webern, as this fugue was intended only for two hands at a keyboard (most likely a Silbermann piano-forte, as it was the favorite keyboard instrument of Frederick the Great, who ordered the fugue—he had sixteen of these instruments).

Even if we wanted to hear music of the early eighteenth century exactly as we imagine the composer would have played it, public performance in large halls will force us consciously or unconsciously to compromise in order to make the work not only effective, but simply intelligible to our contemporary listeners. We are told that Bach once played through one book of the *Well-Tempered Keyboard* for a pupil. Playing a piece oneself or sitting by the performer and looking at the music is very different from listening to a work with hundreds of others in a large space, and the problems of comprehension are magnified when it is music that one has never heard before or does not know well. No performer of Bach today on the piano with any conscience will resist setting in relief certain aspects of the music, bringing out what is interesting but hard to hear—or, indeed, imperceptible—, even when such attempts to inflect and highlight the score would have been either impossible or extremely inconvenient on the instruments available to the composer. Nevertheless, such distortions of the text are only making audible what was really there for Bach's contemporaries, what every performer could hear—or imagine and under-stand—and enjoy!—when playing. Surely, when performing in public, it is a simple act of generosity to make available to the listeners what gives pleasure to the performer. In such cases, a dogmatic or absolute fidelity to the limitations of the past is morally self-defeating, a form of obfuscation in the name of aes-thetic purity as indefensible as, for example (to go to the other extreme), Ferruccio Busoni's transformation of the modest return of the sarabande theme at the end of the *Goldberg Variations* into a turgid Lisztian apocalypse. Some years ago,[2] I remarked on an interesting exchange between Edward T. Cone and Richard Taruskin, sparked by Cone's observation that it was generally close to impossible on a harpsichord to bring out the theme in an inner voice

2. *Critical Entertainments* (Cambridge, Mass.: Harvard University Press, 2000), p. 216.

of a Bach fugue. Taruskin objected indignantly that a generation of harpsichordists had sweat blood in order to be able to do just that. Indeed, modern harpsichordists, striving to set details in relief on their instruments just like pianists, do occasionally manage to achieve this kind of highlighting by phrasing and rhythm. In the eighteenth century, of course, no harpsichordist would ever have bothered to try to accomplish anything of the sort, because a Bach fugue on the harpsichord would have been played for oneself or for someone else perhaps looking on the music over the performer's shoulder—at least, no question of making the work effective for a public was ever raised for music of this kind. There would have been no point to set in relief a detail evident to everyone present, above all a detail for which the charm lies in the way it is hidden and enclosed within more immediately audible lines. If one plays the fugue oneself, one can, so to speak, hear the inner voice through the fingers. I raise this interesting controversy once again to illuminate the way our thinking of performance style is defined and hedged by our modern experience of public music as the norm. In music of dense contrapuntal texture, it is doubtful that any performance will make every interesting detail perceptible to the ear. Of course, when looking at the score while listening, eye and ear cooperate, and we may easily convince ourselves that we hear what our eyes inform us is present.

Even the nature of public performance has changed over the years. Only a little over half a century ago, it was likely that a large proportion of the listeners at piano recitals in large cities in Europe and America had learned to play the piano, and some of them may have tried to play or even studied a few of the pieces on the program. At least they had an inkling of the physical and mental challenges involved in turning a written score into a performance. The audience, therefore, was still taking an active part in a more than four-hundred-year-old tradition of playing a keyboard instrument. To some extent playing Beethoven in public today is like performing Shakespeare for an audience for whom English is a language only incompletely familiar.

4

We are sometimes warned against turning our opera houses or recital halls into museums, which merely exhibit the most cherished works of the past—as if they were bottled in formaldehyde, stuffed by a taxidermist, or preserved by painstaking restoration. Nevertheless, works of music or the theater need to be kept alive by performance; and this gives them both an advantage and a disadvantage compared to works of the visual arts. Opera houses and repertory theaters must indeed function partly as museums. Yet an opera or a play is not a solid unchanging object from the past. A performance is insubstantial and fleeting; it disappears as it takes place to be recaptured only imperfectly by memory. It can be fixed by film or recording, but these are, as I have said, secondhand substitutes that never completely realize the immediacy of the direct experience. (At a live concert, the Adagio introduction to the finale of Mozart's G Minor Viola Quintet may bring tears to my eyes, but even a splendid recording will not make me weep.) We would also like our art museums as well as our opera houses to be an active part of our culture, but we do not expect them to repaint the pictures to make them more acceptable to modern taste, or to remodel the statues regularly to bring them up to date and expose their relevance to the contemporary life. Yet we now demand such original interpretations and astonishing disfigurements of operas and dramas at all cost from our performers and stage directors.

A performance of *Hamlet* or the *Appassionata* sonata is just as much a critical interpretation of these works as a journalistic or scholarly essay on them. When writing about an all-too-famous work of the past, every critic naturally would like to pen (or compose on a computer) something original, to make a point never thought of before. Still, anything absolutely new that one can say about works that have enjoyed universal esteem for so many years is not likely to have anything to do with why the work has been so much admired throughout history; in fact, a truly novel interpretation that has never been thought of before has a good chance of being trivial and unimportant. There are, indeed, modest ways to escape this problem,—that is, first, to find something apparently new and unremarked about a famous classic and claim that it was one of the reasons for its prestige in the past, but that spectators and listeners today no longer understand its earlier reception history, as Hermann Abert insisted on the difficult and ambitious element in Mozart that shocked the composer's contemporaries but that was largely forgotten and overlooked in the nineteenth century. Or, even better, for the critic to discover an important aspect of the work only obscurely or unconsciously appreciated today that nevertheless continues to act upon our sensibilities while we remain largely unaware why we are so affected or moved (as Bernard Shaw uncovered the revolutionary political aspect of Wagner's Ring cycle, and Edmund Wilson remarked on the sexual symbolism used by Henry James in *The Turn of the Screw*). Any truly original interpretation, if it is not to seem either perverse or negligible, must make one or other of these claims, not often successfully supportable.

That is why the radical and imaginative stagings of opera or drama encouraged in our time by impresarios and journalists seem so often to be willfully eccentric, or incongruously inventive stagings. In a recent production of *Hamlet,* the hero rapes Ophelia on the stage, and his mother, Queen Gertrude, is drunk throughout the play.

Of course, defacing the reproduction of a visual work of art is perfectly acceptable, since the original remains unharmed and available. And the plot of a Jane Austen novel can be rewritten and filmed as an American high school comedy without serious damage to the original novel for future readers. However, an opera or a play depends on ephemeral reproduction,—in other words, on performance. To most people, even to most musicians, an opera is not fully available without a staging. Reading the score and imagining the spectacle is not a fulfilling experience. A fine recording is a deeply imperfect substitute, even though it may reveal details generally lost in the oversize hangars that now serve as opera houses.

The attempts by stage directors who wish to be seen as creative to make stage works of the past more immediate for a contemporary public result most often in our seeing the old play or opera dimly through a haze of irrelevant associations. A 1995 film of Shakespeare's *Richard III* with a brilliant performance by Ian Maclaren was updated by having Richard's soldiers in modern uniforms goose-stepping and giving Fascist salutes. This made Shakespeare's treatment of the history seem oddly vacuous; as his hero-villain had no political philosophy at all, and his obsessions were not ideological but simply dynastic: to kill all of his relatives who stood in the way of his inheriting the throne. He does not murder the little princes in the tower and drown his cousin Clarence in a butt of Malmsey in order to install a new kind of regime or for any political goal except becoming the legitimate heir. I do not see why creating a Fascist government should be more gripping to a modern audience than disposing of one's inconvenient relatives. In any case, introducing Fascism as a central element of the drama does not make Shakespeare seem more profound or prophetic but only oddly inattentive to the action in the play. On the other hand, the famous Mercury Theater production of *Julius Caesar* by Orson Welles used modern costumes and uniforms to great advantage, since this drama has politics at its center and the conspirators who kill Caesar are openly trying to prevent the installation of a dictatorship. Like the tempos of Mozart and Beethoven during the nineteenth century, performances of Shakespeare have been getting considerably slower since 1950. Perhaps the reason is a concern that Shakespeare is now too difficult to understand at a lively pace. Above all, there seems to be an idea that an audience today will only submit to the scenic illusion if they believe the actors are conversing in colloquial modern prose. Stage directors are evidently terrified that the public will think the actors are intoning iambic pentameters. Every speech is now chopped into separate clauses with emphatic breaks while the actors pause for reflections that make me think of the joke in a novel by Peter de Vries about Harold Pinter's plays, "No, mother, that is not the actors forgetting their lines; those are significant pauses." Racine is now also played the same way at the *Comédie Française*. The plays of both, in fact, only make full sense and keep their excitement if we are carried along by the swing of the poetic rhythm. Pausing even briefly to let the audience reflect and catch the meaning of the last clause is deadly. It does not pay to assume that the audience is a pack of ignoramuses, even when that happens to be the case. Treat the spectators as intelligent, and they will understand well enough. I very much doubt if an Elizabethan public fully grasped every word of the immensely complex speeches of Leontes in *The Winter's Tale,* difficult to comprehend even when read slowly from a book, but they were carried along with the sweep of the verse and the action, as I was a half century ago in a production by Peter Brook with John Gielgud, who played the scene of insane jealousy as if on the verge of an epileptic fit. Roland Barthes remarked that Racine made no sense unless the verse was read with great formality, which made the dramatic force irresistible. Modernizing Shakespeare by covering up his poetic genius only destroys the dramatic power. This explains why most productions of Shakespeare today have to cover up the crippling loss of interest by a huge dose of unmotivated physical horseplay.

There is no rule of thumb to determine what aspect of a past tradition needs to be preserved in order to remain intelligible, or what has permanently lost all possible sense for today's public and needs to be eliminated for the works to be able to speak to us effectively. It is probably not useful in a production of Shakespeare's *Antony and Cleopatra* today to insist that Cleopatra be played by a teenage boy—even though, in fact, one detail of the text had a much more powerful impact when this was the case. As Cleopatra chooses suicide over captivity, she pictures her arrival in Rome if she surrenders to Octavius Caesar:

> The quick comedians
> Extemporally will stage us. . . .
> . . . . and I shall see
> Some squeaking Cleopatra boy my greatness
> I'th' posture of a whore

When she was played by a boy, these lines were obviously more ironically effective, but a modern audience would still prefer the more matronly actress who generally fills the role. Furthermore, the English in Shakespeare's day was spoken with an accent close to a strong Irish brogue. In spite of the dependence of poetry on sound, I doubt that anyone would seriously advocate reviving the old vowel sounds on the stage today.

Nor do I think that we would contemplate reviving the technique of conducting an opera of Rameau or Lully by banging on the floor with a heavy stick, although this surely was an important acoustic element in the contemporary experience of these works, adding rhythmic definition, but it was certainly filtered out of the listeners' consciousness even if it contributed subliminally to the perception of the music.

There are, however, works of the past that require an absolute reproduction of some aspects of the original presentation. The comedies of Georges Feydeau are one example, particularly the ones in which the second act finds several characters in a hotel blundering into the wrong rooms and being discovered embarrassingly in the wrong beds. The text presents us with the most specific stage directions: where each actor must stand, what gestures are to be used, what tone of voice is required (Feydeau even once indicated the musical pitches he wanted). These prescribed stage directions are as important as the dialogue in this style of comedy; any attempt to change them and add an original touch results in a loss of effectiveness. A great director, Roger Planchon, when young staged Racine's *Bérénice* so powerfully that I could hardly see some of the final act for tears, and mounted a farcical production of *The Three Musketeers* that was enchanting and an enormous popular success. When older, however, he became more ambitious and creative, trying his hand at Feydeau's *Occupe-toi d'Amélie* at the Comédie Française, altering the directions and adding some *tableaux vivants:* as a result all the verve and most of the comedy went out of the play.

A production by Planchon of Molière's *Tartuffe* also showed the danger of original thought on the part of a brilliant director. In this work, the hypocrite Tartuffe, who dazzles and hoodwinks the bourgeois Orgon by his ostentatious piety and who almost destroys Orgon's family with his wicked machinations, is traditionally played as disgustingly fat (he is described in the text as *gros et gras*). Planchon was inspired to make Tartuffe very seductive (and he played the part himself), suggesting homosexual attraction on the part of Orgon. This certainly brought the play up to date and destroyed all its moral significance, as the subject is simply the dangerous temptation of exaggerated and feigned piety.

Originality is, however, still possible without essentially distorting this work, and this was shown some years before Planchon's production by a great performance of the actor Fernand Ledoux at the Comédie-Française as Tartuffe, and who did appear authentically greasy and repellent. The originality lay in the details, not in a pretentious staging that amounted to a fundamental rethinking and rewriting of the play. One small gesture of Ledoux vastly increased the power of the text. In perhaps the most celebrated scene of the play, Tartuffe tries to seduce Orgon's wife, Elvire, as they sit at a table under which Orgon is hiding to spy on them, and he puts his hand on her—I have always presumed that it is on her thigh. The dialogue goes:

Elvire: Que fait là votre main?
Tartuffe: Je tâte votre robe
L'étoffe en est moelleuse

Elvire: What is your hand doing there?
Tartuffe: I am feeling your dress
The cloth is luxuriously soft

Ledoux played this scene giving the impression that his hand was completely independent of his volition, as if it were a separate little animal. When asked what his hand was doing there, he glanced at it with great surprise. The effect brought down the house and illuminated the text, and gave a life to it that it had never had before but was completely motivated by the play. It transformed the scene. The first entrance of Ledoux also astonished a public that almost to a man or woman knew the play from having been forced to read it at school, as he came in walking backward, speaking to his valet off stage, "Laurent, fold up my hair shirt with my flagellation whip." In general, small details of this kind can restore the vitality of a well-known classic and give a personal dimension to the conception. Rethinking the entire work to give it a novel meaning undreamt of before is the easier and cheaper route, but only speciously creative. It is true that we need a vision of the large form, but one that respects its historical integrity and authority without necessarily insisting upon a routine repetition of the realizations of the past.

5

A work of literature, art, or music can seem to undergo an almost physical transformation with variations of critical fashion. For the biographical interpretation that held sway for much of the nineteenth and twentieth centuries, the work became a document in the life of the artist, and each book, symphony, or painting was interrogated as a witness to a personal crisis. With the rival system of interpretation in terms of national styles that also reigned from 1800 to our day, each work gives us access to the German soul, the American psyche, or the allure of Gallic culture. Both approaches have increased our understanding and pleasure: any work is bound to reflect both the life of the maker and the culture of the land in which it was produced. Nevertheless, they can obscure as well as enlighten. Biography can be an inspired guide, but a book or a sonata or a painting is not always an exposé of the life that produced it, and the art may preserve a reticence that cannot be broken down without falsifying the work. The biographical critic, frustrated by the refusal of the work to speak unequivocally of the creator's life, is sometimes tempted to force a confession. When one music historian, distressed by Mozart's failure to write an elegiac piece after the death of his mother, called the sonata with the jolly percussive effects of drum and triangle in the Turkish Rondo a tender and affectionate souvenir of his dead mother, he desperately stretched the limits of biographical significance. Edmund Wilson was convinced by his reading of *A la Recherche du Temps Perdu* that Proust could not possibly be homosexual, and this is generally thought to be a lapse of critical judgment, but he was at least half right to believe that that is what the book was saying. It was not intended, in any case, to open the closet door.

Biography is relevant to the disputed subject of authorial intention; does the artist have the final authority to determine the meaning of the work? We have been warned of the dangers of this position as long ago as Plato, who claimed that the poet knew less about the meaning of his verses than the professional who recited them. Many centuries later, Montaigne would observe that poetry often contained effects and meanings that the poet did not understand and of which he was not even aware. This question has its practical political side as well: must the Supreme Court abide by the authorial intention of the framers of the Constitution, or should a modernized interpretation be permissible? The topic is similar to the one raised at the opening of this essay: must we play Mozart as he played it, or may we bring it up to date?

Having chosen a method of analysis, a critic is all too easily convinced that it must always provide an answer. National styles are patent enough for all to see, but they can lead the obsessed critic into quicksand. Chauvinism naturally rears its head in any discussion of this topic. Writing in 1919 after the German defeat of World War I, Abert's insistence that Mozart was not an Austrian composer but Swabian (his family came from Augsburg, near the Swabian capital, Stuttgart) was an attempt to recoup a little national honor for his native Germany. At the end of the nineteenth century, Henri Bouchot mounted a famous exhibition of the then still unfamiliar great northern European painting of the fifteenth century; perhaps discouraged by the crushing predominance of Flemish artists, he called Jan Van Eyck "the most Parisian painter of all." Much later, the distinguished French art historian Charles Sterling, examining the Flemish and Franco-Flemish illuminated manuscripts of the fifteenth century, became concerned about the absence of purely French manuscripts. His solution was ingenious and comic: first, to determine the characteristics of the Franco-Flemish and then the characteristics of the Flemish works; finally, subtracting the Flemish characteristics from the Franco-Flemish, we would know what the French manuscripts would look like,—if there were any. A critical method takes on a life of its own, independent of good sense. We continue to ask the usual questions about works of art, even when the answers are irrelevant or of no interest. This explains Adorno's comic exasperation at discovering that there is no sonata form in Beethoven's *Missa Solemnis,* concluding absurdly that it was a poor work since one of his most cherished tools of analysis produced no results.

New fashions have partially displaced biography and national styles in recent decades, and modernized our views of the past. Sociological investigations provide insights on the economic organization of artistic life, and gender studies illuminate the role of the sexes throughout history. In music, the exceptionally fine work of Jeffrey Kallberg on the development of the style of keyboard music has demonstrated the crucial influence of women, who dominated piano performance in the private sphere throughout the nineteenth century. With gender studies, however, as with every novelty, the intoxication of the new can lead in strange directions. The male chauvinist piggery of Schumann's masterpiece, *Frauenliebe und Leben,* where the woman is dazzled by the first sight of her love, rejoices in her marriage and the arrival of a baby, and regrets only the death of her husband, has led one concerned musicologist to propose that the singer demonstrate her disapproval of the whole affair by her performance of the work. (It is not clear just how this should be done: by singing off pitch? by making funny faces of distaste?) It is of course humbling for musicologists to reflect that their insights, however brilliant, are unlikely to have any influence on performance.

6

No form of serious music has captured the interest of both popular and sophisticated taste so solidly as opera. Nevertheless, perhaps more than any other form of art, it has traditionally drawn its financial support largely from the pockets of taxpayers. Only briefly in the eighteenth century, modest comic operas with little scenery and a small cast of singers could break even without government help. Soon after the invention of opera in the late 16th century, lavish scenery, dance sequences, special scenic effects, and highly paid international stars attracted the fanatic devotion of any member of the public from all walks of life who could afford the price of a ticket—a price generally kept within the means of at least the middle class by government subsidy.

The past fifty years have seen a radical transformation in the production of opera. Throughout the nineteenth century and most of the eighteenth as well, the singers were the main attraction, and even the ballet took second place, and publicity focused on the diva. Around 1900, a more earnest and pretentious concern for the values of the musical work as a whole made the conductor a star, beginning with Gustav Mahler and Arturo Toscanini. Music lovers spoke as readily about Beecham's *La Bohème* and Reiner's *Salome* as they did about

Ponselle's Aida or Flagstad's Isolde. Those days are gone. An opera is no longer owned by singer or maestro; it now belongs officially to the stage director, a minor functionary in the nineteenth century (or a post filled temporarily by the librettist) who kept the singers from bumping into each other and indicated where to go on entering or leaving the scene.

The change is a sign of how uncertain and ill-at-ease we have become with the production of opera. The spectacle is costly, and was almost always so, particularly in the nineteenth century, when there would be special effects like hell-fire from a trapdoor into which the devil would disappear, slow-motion background scenery to illustrate a walk through the forest for Parsifal and Gurnemanz, or an elaborate macabre ballet of dead but resuscitated debauched nuns. Later, *Aida* would reinforce the grand tradition by a parade of elephants, but, starting with Puccini and Mascagni, composers made more modest demands. Today we should be able to achieve spectacular visual shows more easily and economically with lighting and film. But, uncertain of, and even frightened by, the customs of the past, we are no longer sure that divas or star conductors or even scenic effects will attract a public unless we can spruce the superannuated classics up to date.

To modernize the antiquated operatic specimens, it seems not to be an option to rewrite the music. But if we cannot jazz up the music, then it is difficult to rewrite the words, and that seems to leave little space for our creative improvements. But we can change the stage directions and make the words and music tell a different and, we hope, a more exciting story. As a model for rehabilitating an opera, there are examples from the theater: without altering the text of Shakespeare, we can transform Capulets and Montagues into twentieth-century New York street gangs. After all, nineteenth-century composers and librettists were often enough forced by censors to change the venue of their operas—from Stockholm to Boston in one famous case. Jonathan Miller had a great success when he transferred *Rigoletto* from Renaissance Mantua to Prohibition-era Brooklyn (but then, Verdi had already been forced to alter the scene from the royal court in France to a ducal residence in Mantua, since it was less politically inflammatory to have a villainous duke than a corrupt king.) Miller's success was justified and confirmed by a stroke of genius: in the last act, when the tenor entered the Brooklyn bar that replaced the original Renaissance inn, he walked directly to the juke box and put in a coin. The juke box blazed with light, and the orchestra triumphantly attacked the first bars of "La donna é mobile." The effect was electrifying and perfect, as the aria was calculated as a hit song before anyone had even heard it, and the staging made it, if possible, more effective than ever.

Equally remarkable was Miller's tactful staging of Bach's *Passion According to Saint Matthew,* deeply moving without interfering with the music. Never a concert piece, but a religious ceremony, this work has theatrical aspects built into text and music. Not all such efforts to displace a work from church or concert hall to theater are convincing. I have not found the transformation of Berlioz's oratorio *Damnation of Faust* into an opera anything but awkward; the powerful drama conveyed by the music is not enhanced by visual realization.

Most attempts to update an old opera result in a puzzling charade. It has now become obligatory to dress the Norse gods and primitive Germans of *The Ring of the Nibelungs* in modern business suits: of course, Bernard Shaw explained to us more than a century ago that the gods are an analogue for aristocratic capitalists exploiting the proletarian dwarves, while the world will ultimately be saved by an orphaned hero born from incestuous twin siblings, who were produced by an adulterous liaison of the leading capitalist with a bourgeoise. Yet Wagner's music combines extraordinary modern sophistication with a clearly implied vision of a primitive spear-carrying tribe from a legendary past. The point was to see our world suggestively mirrored in a distant and mythical ancient society. The drama is vitiated by making Valhalla look like Wall Street. Now that translated subtitles are available in so many opera houses, so that the spectators can understand the words, it has become disconcerting to read what Brunhilde sings to her horse (when she immolates herself by riding into the flames that consume Siegfried's body) when we see that there is no horse. No one would wish to return to the stodgy realism of Wagner's own staging, against which his greatest admirers already protested during his lifetime. The proposals of Gordon Craig and Alphonse Appia of more than a century ago to produce Wagner's operas as symbolic art, using lighting and a stripped-down décor, bore fruit for some years in the 1960s at Bayreuth, but more recent productions have come up with a modern realism even more inappropriate and far more grotesque than the comic old-fashioned style I saw as a child.

A fanatically authentic reconstruction of past methods of staging that have long outlived their usefulness will not satisfy anyone except a dogmatic antiquarian, but we may require that an original style make sense. It is already commonplace nonsense to watch Mélisande lean out of the window in Debussy's only opera as Pelléas below says that her hair covers his face, and to realize that she has a short haircut. I have been present at a *Magic Flute* in Paris at the Theatre des Champs Elysees, where the Sarastro could not sing the low notes (surely the principal requirement for hiring a singer for this part), but could balance on a trapeze. I do not see why *Cosi fan tutte* should take place in a kitchen, or why Figaro and Susanna should be measuring the place for their bed in a busy office corridor. And what are we to say to a production of *Siegfried* filmed in Stuttgart and shown on television, in which Brunhilde is not awakened behind a wall of fire but in a motel bedroom, displays an odd desire to go back to bed immediately after having been asleep for more than sixteen years, and moves to the wash basin and brushes her teeth while Siegfried expresses his love?

The limit of senseless modern interference with tradition was in New York at a recent production of *Tristan und Isolde* to which I was invited, and went with misgivings that turned out to be justified. In the third act, perhaps the most remarkable dramatic sequence of any operatic creation, almost nothing happens at all for three-quarters of an hour to the most affecting and powerful music Wagner ever wrote: everyone waits for a boat to come with Isolde to cure the wounded and dying Tristan. The dramatic power depends on the frustration of action. In this production, the scenic design appeared to represent the corridor of an airline terminal with plastic walls. There was even a moving sidewalk to confirm the impression. At the back of the stage, Tristan lay spread-eagled on a rug which began to move slowly forward and deposited him near the orchestra pit. When the boat finally arrived, people emerged oddly from tiny trapdoors in the terminal floor. Tristan is supposed to tear off his bloody bandages in a paroxysm of excitement, and Isolda should rush forward and catch him in her arms as he dies. Not any longer. Tristan did not tear off his bandages; Isolda did not rush forward but moved in a stately and majestic pace, like Margaret Dumont in a Marx Brothers farce; Tristan did not die in her arms but just lay down in a fetal position, and she patted him on the head. I could not discover any reason for the novel stage effects.

The pressure put on stage directors to invent new business at all costs is corrupting the form of opera throughout the world. Even seemingly innocuous invention can have an unfortunate effect. When Jonathan Miller tried to humanize the Countess in *The Marriage of Figaro* by giving her children, he only succeeded in strengthening the misconception of the Countess as an aging unsatisfied wife. There is nothing maternal about the Countess: she was married in *The Barber of Seville* when she was sixteen years old, and we have no reason to think she has been married very long. She is surely no older than Susanna. Nothing in Mozart's music or da Ponte's libretto encourage us to believe she is motherly. It is true that the singers are generally all too mature. The Count, too, is not an elderly roué, but a young man in his early twenties, younger than Figaro. In a glorious staging by Giorgio Strehler at the Paris Opéra many years ago, the Count was a great and famous singer in his late fifties, Gabriel Bacquier, and there is nothing a stage director can do about that.

Mozart's singers were generally very young, except for an elderly tenor in *Idomeneo* (who did not like to sing Mozart's innovative ensemble, because he could not show off his voice as in an aria). The first Don Giovanni was twenty-one years old—he must have seemed remarkably enterprising from an early age to have totaled 1,003 female conquests in Spain alone, not counting the rest of Europe. The little gardener's daughter in the last act of *The Marriage of Figaro* was only twelve years old at the première, but her aria was perfect for a little girl. What is more to the point, seven years later she was the original Pamina in *The Magic Flute*!

This may help to explain one of the problems that make it so difficult to achieve an adequate production of a Mozart opera. The texture of his music is far more complex than that of any of his contemporaries, and to hear everything clearly, it should never be performed in a theater that seats more than 750, the size of the theater in Prague where *Don Giovanni* was done for the first time (*Idomeneo* was written specifically for the Munich theater that accommodates little more than three hundred). Famous singers, however, command a high price, and to meet their fees even with heavy subsidies and the status of a tax-exempt business granted to most opera houses, the management must be able to sell three thousand seats. Talented younger singers in a smaller house might give us a more satisfactory musical and dramatic experience. Why pay for international stars in a hall where they cannot perform properly?

Most opera halls of a size to suit Mozart are set in some distant rustic landscape like Glyndebourne, and are meant for the very wealthy who can travel for their day at the opera, and pack a picnic hamper for the intermission. Establishing a fine opera company for younger singers and building a house of the proper size in a major city like New York, London, or Paris would be the best way to make the performance of eighteenth-century and even many nineteenth-century operas musically viable, both to honor the tradition and bring it up to date. An uncritical effort to revive outmoded practices at all cost or a ruthless attempt to modernize that shows little respect for the historical aura of the music are equally disastrous. We need new approaches that are sensitive to every detail of the music and respect the logic and sense of the dramatic action.

7

A dogmatic insistence on preserving or restoring the purity of style of an old work can lead to disaster. Disapproval by advocates of authenticity of the stylistic changes inflicted on ancient architecture over the centuries has often resulted in the disfigurement of important monuments when the authorities had enough money to try and reconstruct the original appearance of a building. In Milan, during the nineteenth and twentieth centuries, the venerably ancient paleochristian church of San Babila was disencumbered of all the changes successively brought on through medieval, Renaissance, and baroque changes of style, and now has almost no stylistic character at all except for a slight resemblance to the austerely simple Fascist brutalism of the 1930s.

A respect for antiquity need not refuse to acknowledge an interest in the way that history has distorted and transformed the past, but it is difficult to overcome our prejudices. For example, one of the volumes of that indispensable series of French tourist guides of some decades ago, the *Guide Bleu,* the volume that informs us about Flanders, Hainaut, and Picardy, printed in 1966, still gives most of its aesthetic admiration to the Middle Ages, and becomes almost comic in its moral disapproval of any later attempts at modernization. Nevertheless, we can sense the clash of allegiance when an inauthentic modernization seems attractive and catches the fancy of the authors of the guide. The interior of a modest thirteenth-century Picardy church in a village with the picturesque name of Ham was redecorated during the reign of Louis XIV with stucco, and the guide becomes ill-at-ease because it cannot wholly condemn the result. We read:

> In the interior, the imposition of the classical decoration on the medieval architecture is curious, although regrettable; in the nave, 32 bas-reliefs in stucco retrace the scenes of the New Testament. The parasitical decoration does not succeed in dissimulating the beautiful architecture of the choir (beginning of the 13th century)

Clearly, the guide displays uneasy guilt at finding the modernization of the seventeenth century even interesting or curious. We need to cultivate a more eclectic tolerance.

Dealing with venerable architectural monuments, our practice has become more sophisticated over the ages. For many centuries, when repairs were necessary, an old church would be partially rebuilt in a new and more up-to-date style. Then, in the nineteenth century, historical authenticity became the rage, and attempts were made to restore to the monument its original appearance, making it look new and shiny. We must remember the great historian Louis Dimier's sardonic exclamation at Viollet le Duc's restoration of (or invention of) the medieval ramparts at Carcassonne: "Flambant neuf et prêt à servir" (Brand new and ready for use!). We are now aware that a work should reflect its passage through time. New construction may be necessary to keep a cathedral from falling down, but we no longer try to hide the traces of time that centuries have inflicted upon it. We allow the old to have the beauty of age, the ruin to appear as a ruin.

We must become equally sophisticated with our critical interpretation of literature, art, and music, and with performances of music and literature intended for public display. We ought to acknowledge what has become dead in a work over time, and what has been given new meaning by its later history. What part of Shakespeare's *Love's Labour's Lost* is still alive for us today and what part has been buried in the rubble of fashionable Elizabethan euphuistic style? How much account must we take of the conditions of the stage of the time?

Flaubert thought if people had read and understood his *L'Education Sentimentale* dealing with the revolution of 1848, that the revolution of 1870 would never have happened; how much of that book is relevant to today's politics? How much of Handel is effective today without the elaborate decoration improvised or otherwise added by singers and other musicians in his time? Where is this embellishment absolutely needed for musical sense? What Protestant theology is required for our understanding and enjoyment of J. S. Bach's church cantatas and chorale preludes? We have seen that with the Quartet op. 131, Beethoven wrote music that demanded a radical change in the performance conditions of his time, a change eventually imposed throughout the concert world.

A double approach to a work of the past increases not only knowledge but delight. Any work becomes richer and more interesting when we cease to restrict our vision either to the conventions of the past or to the demands of the present. We must abandon the view that an acceptable interpretation is reachable either by a one-sided attempt to impose an "authentic" view or by a rigorously "modern" reconception. The most satisfactory and enjoyable approach will always be a juggling act that keeps the nostalgia of the past and the exigencies of the present in balance.

Credits

Chapter 1 was published in Dutch translation in *Nexus* no. 54 (2010)

Chapter 2 was originally published in the *New York Review of Books,* November 6, 2003.

Chapter 3 was originally published in the *New York Review of Books,* December 20, 2001.

Chapter 4 was originally published in the *New York Review of Books,* May 9, 1996, as "The Scandal of the Classics."

Chapter 6 was originally published in the *New York Review of Books,* October 25, 2007, as "The Best Book on Mozart."

Chapter 7 was originally published in the *New York Review of Books,* September 21, 1995, as "Beethoven's Triumph."

Chapter 8 is excerpted, revised, and expanded from a review of *Mozart's Piano Concertos: Text, Context, Interpretation* by Neal Zaslaw, in *Journal of the American Musicological Society,* vol. 51, no. 2 (Summer 1998), pp. 373–384, © 1998 by the American Musicological Society. Published by the University of California Press.

Chapter 11 originated as the Tanner Lectures on Human Values, delivered at the University of Utah, April 11, 2000, and published by the University of Utah Press.

Chapter 12 was originally published in the *Times Literary Supplement,* March 19, 2004.

Chapter 13 was originally published in the *New York Review of Books,* March 12, 2009.

Chapter 14 was originally published in the *New York Review of Books,* June 24, 2010, as "Happy Birthday, Frédéric Chopin!"

Chapter 15 was originally published in the *New York Review of Books,* December 23, 2010, as "Happy Birthday, Robert Schumann!"

Chapter 16 was originally published in the *New York Review of Books,* June 21, 2001, as "Within a Budding Grove."

Chapter 17 was originally published in two parts in the *New York Review of Books,* February 23 and March 9, 2006, as "From the Troubadours to Frank Sinatra." The Chapter 17 Postscript was originally published in the *New York Review of Books,* April 7, 2011, as "Music and the Cold War."

Chapter 18 was originally published in the *New York Review of Books,* October 24, 2002, as "Should We Adore Adorno?"

Chapter 19 was originally published in the *New York Review of Books,* May 31, 1979, as "Too Much Opera?"

Chapter 20 was originally published in the *New York Review of Books,* April 22, 1993, as "The Ridiculous and Sublime."

Chapter 21 was originally published in the *Times Literary Supplement,* November 7, 2008.

Chapter 22 was originally published in the *New York Review of Books,* February 14, 2008, as "The Genius of Montaigne."

Chapter 23 was originally published in the *New York Review of Books,* December 18, 1997.

Chapter 24 was originally published in the *New York Review of Books,* June 9, 2005, as "The Fabulous La Fontaine."

Chapter 25 was originally published in the *New York Review of Books,* May 20, 1999, as "Mallarmé the Magnificent."

Chapter 26 was originally published in the *New York Review of Books,* April 8, 2010, as "Radical, Modern Hofmannsthal."

Chapter 27 was originally published in the *New York Review of Books,* November 20, 2008, as "What Happened to Wystan Auden?"

Index of Names and Works